Economic Liberalization and Integration Policy

Harry G. Broadman · Tiiu Paas
Paul J. J. Welfens
Editors

Economic Liberalization and Integration Policy

Options for Eastern Europe and Russia

With 93 Figures and 52 Tables

Springer

Dr. Harry G. Broadman
World Bank
1818 H Street, NW
Washington DC, 20433
USA
hbroadman@worldbank.org

Professor Dr. Tiiu Paas
University of Tartu
Institute of Economics
Narva mnt. 4
51009 Tartu
Estonia
tiiu.paas@ut.ee

Professor Dr. Paul J. J. Welfens
University of Wuppertal
EIIW – European Institute for International
Economic Relations
Rainer-Gruenter-Straße 21
42119 Wuppertal
Germany
welfens@eiiw.uni-wuppertal.de

Cataloging-in-Publication Data
Library of Congress Control Number: 2005934893

ISBN-10 3-540-24183-3 Springer Berlin Heidelberg New York
ISBN-13 978-3-540-24183-6 Springer Berlin Heidelberg New York

Springer is a part of Springer Science+Business Media

springeronline.com

Printed in Germany

Hardcover-Design: Erich Kirchner, Heidelberg

SPIN 11371670 43/3153-5 4 3 2 1 0 – Printed on acid-free paper

Contents

Introduction

The New Russia has achieved considerable growth in the seven years following the 1998 debt default, ruble devaluation and economic crisis. Political stability, strengthened economic institutions, and high oil prices, coupled with significant import substitution and export competitiveness, have contributed to Russia's strong economic growth. The Russian authorities have maneuvered the levers of fiscal and monetary policy adeptly, at the same time introducing a flat income tax rate and reducing import tariffs, with further external liberalization anticipated in the context of the envisaged WTO membership. EU accession of eastern European countries has caused only modest trade diversion in the short run, since the growth-enhancing effects of EU membership tend to stimulate overall imports of accession countries, and Russia thus stands to benefit through growing exports. Moreover, there are new opportunities to import modern machinery and equipment from eastern Europe. At the same time, Russia looks towards Asia, where China is increasingly becoming a new economic gravity center. While China's expansion is trade creating in Asia (including Russia), it is more doubtful whether Russia is not suffering from foreign direct investment diversion in a period in which China continues to attract massive FDI inflows, not to mention that Russia's FDI policy regime greatly needs improvement in its own right. Moreover, Russia will have sustained economic growth only if the expansion of the oil and gas sector is accompanied by solid growth of a modern manufacturing sector for which capital accumulation and innovation play a crucial role. If Russia does not achieve a diversified production and export structure, it could face serious long run problems if there is a sustained current account surplus which translates into a real appreciation of the currency. There remains, therefore, a fundamental challenge for Russia's economic policy-makers: implementing economy-wide, cross-sectoral structural reforms and building durable market institutions that will transform the Russian economy into one that is flexible, diversified and integrated, not only domestically but also internationally.

There is little question that Russia has made significant progress in dismantling the central planning system, which, during the Soviet era, had directly governed Russia's industrial structure, conduct and performance. But, to date, the development of these basic market institutions to take the place of central planning remains nascent – especially in regional markets, where day-to-day business transactions are actually conducted. This is the principal factor making the costs of doing business in Russia excessively high and impeding enterprise formation and restructuring. While there has been much debate as to why – at the national level – the restructuring of Russian enterprises has been partial and new private sector start-ups are struggling to emerge, little systemic analysis has been carried out to assess the state of basic market institutions in Russia's regions. The paper by

Harry G. Broadman helps to fill this gap. His analysis focuses on the business environment of 13 of Russia's 89 regions and examines four key issues that Russian firms face in carrying out business transactions: (i) the state of inter-enterprise competition; (ii) the regulatory regime governing the delivery of infrastructure services (with a focus on the telecom and Internet sector); (iii) the sources and use of corporate finance; and (iv) the efficacy of the court system in fostering the settlement of commercial disputes. The paper formulates policy recommendations for each of the areas analyzed, and in so doing sheds light on salient inter-regional differences in existing policy frameworks and in the structure and nature of the country's enterprise sector, as well as on how regional governments and firms both respond to and shape these differences.

As regards economic opening up of Russia it is obvious that there is a considerable expansion of the tradables sector, but there also is high unemployment and a special role of the natural resources sector. Paul J.J. Welfens takes a closer look at some of the key issues of opening up and growth in a resource-based economy. Moreover, the focus is on the Balassa-Samuelson effect, the role of innovation in the Mundell Fleming model and key aspects of long run exchange rate dynamics. The analysis shows that the role of unemployment and innovation should be integrated in the standard analysis of economic opening up and growth.

Evgeny Gavrilenkov's contribution is on the role of reforms for long run growth and the problems of low monetization of the Russian economy on the one hand, on the other hand his focus is on issues of political governance and the efficiency of government spending. Russia's macroeconomic prospects are favorable as long as there is sustained investment dynamics and a growing monetization of the economy. In this respect, Russia has achieved considerable progress. Gavrilenkov also analyzes the structure of the revenues and expenditures of the Russian government. Financial sector development will remain a major challenge on the agenda, and the new Russia will have to cope both with financial market volatility and considerable oil price dynamics.

The higher the degree of Russia's economy – with international links through trade, foreign investment and portfolio capital flows – the higher the exposure of Russia to the global economic dynamics; and with Russia growing strongly the economic weight of the country in the world economy is growing. Hans Gerhard Strohe and Noer Azam Achsani analyze the interdependency of fluctuations between Russia, Europe, Asia and the US. Methodologically they use correlation analysis, Granger causality and VAR analyis. The various approaches suggest different patterns of international interdependencies. It is quite interesting to see not only how Russia's economic development is dependent on international impulses but also to understand the role of Russian economic shocks for eastern Europe.

Similar to Russia the Ukraine has experienced economic and political transformation where the country's recent political developments emphasize the role of democracy. Both countries have not only major international economic relations with the EU25 but also with the US: Trade and capital flows play an important role where part of US foreign direct investment in both countries actually comes from US subsidiaries in the EU. Hence the extensity of US links with Russia and the Ukraine is often underestimated. Olga Nosova analyzes the links between the

United States and these two countries and finds a gradual growth of trade flows and capital flows.

Russia is a market economy with some special features, including a rather dynamic shadow economy and a wide range of government administered prices – these include not only domestic prices of oil and gas but also many government services. Moreover, in a country which is as large as Russia there are considerable regional price differentials which mainly concern nontradables. Given the dominance of short-term contracts in many sectors of the economy (including housing and office rental) there also exists remarkable price flexibility. From this perspective, the measurement of inflation is rather difficult and the concept of core inflation quite important. Irina Eliseeva analyzes with great care and based on broad data sets the concept of core inflation and crucial aspects of the inflation process in Russia.

For decades Russia – and the former Soviet Union – has emphasized the production of energy. In the socialist era, availability of cheap energy was a key ingredient for sustained growth, and energy exports at favorable prices (below world market prices) helped to create a system of economic dependency within the Council of Mutual Economic Assistence. The New Russia still emphasizes the role of the energy sector whose structure is shaped by energy giants and the results of the partly strange privatization procedure in the early 1990s; there have been recurrent conflicts between oil and gas tycoons and the Putin government and the judicial system, respectively. It certainly is difficult to establish the rule of law in the context of these conflicts given the particular initial distortions on the one hand and the enormous stakes in terms of economic and political power on the other hand. Government apparently wants control over key facilities of the oil and gas sector, at the same time government is interested in foreign direct investment inflows and technology transfer which help to reduce exploration costs and to give better access to downstream markets. Ruslan Grinberg's contribution highlights the key elements of the government's energy strategy and gives an interesting picture of the various interests relevant in the oil and gas sector.

Roland Götz also takes a critical look at Russia's energy strategy and the links between Russia and the EU in the field of energy policies. His main focus is on the oil sector on the one hand, on the gas sector and the various alternatives for modernization of the energy sector and of rising international energy trade on the other. He discusses the investment needs relevant for various strategies and highlights western European needs to import energy from Russia.

Thorvaldur Gylfason presents a careful and thought-provoking analysis of potential Dutch disease problems, namely the particular problems of structural change and modernization in resource-rich countries. His analysis points out the main problems of resource rich countries, but also looks at the experience of selected countries, including the OPEC Countries and Norway. A key concept developed in this contribution is the comparative analysis of human capital, physical capital, financial capital and natural capital. The author clearly argues that sustained economic growth cannot be achieved without a careful strategy for a long term diversification of the economy. Given problems of path-dependency and political economy, it certainly is a crucial challenge for Russia and other resource rich countries to adopt a consistent strategy for modernization cum diversification.

Russia and many other postsocialist transition countries face the problem of modernizing public infrastructure, and most sectors of the economy indeed stand to benefit from an upgrading of infrastructure. It is not necessesarily the energy sector with its supranormal profits which causes major problems in the form of corruption in Russia; there are also other sectors which are relevant, and corruption is a major problem in many OECD countries as well. Frank Bohn suggests an interesting new model for analyzing corruption and public investment under political instability. It is quite important to use innovative theoretical modeling for gaining a better understanding of the recurrent problems with corruption.

Nina Oding's contribution puts the focus on the role of transportation policy, where major attention is devoted to maritime transport issues and trade. Given the geography of Russia and the enormous regional differences in terms of population density and proximity to major international markets it is obvious that modernization of the transport sector is a key policy challenge. The transportation infrastructure has regional, national and international aspects; and there is a considerable long term need for investment. What is most important is not so much the infrastructure itself but the quantity and quality of transportation services which can be achieved through infrastructure modernization – part of the benefits are determined by the scope of privatization strategies and by competition policies adopted.

Countries eager to achieve long run economic growth in a diversified economy clearly face challenges in the field of education as well as human capital formation. The paper by Dora Borbély and Christopher Schumann sheds light on this important topic by looking at the EU-15 countries, some eastern European accession countries and Russia. The contribution is an empirical analysis of the factors that have contributed to the growth of the East European transition countries and the EU-15 countries in the course of the 1990s. The underlying extended neoclassical growth model includes variables representing macroeconomic stability, government size and trade openness. In the pooled mean group estimations of the panel data set, we find strong empirical support for the neoclassical elements of growth theory such as capital and population growth also during the transition period. Furthermore, the analysis confirms that the accumulation of human capital is extremely important for enhancing economic growth. Convergence is clearly observable within the selected group of countries. While the EU accession countries perform similarly, Russia follows rather different patterns throughout the estimations.

Albrecht Kauffmann conducts innovative research on the link between telecommunications, trade and growth. He presents new findings from gravity modeling which take into account the role of telecommunications on international trade dynamics thus extending existing literature in an interesting way. Investment in the telecommunications sector and better and cheaper digital services could stimulate trade and growth. His analysis of trade dynamics in the countries of the Former Soviet Union present new insights into the dynamics of the real economy.

The contribution of Alexander Libmann is an interesting piece of institutional analysis applied to Russia's integration into the world economy. His approach is based on interjuridictional competition and carefully analyzes the various incentives and opportunities for integration. Given the many distortions existing it is not easy to generate a reform and integration process which leads to efficient and sustained integration. Adequate institutional reforms and sustained integration of Russia's economy require careful analysis and prudent choices – quite difficult in a situation with many initial distortions.

The Forum: Russia's Economic Perspectives gives some key insights of the analysis of Tiiu Paas, Tatiana Sedash and Ralf Wiegert.

We hope that this book will stimulate national and international discussion about Russia's economic situation and the integration of this country into the world economy. Moreover, one should get a better understanding of potential Dutch disease problems and the role of economic opening up in countries with unemployment. Economic catching up in countries with major initial distortions is not easily achieved: infrastructure modernization, structural change and adequate institutional adjustment as well as careful policy choices are crucial in a long run perspective. Europe, the US and Asia need a better understanding of the considerable dynamics and challenges in the new Russia. The European Institute for International Economic Relations will continue to monitor and analyze the Russian transformation process with these issues in mind.

We are grateful to the Higher School of Economics which hosted the international workshop at which most of the papers contained in this volume were presented; also included are papers from the Transatlantic Transformation and Economic Development Research Group (Trans@lantic-Transfo.Net). We also thank the Alfried Krupp von Bohlen und Halbach Foundation for their support for the underlying research project – for details of the projekct see our project website www.progressinfo.net; our research is not only theoretical, it also has a clear policy focus and is dedicated to promoting growth and stability in Russia and prosperity in Europe as a whole.

Finally, we greatly appreciate the editorial assistance provided by Michael Agner, Ekaterina Markova, Chistopher Schumann and Stephanie Kullmann. Christopher Schumann has been an excellent project manager throughout the course of the project.

Washington DC, Tartu and Wuppertal, July 2005

Harry G. Broadman, Tiiu Paas and Paul J.J. Welfens

The Regional Dimensions of Barriers to Business Transactions in Russia

Harry G. Broadman[1]

---

[1] This paper draws from the first chapter of Broadman, Harry, ed. Unleashing Russia's Business Potential: Lessons from the Regions for Building Market Institutions, The World Bank, Washington, DC.

1 Introduction

Growth is finally underway in Russia.[2] But is this new-found growth – initiated largely by the import-substitution effects from the devaluation of the ruble and increased world oil prices – sustainable? Russia still faces the daunting challenge of restructuring its enterprises and engendering new business investment. While privatization initiatives successfully changed the ownership of many of the country's firms, they have not led to major restructuring of most incumbent enterprises. The mode of privatization most commonly used relied on worker-management buyouts and the resulting insider-controlled firms faced weak incentives to restructure, especially against the backdrop of a policy framework that, up until relatively recently, permitted soft budget constraints. At the same time, the growth of *de novo* private sector businesses in Russia, especially small and medium enterprises (SMEs), is strikingly low, particularly when compared to other transition countries in Central and Eastern Europe. Moreover, the vast majority of new businesses that have taken root are located in the largest, wealthiest cities, such as Moscow and St. Petersburg, exacerbating the already skewed pattern of development of Russia's regional geography.

An incentive framework that engenders efficiency and predictability in business transactions is crucial for sustained enterprise development. In developed market economies, these incentives are conditioned by a set of basic market institutions that work to facilitate and reduce firms' costs of transacting, whether in terms of new investments or restructuring of existing operations. These institutions include vigorously enforced competition policy to keep in check market power exercised by dominant incumbent firms and facilitate the entry of new enterprises; a regulatory regime that ensures that tariffs for and access to infrastructure utility services are market-oriented while protecting the public interest through a decision-making process that is transparent, rules-based and independent; an efficient system for the intermediation of savings into investment capital and the provision of finance to businesses on commercial terms; and an effective legal system to foster the settlement of commercial disputes.

There is little question that Russia has made significant progress in dismantling the central planning system, which, during the Soviet era, had directly governed Russia's industrial structure, conduct and performance. But, to date, the development of these basic market institutions to take the place of central planning remains nascent – especially in regional markets, where day-to-day business transactions are conducted. This is the principal factor making the costs of doing business in Russia excessively high and impeding enterprise formation and restructuring. While there has been much debate as to why at the national level the restructuring of Russian enterprises has been partial and new private sector start-ups are struggling to emerge, little systemic analysis has been carried out to assess the state of basic market institutions in Russia's regions. This study helps to fill this gap.

---

[2] We use the term "Russia" for the "Russian Federation" throughout the contribution.

Assessing the development of market institutions at the regional level is of paramount concern to the Russian authorities as they increasingly focus on ways to reform the fundamental underpinnings for fostering business investment and sustaining growth and move beyond the narrow and less intractable issues such as how to reduce administrative barriers to firm registration and licensing. Indeed, deeper economic diagnosis of how basic market institutions create incentives and constraints on business transactions at the regional level in Russia is essential for the design of "second generation" medium term structural policy reforms. The focus on local[3] market institutions is thus a key and novel aspect of this study, given that, in practice, reform in the regions will have the most direct impact on Russian enterprise behavior and growth.

This study is based principally on the analysis of original in-depth company case studies and interviews of general directors and other senior managers of more than 70 enterprises, infrastructure monopoly utilities, and banks, as well as of senior regional government and chamber of commerce officials, carried out in the field during the spring, summer and fall of 2000 and the summer of 2001 among thirteen Russian regions: Krasnodarskii Krai, Leningradskaya Oblast, City of Moscow, Moscovskaya Oblast, Omskaya Oblast, Novgorodskaya Oblast, Novosibirskaya Oblast, Primorskii Krai, City of St. Petersburg, Samaraskaya Oblast, Saratovskaya Oblast, Sverdloskaya Oblast and Volgogradskaya Oblast. In order to foster a frank discussion of the prospects and problems of the business environment, all individuals and institutions that participated in the case studies were guaranteed anonymity. The study team has supplemented the results of the field case studies and interviews with data from secondary sources and from earlier firm-level surveys with which they have been associated.

The objective of the study is to facilitate the formulation of new policy initiatives in order to improve Russia's business environment – especially in regional markets. In so doing, it sheds light on salient *inter-regional* differences in existing policy frameworks and in the structure and nature of the country's enterprise sector, as well as on how regional governments and firms both respond to and shape these differences. To give added focus in developing these policy recommendations, the study focuses on certain *industry sectors*. In the analysis of competition, for example, the study compares the evolution of competitors in the "new" versus the "old" economy sectors; and in the analysis of the regulatory regime, the focus is on the telecommunications and Internet sectors. The study also highlights the evolution of inter-regional policy and economic changes *over time*. Thus it assesses the extent to which, two years after the 1998 crisis, enterprise restructuring, import-substitution, export expansion, and job creation/destruction at the local level has been affected by the devaluation to the ruble.

The structure of this study – and the thematic focus of the following chapters – is organized around the four areas of institutional development highlighted above: (a) determinants of inter-enterprise competition and market structure and the policy framework governing them at the local level; (b) the regulatory regime govern-

[3] The terms "local" and "regional" are used interchangeably throughout this contribution to denote sub-national or sub-federal activities and entities.

ing the price, supply and access to local infrastructure services; (c) access to corporate finance in regional markets; and (d) the legal system for resolution for commercial disputes. Policy recommendations for each of the respective areas are outlined at the end of each chapter.

This chapter presents a brief description and analysis of the various regions under study. It then provides an integrated overview of the main points of the thematic chapters.

2 Description of the Studied Regions

Among the thirteen regions under study, there is substantial heterogeneity in their basic attributes, as illustrated in Tables 1 and 2.[4] The regions span most of the key geographical dimensions of Russia, from the cities of Moscow and St. Petersburg in the West and North West, respectively, to Volgogradskaya in the South, Primorskii in the Far East, and Novosibirskya in Central Siberia.

As Table 1 indicates, some of the regions are very densely populated (Moscow and St. Petersburg Cities), while others are relatively sparsely populated (Volgogradskaya, Novgorodskaya, and Primorskii). All the regions are relatively urbanized, with more than half of their populations living in urban areas – although Moscow and St. Petersburg are at one extreme, with 100 percent urbanization, while just over 50 percent of Krasnodarskii's population lives in urban areas. Moscow City stands out as the wealthiest region, as measured by Gross Regional Product per Capita, followed by Samaraskaya and St. Petersburg; most of the rest of the 13 regions are in the same range, except for Saratovskaya, Volgogradskaya, and Omskaya, which are the poorest regions under study. While there is a fair amount of regional uniformity in terms of share of the population that is of working age, there are much greater differences with respect to proportion of the population completing higher education. Self-financing for budgetary expenditures from locally-raised revenues also varies greatly among the regions.

Table 2 contains data describing various enterprise-related aspects of the regions. Sverdlovskya and Samaraskya are the most industrialized of the regions under study, as measured by the share of workers employed in the industry sector. Owing to the prominence of the service sector in Moscow City and of the agriculture sector in Krasnodarskii, these two regions rank as the least industrialized of the 13 regions. The share of the employed population working in SMEs is highest in the cities of St. Petersburg and Moscow (at levels between 20 and 25 percent), which is not surprising inasmuch as these two locales account for the overwhelm-

---

4 As all researchers working on Russia know, systematically comparable data on Russia's regions are generally not available contemporaneously; indeed, there is usually a two to three year lag. Hence, the data presented in Tables 1 and 2 are not as recent as one would like, but they are essentially the most recent data available.

ing bulk of SMEs for the country as a whole;[5] for the other 11 regions, the share of employment accounted for by SMEs is at most around 7 percent or less..

Table 1. Socio-Economic Comparisons of the Regions

Region	Population (Thousands of Persons) (2000)	Population Density (Thousands of Persons per Sq. Km.) (2000)	Gross Regional Product per Capita (1000 Rubles) (1999)	Share of Population in Urban Areas (1999)	Share of Population of Working Age (1999)	Population Possessing Higher Education (per 1000 Aged 15 or Older) (1997)	Share of Consolidated Regional Budget Expenditures Covered by Own Revenues (1999)
Krasnodarskii Krai	5,007	65.9	21,525	53.7	55.5	115	52
Lenigradskaya Oblast	1,666	19.7	25,396	66.0	58.2	108	69
City of Moscow	8,537	7,192.0	78,488	100.0	58.2	299	61
Moskovskaya Oblast	6,464	140.8	24,510	79.8	58.3	161	63
Omskaya Oblast	2,164	15.5	18,702	67.3	57.8	117	50
Novgorodskaya Oblast	727	13.1	22,418	71.1	56.2	104	47
Novosibirskaya Oblast	2,740	15.4	21,218	74.0	58.5	135	44
Primorskii Krai	2,172	13.1	25,071	78.3	62.3	146	37
City of St. Petersburg	4,661	3,329.3	34,334	100.0	59.7	247	67
Samarskaya Oblast	3,295	61.5	36,736	80.5	59.2	135	62
Saratovskaya Oblast	2,709	27.0	17,888	73.2	57.6	141	51
Sverdlovskaya Oblast	4,603	23.6	26,685	87.5	58.4	109	54
Volgogradskaya Oblast	2,677	23.5	18,603	74.1	56.8	121	56

Source: Center for Fiscal Policy (2001), Goskomstat (2000), Orttung (2000), and Broadman and Recanatini (forthcoming).

[5] See Broadman (2000).

Table 2. Enterprise-Related Regional Comparisons

Region	Share of Workers Employed in Industrial Sector (1999)	Share of Population Employed in SMEs (1999)	Share of Enterprises that are State or Municipally Owned (1999)	Share of Enterprises that are Loss-Makers (mid 1998)	Cumulative FDI (US$ mln) (1999)	Cumulative FDI per Capita (US$) (1999)	Unemployment Rate (ILO Definition) (1999)
Krasnodarskii Krai	16.6	4.9	14.1	50.4	704.4	138	15.9
Leningradskaya Oblast	25.0	7.2	10.6	46.9	466.5	274	14.8
City of Moscow	15.1	20.3	2.7	31.7	7,764.8	902	5.6
Moskovskaya Oblast	23.5	5.4	10.2	42.1	1,718.3	264	10.7
Omskaya Oblast	19.6	5.5	10.3	63.1	19.7	9	15.0
Novgorodskaya Oblast	24.1	3.7	19.7	46.5	76.7	110	14.5
Novosibirskaya Oblast	20.4	7.4	11.3	49.7	371.8	133	15.0
Primorskii Krai	19.6	4.6	11.4	48.8	215.5	98	13.7
City of St. Petersburg	22.7	23.7	3.4	31.5	939.9	200	11.0
Samarskaya Oblast	30.8	6.6	9.2	39.7	404.7	123	12.4
Saratovskaya Oblast	21.6	4.8	13.1	41.2	57.3	21	11.2
Sverdlovskaya Oblast	32.2	5.6	10.4	48.8	280.0	61	13.9
Volgogradskaya Oblast	29.7	5.0	12.3	36.6	199.5	154	12.5

Source: Goskomstat (2000), Orttung (2000), and Broadman and Recanatini (forthcoming).

There are dramatic differences among the regions with respect to the extent of registered foreign direct investment (FDI), both in terms of the absolute stock of FDI and the stock of FDI normalized by population levels. Enterprise performance, as measured by share of firms exhibiting losses, also displays wide variation among the regions, with Moscow and St. Petersburg registering the fewest proportion of loss-making firms, and Omskaya, Krasnodarskii, Primorskii and Sverdlovskya registering the greatest proportion.[6] However, in terms of measured unemployment, apart from Moscow City, which registered the lowest unemployment rate by a substantial margin, the unemployment rates among the remaining regions does not vary significantly.

3 Competition in the "Old" and "New" Economy in Russia's Regions

In their analysis of competition, Broadman, Dutz and Vagliasindi undertake an approach that assesses the incentives and constraints on inter-enterprise competition. They focus on factors that give rise to barriers to new competitive entry and that permit restrictive business practices by incumbent firms able to exercise market power, as well as by state executive bodies who undercut competition through powers they possess by dint of their legal authority. An important feature of their analysis is comparing firms in Russia's "old" and "new" economy. This approach allows them to explore the extent to which businesses belonging to the "old" economy continue to be shaped by, or have overcome, the planning legacy of the Soviet era, influencing the extent to which they have been able to restructure into competitive enterprises. At the same time, the taxonomy enables an assessment of how much "new" economy businesses have been able to exempt themselves from the Soviet inertia, the influence of vested interests and transition-related distortions; in short, how much they have been able to grow and prosper more in line with competitive forces, unencumbered by the problems that have plagued their older counterparts. While there are – necessarily – many "old" economy sectors in Russia on which such an approach can focus, the authors concentrate on construction materials, food and beverages, wood processing, fishing, machine building, metal fabrication, electronics and textiles. As a representative of the "new" economy, they selected the software industry.

The authors' case studies result in a variety of findings on the state of competition in Russia's regional markets. The extent of state/government involvement in business affairs continues to make a significant difference in the strength of competition – particularly in the "old" economy sectors. In most of the regions visited, there is a continuing – albeit metamorphosized – direct role of government in the marketplace, which more often than not has a negative impact of diminishing new business entry, largely benefiting the "old" economy firms. In particular, the case studies reveal incestuous "captured" relationships between government agencies and incumbent businesses, where their *joint* actions directly influence the extent to which new competition can thrive.

---

6 In light of the crisis that occurred in 1998, this is hardly a representative year for which to measure enterprise losses. However, more recent data on a cross-regional basis are not available and the losses depicted here are as of mid-1998, prior to the eruption of the crisis.

Some regional administrations employ protectionist policies to insulate "local champions" from competition – not only competition from within an oblast but from firms domiciled in "foreign" oblasts. For example certain oblasts have devised local registry stamps – under the guise of "ensuring quality control" – that have to be purchased and placed on beverage containers for the beverages to be sold within the oblast. Regional air transport provides another example. Collusion between local airlines and airports gives rise to effectively exclusive landing rights for local carriers: runway repairs are temporarily halted for local airlines to land, but for non-local airlines, the repairs are either stopped at inconvenient hours or not at all. Clearly, the cozy relationships between local firms and local administrations hamper inter-regional trade and investment flows, reducing the prospects for competitive pressure. But there are cases where government is playing an indirect, competition-reinforcing role in the market. More progressive and reform-oriented regional administrations, such as Novgorod's, have promoted new business entry, enterprise restructuring and a more flexible labor market through judicious economic and fiscal policies, bolstered by greater policy stability and transparency.[7]

In the "new" economy, Broadman et al find that government has yet to catch up with the market; as a case in point, the software industry benefits from the lack of sector-specific regulation. Lingering social obligations burden enterprises – especially those in the "old" economy – and serve to undermine the free play of competitive forces.

Yet unanticipated distortions are being engendered through some of the more celebrated enterprise reforms in Russia – particularly the policy to foster SME development. This industrial policy is, in fact, artificially constraining business growth. For example, certain SME tax incentives create palpable inducements for businesses to remain at certain scales, lest they not enjoy tax concessions. These distortions are hampering exploitation of SME economies of scale.

The 1998 debt default, economic crisis and ruble devaluation have prompted significant enterprise restructuring and changes in competitive strategy – especially in the "old" economy sectors – that are likely to change the face of certain market structures. Many firms interviewed for the case studies – particularly those in the tradeables sectors, such as wood processing, textiles and food – have embarked on restructuring (and expansion) strategies to take advantage of the void created by now-expensive imports and new opportunities of hitherto "off limits" export markets and are targeting sales to increase market share and profits. Restructuring is manifested in significant diversification of product lines, rationalization of production and integration and conglomeration through mergers and acquisitions (both vertical and horizontal), reduction in the share of barter and offsets as means to effecting commercial transactions, diversification of sources of supply, seeking out and responding to institutional investors (both foreign and domestic), and changes in the skills mix in staffing the workforce.

In the "new" economy, Broadman et al find that government has yet to catch up with the market; as a case in point, the software industry benefits from the lack of

7 See Broadman and Recanatini (2003) for an empirical analysis of enterprise restructuring and job creation and destruction in Russia.

sector-specific regulation. Lingering social obligations burden enterprises – especially those in the "old" economy – and serve to undermine the free play of competitive forces.

Yet unanticipated distortions are being engendered through some of the more celebrated enterprise reforms in Russia – particularly the policy to foster SME development. This industrial policy is, in fact, artificially constraining business growth. For example, certain SME tax incentives create palpable inducements for businesses to remain at certain scales, lest they not enjoy tax concessions. These distortions are hampering exploitation of SME economies of scale.

The 1998 debt default, economic crisis and ruble devaluation have prompted significant enterprise restructuring and changes in competitive strategy – especially in the "old" economy sectors – that are likely to change the face of certain market structures. Many firms interviewed for the case studies – particularly those in the tradeables sectors, such as wood processing, textiles and food – have embarked on restructuring (and expansion) strategies to take advantage of the void created by now-expensive imports and new opportunities of hitherto "off limits" export markets and are targeting sales to increase market share and profits. Restructuring is manifested in significant diversification of product lines, rationalization of production and integration and conglomeration through mergers and acquisitions (both vertical and horizontal), reduction in the share of barter and offsets as means to effecting commercial transactions, diversification of sources of supply, seeking out and responding to institutional investors (both foreign and domestic), and changes in the skills mix in staffing the workforce.

In general, Broadman et al find that firms face few effective competitors in their markets and that concentration seems to be increasing. At the *national* level, the degree of concentration of industrial output in Russia appears to suggest an absence of a structural competitive problem. The average national 4-firm concentration ratio (the sum of the market shares of the top four producers) is about 60%. For many industries, Russia and more industrialized countries (such as the U.S.) have similar 4-firm concentration ratios, and the largest Russian manufacturing enterprises (measured by number of employees) are not unusually large compared to firms in more industrialized countries. However, this aggregate-level analysis masks important underlying attributes of Russia's industrial landscape. Large Russian enterprises tend to be configured as single integrated multi-plant establishments, often located in or near a single city. In contrast, in industrialized economies a given enterprise usually has multiple establishments and they are located across domestic regions and often abroad. On an establishment basis, the largest Russian enterprises are significantly *larger* than their counterparts in other countries. Survey data from 1997 indicate that the average market share at the *oblast* level is 43%. Recent data on concentration indicate that at the *oblast* level, the average 4-firm concentration ratio is above 95%. Many of the dominant enterprises in Russia are also highly vertically integrated. Excessive levels of vertical integration superimposed on (horizontally) concentrated product markets can foreclose the entry of rival firms. The high degree of observed vertical integration largely reflects inertia of the uncertainties and chronic shortages of the old Soviet supply system. But vertical integration is also increasing, occurring usually through mergers and acquisitions rather than through *de novo* expansion.

In the case studies, concentration in market shares appears to be more frequently due to few firms rather than many firms of very unequal size. While it is difficult to generalize, in almost every sector analyzed, businesses indicated they faced a maximum of 3-6 competitors in their oblast/regional market. Not surprisingly, many of the firms indicated they had relatively sizeable market shares (at the regional level), indicating a moderate degree of horizontal dominance, often brought about through horizontal integration, i.e., horizontal mergers. The case studies also reveal an appreciable degree of vertical integration – particularly in "old" economy sectors; for example, some construction firms made bricks and other construction materials and were building and selling apartment buildings (to regional governments). In most cases, if there was not vertical integration, there were exclusive buyer-seller relationships through contracts.

Our case studies suggest that firms' ability to exercise market power is enhanced with concentration. One manifestation of this is that many of the firms we studied had plants that appeared to be above "minimum efficient scale" (i.e., the production level where unit costs are lowest). Indeed, during site visits our attention was often drawn to facilities that a general manager would proudly proclaim as being "the biggest in Europe". The fact of the matter is that such excess productive capacity serves as a credible threat to deter potential rivals from entering the market.

Much has been written about the problems posed by so-called "administrative barriers" to businesses in Russia, and policy-makers have given sizeable attention to these issues. To be sure, these problems are real. But Broadman et al find that a systemic examination of business transactions in Russia's regions reveals far more fundamental and sometimes less visible impediments to business start-ups and expansion in the underlying competitive fabric of markets. The case studies suggest that the competitive success of many (though not all) of the firms investigated was significantly determined by privileged relationships they enjoy with governmental authorities – especially local administrations, less so federal agencies – rather than their ability to serve effectively customers. Indeed strong political economic power is wielded by regional authorities.

This power manifests itself, in part, by preventing entry from firms in neighboring oblasts in order to protect the market shares of local champions. Among other means, entry is deterred through local government practices involving subsidies, anti-competitive disposition of marketing rights, access to land and real estate, and so on (recall also the example above regarding local air transport exclusivity). A key constraint new start-ups and expanding medium sized firms face in the industrial sectors is the market power exercised by large, dominant incumbent enterprises that occupy concentrated market segments through their pricing, investment and marketing strategies. By the same token, a critical bottleneck constraining entry is the market power exercised by infrastructure service providers and the regulatory regime governing their service offerings. In addition an important barrier to entry and expansion that stands out from the majority of case studies in the "new" economy software sector is the uneven playing field determined by lack of enforcement of intellectual property rights that lead to piracy. Problems of excessive inspection intervention, indeed the political economy use of inspections, in business activities by various governmental bodies – especially federal agency branch offices in the regions – are highly problematic.

Broadman et al's case studies show that that lack of competitive access to warehousing and distribution facilities, due to monopolization and corruption, also is stifling competitive entry in Russia's local markets. In addition, the inability to secure competitively priced financing and for a sufficiently reasonable term is a significant impediment. There is also a difficulty in finding expert workers. Indeed, many of the managers in the studied firms indicated that despite stronger demand for their products following the ruble devaluation, their attempts to expand production capacity are hampered by the lack of labor trained in modern management techniques and in specialized areas such as use of computer programs. Although most firms acknowledge that a large part of the problem is that they are unable to offer competitive wages, the shortage also is the result of institutional constraints that engender limited regional mobility within the country.

In devising policy recommendations, Broadman et al note that although business competition in Russia's regions has intensified significantly in the wake of the 1998 crisis, the incidence of competition varies considerably across sectors and across regions, which is not surprising in an economy undergoing transition and as heterogeneous as Russia's. Still, it is not clear the extent to which the new competitive pressures are enduring.

The case studies suggest that it is important for Russia's competition policy regime to place emphasis on dealing with horizontal and vertical structural market imperfections among incumbent industrial firms to create economic space for new entrants. Priority attention and resources – both human and political – would be best directed toward those markets where there is already significant concentration and structural dominance; other markets can be dealt with subsequently. Moreover, policy emphasis on preventing *further* horizontal and vertical consolidation through mergers and acquisitions in markets where concentration and structural dominance are already excessive would be highly desirable. In this regard, more explicit and well-defined merger guidelines could be developed to establish general policy parameters for distinguishing between pro-competitive and anti-competitive mergers based on similar guidelines used in industrial countries, such as the EU and the US. But a balance must be struck between, on the one hand, prohibiting excessive enterprise integration that engenders the exercise of market power, and on the other, fostering sufficient integration that permits the realization of technical economies of scale and scope.

Equally important is the need to create bona fide economic competition both within and among regions. This would include the removal of regional government barriers to inter-regional trade and investment. Indeed, the use of licenses, taxes, loans, debt forgiveness or other instruments to favor some local enterprises over others should be harshly penalized under the existing provisions disciplining anti-competitive acts by state executive bodies. To facilitate trade and investment within the country, all requirements that unduly obstruct economic activity, such as bans on the import or export of goods and services across localities and oblasts, unequal price controls or taxes for local versus non-locally produced goods, or the granting of other unequal privileges to some enterprises and not others should be removed based on enforcement of the provisions related to state executive bodies. The current SME tax concession regime needs to be reformed so as to reduce the incentives for firms to remain at small scales so as to qualify for tax benefits. Consideration might be given to provide the SME tax credits along a sliding and less graduated scale.

The regional branches of the Ministry of Antimonopoly Policy and Support for Entrepreneurship (MAPSE) needs to play a stronger role. Clearly stronger enforcement is needed at the regional level against anti-competitive conduct by incumbent dominant firms. As part of their competition advocacy mandate, regional MAPSE offices would do well to undertake more regular educational activities aimed at ensuring that the public at large as well as all enterprises, especially start-ups, are aware of the importance of the competitive process in practice, and the objectives and content of the competition law. Consideration should be given for a new policy of making federal transfers to the regions conditional on progress in removing barriers to inter-regional trade and investment. This could help counteract the captured relationships between local government agencies and incumbent businesses.

At the same time, in order to foster new business entry, it is essential to improve access to distribution, warehousing and infrastructure services. Facilitating access to distribution channels and warehouses requires the competitive restructuring of powerful incumbent monopolies (often government sanctioned) and combating the corruption that is prevalent in these sectors. With respect to infrastructure services, regional transport facilities – especially road, rail and air networks – need to be modernized, prices need to be set in accordance with cost, and access allocated competitively. With a more competitive telecommunications network will come increased availability and affordability of data and information services, and the development of e-commerce, which can significantly lower transactions costs across oblasts and facilitate downstream entry. Facilitating private access to real estate is a policy priority to enable new entry. To this end, rapid implementation of the new Land Code at the local level is needed. Now that the legal constraints on private ownership have been removed, local governments need to realize that the commercial, fiscal and economic benefits of divestiture far outweigh those from continued government ownership.

Breaking the nexus between incumbent firms and regional governments to foster competition will require fundamental reforms, such as in the civil service, so that salaries are appropriately increased and performance-based reward structures are introduced. But other reforms will be necessary, for example, prohibiting the use of fine-generated resources to fund inspection bodies or preventing tax inspectorates from using the revenues from fines to meet their tax revenue quotas. There is a need to establish independent monitoring systems as a check on reform implementation. As an example, monitoring mechanisms in the area of business inspections could thus include: (i) quarterly public reporting by inspection/ supervisory agencies about their inspection activities; (ii) introduction of inspection logs at enterprises and organizations; and (iii) establishment of coordinating boards to organize inspection activities (these boards would be responsible for monitoring and summing up the results of all inspections, as well as for maintaining a database of such inspections). An important lesson from international experience is that transparent and participatory regulatory impact assessments (RIAs) should be institutionalized for new regulations, in order to subject any proposals to cost-benefit scrutiny.

Clearly, continuation by the government of its current well-designed efforts to de-bureaucratize and reduce administrative barriers, such as reform of the registration and licensing regime for new firms, would be helpful. These will surely help reduce one component of the impediments business start-ups face in Russia. Of course the key to success of such legislative initiatives is the extent to which once they are enacted, they are implemented and their provisions are actively enforced. Appropriate incentives and disincentives thus need to be created in order to ensure satisfactory results. This is particularly challenging at the regional level, where there is a long history of discretionary actions by local officials and collusion between them and incumbent firms.

Finally, Broadman et al argue that more effective protection of intellectual property rights is required to address the R&D market failures and uncompensated benefits and costs. This should stimulate entry and expansion, especially by producers in the "new" economy through the recapturing of market shares stolen by pirates. Russia is making steps towards protecting companies' intellectual property rights as it strengthens its legal framework in preparation for WTO membership. Indeed, more generally, competition in Russia's markets will be significantly enhanced from the liberalization of the trade and investment regimes that will come with accession to the WTO, and thus this objective should be a policy priority for the government.

4 Infrastructure Regulation in Russia's Regions: The Telecommunications and Internet Sector

The operations and structure of the network infrastructure services sector in Russia – encompassing the energy utilities, transport operators, and telecommunication providers, among others – condition the development of the country's "real" sectors. Indeed, there is accumulating evidence that one of the principal burdens on efficient enterprise entry, expansion and innovation in Russia is the extent to which infrastructure service providers pose bottlenecks to broader commercial activity. In principle, one of the tasks of the economic regulatory regime governing infrastructure firms is to minimize such bottlenecks. Of course, as in all economies, while such "utility" regulation should enable government to provide important economic and social protections to the users of the services – both the population at large as well as businesses – it invariably also imposes costs. In Russia these costs arise not only from inappropriate *rules* (for example, prices not being in line with market incentives and social cost valuation), but also inappropriate *application* of utility-related rules (for example, some enterprises within the same industry are entitled to special privileges, whether in terms of access and/or pricing). There are several benefits for Russia of fostering liberalization of the infrastructure sectors, accompanied by transparent and clear "rules of the game." First, these sectors are important sources of employment and innovation in their own right. Moreover, more efficient provision of infrastructure services, in turn, will allow the development of the downstream (real) sector, as the latter depends crucially on more efficient infrastructure. Finally, transparent regulation will help to reduce incentives and opportunities for corruption and preferential privileges for certain operators both at the upstream and downstream sector.

Much has been written about the regulatory problems – both political and economic – and about the debate concerning reform initiatives in the "traditional" infrastructure sectors in Russia, such as electric power, natural gas, and rail transport. But there has been relatively little analysis of arguably the most dynamic Russian infrastructure sector – the telecom network, especially enhanced telecom services, such as Internet services. Dutz, Vagliasindi and Broadman focus on the role of the telecommunications and Internet sector and its regulation in Russia. The sector is increasingly becoming a key facilitator of inter-regional – and international – trade and investment in the country, and how it develops will be crucial in reducing business transactions costs and allowing for exchanges that otherwise would not take place.

The Russian telecommunications industry structure is generally characterized by market and competitive fragmentation, largely due to the lack of a transparent and clear sector strategy. Although consolidation is rapidly underway, the traditional fixed-line market is currently organized into 89 regions, each of which has an incumbent operator. All of these operators provide local, long-distance and international voice services, and many also offer data transmission, mobile and Internet services. The telecom holding company Svyazinvest controls the majority of these. Only three regional operators (MGTS, which serves the city of Moscow; PTS, which serves the city of St. Petersburg; and Moscow Electronsvyaz, which serves Moscow region apart Moscow itself) have more than 1 million access lines accounting together for approximately 27% of total access lines in Russia. Competition to the traditional incumbents is starting in many regions, particularly in Moscow and St. Petersburg. The announced sector consolidation through the creation of seven new enlarged supra-regional telecom operators is proceeding ahead of schedule, with the merger terms already announced for all companies. In particular, the swap terms for all seven enlarged regionals have been approved by all shareholders except for those in the Central region, where the process is expected to be formally completed before the spring of 2002.

The Russian Internet sector is still in the early stage of development, with penetration just around 3% compared to an average of over 20% in Europe. On the other hand, the Russian market is now growing at exponential rates, comparable to the fast growth in the US after 1995. Still, the Internet business in Russia is highly fragmented. There are around 300 companies licensed to provide Internet access services. More than half of the Internet Service Providers (ISPs) are based in Moscow and St. Petersburg. Quality of the service varies significantly throughout Russia depending mainly on the public network involved in the transmission process.

The telecom industry is generally overseen by the Ministry of Communications (MoC). However, the Ministry of Antimonopoly Policy and Support for Entrepreneurship (MAPSE) and the regional administrations also exert some power, such as the setting of tariffs. In September 2001 President Putin signed a decree setting in motion the creation of a new Unified Tariff Body (UTB) with sectoral jurisdiction over regulation of effectively *all* infrastructure prices in Russia, including telecommunications. The UTB would be based on the existing Federal Energy Commission (FEC), and in the case of telecom rate-setting, absorb the authority currently vested in MAPSE.

In their analysis of the regulatory framework, Dutz et al highlight several problems emerging from the case studies. The key issue identified by the telecom operators is the lack of transparency on the procedural aspects of licensing, aggravated by the lack of formalized and specific appeal procedures. For example, formal technical requirements are very unclear and, in some cases, inconsistent with each other. The unpredictability in terms of changes in licensing terms at the time of renewal is extremely high. This dramatically reduces ex-ante incentives to invest in view of the ex-post renegotiation of licensing conditions. In addition, users and operators are given the right to interconnect their network and terminal equipment to the public switched telephone network (PSTN) if they meet the "interconnection requirements" set out by the government, which are provided by the common carriers or stipulated in the license. Since the list of conditions under which access can be denied includes lack of technical capabilities, many carriers experience delays and difficulties. There are provisions of non-discrimination among operators when issuing technical requirements for interconnection, but the criteria to assess discriminatory behavior are not defined, nor is the role for the regulator to detect and deal with discrimination. Lack of transparency and reasonableness with respect to fees prevail as well. These problems appear to be particularly severe in less developed oblasts, very likely due because of the quasi-monopolistic structure for interconnection providers.

Given the fixed nature of regulatory costs imposed on enterprises irrespective of company size, the burden of administrative and utility regulation falls most heavily on smaller start-ups. Costs can be substantial relative to revenues generated by a small enterprise, generally in the range of 10% of annual revenues. There is also the continuous uncertainty of new regulations. The uneven playing field penalizing smaller ISPs is aggravated by the problems on the demand side. Such problems include targeting less attractive customers that also view the Internet as less essential for their work, as the largest customers are served by the few privileged ISPs. However, very limited problems of non-payment are experienced, because of pre-paid tariffs – increasingly used after the financial crisis (especially in the case of riskier customer groups) – and due to the practice of dealing only through agencies that guarantee for the payment of associated enterprises. Another problem is lack of proper support for the equipment. Some telecom operators switch suppliers despite the considerable costs. Even the largest clients, despite being in a very privileged position – by receiving favorable discounts, credit terms, and distribution agreements – complain about the lack of customer care of equipment.

As to policy recommendations, Dutz et al note that delays by regional administrations in introducing more rational policies towards the telecoms sector stifle urgently needed investments in network infrastructure, adversely affecting all operators. The fact that tariffs for local calls for residential customers are so low has starved regional operators of funds for urgent investments, in turn exacerbating the problems surrounding access to the network infrastructure. Starting from November 1999, MAPSE started to raise telecom tariffs. The increases exceeded inflation and ruble depreciation, with tariffs starting to grow in real and dollar terms. However, tariff regulation continues to lack predictability, as there is no clear tariff formula and increases are authorised sporadically. Moreover, the process of tariff changes is open to political interference. In practice, regulation of private operators means including them on the government's list of "natural monopolies". However, it is not clear that the laws on natural monopolies and on competition provide for the inclusion of private telecom operators into the natural monopoly list in the way that MAPSE intends. If the government wants to find investors for Svyazinvest and its seven pan-regional subsidiaries, it will have to convince them that there will be less political interference in the sector.

A priority for reform of the telecom and Internet sector would include promoting further private sector involvement, with specific measures to stimulate competition. Options include unbundling Svyazinvest by separating and liberalizing international long distance and local calls; consolidating local telecom operators and allowing them to compete with each other; and licensing additional wireless local loop operators as alternative access providers. Of equal importance is the need to establish an improved, independent, transparent and publicly accountable regulatory oversight process and institutions, and bringing Russia closer to meeting WTO and EU requirements. In this context, Russia should consider giving the regulatory power for interconnection to the same institution responsible for price regulation, ideally vesting both functions in a new sector-specific regulatory agency.

With the creation of an independent sector regulatory agency, MAPSE would no longer be responsible for tariff-setting processes and supervision, leaving technical and pricing regulation to the specialized agency. On the other hand, MAPSE could play a more forceful role in the determination of the appropriate scope of the regulatory authority, of the appropriate market structure of the telecommunications markets, and focus on controlling anti-competitive conduct by dominant enterprises. It is still too early to assess the likely impact of the establishment of the Unified Tariff Body, but it raises several key issues that need to be resolved. One is the potential benefits and costs coming from the establishment of a single cross-sectoral regulator. Worldwide, sectoral agencies are considered to be more desirable because of the presence of strong economies of specialization and because they diversify the risk of institutional failure. Another key issue to be resolved is the definition of the (sub)sectors that can be considered as "natural monopolies" and should as such be subject to regulation at all. In telecommunications, technological progress has rapidly eroded monopolistic practices and "protected markets", even for fixed line local providers, so no segment of the sector can any longer be considered a natural monopoly.

There is also a need to strengthen coordination among the institutions charged with oversight of the sector, such as the Ministry of Communication and MAPSE, especially the latter's oblast branches that appear to lack authority in addressing cases of abuse of dominant position and discriminatory licensing or providing access to the network. In addition, uniform inter-regional guidelines are needed for licensing, along with clear terms for licensing renewal. At the same time, non-discriminatory terms are needed for interconnection. All public network operators should be obliged to interconnect their networks with one another. Those operators with the ability to abuse their market power should be subject to special rules (ex ante regulation) to ensure that they do not abuse their dominance.

5 Corporate Finance in Russia's Regions: Demand and Supply Constraints

Many of the bottlenecks that businesses face in Russia to get started and grow are finance related. Finance is aggravating regional business development in several ways. On the supply side, the volume of financing is very limited, as banks have small deposit and capital bases. A series of crises, most particularly the 1998 crisis, has eroded the confidence of the public in the fledgling banking sector, with only Sberbank and a few large banks enjoying any trust today. Short-term bank credit is scarce and highly priced, and requires liquid collateral of up to two times loan amounts. The limited contract enforcement environment discourages banks to lend, except to those enterprises in which they have shareholdings or another relationship. Most banks and other financial institutions – especially in the regions – do not have the expertise or skills to properly assess risks and structure financial products and services which meet the needs of the real sector. Furthermore, the banking sector is highly concentrated in urban centers, further limiting the access of many enterprises to finance.

Against this backdrop, Claessens and Ulgenerk analyze the various constraints to business finance on the supply side and show how demand from potentially viable enterprises at the regional level is often not met. Their examination highlights how the formal financial system has little to offer to most firms, especially to *de novo* firms. They note that the Russian financial system is small in absolute and relative terms and underdeveloped compared to countries with similar per capita income. The small size of the Russian financial system can largely be attributed to a lack of trust of households and enterprises in the financial sector, a lack that arises from past experiences with hyperinflation, the government's default on its domestic currency debt, and a weakly governed and fragile domestic banking system. The Russian banking sector is also very small in absolute size. The numerous, small banks have limited deposit and funding bases to lend to the new and existing enterprises. Most of the banks are too small to cater to the financing and investment needs of the large and medium Russian enterprises in energy, telecommunications, chemicals, transportation and utilities. The banking system also has a very limited outreach. As of end 2000, banks operating in Russia had only

2.8 branches per 100,000 inhabitants. This compares to an average for the EU of 48 per 100,000 inhabitants. The government-owned savings bank, Sberbank, dominates the branch network, with 1,564 branches and over 34,000 small outlets throughout the country. The majority of the banks are concentrated in Moscow and St. Petersburg.

Claessens' and Ulgenerk's assessment from the regional case studies reveals a ranking as to what are the most important forms of financing available for *de novo* firms and capital investments for existing firms. There is clear evidence that the most important source of capital for investment is internal financing. Leasing has been used to some extent to finance equipment. Indeed, one of the few formal financing structures, which are used more broadly in Russia, is leasing. Lease terms are more affordable than bank loan terms for comparable sums and maturities, as well as more flexible, faster, and simpler in terms of arrangements. After own financing, leasing is the second most popular source of equipment financing. Still, leasing activity in Russia is relatively very small, financing only 1.5% of capital investment, compared to some 30-40% in OECD countries.

Government-supported credit lines have had a mixed record. Where they have been most effective are initiatives for start-ups on the regional and municipal levels. Novosibirsk's regional authorities are discussing the implementation of business incubators, as well as the setting up of a system for transfer of state and regional property to start-ups at favored conditions. In Vladivostok, the regional government has set aside a notional sum for financing a Fund for Support of Small Business. Donor credit lines remain small as well, but they show that there is scope for viable lending. Private and donor-funded initiatives have also been a source of finance for the small and medium enterprises.

Normal trade credit is virtually non-existent in Russia. Today, businesses in Russia rarely use normal forms of trade financing. To the extent, trade credit is being offered, it is either for within the same business group or to buyers with whom there is a long-term relationship. In an environment of limited bank finance and no formal trade credit and liquidity, non-monetary forms of payment provide the liquidity and credit for the exchange and sales among enterprises. To a large extent, enterprises build-in premiums or discounts into the prices of the goods or liabilities exchanged, thus substituting trade terms (payment and interest) for price gains, and where the exchange of goods or offsets serves as immediate collateral. Although declining, non-monetary payments are still much used in Russia, especially in the remote regions for conducting trade transactions, to resolve arrears or for continued non-transparency reasons as well as to sustain non-viable enterprises.

In their discussion of policy recommendations, Claessens and Ulgenerk note that the weaknesses in Russia's creditors' rights and enforcement are important determinants of its ill-developed financial system. Similarly, Russia's capital market development is impeded by very weakly enforced equity rights. Adopting market economy accounting standards and applications in both the real and financial sectors would decrease the non-transparency and allow financial institutions to start intermediating funds more productively. Tax and audit reforms are also necessary to encourage transparency and full disclosure of information by the corporations. Increasing confidence in and capitalization of the financial system is a must for the longer term.

The development of a fully functioning financial sector in Russia will be a long-lasting effort. One crucial prerequisite for any meaningful reform is the full political commitment of the Russian government, including the Central Bank and the Ministry of Finance, to banking system restructuring and financial reform. This will be a necessity to create greater confidence over time among households and investors in the Russian financial system, thereby increasing the available financial savings and capital, and thus make greater financing available for the corporate sector. Indeed, building confidence requires that the government enforce its own set of rules. Enforcement of existing rules includes the closure and liquidation of insolvent banks according to already set procedures. Up to the present, instead of liquidating insolvent banks the government has, through various means, supported favored banks and through generally limited actions allowed other insolvent banks to remain in business as "zombies." The government also has only made limited efforts in stopping asset stripping in defunct or even officially intervened banks. Before any active restructuring, the liquidation of insolvent banks has to proceed first.

Recent changes in banking legislation are steps in the right direction, but questions still remain about their implementation. The State should be the regulator and supervisor of the financial sector, rather than a direct participant. The large state dominance in the banking sector continues to stifle competition and encourages directing the funds of the state banking sector into politically important projects. Encouraging further foreign bank entry in general would also increase the available capital and confidence in the banking sector.

6 Dispute Resolution in Russia: A Regional Perspective

In their chapter on the role of the courts in facilitating resolution of economic disputes, Hendley and Murrell argue that the *arbitrazh* courts play a beneficial role in the Russian economy that is widely underestimated. They are used extensively and they are viewed relatively benignly by business. Of course, the authors do not find that the *arbitrazh* courts are without problems, indeed far from it. But this is to be expected, since the courts are embedded in a society in which the historical legacy is far from helpful for legal processes, in which many of the institutions that are complementary to the *arbitrazh* courts function poorly, in which the central government has frequently reneged on financial commitments, and where conflicts between central and regional governments can cause problems even for the best designed institutions.

Russia's *arbitrazh* courts, which are the state-sponsored tribunal charged with resolving economic disputes, hear two types of cases: disputes between legal entities (including bankruptcy) and disputes between legal entities and the government. As market reforms have progressed, the disputes submitted to the *arbitrazh* court have grown more complicated, and not surprisingly, cases now take longer to process. Moreover, the increased use of penalties means that the amounts being demanded are no longer symbolic; yet the inability to enforce judgments is the single biggest shortcoming of the *arbitrazh* courts. The large number of cases that come before the *arbitrazh* courts is striking, and if enterprises are shunning the courts in favor of private enforcement, as is commonly stated, then the authors' data on use of the courts do not seem to reflect a lack of demand for the courts. While the number of cases decided decreased significantly from 1992 to 1994 in all of the studied regions, by 1997 the level of demand for the courts had risen above the 1992 level on a national basis, and by 2000 the level of demand was above 1992 levels in all regions under study. The number of claims brought by enterprises against state agencies has increased steadily, suggesting that suing the government is not regarded by enterprises as futile or quixotic.

The law requires that court cases be resolved within two months of being filed. Contrary to conventional wisdom, Hendley and Murrell show that delays have not been commonplace. Nationally, delays have never exceeded 5%. Of course there is regional variation in the levels of delays. The disparate levels of delays likely results from poor management and/or inadequate staffing and/or the complexity of the cases heard. Indeed, court personnel constantly complain about meager funding, and the difficulties in filling vacancies on the *arbitrazh* courts are well-known. Complexity is a likely explanation for the higher level of delays that are observed for Moscow City courts. Still, since the popular image of private enforcement is speed without concern for due process and procedure, it is remarkable that in three of the regions under study the *arbitrazh* courts are rated as superior to private enforcement even on speed. Russian enterprise managers usually emphasize the advance filing fees as a key obstacle to using the courts (second in importance after problems with enforcement), despite the use of a sliding scale for the fees (based on the amount being sought in the case).

The authors' data show, however, that firms are increasingly successful in getting judges to waive the requirement that the fees be paid when the case was filed in favor of collecting these fees from the losing party at the conclusion of the case. While the weak competence of judges is a barrier to the use of the courts, the evidence suggests that competence of judges is less of an obstacle to using the court than either lack of speed or expense. The difficulty of enforcing judgments is regarded as the greatest barrier to using the courts in all the regions studied. Of course, although the problem of enforcement is often laid at the door of the courts, the reality is that, in Russia (as in most countries), judges have no responsibility for enforcing their decisions. Indeed, judges share the frustration of litigants, complaining that their hard work is in vain if the end result is a decision that is never enforced. From 1998 on, enforcement has essentially become the province of state-sponsored "bailiffs", who are subordinate to the Ministry of Justice. There is a decided lack of attention to the special skills and knowledge needed in the Russian bailiff system in order to get enterprises to pay judgments, which no doubt contributes to the less-than-stellar record of enforcement.

Hendley and Murrell conclude their analysis with guidance for reform of court procedures. First, proposals to introduce a new mandatory stage in the judicial process for preparing a case for a hearing, such as having the parties meet with the judge to explore the possibility of working out a settlement, is unlikely to be effective in Russia. The majority of civil cases in Russia (at present) involve nonpayments and most are often settled at the first hearing. So mandating a pre-hearing step will not achieve much. Second, the ability of the *arbitrazh* courts to operate effectively has been undermined by the tendency of litigants and their counsel to appear for hearings without being fully prepared. Other countries have found that imposing fines on those who appear unprepared serves to discourage such behavior. Third, the "bailiffs" charged with implementing *arbitrazh* court decisions ought to be institutionally distinct from their colleagues charged with implementing the decisions of courts of general jurisdiction and/or protecting judges. Finally, while substantial expansion in *arbitrazh* court personnel is needed, at the same time it is critical to make sure there is adequate funding for salaries and office space. To mandate an increase in the number of such officials by statute, and then be unable to carry through, would likely have the effect of undermining confidence in the courts.

7 Conclusion

We posed the question at the outset as to whether Russia's new-found growth is sustainable? The analysis undertaken in this study suggests that the prospects for robust business development and, in turn, enduring economic growth in Russia depend on strengthening a set of fundamental market institutions – at the regional level. To be sure, the notion that building strong market institutions in Russia is key to growth is not novel, and most *federal* policy makers in Russia and observers of the country's economic reform process at the *national* level over the past decade will not be surprised by this finding. But what is new is the study's insights that the most critical market institutions in need of reform (in terms of development impact) are those in the *regions*. Insufficient competition among enterprises, both within and across local markets, blunt incentives for efficient allocation of new investment, sound corporate performance and innovation. The strong political economy nexus that often binds regional governments and incumbent enterprises plays a large role in inhibiting business startups. The regulatory regime governing infrastructure services providers at the regional level (in this case, the telecom and Internet sector) lacks transparency, is not subject to systematic application, and development of its procedures lags the market. The commercial banking sector remains underdeveloped, with little intermediation of savings into investment taking place. The sector is also lacking in competition, especially in local markets. For most Russian firms, the banking system is virtually irrelevant in satisfying investment needs. Russian businesses are increasingly using *arbitrazh* courts, which have become more effective over time, to settle commercial disputes. But, enforcement of judgments remains problematic. The training of judges and the scale of institutional resources made available to the court system, especially at the regional level, are substantially inadequate.

While some reforms to rectify these problems have been underway, the findings from this study indicate that in most cases, *second generation* institutional and structural policy changes are now needed. And such reforms need to be implemented locally (of course nested within consistent reforms made at the federal level). For example, reducing so-called administrative barriers through streamlining business registration and licensing procedures will help facilitate new business startups. But in the absence of resolving regional anti-competitive market structures or removing deep-seated incentives for anti-competitive conduct by incumbent firms – often in collusion with local governments – such administrative reforms will be for naught and may well be counter-productive. Indeed, the illusion that alleviation of administrative barriers will bring forth new investment is already breeding cynicism about the drive for reform among some businesses and policy makers. It is increasingly clear that only by tackling more fundamental institutional reforms will policy credibility be ensured. Similarly, improvements in the procedures of *arbitrazh* courts will surely facilitate the processing of commercial disputes. Yet only if the bailiff system at the local level is strengthened will enforcement of *arbitrazh* court decisions become truly effective and instill widespread confidence among businesses that it is worth taking the risk of making investments in Russia. Overall, the specific policy lessons distilled from the variety of business case studies analyzed in this monograph can greatly inform and shape both the agenda for, and content of these types of second generation reforms.

Of course the challenge of changing long-lived behaviors and building the proper institutions should not be underestimated. As our analysis shows, some vested interests – in business and in government – are strong and, at least in the short run, will likely view needed reforms in public policy to run counter to their own private interests. In this respect the reform agenda is likely of a medium-term nature. But as the case studies also demonstrate, there are in fact parties that are cognizant of strong incentives for reform now – and are acting on them. For example, some local government officials recognize the tax revenue and job creation benefits of allowing for greater enterprise competition and thus are reducing protection of local champions. Similarly, some regulators of infrastructure services, especially in the telecommunications and Internet sector, have gotten the message that realization of the potential dynamism and scale economies of the geographically large Russian economy hinges on modernization of network systems and that only if tariffs are set in line with market signals will needed investments be made by the private sector. As the resonance of these types of incentives grows and more actions are taken producing positive benefits, the greater the momentum will be for further reform.

References

Broadman, H. (2000) "Reducing Structural Dominance and Entry Barriers in Russian Industry", *Review of Industrial Organization,* 16, (3), September.

Broadman, H. and F. Recanatini (forthcoming) "Where Has All the Foreign Investment Gone in Russia?", *Eurasian Geography and Economics*.

Broadman, H. and F. Recanatini (2003) "Is Russia Restructuring?, *Journal of Corporate Ownership and Control,* Vol. 1, No. 1, November.

Broadman, H., ed. (2002) Unleashing Russia's Business Potential: Lessons from the Regions for Building Market Institutions, The World Bank, Washington, DC.

Center for Fiscal Policy (2001) "Local Governments in the Russian Federation", Moscow.

Goskomstat (2000) *Regions of Russia,* Moscow.

Orttung, R. W., ed. (2000) The Republics and Regions of the Russian Federation: A Guide to the Politics, Policies, and Leaders, New York: East West Institute.

Macroeconomic Aspects of Opening up, Unemployment and Sustainable Growth in Transition Countries

Paul J.J. Welfens[1]

---

[1] I am grateful for discussions with participants at an IMF seminar (May 28, 2004); in particular I appreciate the suggestions by Timothy Lane. I also gratefully acknowledge technical support from Dora Borbély and Andre Jungmittag, EIIW at the University of Wuppertal and Albrecht Kauffmann, EIIW Center at the University of Potsdam; many thanks also go to Mario Fantini, European Commission, Thorvaldur Gylfason, University of Iceland and Bernhard Eckwert, University of Bielefeld. The usual disclaimer applies.

1 Introduction

Economic opening up has been a natural element of systemic transformation in the former Soviet Union and the smaller post-socialist countries of Eastern Europe. After high inflation rates and a massive transformational recession in the early transition stage – reflecting obsolescence of part of the capital stock and adjustment costs in the course of restructuring – in the first transition stage, most transition countries have achieved considerable economic growth. Countries with relatively low per capita income, a well educated labor force and a functioning banking system should indeed be able to record considerable economic growth if stable and efficient institutions, competitive pressure and opening up are combined in a sustained manner. It is not easy for transition countries with a young democracy to come up with the right combination of constitutional foundations and efficiency enhancing political learning, in particular since governments eager to generate quick improvement in some fields might favour short-term political action over long term growth strategies.

This analysis will focus on economic catching-up in the sense that we consider economies which become open for trade, foreign direct investment flows and technology transfer. We assume that the first stage of economic opening up is accompanied by a rise in price elasticities. However, in a second transition stage during which firms increasingly specialize in more technology intensive (and less price sensitive) products, requiring a higher share of sunk costs in investment, labor demand elasticity will be assumed to fall. As regards innovations, we will focus partly on process innovations, but more important here are product innovations in countries catching-up. Product innovations are new for the respective poor country but not new to the world economy so that from the perspective of a leading global economy, we focus on international diffusion phenomena. The following analysis presents certain analytical building blocs but not an integrated model, although one may combine the various blocs to a consistent meta model. Moreover, there will be no microeconomic foundations of behaviour at the macroeconomic level. This certainly is possible but as we will consider only minor – but powerful – modifications of well-known models, we are not so much interested in the aspects of microeconomic foundations.

We will emphasize that for certain analytical purposes, it is useful to take a look at the macroeconomic impact of both supply-side and demand-side impulses. In every economy, output dynamics can be understood to be a mixture of the impact of the supply side – its macroeconomic equivalence is the production potential $Y^{pot} = K^{ß}L^{1-ß}$ (K is capital and L is labor) – and of aggregate demand Y^d. In transition countries, both supply-side dynamics and the demand side are important with some sectors being dominated by supply-side developments while others are shaped by demand side dynamics. A hybrid approach can be written as follows:

$$Y = \alpha Y^{pot} + (1-\alpha) Y^d \tag{1.1}$$

An important question is what determines α (in the interval 0,1), the size of the relative supply-side impact parameter. It will reflect various forces, including expectations. The most simple form to think about α is to consider it identical with 1-u (with u denoting the unemployment rate). In a full employment economy, u is zero and hence only the supply side dynamics – that is, the accumulation of input factors – will determine actual gross domestic product. If u were rather high, it is clear that supply-side dynamics would hardly influence actual output while the demand side would have a strong impact on Y. A more refined way would be to replace a with u^{χ}, where the parameter χ is assumed to be positive. In a small open economy – which asymptotically faces a totally elastic world demand curve – k (k =: K/L), the impact of the supply-side, should be relatively high.

It is obvious that for the case of a closed economy the fiscal multiplier for the case of standard specification of the demand side is smaller than the standard textbook case of 1/s; with α =1-u, the fiscal multiplier is

$$dY/dG = 1/[1-uc] \text{ (see appendix).} \tag{1.2}$$

An exogenous increase in the production potential raises actual output by

$$dY/dY^{pot} = (1-u) + u\partial Y^{d}/\partial Y^{pot} > 0. \tag{1.3}$$

For the special case of an increase of the production potential through one unit of net investment and assuming an exogenous real interest rate, we have $\partial Y^{d}/\partial Y^{pot} = r$ and hence

$$dY = [(1-u) + r]dK \tag{1.4}$$

Economic catching-up (associated with both supply-side effects and demand dynamics) is subsequently understood as moving up the technology ladder of products (i.e., the adoption of more sophisticated quality products over time). Product innovation rates will largely be considered exogenous so that we leave open the explanation as to why and at what time firms in the respective countries will upgrade product assortments (e.g. this may be linked to foreign direct investment inflows or to a rise in the ratio of government expenditures on research and development relative to GDP). The analytical focus will be on a one sector model or a two sector approach with tradables and nontradables. Moving up the technology ladder thus means that the share of high quality products in overall exports or total output increases in the respective transition country. An interesting theoretical challenge is to consider both product and process innovations which we will undertake in one simple model – a more refined approach includes endogenous process innovation (and possibly endogenous product innovations).

While the political reforms in transition countries will affect opportunities for economic growth there are naturally favourable prospects of economic catching up in the context of economic opening up. Once those countries have opened up for trade and capital flows they can benefit from:

- competitive pressure from world markets stimulating efficiency-enhancing economic restructuring;
- productivity stimulating effects from OECD imports of intermediate products used for production of final goods, including export goods;
- import of investment goods with embodied technological progress;

- exploitation of scale economies in the context of rising exports in scale intensive industries;
- inflows of foreign direct investment (FDI) which raise the capital stock in the case of greenfield investment and raise factor productivity in the context of international mergers and acquisitions.

For economic analysis it is rather useful to make a distinction between the non-tradables (N-) and the tradables (T-)sector.

- Rising trade will naturally only affect the tradables sector, however the tradables sector will typically be the main impulse for structural change.
- FDI inflows can be in both the T-sector and the N-sector. A major effect of FDI inflows should be productivity growth. The structure of FDI inflows will thus partly determine the relative price of tradables, namely to the extent that productivity determines the relative price. If FDI is affecting both sectors in a parallel way with respect to productivity growth, we should expect a smaller rise in the relative price of nontradables compared to the case that FDI inflows are concentrated in the tradables sector.

Foreign Direct Investment

It is an interesting question as to whether asymmetric FDI inflows – eg. a dominance of FDI in the tradables sector – will cause any problems for the economy. More generally put, to what extent large differences in productivity growth could be a problem for balanced growth and full employment? Furthermore, to what extent will the production elasticity of domestic capital affect the long term ratio of domestic capital to foreign capital (K**) employed? We consider the production potential to be given. We take up the latter question first and assume that output is determined on the basis of domestic capital input K and the stock of foreign capital K** (production function and gross domestic product, respectively, is $K^{ß}K^{**1-ß}$) while demand consists of domestic investment – assumed to be proportionate to national income - and net exports X' which we assumed to be proportionate (proportionality factor z") to cumulated foreign direct investment inflows K** in country I: the higher the stock of cumulated FDI inflows the better the access to the world market will be – to provide just one simple reasoning for the proposed specification.

$$ß\, K^{ß}K^{**1-ß} = z''\, K^{ß}K^{**1-ß} + z'K^{**} \tag{1.5}$$

Here we have assumed that both domestic capital K and foreign capital K** are rewarded in accordance with the marginal product rule so that national income is ß times gross domestic product.

$$(1-z'')ßK^{ß}K^{**-ß} = z' \tag{1.6}$$

Hence it holds:

$$[K/K^{**}] = \{z'/[1-z'']ß\}^{1/ß} \tag{1.7}$$

The ratio of domestic to foreign capital employed in the country is therefore positively correlated with z'/(1-z") and negatively correlated with the output elasticity of domestic capital ß.

One should emphasize that a combination of trade and FDI liberalization – observed in the reality of catching-up economies - takes us outside of the familiar Heckscher Ohlin model, and we clearly have a lack of modelling when it comes to taking into account both trade and FDI effects. There are also other potential problems associated with economic opening up, in particular there could be the problem of:

- high current account imbalances; indeed high deficit-GDP ratios can be a problem as foreign indebtedness is rising – however, a large sustained current account surplus also can be a problem since it will go along with "unnatural" net capital exports and a strong temporary boom which could raise the price of nontrables relative to tradables strongly;
- volatile short term inflows which raise the exposure of the respective country in the sense that high outflows might follow in the future: an exceptional period is represented by election years as these may be associated with political instability and large ideological swings in the case of a change in power.

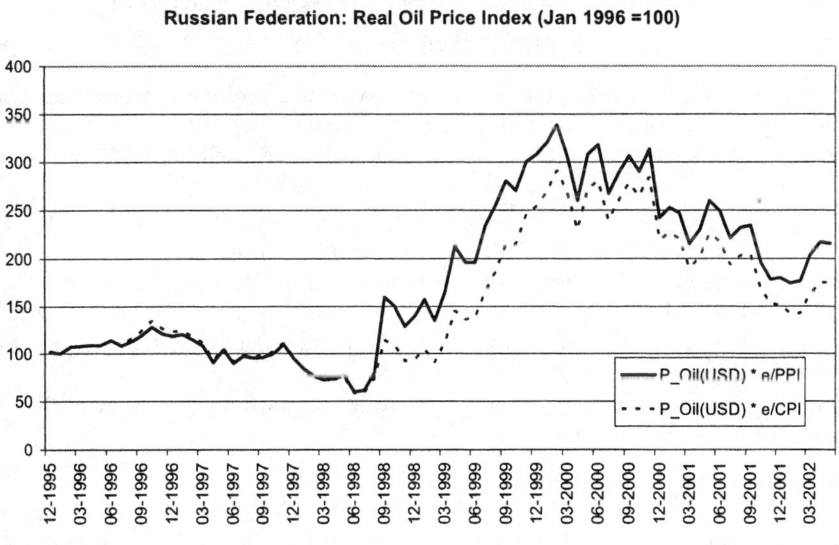

Fig. 1. Relative Price of Oil

Data Source: www.recep.org

Transition countries differ in many ways including the size of the respective country and factor endowment. Russia, Romania and Kazachstan are resource rich countries while other transition countries are relatively richly endowed with labor (and in some cases capital – taking into account countries which have attracted high FDI inflows). Countries which are relatively abundant in natural resources should clearly benefit from economic expansion in periods in which the relative price of resources is high – as was the case in the late 1990s.

One should not overlook that many resource abundant countries have a tendency for artificially low prices – for instance oil and gas prices in countries with rich oil or gas sites. If prices were raised to the world market price level there income levels from the natural resources sector would be high, however a fast price convergence would undermine the viability of energy-intensive firms and could raise unemployment. Countries rich in oil and gas also tend to have high nontradables prices and strong Balassa-Samuelson effects in the sense of a relative rise of nontradables prices. The latter may, however, not so much reflect technological economic catching-up but rather a pure natural resources boom effect. As regards the impact of a relative rise of energy prices on employment the effect will be negative in the non-energy sector and positive in the oil and gas sector. Assume that the energy sector uses only capital K' and labor L' while the non-energy sector (NE) uses factor inputs capital K and labor L, namely according to $Y^{NE}=K^{ß}E^{ß'}L^{1-ß-ß'}$. In the short term we can assume a constant capital stock and obtain from profit maximization and assuming competition in goods and labor markets so that factors are rewarded according to the marginal product rule (we denote the energy price as P", output price in the non-energy sector as P):

$$w=[1-ß-ß''][K/L]^{ß/1-ß'} (ß'/[P''/P])^{ß'/1-ß'} \qquad (1.8)$$

Hence, labor demand in the non-energy sector is a positive function of capital intensity and a negative function of the real energy price P"/P. However, in the energy sector – with output $E=K''^{ß''}L''^{1-ß''}$ – we will have (defining W/P"=w")

$$w''= [1-ß''][K''/L'']^{1/ß''} \qquad (1.9)$$

Overall labor demand is L'=L"+L. For countries which are richly endowed with natural resources a rise of the oil price could indeed raise overall labor demand and overall real income which is, expressed in terms of the non-energy good: $Y''=(P''/P)E+Y^{NE}$. The option is all the more attractive if the country considered enjoys alone or with other countries together – as in the case of OPEC – some international market power (then profit maximization leads to a slightly modified labor demand schedule).

Transition and Unemployment

As regards the dynamics of unemployment in transformation countries the unemployment rate is high in many transition countries (e.g. in Poland it has risen continuously in the first twelve years of transformation reaching a specific unemployment rate of close to 30% in 2004). In the following table, countries are ranked according to the degree of economic openness: It seems that small open economies face less problems in the field of unemployment than large economies – except for Russia which has benefited after the 1998 crisis from strong economic growth, stimulated strongly by high real oil prices.

Table 1. Openness (Trade/GDP), Growth and Unemployment in Transition Countries

	2000			2001			2002		
	Open-ness (% of GDP)	GDP growth (%)	Un-empl. Rate (%)	Open-ness (% of GDP)	GDP growth (%)	Un-empl. Rate (%)	Open ness (% of GDP)	GDP growth (%)	Un-empl. Rate (%)
Estonia	172.2	6.4	14.8	182.5	6.5	12.6	177,7	6,0	NA
Slovak Republic	149.6	2.2	18.9	156.5	3.3	NA	152,7	4,4	NA
Czech Re-public	146.6	2.9	8.8	144.2	3.1	NA	132,7	2,0	NA
Belarus	137.2	5.8	NA	137.1	4.7	NA	143,4	4,7	NA
Hungary	129.2	5.2	6.5	150.2	3.8	5.7	131,1	3,3	5,8
Bulgaria	122.5	5.8	16.3	118.7	4.1	NA	112,9	4,8	NA
Slovenia	121.8	4.6	7.5	116.5	2.9	5.9	114,4	3,0	13,8
Latvia	100.1	6.6	8.4	100.0	7.9	7.7	101,5	6,1	NA
Lithuania	96.7	3.9	11.1	107.3	6.5	12.9	113,9	6,7	NA
Romania	73.9	1.6	10.8	74.4	5.3	NA	76,7	4,3	NA
Russian Federation	70.7	8.3	11.4	59.8	5.0	NA	58,7	4,3	NA
Poland	61.8	4.0	16.7	59.8	1.0	16.2	59,5	1,4	17,8

Data Source: WDI 2002, WDI Online (Openness and GDP Growth 2001, 2002), IFS (Unemployment Rate 2001, 2002).

A typical phenomenon of transition countries is that the specific unemployment rate of unskilled labor is rather high, although labor markets seem to be quite flexible in most of these countries. This has to be explained, and our analysis will present a simple model which is mainly related to the interaction of the tradables and nontradables sectors.

Another element of transition and economic catching up is that firms will upgrade in terms of technology and specialize according to comparative advantages – here analysis shows that revealed comparative advantage is changing relatively quickly in countries with high foreign direct investment inflows. Shifts in revealed comparative advantages of different types of industries, ordered in accordance with technology intensity, are observed (Borbély, 2004). In the course of technological upgrading and specialization one may expect that factor demand becomes more inelastic; which consequences this might have for labor has to be analyzed. Unemployment also has other effects crucial for macroeconomic analysis, as will be shown subsequently.

Patterns of economic catching up are difficult to reconcile with Heckscher-Ohlin-Samuelson (HOS) modelling. Successful catching-up seems to be comprised of two elements where one indeed is HOS-compatible. A typical pattern of economic catching up in the context of EU southern and EU eastern enlargement (EU eastern enlargement effectively started with the EU association treaties with postsocialist countries of eastern Europe) is that poor countries specialize in labor intensive products which is consistent with the Heckscher-Ohlin-Samuelson approach. Poor countries are relatively labor abundant and thus should specialize in labor intensive products – economic opening up will raise the share of labor intensive production and exports will concern labor intensive products. Indeed countries such as Spain, Portugal, the Czech Republic, Poland and Hungary show a revealed comparative advantage (RCA) and high export unit values in part of labor intensive production: This combination of a high RCA and high export unit values in labor intensive production represents profitable exports in this field.

However, there is a second element of successful catching up, namely a gradual rise of the RCA in science-intensive and human-capital intensive products: if in such sectors a high and rising export unit value can be obtained this will stimulate long term expansion of these sectors (narrowly defined) and related sectors into which firms might move in the course of product differentiation (broadly defined) and catching-up. Such developments are associated with product innovation dynamics where a product innovation in a poor country typically will stand for diffusion when defined from the perspective of a leading OECD country. It is unclear whether the ability to achieve positive RCA in technology-intensive and science-intensive goods and differentiated goods (largely electronics) depends mainly on domestic human capital formation or mainly on foreign direct investment. A quick product upgrading and hence rising RCAs can hardly be expected without foreign direct investment inflows in those sectors unless there is considerable domestic research and development; and it requires active human capital formation policies and government support for research and development. Such traits are not only found in catching-up dynamics of Spain and Portugal in the 1980s and Hungary, Poland and the Czech Republic in the 1990s but also in Asian Newly Industrializing Countries in the 1970s and 1980s. One may argue that this second element of catching-up – it may be dubbed the DUNNING-SCHULTZ-SCHUMPETER element – is of general importance for product innovation and technological upgrading: Once labor intensive profitable production contributes to reducing unemployment and rising technology-intensive plus human-capital-intensive production contributes to growth of net exports of goods and services there is a broad potential for future structural change and shifts towards high-value added sectors. This amounts to favourable prospects for sustained long term economic growth. A crucial sustainability test for economic catching up is the phase of continuous real appreciation which will stimulate firms to upgrade product quality and to move towards industries which are more technology intensive and hence less price sensitive.

Taking simply a look at the output structure of countries in eastern Europe or Asia can be misleading, particularly if there is a high share of technology intensive production and positive RCAs in this field (positive RCA means that it should exceed unity if it is defined as sector export-import balance relative to the national export-import balance or exceed zero if one uses the natural logarithm of this variable). There is a caveat which concerns vertical multinational investment: e.g. even if computers were manufactured in Hungary or Poland one must analyze whether production statistics showing computer manufacturing are not hiding the fact that high tech components are imported and that value-added is mainly from "screw-driving factories" so that ultimately there is labor intensive production taking place. Production and export of intermediate inputs can, however, lead to more complex long term production and upgrading: e.g. Portugal initially developed intermediate product assembly for the automotive industry abroad, but later was able to attract final assembly in the automotive sector – not least because it had developed a competitive supplier industry. From this perspective technological upgrading does not only mean to switch to more advanced products but also to shift more into final product assembly. Another example is Toyota in Japan which started out decades ago as a producer of textile machinery before it became a very innovative and profitable automotive firm. We leave open here how upgrading in production takes place – in subsequent modelling the idea is basically that it is associated with foreign direct investors and that international technology transfer occurs (for simplicity) at zero marginal costs.

In the following analysis we want to highlight selected macroeconomic problems of transition and economic opening up. In particular, we are interested in innovation issues. We suggest new ideas in three different fields of transformation: (i) we state the hypothesis that there is a link between the Balassa-Samuelson effect and unemployment of unskilled labor; (ii) we argue that product innovations are crucial in the course of economic catching up and opening up – and we show how product innovations can be integrated into the Mundell Fleming model; (iii) it is shown in a simple dynamic model how the current account and relative innovation performance affect the long term real equilibrium exchange rate. In addition our analysis recalls standard sceptical approaches to high output growth in resource-rich countries when they based growth largely on depletion of non-renewable natural resources. As regards policy conclusions, government promotion of product innovation seems to be rather important in transition countries and NICs.

2 Growth, Resource Dynamics, Balassa-Samuelson Effects and Unemployment

2.1 Growth, Natural Resources and Economic Welfare

Before we take a closer look at innovation aspects of catching-up we briefly look into the issue of countries which are abundant with natural resources. In transition countries aggregate output can typically be described by a standard production function which for simplicity can have the arguments capital K, labor L, technology A – assumed to be labor augmenting – and natural resources dR/dt where R is the stock of natural resources. In the case of a Cobb-Douglas production function we can write:

$$Y=K^{ß} R'^{ß'}(AL)^{1-ß-ß'} \tag{2.1}$$

Hence output growth is – with g denoting growth rate and R'=dR/dt - given by

$$g_Y = ßg_K + ß'g_{R'} + (1-ß'-ß'')[g_L + g_A] \tag{2.2}$$

As we have a homogenous production function we also can write

$$Y = Y_K K + Y_{AL}(AL) + Y_R \,|dR/dt| \tag{2.3}$$

If factors are rewarded according to the marginal product rule we have

$$Y= rK + w[AL] + [P^R/P]|\,dR/dt| \tag{2.4}$$

If resources are non-renewable resources an adequate measure of welfare – or of "modified net national product" – would be (assuming that capital depreciation is proportionate to K) the following term Z':

$$Z' = Y - \delta K - A''|\,dR/dt| \tag{2.5}$$

A" is a real shadow price variable which reflects the value of resource depletion in terms of consumption goods; A" should be determined on the basis of a sustainable growth model – at a given level of technology (not discussed here). If there are negative external effects from oil production and transportation (problems of oil spills due to pipeline ruptures – causing serious health problems for the local population; e.g. the case of Russia) the variable A" is raised(!).

In a broad perspective this concept corresponds to the logic of net value added. One has to deduct capital depreciations and resource depletion if one wants to focus on value added along with maintaining the stock of capital and natural resources, respectively.

The term adR/dt catches the depletion of natural resources which are considered as a natural asset here. Combining equations (2.4) and (2.5) yields

$$Z'= rK + w[AL] + \{[P^R/P]|\,dR/dt| - A''|\,dR/dt|\} - \delta K \tag{2.6}$$

If the relative price of natural resources were identical to the parameter a, an adequate welfare measure would be simply the sum of capital income and labor income. The analysis is rather complex in reality since the first element in the term

$\{[P^R/P]|\ dR/dt| - A"|\ dR/dt|\}$ refers to the physical use of resources while the second term dR/dt should effectively be corrected by a factor (1-b"), where b" is a technological progress parameter allowing a better exploitation of existing stocks of resources. As b" can be assumed to be relatively large in transition countries one should not overemphasize the problem of natural resources depletion in the medium term. However, in the long run this aspect is clearly important.

$$Z' = rK + w[AL] + \{[P^R/P]|\ dR/dt| - A"(1-b")|\ dR/dt|\} - \delta K \quad (2.6')$$

If the relative price of oil is increasing (as was the case in the late 1990s) we can expect a rise of Z'.

In any case we may emphasize that resource rich countries are well advised to take into account the problem that early growth dynamics can only be sustained if there is long term industrial diversification in production and exports. This view does, of course, not rule out that proceeds from the export of natural resources can be quite useful to finance the import of machinery and equipment as well as technology useful for the expansion of manufacturing exports in the long run. There is also a risk that strong wage growth from the resource sector – in periods of high international resource prices – spills over to other sectors and thus could raise unemployment. Russia, Kazakhstan, Azerbaijan and Romania are crucial countries in this respect.

2.2 The Balassa-Samuelson Effect, Unemployment and Exports

The catching-up process of poor countries will be accompanied by relatively high growth rates which in turn will raise the relative price of nontradable (N) goods. The relative price of nontradables – including rents – will increase in the course of rising real per capita income; this is the Balassa-Samuelson (1964) effect which we assume to work in transition countries. The price index is $P=(P^N)^b\ (P^T)^{(1-b)}$. If we assume a fixed exchange rate and an exogenous and constant world market price of tradables the domestic price of tradables is exogenous – the price level is determined by the Balassa-Samuelson (BS) effect and the rise of the nontradables price. The assumption of a constant exchange rate might be inadequate in resource abundant countries, which in a regime of flexible exchange rates will face considerable appreciation pressure in periods of a rise of the world market price of natural resources. Rather, one would expect long term appreciation – bringing about a rise of the nontradables price in the context of stable nontradables prices and a fall of the domestic price of tradables (due to strong appreciation) – in combination with high volatility of the exchange rate.

Now let us take a look at the labor market for unskilled workers. A first issue concerns the size of the true unemployment rate; if state-owned firms have a policy of not laying off excessive workers such firms stand for hidden unemployment. Other distortions also could be important: In poor countries government and state-owned firms, respectively, tend to distort international trade by buying – often for pure prestige reasons – the latest technology in OECD countries while a private company often would have preferred instead to buy older vintages of machinery and equipment because this is cheaper and represents a higher labor intensity (with labor abundance it makes no economic sense to buy the latest technology which is developed in capital intensive countries) than ultra-modern equipment. From this perspective one should not be surprised if empirical analysis of international specialization would not exactly find Hecker-Ohlin dynamics in poor countries.

Tradables and Nontradables

Next we turn to the role of tradable goods versus nontradable goods. Assuming that consuming nontrables is a basic necessity for survival – think for instance of housing – one may argue that the reservation wage (the beginning of the labor supply curve) is determined by the absolute price of nontradables. Hence the Balassa-Samuelson (BS) effect will shift up the labor supply curve over time. At the same time we may assume that there is labor saving technological progress in both the tradables and the nontradables sector. We have sectoral neoclassical production functions for T (sector 2) and N (sector 1) with the inputs unskilled labor L, capital K and labor augmenting technological progress A; in addition we assume that skilled labor H is employed in the T sector (an alternative would be to assume that only skilled labor is employed in the T sector, then full employment in the presence of any excess supply of L in the nontradables sector can be only eliminated through retraining efforts and skill-upgrading which is costly)

$$T^s=T(L^T,H,K^T,A^T) \qquad (2.7)$$

$$N^s=N(L^N,K^N,A^N) \qquad (2.8)$$

where A^N is assumed to be governed by positive spillover effects from A^T because the tradables sector typically is the more dynamic sector and indeed often has technology spillover effects. Let L^{Ns} denote the short-term labor supply of unskilled labor in the N-sector which is supposed to depend positively on the sectoral nominal wage rate W^N and negatively on the price level and the nontradables price P^N. We will consider a rise in the price of nontradables which implies a leftward shift of the labor supply curve in W^N,L^N space. Assume a constant capital stock K^N in the nontradables sector, then the – exogenous or endogenous (for instance determined by the level of international trade relative to output in the tradables sector) – spillover effect from technological progress in the T-sector: labor-saving progress in the T-sector, A^T, is assumed to have a positive spillover to A^N, that is to trigger labor-saving progress in the N-sector, and this rise of A^T implies a leftward shift of the labor demand curve in the N-sector. In the subsequent diagram we assume this leftward shift to dominate the rightward shift associated with a rise of the nontradables price. The effect is a reduction in employment in the N sector and to the extent that in the short run labor is immobile across sectors (or regions in the case that N and T are located in different regions), we will have quasi-unemployment, namely the difference between initial employment L^N_0 and L^N_1. Strictly speaking we have voluntary unemployment but those losing their job will certainly register as unemployed although they do not want to work at the going wage rate in the official economy. They might, however, be interested in working in the unofficial economy provided that the official economy is subject to considerable burdens in terms of income taxes and social security contributions. If there is full labor mobility across sectors one might argue that unemployed workers from the N-sector could find a job in the T-sector. However, this argument is not very convincing if physical capital and human capital are strongly complementary – hence the expansion of the tradables sector is accompanied with only a modest increase in the demand for unskilled labor.

The result could be that there is economic growth and poverty at the same time, and indeed a high share of the population may suffer from malnutrition. The rise of the relative price of non-tradables will not only be a problem for unemployed people but also for pensioners who cannot expect to automatically get annual increases of benefits in line with inflation.

As regards medium term labor dynamics, labor is assumed to be mobile across sectors, and in the long run a certain fraction of unskilled workers can be transformed through training and education into skilled workers. Retraining efforts require investment in human capital, however, it is unclear whether there are financial resources available for this. If there are low mobility costs and excess unskilled labor from the N-sector can easily move towards the T-sector, unskilled labor unemployment should decline over time. There is, however, a problem if production in the T-sector is using skilled labor intensively and if government is unable or unwilling to subsidize training and human capital upgrading adequately.

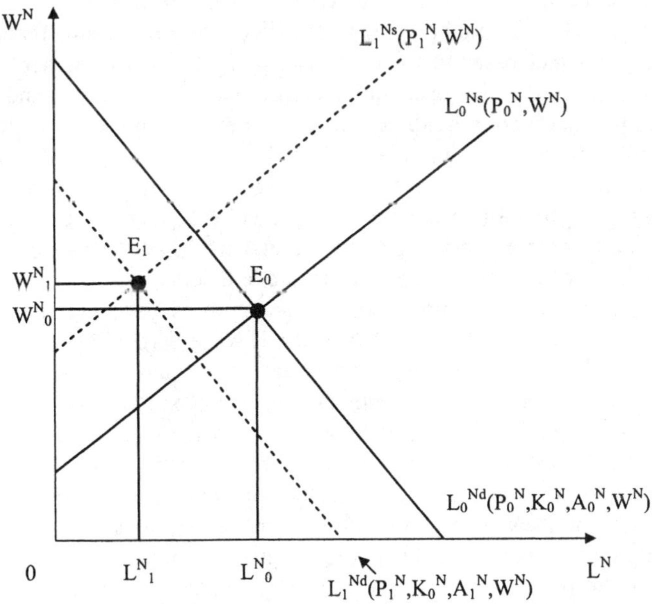

Fig. 2. Balassa-Samuelson Effect, Technological Progress and Quasi Unemployment

Moreover, if there are barriers to mobility, e.g. excess demand in regional housing markets or administrative barriers, this will make unemployment of unskilled labor a sustained problem. Moreover, to the extent that structural change, stimulated by economic opening up and FDI inflows, favors expansion of sectors with a relatively high demand for skilled labor, the excess unskilled labor from the N-sector will find it difficult to get a new job. The real adjustment dynamics in poor countries opening up in a world with trade and FDI flows indeed does not often show a general expansion of labor intensive production which would absorb unskilled labor. Rather we see some expansion and positive revealed comparative advantage in labor intensive sectors, while sectors with high FDI inflows are often sectors which are technology-intensive or skill-intensive. In a nutshell these problems are found in many transition countries and certainly also in many Newly Industrializing Countries and in developing countries.

2.3 Wage Bargaining as Inherent Source of Unemployment?

The reasons for long term high unemployment in transition countries are not well understood, and it is unclear how economic and institutional developments in the course of catching-up will affect employment and unemployment, respectively. Keynesian models suggest that a lack of effective demand is a major reason for high unemployment as neoclassical models emphasize a lack of investment and problems in labor markets. The following analysis emphasizes problems of wage bargaining and argues that it might be rather difficult to implement a policy framework which gives incentives to trade unions to target full employment. An important point of departure is that trade unions represent both employed and unemployed workers where for an individual trade union organization (O_i in sector i) an unemployed member might be more important in terms of membership fees than a member with a job who will change with a certain probability from sector I to sector j and thus leave the initial trade union organization O_i and join O_j instead. It is clear that unemployed members pay a lower membership fee to the trade union since membership fees typically are proportionate to income.

It is often argued that trade unions have a tendency – in particular in large countries – to lobby for excessively high wage rates. If wage bargaining leads to a wage rate w_1 above the market-clearing wage rate w^E, we have a situation in which workers obtain wages $w(1-\tau)L$ – with the tax rate τ partly or fully determined by the costs of unemployment and unemployment benefits paid; in addition unemployed workers will obtain unemployment benefits which are proportionate to their former income (see the shaded area in the following graph). As regards unemployed workers, an alternative assumption considered subsequently is to assume for simplicity that unemployment benefits are proportionate to the wage rate fixed in the bargaining process, and indeed this simplifying assumption will not change the basic results as long as labor supply is inelastic. While we will not consider an explicit model with tradables and nontradables, this assumption can be defended on the grounds that with wages fixed above the market-clearing rate the (overall wage) income is higher than under market-clearing which in turn leads to higher nontradables prices, eg housing prices and rents, than under market-clearing so that government and parliament will have a natural incentive to consider a rule under which unemployment benefits are implicitly proportionate to the going wage rate.

The incentive for trade unions to strive in wage bargaining for a wage rate above the equilibrium wage rate will increase over time if technological upgrading and specialization makes labor demand less elastic. The graphical analysis in panel a) shows that in the case of labor demand curve L^d_o switching from a market-clearing wage rate to a higher real wage rate w_1 has two effects: It reduces labor income due to the fall in employment, namely by the area $GE_0L_0L_1$, but labor income will be raised in line with the rise of the wage rate (area $FGw^E_0w_1$). The net effect of the fall in employment and the rise in the real wage rate is ambiguous, however, if the labor demand becomes more elastic the income-enhancing effect from the rise in the real wage will become more important (the theory of efficiency-wage bargaining suggests that firms also may have a tendency to support strong wage pressure – we will, however, not consider these effects here).

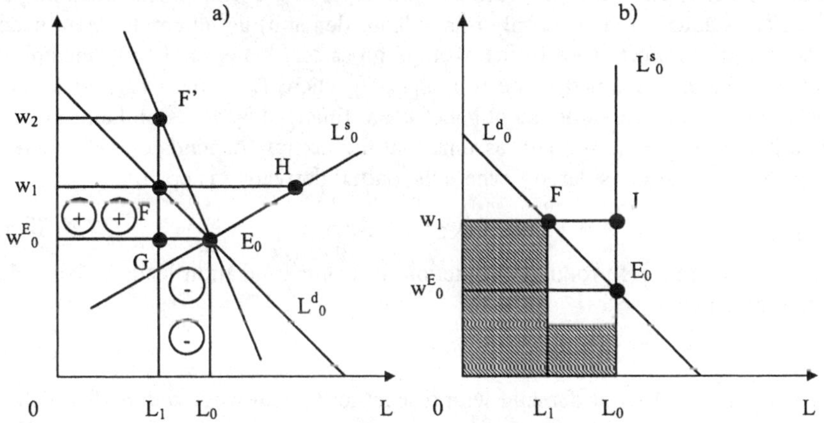

Fig. 3. Wage Rate Fixing above the Market-Clearing Rate

Economic caching-up of the transition countries is associated with increasing specialization of firms – partly reflecting the very impact of opening up and international competition – the demand for labor becomes less elastic and hence the risk is rising that wage bargaining will lead to excessive wage rates and unemployment. Part of the problem is, of course, related to the degree of wage centralization and the strength of trade unions and employer organizations. The problem considered might effectively be rather negligible in small open economies where fixing wage rates above marginal labor productivity will lead to large visible losses in world market shares which renders part of the capital stock obsolete and thus shifts the labor demand curve to the left: Labor income and national income will reduce in parallel. However, in a large economy the trade-GDP ratio is much below that in small open economies which implies – along with a home bias of consumers with respect to tradables goods – that a period of excessive wage fixing will not be followed by as quick a fall of overall market shares of firms in the tradables sector as in a small economy. Since incentives in a large economy to fix the wage rate at the equilibrium level are weaker than in a small economy the risk of neoclassical unemployment is rather strong in large transition economies.. This holds except for large countries in which wage bargaining is rather decentralized and in which trade unions are relatively weak (see for instance the US). A priori it is unclear, in transition countries, whether the influence of trade unions will rise over time and how their behaviour will develop.

The Model

Taking a closer look at a simple model of wage bargaining can shed some light on the issues raised. In the following analysis we assume that firms are profit-maximizing and the economy is characterized by a Cobb-Douglas production function $Y = K^{ß}L^{1-ß}$ where Y is output and capital K and labor L, respectively. Labor demand L is derived from profit maximization of the firm. Those unemployed (L' which is equal to labor supply minus labor demand) get unemployment benefits which are proportionate to the average gross real wage paid (w); unemployment benefits are assumed to be $w(1-z)[L_o-L]$ where L_o is the exogenous labor supply and $0<z<1$. Unemployment benefits are financed by taxes on labor income where the tax rate is τ. We will assume that the tax rate depends on w – alternatively wL might be considered – where the partial derivative is positive.

$$\tau = \tau(w) \tag{2.9}$$

With a Cobb-Douglas production function profit-maximization leads to labor demand L given by

$$L = [(1-ß)/w]^{ß} K \tag{2.10}$$

The elasticity of labor demand with respect to the real wage rate is -ß which in absolute terms is below unity. Pure gross wage income is $wL = [1-ß)]^{ß} Kw^{1-ß}$ so that the elasticity of pure labor income – income earned in the market – is below unity. Trade unions are assumed to aim at maximizing the sum Z of net wage income $w(1-\tau)L$ and the quasi-income of unemployed which is defined as $w(1-z)(L_o-L)$; however, as trade unions are averse to unemployment we will use a slightly modified expression, namely $\alpha w(1-z)(L_o-L)$. The parameter α indicates how strongly the trade union weighs the unemployment benefits and unemployment. If this parameter were zero or the effective replacement ratio $(1-z)=z'$ zero, the trade union would disregard the income accruing to unemployed workers. Trade unions are thus assumed to maximize (see also appendix):

$$Z = w[1-\tau(w)]L + \alpha w(1-z)(L_o-L) \tag{2.11}$$

The solution for maximizing Z is shown in the appendix. This solution has to be compared to the full employment wage rate so that one can draw conclusions with respect to an adequate replacement parameter $z'=(1-z)$ – the parameter has to be fixed by the political system – which would lead to full employment. To the extent that the full-employment enhancing z' is very low and imply an income of unemployed below a critical minimum, government may want to consider giving unemployed workers a fixed per capita unemployment benefit – regardless of the previous income of those who lost their job. There are also other ways of providing an incentive compatible labor market regime: eg those regions and sectors which exhibit unemployment rates below average would have lower contribution rates to the unemployment insurance system than regions and sectors with unemployment rates – or job loss rates – above the national average; or some other benchmark figure.

Unemployment and Current Account Position

Economic catching-up is associated with growing exports and imports, where poor countries typically record net imports for an extended period – later a current account surplus emerges as firms in the tradable sector become more competitive. However, we will argue that macroeconomic developments play a role for the current account, too.

We assume that there is a move from full-employment to a situation with a high unemployment rate. How does this affect the current account? An answer to this question should help us to understand changes in current account positions. In particular we will see in a simple model – with all goods assumed to be tradable – that a high current account surplus is not always an indicator of high competitiveness of countries. The basic point can be shown in four equations: Assume that consumption C and Investment I are proportionate to real income Y and are negatively affected by the number of unemployed L' (the unemployment rate u is defined as the ratio of unemployed L' to those employed L).

Furthermore real government expenditures G are written as

$$G = \gamma Y + n'L' \tag{2.12}$$

where n' is the replacement ratio paid by the unemployment insurance system to the unemployed. Hence we have two behavioural equations for real consumption C and real investment I plus the equilibrium condition for the goods market where X' denotes net exports of goods and services, Y^{pot} is the production potential, while actual output supplied is assumed to be $(1-\omega u)Y^{pot}$ which implies that with a positive unemployment rate u (u is defined as unemployed L' over employed L) there will also be underutilization of capital and labor in firms – this is quite a realistic assumption. Our approach – with parameter $\omega>0$ and $\omega u<1$- implies that output supply will be equal to the production potential once u converges towards zero. Moreover, the proposed specification allows the building of models that represent medium term approaches for a situation with unemployment and looking in a consistent manner at long term growth. The term $(1-\omega u)$ affects the level of output but not growth as e.g. the fall of the number of unemployed must be equal to the rise in the number of new jobs (du is zero!). Our simple consumption function and the investment function are as follows:

$$C = cY - fL'; \; f>0 \tag{2.13}$$

$$I = bY - b'L' \; ; \; b'>0 \tag{2.14}$$

Note that one might introduce the assumption that b=b(r,q) so that the investment function to some extent becomes more similar to the traditional investment function in Mundell Fleming models; and to take into account the impact of FDI inflows along the lines suggested by (Froot/ Stein, 1991). Moreover, in an open economy with FDI inflows and outflows it would be adequate to assume that investment depends on the ratio of the marginal product of capital at home to that abroad which implies – relying on the case of a Cobb-Douglas production function which has proportionality of marginal product and average product of input factors – that I=I([Y/K]/[Y*/K*] so that I=I(q,Y,Y*...): This would imply a net export function X'(q,Y,Y*) with familiar partial derivatives! In Addition to the goods market one might, following (Artus, 1989, p. 45), consider the money market equilibrium and assume a money demand function m^d where the demand for real money balances m depends on output, the interest rate and the unemployment rate; the partial derivative for the unemployment rate is positive since higher unemployment raises the demand for liquidity: higher u means higher uncertainty. Thus a modified Mundell Fleming model in r-u-space:

$$M/P = m^d = -\sigma[i^* - \alpha' \Sigma X'/L] + \sigma' u + \sigma'' k \tag{2.15}$$

Here we have assumed that the domestic interest rate i depends on the foreign nominal interest rate i* plus an implicit risk premium related to cumulated net exports per capita; the money demand also depends on u and on the capital intensity k so that the LMU curve is money market equilibrium.

The approach proposed also easily lends itself to combining a goods market quasi-equilibrium condition with Phillips-curve analysis; moreover, the capacity effect of investment could be incorporated as well, however, these possible extensions are not pursued here. We state our basic idea for output supplied as follows:

$$Y^s = (1-\omega u)Y^{pot} \tag{2.16}$$

Equation (2.14) states that output supplied is proportionate to the production potential but also is negatively affected by the unemployment rate u; if there is a positive unemployment rate firms will realize some labor hoarding for various reasons so that output is less than the number of employed people normally would suggest. Potential output is defined as follows:

$$Y^{pot} = K^{\beta} L^{1-\beta} \tag{2.16'}$$

The quasi-equilibrium condition– output is not at the full employment level – for the goods market can be written as follows:

$$(1-\omega u)Y^{pot} = (b+c+\gamma)Y - (f+b'-n')L' + X' \tag{2.17}$$

Dividing equation (2.16') by L and taking into account the production function – and denoting K/L as k – we get for net exports per worker:

$$X'/L = (1-\omega u)[1-c-b-\gamma]k^{\beta} + (b'+f-n')u \tag{2.18}$$

Hence net exports per capita are – for a given capital intensity – a positive function of the unemployment rate if (b'+f-n') >ω [1-c-b-γ]$k^{ß}$. Therefore a rise of net exports per worker thus must not simply be interpreted as a rise of competitiveness. It simply may reflect a rise of the unemployment rate and the associated fall in domestic absorption – corrected for supply effects related to changes in the unemployment rate. This case of a positive impact of the unemployment rate on net exports per worker is shown in the subsequent graph (ISU curve).

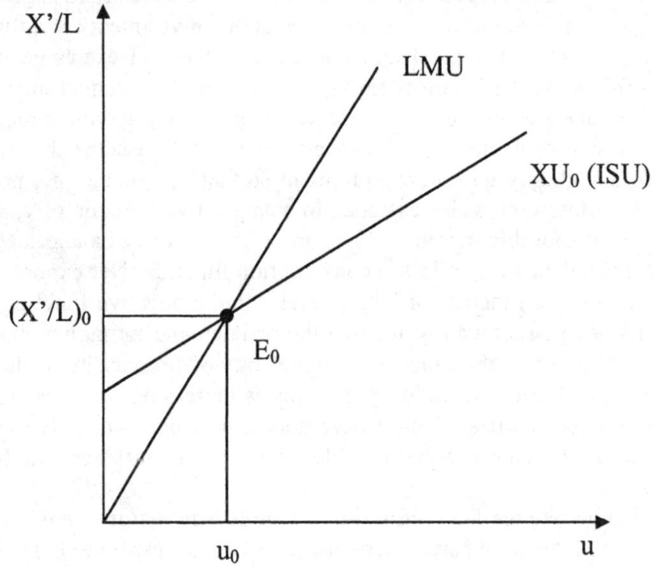

Fig. 4. Net Exports and Unemployment Rate

3 Product Innovation and Macroeconomic Developments: Schumpeter and the Mundell-Fleming Model

3.1 Medium Term Issues Product Innovations, Output and the Exchange Rate

As countries catch up, the export-GDP and the import-GDP ratio will grow while the share of intra-industrial trade will increase. Moreover, foreign direct investment inflows will rise – and in the long run there will typically be two-way FDI flows. Firms will become more innovative and will emphasize product innovations; the rate of product innovations will be denoted as v. Note that the term product innovation is understood here in the sense that the respective product is new from the perspective of the respective catching-up country (from the perspective of a global technology leader country this looks like product imitation). The term v may be understood as the country's product innovations relative to that of foreign countries: v is a stock variable, that is the share of product innovations given the overall number of products n_0. In the following analysis we will raise the issue of how product innovations will affect output, the interest rate and the exchange rate. The following macroeconomic model set up is a "Schumpeter-Keynes" approach in the sense that product innovations are integrated into the familiar Mundell-Fleming model. Hence the price level at home and abroad is given.

As regards the goods market our basic assumption is that investment I is a function of the real interest rate at home I and abroad (r*), the real exchange rate q*(that is eP*/P) - following the Froot/ Stein argument – and the product innovation rate v which is exogenous in the model. Hence we implicitly assume a model with foreign direct investment inflows. Moreover, we basically assume that new products can be produced only with new equipment so that investment is a positive function of v. Consumption is also assumed to be a positive function of v; and a positive function of disposable income Y(1-τ) and of real money balances M/P so that we have a real balance effect in the consumption function. Net exports X' are assumed to be a positive function of Y*, q* and v, but a negative function of Y. As regards the money market we assume that the real demand for money m depends positively on Y and v – the latter as a higher rate of product innovations suggests that the marginal utility of holding liquidity is increasing for consumers looking for shopping opportunities of innovative goods; m depends negatively on the nominal interest rate I which is equal to r plus the expected inflation rate (assumed here to be zero).

The foreign exchange rate market equilibrium requires here that net capital imports Q(i/i*, v, q*) – with positive partial derivatives of Q with respect to both i/i*, q* and to v – plus net exports of goods and services are equal to zero. Net capital imports react positively to a real depreciation in line with the Froot/ Stein argument. Net capital imports are assumed to depend positively on v because a higher rate of product innovations will stimulate FDI inflows – foreign investors become more active as they are anticipating higher profit opportunities. Linearizing the consumption function as

$$C = c(1-\tau)Y + c'(M/P) + c''v \qquad (3.1a)$$

and using a simple investment function for an open economy (with foreign direct investment inflows so that investment depends both on the domestic real interest rate and the foreign interest rate; and the real exchange rate in line with the Froot-Stein argument)

$$I = -hr - h'r^* + h''v + h'''q^* \qquad (3.1b)$$

and a net export function

$$X' = xq^* + x'Y^*/Y + x''v \qquad (3.1c)$$

we have the following three equations (3.1d, 3.2, 3.3) as the equilibrium condition in the goods market, the money market and the foreign exchange market, respectively (G is real government expenditures):

$$Y = c(1-\tau)Y + c'(M/P) + c''v + G - hr - h'r^* + h''v + h'''q^* + xq^* + x'Y^*/Y + x''v \qquad [IS] \quad (3.1d)$$

$$M/P = m(Y,r,v) \qquad [LM] \quad (3.2)$$

$$Q(i/i^*, v, q^*) + xq^* + x'Y^*/Y + x''v = 0 \qquad [ZZ] \quad (3.3)$$

Product innovations shift the IS curve to the right, the LM curve to the left and the ZZ curve downwards; the latter holds since net exports of goods and services will increase as a consequence of a higher v: an initial negative trade balance will thus be reduced so that required net capital imports will fall. If one would assume that foreign direct investment inflows and hence Q depends positively on Y/Y* – that is the relative size of the market – the implication is that the balance of payments equilibrium curve (ZZ) can have zero slope even if $\partial Q/\partial(i/i^*)$ is not infinitely in absolute terms; and hence the domestic interest rate could diverge from the foreign interest rate.

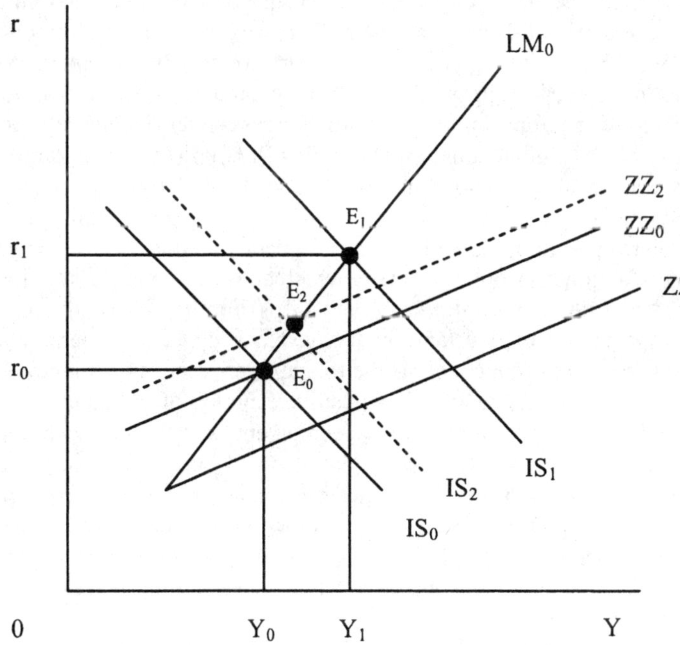

Fig. 5. Rise of Product Innovations in the Mundell-Fleming Model

If m_v is zero the LM curve is not directly affected by a change of v so that product innovations clearly raise both equilibrium output and the interest rate. Under flexible exchange rates there will be an appreciation of the currency in point E_1 – as this point is above the ZZ line – so that the IS_1 curve (driven by reduced net exports of goods and services) will shift a little to the left (IS_2) while the ZZ_1 curve will shift upwards (ZZ_2). It remains true that product innovations raise the output level and the real interest rate, and contribute to a current account surplus. This situation could continue until there is a new intersection point in the initial equilibrium E_o (note that in a system of fixed exchange rates point E_1 implies higher net capital inflows and an excess supply in the foreign exchange market. The stock of money M will increase, the LM-curve and the IS-curve, the latter due to higher consumption, will shift to the right).

This, however, does not mean that government promotion of policy innovation is inefficient since in a medium term perspective the capital stock K will increase as the consequence of net investment – actually increased net investment in the context of product innovations. Indeed, a modified simple medium term model could consider that consumption $C= c(1-\tau)Y+c'[(M/P)+(P'/P)K] +c''v$ where the term c'[…] is a broader real wealth effect on consumption, namely including the real value of capital stock; P'/P is the ratio of the stock market price index P' to the output price index P. A consistent medium term export function would read $X= xq^* + x'Y^*/Y +x''v + x'''K$ where the term x'''K (with x'''>0) is a supply shift variable in the export sector. This term will then shift both the IS curve to the right and the ZZ curve downwards as K is raised. Thus the general equilibrium point in our diagram will shift to the right over time where we assume that monetary policy raises the money supply in parallel with the capital stock K, so that medium term money supply equilibrium is given for the case of an income elasticity of output of unity by the simple equation $(M/P)/K = [Y/K]m'(i,v)$. In a noninflationary economy it is equal to the real interest rate r which under profit maximization and a Cobb Doublas production function $Y=K^{ß}AL^{1-ß}$ (with L standing for labor and A for Harrod-neutral technological progress) is equal to ßY/K so that Y/K=r/ß. Hence a monetary policy strategy which aims at a constant ratio [M/P]/K is then consistent with a constant money demand {[r/ß]m'(i,v)} – assuming that v and i and r, respectively, are constant; read: have reached an equilibrium value. An interesting long term question concerns the relation between product innovations v and the process innovations A. If A is a positive function of v – since new products can often be produced only with new equipment (and the innovation system may be assumed to be responsive to the higher demand for A) – an exogenous rate of product innovations dv/dt>0 would indeed generate a continuous growth process. A more realistic picture would emerge if we would also consider a quasi-depreciation rate of the stock of product innovations or a vintage type approach to product innovations so that in each period the oldest product generation is removed from the shelf and production.

As endogenous variables we have Y, r and e (changes in e stand for a real exchange rate change as long as P or P* are not changing). So we are interested in the medium term multipliers for Y, r and e with respect to v, the product innovation rate. Using Kramer's rule we obtain (with ζ = i/i*) after differentiation of (3.1d), (3.2), (3.3):

$$dY/dv > 0 \text{ (sufficient condition is } m_v=0) \tag{3.4}$$

$$dr/dv > 0 \text{ (sufficient condition is } m_v=0) \tag{3.5}$$

de/dv <0 if (see appendix; the system determinant is negative; the following expression shows the nominator expression of the multiplier de/dv) Q_φ and m_r are sufficiently small, so that

$$\left\{\left(1-c^{'}(1-\tau)+\frac{x^{'}Y^{*}}{Y^{2}}\right)m_r\left(Q_{q^{\cdot}}+x\right)-hm_Y\left(Q_{q^{\cdot}}+x\right)\right\}>\left\{\left(h^{'''}+x\right)\left(m_Y Q_\zeta-m_r\frac{x^{'}Y^{*}}{Y^{2}}\right)\right\} \tag{3.6}$$

and Y^* exceeding Y_0^* (home country is relatively small). Product innovations will bring about a real appreciation. One may also note that it raises equilibrium output. This is much in line with original reflections of Schumpeter who has argued that firms facing the pressure of economic recession will launch new products in order to generate more sales. From a policy perspective our analysis suggests that government could stimulate product innovations in recessions in order to raise output; indeed one may split government expenditures G into government consumption G' plus government R&D support (G") for product innovations. Such an approach is certainly rather appropriate in countries catching-up, as for them a higher rate of product innovations largely means to accelerate the speed of international imitations of foreign product innovations. As regards advanced countries it is questionable whether higher government R&D subsidies could strongly stimulate product innovations in the short term so as to easily overcome a recession. At the bottom line, the model presented clearly suggests that the structural breakdown of government expenditures is crucial. Since the ratio of R&D expenditures to GDP has increased in the long run in OECD countries, it is obvious that innovation issues have become more important – while standard macroeconomic modelling largely ignores innovation issues.

Total Multiplier Effect

The distinction between different types of government expenditures is crucial as we will show subsequently and is totally ignored in the traditional macro models. Real government expenditure G is split here into government consumption G' and expenditures G" on the promotion of product innovations:

$$G = G' + G'' \tag{3.7}$$

Expenditures on the promotion of product innovations mean in the case of leading OECD countries that development of true product innovations is stimulated; and no short-run results can be expected. However, for catching-up countries this could mean mainly acceleration of imitation of foreign product innovations which in many cases should be possible within one or two years. We assume subsequently that there is a link between government expenditures on research & development – with a focus on product innovations – that can be described by

$$v = \Omega G'' \tag{3.8}$$

Hence we have a link between two exogenous variables. As regards multipliers for G" they clearly differ from that for G' since a change in G" will not only affect aggregate demand (direct impact) but also the product innovation rate v (indirect impact) so that the overall multiplier for any endogenous variable Z_i (=Y, r, e) can be written as

$$dZ_i/dG'' = [dZ_i/dG] + \Omega dZ_i/dv \tag{3.9}$$

The first RHS term in brackets is the same for dG=dG' and dG=dG", but the second term is relevant only with respect to a change of G". The output multiplier dY/dG" for a rise of G" is clearly larger than that for a rise of government consumption G'.

There is another link between exogenous variables in the context of product innovations which imply an effective fall of the price level P – a problem which theoretically comes under the heading of hedonic price measurement. Using a simple approach – with the hedonic parameter H (H>0) - we can thus write

$$dP = -Hdv \tag{3.10}$$

Product innovations are indeed a nonmonetary aspect of the price level. At the bottom line the complete multiplier analysis for the impact of a rise of G" is given by

$$dZ_i/dG'' = [dZ_i/dG] + \Omega dZ_i/dv - HdZ_i/dP \tag{3.11}$$

The following graphical analysis shows both the direct effect of a rise in government expenditures promoting product innovations and the indirect effects of this policy which consists of a double rightward shift of the IS curve related to the impact of G" on v and of v on P and M/P, respectively; the effective rise of M/P amounts to a hedonic real balance effect. Moreover, there will be a rightward shift of the LM curve which is to say that product innovations are equivalent to a rise of M/P unless there is a dominant money demand effect.

In a more general perspective it is true that the impact of v on P must be considered with respect to all multipliers dZ_i/dv so that these multipliers are composed of a direct effect and an indirect effect related to a change of the price level. Thus a consistent analysis of the multipliers for Y, r and e is achieved. As regards the change in the "hedonically adjusted" real exchange rate one has to take into account that d(eP*/P) is given for a constant foreign price level P* normalized to unity by $(1/P)de/dv - (e/P^2)dP/dv$. Our analysis offers a new and broader analytical picture of important policy issues (for more details see appendix).

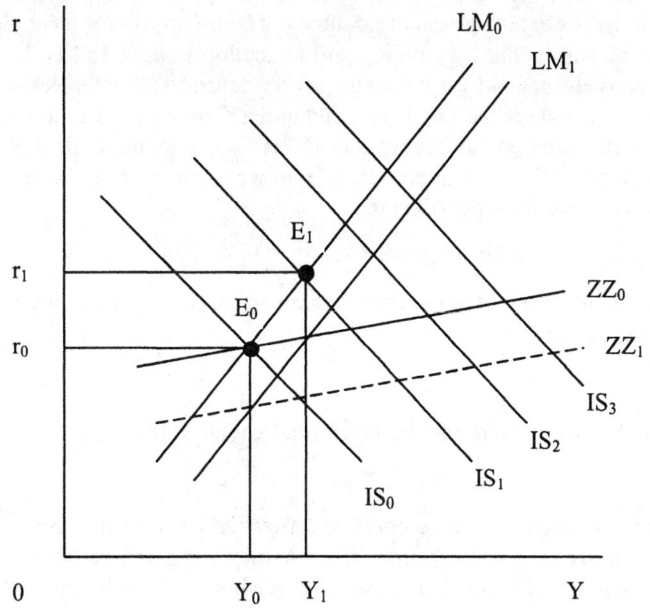

Fig. 6. Direct and Indirect Effects of Product Innovation

3.2 Economic Catching-up and Long Term Real Exchange Rate Dynamics

From a theoretical perspective, we expect a long-term real appreciation of the currency of accession countries which are assumed to catch up in economic and technological terms with EU-15. Thus, the Balassa-Samuelson effect would work. However, how will this effect indeed be realized? One may ask whether it is mainly a nominal appreciation which brings about the BS effect, thereby requiring flexible exchange rates or whether it is a rise of the price level relative to the foreign price level (in a setting with a constant or stable nominal exchange rate). A rise in the domestic price level could bring problems with respect to the inflation convergence criterion and the interest rate convergence criterion of European Economic and Monetary Union. From this perspective, it is clear that countries eager to join the monetary union quickly might prefer an extended period of flexible exchange rates and enter the Euro zone only after a transition period of several years.

A Simple Long-Term Approach

In the following approach, we assume that net exports X' positively influence the real exchange rate q=:[P/(eP*)] (parameter b>0) and that it is a negative function of the relative innovation differential a*". On the link between the real exchange rate and the current account consistent models are available. A relative rise of innovativeness abroad (country II) – we focus here mainly on product innovations – will lead to relatively lower export prices of country I. The prospects for technological catching-up depend on technology policy and education policy, and both can be expected to negatively depend on the share of the natural resource sector in the overall economy. As regards the link between q and a*" one may also note that net capital exports will be larger the higher our a*" is (i.e., a technological progress differential in favour of the foreign country). Here we assume a*" to be an exogenous variable. Hence we find the following:

$$dq/dt = bX' - a^{*\prime\prime}q \tag{3.12}$$

We furthermore assume that net exports negatively depend on q where the elasticity η is negative; hence we have:

$$X' = q^{\eta} \quad (\text{with } \eta \leq 0) \tag{3.13}$$

This leads to the following Bernoullian differential equation for q(t):

$$dq/dt = bq^{\eta} - a^{*\prime\prime}q \tag{3.14}$$

In the subsequent graph, we have drawn the first right hand side expression as the BB line and the second expression as the AA line; for given parameters there will be a monotonous real appreciation (see the QQ-line). The solution of the differential equation is – with C_o determined from initial conditions and e' denoting the Euler number:

$$q(t) = \{C_o e'^{-a^*(1-\eta)t} + b/a^{*\prime\prime}\}^{1/(1-\eta)} \tag{3.15}$$

This equation is convergent for q. Hence we have an equation for the long-term real exchange rate with q converging and thus has the steady state value (for t approaching infinity) q#:

$$q\# = (b/a^{*\prime\prime})^{1/(1-\eta)} \tag{3.16}$$

For a small open – non-innovative (!) – economy facing an infinite price elasticity in export markets, the equilibrium real exchange rate is clearly unity (see equation 3.16). If the export demand elasticity is zero, which would reflect the extreme case of a country exporting a very large share of high technology goods, we find that:

$$q\# = b/a^{\prime\prime *} \text{ (case of high technology dominance in exports)} \tag{3.17}$$

If the absolute value of η is unity, we would get as the steady state value $q\#=(b/a''^*)^{1/2}$. Clearly, technological catching-up with a*' being reduced will lead to downward rotation of the AA curve (AA_1 in Fig. 7b); technological upgrading also could go along with a fall of the absolute value of the price elasticity. Both elements could occur simultaneously.

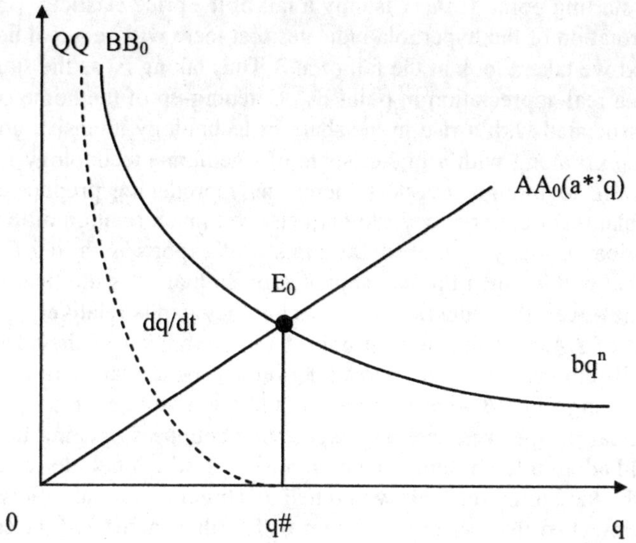

Fig. 7a. Real Exchange Rate Dynamics

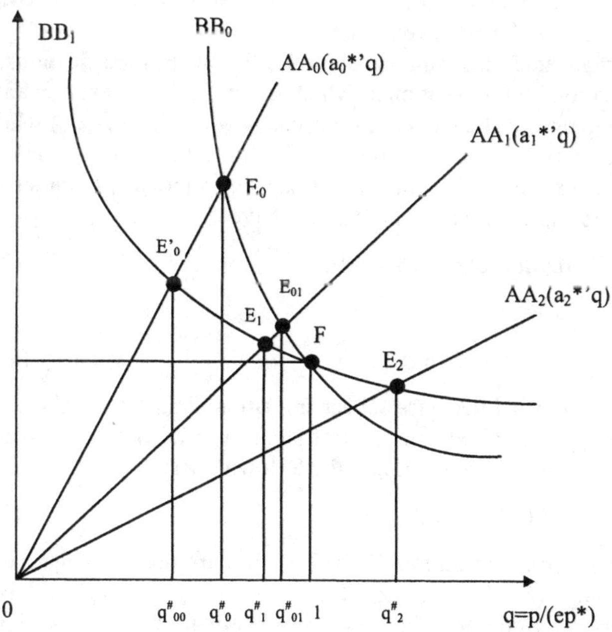

Fig. 7b. Model of the Long Term Real Exchange Rate ($dq/dt=bq^{\eta} - a^{*\prime}q$)

Take E_o as the starting point. If there is only a fall of the price elasticity (in absolute terms) the rotation of the hyperbola indicates that there will be a real depreciation effect. Next we take a look at the fall of a*". Thus taking E_0 as the starting point, we observe a real appreciation in point E_{01}. Catching-up of the home country also will be associated with a rise in the share of technology intensive goods: Should catching-up go along with a higher share of (medium-) technology intensive goods (e.g., due to foreign investors increasingly producing product cycle goods in modern plants for exports to world markets), we find a rotation of the BB curve since the price elasticity – in absolute terms – of exports is falling (BB_1). This elasticity effect will dampen the real appreciation so that E_1 is the final equilibrium point. If, however, the reduction of the technology gap is relatively strong (intersection point of AA is to the right of point F) the reduction of the absolute price elasticity will reinforce the real appreciation effect. Note that there may be cases when a*" is rising and the price elasticity is falling in absolute terms.

From an empirical perspective, we may expect that countries opening up will liberalize trade and adopt internal modernization measures which help to raise per capita income in the medium term. This would help to stimulate capital inflows (in particular FDI inflows) so that per capita output will further increase. (Per capita GNP might increase more slowly than per capita GDP, however, since rising FDI inflows could raise the share of profit transfers relative to GDP.) As per capita income y rises, the share of intra-industrial trade should increase, accompanied by intensified competition. The latter in turn should stimulate static efficiency gains as well as innovation, and government policy may then stimulate innovation through subsidies for research and development.

As a possible further analytical step consider the following modifications. We restate our basic equation by focusing on x' which is per capita net exports and assuming that b is a function of the capital intensity k' – where k'=K/(AL) which is capital per efficiency unit of labor (A standing for Harrod neutral technological progress) because net exports will contribute to an appreciation the higher for a given net export x' the capital intensity is. We thus have

$$dq/dt = b(k')[x'] - a''{}^*q \tag{3.18}$$

We specify

$$b(k') = b'k'^{\Omega} \tag{3.18'}$$

Moreover, we state a modified neoclassical accumulation dynamic which includes foreign direct investment inflows F' per unit of labor in efficiency unit which we assume to be proportionate to y'=-Y/(AL) in the following way:

$$F/(AL) = f(q)y' = q^{\lambda}y' \tag{3.19}$$

The parameter λ is – in line with the FROOT-STEIN argument – negative. Assuming a simple savings function S (where the real exchange rate affects savings but we make no a priori assumption about the partial derivative; with a net foreign debt position a rise of q reduces the burden of the debt and thus might raise the ability to save, with an international net creditor position a rise of q could reduce the savings rate – ultimately, all this is an empirical issue) we have

$$S = sq^{\sigma}Y \tag{3.20}$$

The modified neoclassical equilibrium condition is therefore:

$$\delta K + (dK/dt) = sq^{\sigma}Y + F' \tag{3.21}$$

Dividing by AL and taking into account (3.19) and using a Cobb-Douglas production function $y'=k'^{ß}$ (this production function might include – as a kind of positive external effect of household's money holdings - real money balances M/P if M/P=1) gives

$$dk'/dt + [n+a+\delta]k = sq^{\sigma}k'^{ß} + q^{\lambda}k'^{ß} \tag{3.22}$$

Note that using the equilibrium condition equation (3.20) implies that investment is linked to output and the real exchange rate, but one should note that this equilibrium perspective also is fully compatibly with an investment function I(Y,q) in a disequilibrium approach). We define x' as net exports per efficiency unit of labor and now assume that $x'= q^{\eta}$. The accumulation dynamics for the capital stock are governed by:

$$dk'/dt = [sq^{\sigma}+q^{\lambda}]k'^{ß} - [n+\delta+a]k' \tag{3.23}$$

An analytical solution of this pair of differential equations is quite complex.If a steady state for k,q exists, then we can solve by setting dk'/dt =0 and dq/dt=0:

$$q\# = [b'k'^{\Omega}/ a''*]^{1/(1-\eta)} \tag{3.24}$$

A solution of (3.23) is rather easy if we take a look at the special case $\sigma=\lambda$:

$$k'\# = \{[(s+1)q^{\sigma}]/[n+\delta+a]\}^{1/1-\sigma ß} \tag{3.25}$$

$$k'\# = \{[(s+1)(b'k'^{\Omega}/ a''*)^{\eta'\sigma}]/[n+\delta+a]\}^{1/1-\sigma ß}\text{; we define } 1/(1-\eta)=\eta' \tag{3.26}$$

From this we have

$$k'\#^{\sigma\Omega\eta'/(1-\sigma ß)} = \{[(s+1)(b'/a''*)^{\eta'\sigma}]/[n+\delta+a]\}^{1/1-\sigma ß} \tag{3.27}$$

There is a problem with the interpretation of output Y (or Y/AL) when we have product innovations. However, one may assume that true output Y" – a hedonically deflated nominal output variable – can be written as Yq^{μ} since q is strictly a negative function of a"* (the parameter μ is positive).

A potential variant of this model would be to endogenize the rate of product innovations, e.g. by making it dependent on the per capita income and the real exchange rate. This would be a new line of research in endogenous growth modelling. Moreover, the model can be linked to endogenous growth theory – based on endogenous process innovations (e.g. Welfens, 2003)

3.3 The Role of Risk and Innovation

An important aspect of innovation dynamics concerns risk. As a simple way to take into account risk and innovation one may proceed as follows. We consider a consumption function C where consumption depends on income on the one hand and on wealth A' on the other hand. The expected rate of return on innovation is μ, the variance is σ. There are only two assets considered, namely real capital K and real money balances m (m=M/P). We chose deliberately a specification where K/AL and [M/P]/AL (denoted as m') both enter the consumption function as a variable to the power ß since otherwise the mathematical calculation would become very intricate. All exponents are assumed to be positive. Hence a higher variance of innovation (and investment) yield imply a higher consumption since saving obviously brings relatively uncertain rewards; a higher expected yield on innovation reduces consumption and indeed stimulates savings as the reward for those saving is increased.

$$C/[AL]= cy' + c'[\sigma / \mu]^{\varepsilon} [k'^{\beta} + m'^{\beta}] \tag{3.28}$$

As regards the term $[k'^{\beta} + m'^{\beta}]$ this formulation is rather unusual at first sight; an ideal specification would indeed use $[k'^{\beta} + m'^{\beta}]^2$ but for ease of exposition we will drop the square. Our basic reflection in this context will focus on a special case where $A=A_o=4$ and $L=L_o=1$. Assume that ß=1/2 and the production function contains real money balances M/P as a positive external spillover effect, where real balances factor in as $(M/P)^{\beta}$; hence we have output as $Y=K^{\beta}(M/P)^{\beta}L_o^{\beta}$. One may then indeed state a simple consumption function as

$$C/[AL] = cy' + c' (K^{0.5} + m^{0.5})^2 = cy' + c'[K + 2K^{0.5}m^{0.5} + m] = c''y' + c'[K+m]. \tag{3.29}$$

We will use the Cobb-Douglas output function to replace k'^{β} by y' and a simple CAGAN-type real money demand equation to replace m', namely (with the Euler number written as e' and the semielasticity of the nominal yield on investment denoted as ψ and the expected inflation rate denoted as π'):

$$m'^{d} = e'^{\,-\psi'[\mu+\pi']}\, y \tag{3.30}$$

Let us assume that both σ and μ are positive functions of the product innovation variable v.

The corresponding savings function is therefore as follows:

$$S/[AL] =\{1-c - c'[\sigma(v) / \mu(v)]^{\varepsilon} [1+e'^{\psi'[\mu(v)+\pi']}]\}y' \tag{3.31}$$

We assume that the partial derivative of the expected rate of return with respect to v is higher than that for the reaction of the variance with respect to changes in v. This assumption is sufficient to bring about a rise of savings if v is increased. If we insert this equation in the familiar neoclassical growth model we will get the following steady state result for k'# (note we we use v/v*' instead of a'*):

$$k'\#^{\sigma\Omega\eta'/(1-\sigma\beta)} = \{1\text{-}c - c'[\sigma(v)/\mu(v)]^{\varepsilon}[1+e'^{\psi'[\mu(v)+\pi']}]\}+1) \quad (3.32)$$
$$(b'/[v/v^*])^{\eta'\sigma}]/[n+\delta+a]\}^{1/1-\sigma\beta}$$

This result includes both process innovations and product innovations and represents a much richer approach than traditional models. Domestic product innovations clearly raise the optimum capital intensity and output per efficiency unit of labor.

3.4 Endogenous Product Innovations in Countries with Similar Development Levels

Which research perspective is useful for countries which are of similar sophistication in product innovations? Let us consider two open economies of a similar technological level which are exporting goods and importing goods. Households consume domestic and foreign goods, including new products launched at home and abroad; in addition there is a kind of consumption technology which allows households to develop novel consumption patterns which depend on the interaction of v and v* in the market. The stock of product innovations abroad is v*, in the home country it is v. We assume that there are network effects (in commercial novelties) N' in country I which can be described as follows:

$$N' = (v+v^*+2vv^*)^{\alpha} \quad (3.33)$$

The rights hand side term says that the stock of novelties available depends on domestic product innovations (v), foreign product innovations (v*) and a third term which represents the interaction of both terms. We can rewrite the above equation as

$$N' = (v+v^*)^{2\alpha} \quad (3.34)$$

Abroad we may assume a similar network effect $N'^* = (v+v^*+2vv^*)^{\alpha^*}$. The next question to be raised is how v and v*, respectively, can be explained. Research expenditures H is obviously one relevant variable.

How can we define true quality-adjusted output? One useful definition would be:

$$Y'' = YN'^{\alpha'} \quad (3.35)$$

If the term a' is unity (and abroad a'* is unity) we can calculate relative quality-adjusted output as

$$Y''/Y''^* = [Y/Y^*]N'/N'^* \quad (3.36)$$

There are indeed considerable differences across countries when it comes to the willingness of households to use new products as was shown.

4 Conclusions and Policy Implications

We have analyzed some key issues of transition countries from a theoretical point. From an analytical perspective it is clear that the familiar Heckscher-Ohlin Samuelson framework has to be refined if the challenges of opening up and transition are to be understood. Transformation is not a quick process where a country can jump from the distortions of the old system towards a new full employment market economy. First, it is important to take into account that transition countries differ in important aspects, e.g. the degree of natural resource abundance. Second, there has been high unemployment in many transition countries over decades, particularly high amongst unskilled workers. The analysis presented argues that economic and technological catching-up – accompanied by increasing specialization – will make labor demand less inelastic. This in turn reinforces the problem that wage negotiations may lead to a wage rate above the market-clearing rate where we suggest that government should fix unemployment benefits in a way which effectively leads to full employment. Unemployment in a small open economy (by assumption it can export the excess supply of the tradables sector) in turn is likely to raise net exports so that an improvement in the current account is not necessarily related to an improvement of technological competitiveness. Misinterpretation of the net export position by government and international organizations can have very serious consequences.

As regards medium term modelling of output development in transition countries we focus on the role of product innovations within a Schumpeter-Mundell-Fleming model (product innovations effectively means – from the perspective of leading OECD innovators – diffusion). We argue that the law of one price will not hold in such a model and show that product innovations raise output and bring about a real appreciation. To the extent that government innovation policy (with a focus on promotion product innovations and diffusion, respectively) can stimulate product innovations there is an important policy variable beyond traditional fiscal policy and monetary policy. It would be interesting to have empirical analysis for various countries which shows how important the share of product innovations in overall (net) exports is and how strongly government R&D promotion affects the product innovation rate. As regards policy conclusions government promotion of product innovation seems to be rather important in transition countries and NICs.

Finally, we take a look at real exchange rate dynamics in a setup in which the current account position and the relative rate of product innovation is affecting the real exchange rate. The approach presented argues that catching-up means a reduction of the price elasticity of net exports and a fall of the foreign relative innovation rate. Both effects contribute to a real appreciation of the currency.

The contribution has presented analytical building blocs relevant for transition countries. It is beyond the scope of our analysis to integrate those blocs into one coherent model. However, we have raised several crucial issues relevant for economic catching-up and transition countries. There certainly is need for further research which should help to reconcile real world dynamics with standard economic wisdom.

Appendix 1 Output and Wage Pressure in a Hybrid Supply and Demand Macro Model

One should also note that the hybrid approach suggests an interesting answer to the question of how a rise in the real wage rate will affect output as well as employment. Consider a small open economy which can raise exports in accordance with the growth the potential output - here we assume that all output is tradable. We can rewrite equation (1.1) as follows if one assumes that consumption C=cY – with Y=wL+rK# (assuming that factors labor L and capital K are rewarded in accordance with their respective marginal product; K# is the equilibrium capital stock, r the real interest rate, w the real wage rate); investment I=I(r), government consumption G is exogenous, net exports X' are a negative function of the international real wage ratio (* denotes foreign variables) and a negative function of the real exchange rate q=P/(eP*) – P is the price level, e the nominal exchange rate, W the nominal wage rate and the real wage rate is defined as w=W/P.

$$Y = \alpha\, Y^{pot}(W/P) + [1\text{-}\alpha]\{c[wL + rK^{\#}] + I(r) + G + X'(W/eW^*,\ q) \qquad (1)$$

We assume that the real interest rate r and the exchange rate e are exogenous; denoting eW* as W'* we obtain from differentiation:

$$dY/dW = \alpha\, \partial Y^{pot}/\partial W + [1\text{-}\alpha]\{c[L + r\partial K^{\#}/\partial W] + \partial X'/\partial W \qquad (2)$$

By assumption, the partial derivative $\partial X'/\partial W$ is negative. With P given, the rise in the nominal wage rate is, of course, equivalent to a real wage increase. The impact of a higher wage rate on consumption is positive, namely $c[L + r\partial K^{opt}/\partial W]$, and the overall sign for dY/dW is thus unclear. In a small open economy, the net export effect may be expected to outweigh the domestic consumption effect (and also the effect $\partial Y^{pot}/\partial W$ if it should be negative). Moreover, if α=1-u and u=u(w/[Y/L]), the total differential for (1''') yields even a somewhat more complex result for dY/dW (if dY/dW is negative, the sign for du/dW should be positive). The ambiguity of dY/dW remains, but we can learn from the approach presented that the risk to adopt an excessive wage rate is higher the less open the economy is.

One should not, however, rule out that net exports could be a positive function of W/W'*, namely if the quality and innovativeness of the export basked is a positive function of the relative wage ratio. Such a function implicitly assumes that the country considered can sufficiently move up the quality ladder in line with the rise in the international wage ratio. Analytically we thus enter a world of imperfect competition where the export price P** might well diverge from domestic price P for the same good. Assume that nominal exports XP** (with P** for the export price in domestic currency units; W is the nominal wage rate) negatively depend on the ratio of the wage rate W to marginal market revenue per worker P**ßY/L. We thus consider a relative cost pressure indicator

$$\Omega' = \{[W/P^{**}]/[\beta Y/L]\}/\{[W^*/P^*]/[\beta^* Y^*/L^*]; \qquad (3)$$

Note that real exports are XP**/P while real imports, expressed in domestic quantity, is q*J where J is the quantity of imports. Now let us assume that we have the following pricing rule (with v as a qualityindex or novelty index; σ" is a positive parameter):

$$P^{**} = W(1-ß)+ \sigma' v \tag{4}$$

We furthermore assume (with parameter σ">0) that the quality index realized by exporters is a positive function of the international nominal wage ratio, because a relative rise in wage costs stimulates firms to move up the technology and quality ladder – an argument which might be doubtful in the case of technologically leading countries.

$$v= \sigma'' W/[eW^*] \tag{5}$$

Hence

$$P^{**} = W(1-ß)+ \sigma'\sigma'' W/[eW^*] = W[(1-ß) + \sigma'\sigma''/[eW^*]] \tag{6}$$

$$P^* = W^*(1-ß)+ \sigma'^*\sigma''^* W^*/[e^*W] = W^*[(1-ß^*) + \sigma'^*\sigma''^*/[e^*W]] \tag{7}$$

Thus we can write

$$\Omega' = (1+ \sigma'^*\sigma''^* e/W)[ß^*Y^*/L^*]/(1+ \sigma'\sigma''/eW^*)[ßY/L] \tag{8}$$

Real imports are qJ and J is assumed – with W/W'* denoted as φ" – to be a function

$$J(q, \varphi'', Y) \tag{9}$$

With respect to J, all three partial derivatives Jq , $J_{\varphi''}$ and J_Y are positive; J_q reflects a demand shift effect since the quantity of imports will reduce when their price is raised relative to domestically sold goods; $J_{\varphi''}$ reflect the relative importance of wage income in overall income. J_Y is the familiar increase of imports resulting from higher aggregate income.

Hence we paradoxically find that the ratio of real exports to real imports [XP**/P]/[qJ] could be positively influenced by the international nominal wage price ratio. A critical assumption here is that the price of exports indeed can be raised, which is possible only under imperfect competition in international goods markets and if the firms of the countries considered move up the quality ladder sufficiently. Quality here includes product innovativeness.

In a simplified case in which we assume the quantity of imports to not be reacting to relative price changes and the relative wage position – more or less the case of a country whose imports are dominated by natural resources (as is the case of Japan and a few other countries), net real exports X' are given by

$$X' = [P^{**}X(\varphi'')/P] - eP^*J/P \tag{10}$$

Denoting E as an elasticity we get:

$$dX'/d\varphi'' = [1/P][P^{**}/ \varphi'']E_{P^{**}, \varphi''} + P^{**}\partial X/\partial\varphi''/P - q^*\partial J/\partial\varphi''/P. \tag{11}$$

The expression dX'/dφ" is positive only if the elasticity exceeds a critical value.

Maximization of Total Quasi-Income of Workers through Trade Unions (labor supply L_o is exogenous, parameter $0 \leq \alpha \leq 1$)

$$Z = w[1 - \tau(w)]L + w(1 - z)\alpha[L_0 - L] \text{ mit } z' = 1 - z \tag{12}$$

$$= wL - w\tau(w)L + wz'\alpha L_0 - z'\alpha L \tag{13}$$

$$= (1-\beta)^{\beta} w^{1-\beta} K(1-\tau(w) - z'\alpha) + wz'\alpha L_0 \tag{14}$$

$$\frac{dZ}{dw} = [(1-\beta)(1-\beta)^{\beta} w^{-\beta} K(1-\tau(w)-z'\alpha)] - \tau_w (1-\beta)^{\beta} w^{1-\beta} K - z'\alpha L_0 \tag{15}$$

$$=0$$

$$[(1-\beta)(1-\beta)^{\beta} w^{-\beta} K(1-\tau(w)-z'\alpha)] - \tau(\varepsilon_{\tau,w}(1-\beta)^{\beta} w^{-\beta} K = z'\alpha L_0 \tag{16}$$

$$= K[(1-\beta)^{1+\beta}(1-\tau(w)-z'\alpha) - \tau(w)\varepsilon_{\tau,w}(1-\beta)^{\beta}] \Big/ z'\alpha L_0 = w^{\beta} \tag{17}$$

$$w^{\beta} = K(1-\beta)^{\beta}[(1-\beta)(1-\tau(w)-z'K) - \tau(w)\varepsilon_{\tau,w}]/z'\alpha L_0 \tag{18}$$

$$w^{\beta} = K(1-\beta)^{\beta}[(1-\beta)(1-\tau(w)-z'\alpha) - \tau(w)\varepsilon_{\tau,w}]/z'\alpha L_o \tag{19}$$

The optimum w# is obviously a negative function of ß; (note that ßln=lnK + ß(-ß)[-ß - τ(w) -z'-α –t(w)ετ,w) – ln (z' α L_o). The larger ß (the lower 1-ß), the lower the optimum wage set by trade unions will be. Note, the term [(1-ß)(1- τ(w) -z'- α –t(w)ετ,w]) is assumed to be positive – otherwise the real wage rate would be negative. The wage rate set by trade unions depends negatively on the tax rate, labor supply, the parameter α and z' (w# depends positively on z!): A rise of α which indicates that trade unions weigh the unemployment element in the target function relatively higher implies a lower wage rate; and indeed higher employment. Government can induce trade unions to attach a higher weight to unemployment if government assigns funds to trade unions, for instance, earmarked for training programs, that should be a negative function of the unemployment rate. Compare (19) to profit maximization and full employment, respectively, namely the equation

$$Lo = [(1-\beta)/w]^{\beta} K; \qquad \text{or } w = (1-\beta)(K/L_o)^{1/\beta} \tag{20}$$

Comparing (19) and (20) equation (19) will coincide with (20) only if

$$[(1-\beta)(1-\tau(w)-z'\alpha) - \tau\varepsilon_{\tau,w}]/z'\alpha = 1 \tag{21}$$

$$[(1-\beta)(1-\tau(w)) - \tau(w)\varepsilon_{\tau,w}]/z'\alpha - 1 + \beta = 1 \tag{22}$$

$$[(1-\beta)(1-\tau(w) - \tau(w)\varepsilon_{\tau,w}]/z'\alpha = 2 - \beta \tag{23}$$

Taking logarithms we have – assuming ß and $\tau(w)(1+\tau(w)\varepsilon_{\tau,w})$ and z to be close to zero – we have the following approximation:

$$-\beta(\tau(w)-1)-\tau(w)(1+\tau(w)\varepsilon_{\tau,w}) = -z + \ln\alpha + \ln(2-\beta) \tag{24}$$

Hence government policy should set z according to:

$$z = \tau(w)(1+\tau(w)\varepsilon_{\tau,w}) + \ln\alpha + \beta(\tau(w)-1) + \ln(2-\beta) \tag{25}$$

The larger α, the larger should government choose z in order to obtain full employment. So if trade unions attach a high weight to unemployment benefits, government should counterbalance this by reducing unemployment benefits. Unemployment benefits should be the smaller (hence z would rise) the larger the tax rate and the elasticity $\varepsilon_{\tau,w}$ .If z would be so small that the survival of unemployed would be difficult one may consider a system which basically gives a fixed per capita payment to all the unemployed. Finally, note that maximization of Z requires conditions to be considered that guarantee that the second derivative of Z with respect to w is negative. However, we rather will focus on a refined approach in the next section and then look at both the necessary and sufficient condition for a maximum.

Rational Trade Unions

Next note that the government budget constraint is as in equation (26), and we assume that trade unions take this also into account – this is most likely in small open economies in which there are transparent macroeconomic feedback effects on wage setting. The budget constraint is:

$$\tau(w)wL = w[1-z][L_o-L] \tag{26}$$

where on the left hand side we have tax payments (read: contributions to the unemployment insurance system), on the right hand side we have expenditures on the unemployed. We rewrite the above equation

$$\{\tau(w)+[1-z]\}L = (1-z)L_o \tag{27}$$

Denote 1-z=z', divide the equation by L and separate τ(w):

$$\tau(w) = z'\,(L_0/L-1) \tag{28}$$

Trade unions maximize the following equation (30) while taking into account (12) and profit maximizing labor demand – see (29):

$$L = [(1-\beta)/w]^{\beta} K \tag{29}$$

Trade unions now maximize the equation while taking into account (26) and (29):

$$Z = w[1-\tau(w)]L + w(z')\,\alpha[L_o-L]\text{; we replace the tax rate by (28):} \tag{30}$$

$$Z = w[1-z'\,(L_0/L-1)]\,L + wz'\,\alpha\,(L_o-L)$$

$$= w[L-z'(L_o-L)] + wz'\,\alpha\,(L_o-L)$$

$$Z = wL\,[1+(1-\alpha)z'] - (1-\alpha)wz'L_0\text{; we next insert L from (29):} \tag{31}$$

$$Z = (1-\beta)^{\beta} K\left[1+(1-\alpha)z'\right]w^{1-\beta} - (1-\alpha)z'L_0 w \tag{32}$$

Next we take a closer look at dZ/dw=0 to obtain the optimum w#:

$$\frac{dZ}{dw} = (1-\beta)^{1+\beta} K\left[1+(1-\alpha)z'\right]w^{-\beta} - (1-\alpha)z'L_0 = 0,$$

$$w\# = \left(\frac{(1-\beta)^{1+\beta} K\left[1-(1-\alpha)z'\right]}{(1-\alpha)z'L_0}\right)^{1/\beta}. \tag{33}$$

The larger ß is, the higher will be the optimum w#. The smaller a (that is the higher 1-a), the smaller w# which is rather paradox: The less the trade union cares about income accruing to the unemployed the less it will push for a high real wage rate. The larger z' – that is the smaller z – the lower the desired wage rate w#. This also is rather paradox since it suggests that governments with a generous unemployment system (that is wage replacement regime) will face less the risk of excessive wage pressure. There is, of course, a caveat here since we do have inelastic labor supply and thus are not analyzing how the unemployment insurance system will affect effective labor supply.

Compare (33) to profit maximization and full employment, respectively, namely the equation

$$L_o = [(1-ß)/w]^{ß} K \text{ or } w = (1-ß)(K/L_o)^{1/ß} \tag{34}$$

Hence (33) is consistent with this only if$\{(1-ß)^{1+ß}[1-(1- \alpha)z']/[(1- \alpha)z']=1$; w# will exceed the full employment wage rate if $(1-ß)^{1+ß}[1-(1- \alpha)z']/[(1- \alpha)z']>1$. From (6) in combination with (29) we can derive the z'# which government should chose. If z'# is politically not feasible there will be no full employment.

$$(1-ß)^{1+ß}[1-(1- \alpha)z'] = [1- \alpha]z' \tag{33.a}$$

We now assume that ß and -(1- α)z' and α are rather small so that we can use the approximation ln (1+x) ≈x.

$$-(1+ß)(-ß) -(1- \alpha)z' = - \alpha + z' \tag{33.b}$$

$$\alpha + (1+ß)ß = z'[2- \alpha] \tag{33.c}$$

Hence we obtain the full-employment preserving z# as:

$$z\# = 1-[\alpha + (1+ß)ß]/[2- \alpha] \tag{33.d}$$

There is only a certain range of parameters under which z falls in the interval 0,1. If ß is rising and hence (1-ß) is falling z should fall. However, it is unclear whether government will be able to impose a corresponding z#.

The second order condition for a maximum of *Z* is negative:

$$\frac{d^2Z}{dw^2} = -\beta(1-\beta)^{1+\beta} K\left[1+(1-\alpha)z'\right]w^{-(1+\beta)} < 0. \tag{35}$$

Appendix 2 Fiscal Multiplier in a Hybrid Approach

A hybrid approach can be written as follows: Output is a weighted sum of the production potential and aggregate demand.

$$Y = \alpha Y^{pot} + (1-\alpha) Y^{d} \tag{1}$$

To see the implication of a medium term analysis – with $\alpha = 1-u$ – one may consider the case of closed economy with consumption $C = cY$, investment $I(r)$ and exogenous government consumption G; and production potential $Y^{pot} = K^{ß}L^{1-ß}$ (K is capital, L is labor, $0<ß<1$). Hence we can rewrite equation (1) as follows

$$Y = [1-u]\, K^{ß}L^{1-ß} + u\,\{cY + I(r) + G\} \tag{2}$$

$$dY/dG = 1/[1-uc] \tag{3}$$

Only if the unemployment rate approaches unit we get the familiar Keynesian multiplier $dY/dG = 1/[1-c]$. For any positive unemployment rate below unity the multiplier for fiscal policy is smaller than the standard textbook result.

Appendix 3 Reconsidering Aggregate Output in a Two-Sector Approach

Assume that aggregate demand consists of tradables demand T and nontradables demand N, the relative price between tradables and nontradables is φ. We can thus state, as an equilibrium condition for the goods market (with Y^{pot} denoting potential aggregate output) in a fully employed economy:

$$Y^{pot} = N + \varphi T \tag{1}$$

Instead – and assuming for simplicity $\varphi=1$ - we may state:

$$[Y^{pot}]^{\sigma'(N,T)} = N^{\sigma'(N,T)}\, T^{1-\sigma'(N,T)} \tag{2}$$

The elasticity σ' depends on N and T in a way which is not clear here (more on this subsequently). We can thus state

$$\sigma'(N,T) \ln Y^{pot} = \sigma'(N,T) \ln N + [1-\sigma'(N,T)]\ln T \tag{2'}$$

Thus the elasticity of potential output with respect to N-demand is unity and with respect to tradables demand is $(1-\sigma)/\sigma$. This elasticity should not be confused with the pure output elasticity for the case of a production function (say $Y^{pot} = K^{ß}L^{1-ß}$ where K and L are respectively, capital input and labor input). Why can we state equation Ib? Note simply that for any two variables A and B ($A \neq 0$; $B \neq 0$) the following equation holds – with a specific exponent α:

$$[A+B]^{\alpha} = A^{\alpha} B^{\alpha} \tag{3}$$

Taking logarithms results in:

$$\alpha\{\ln[A+B] - \ln A + \ln B\} = \ln B \tag{4}$$

Hence the above equation (3) holds for

$$\alpha = \{[\ln[A+B]/\ln B] - [\ln A/\ln B] + 1\}^{-1} \tag{5}$$

A useful approximation is $\ln[A+B] - \ln A \approx \ln B - n'\ln A$.

$$\alpha = \{2 - [[1-n]\ln A/\ln B]\}^{-1} \tag{5'}$$

Moreover, for the special case that A+B are normalized to unity α is even simpler:

$$\alpha = \{[\ln A/\ln B] + 1\}^{-1} \tag{6}$$

An interesting application of this theorem in mathematics – with many useful applications in Economics – is the familiar goods market equilibrium condition in macroeconomic analysis (C is consumption, I investment, Y real income):

$$Y = C + I \tag{7}$$

Without loss of generality we can state instead

$$Y^{\alpha} = C^{\alpha} + I^{1-\alpha} \tag{8}$$

Hence

$$\ln Y = \ln C + \{[1/[1/\alpha] - 1\}\ln I \tag{9}$$

If we assume a consumption function C=cY we can state:

$$\ln Y = \ln c + \ln Y - \{[2 - [1-n][(\ln c + \ln Y)/\ln I]]\ln I \tag{10}$$

Hence we can easily calculate the elasticity of Y with respect to a change in exogenous investment I.

Alternatively one can consider an investment function (with e' denoting the Euler number) $I = e^{-\mu' r}$. Basically the equilibrium line for the goods market can be drawn in lnY-r space.

Appendix 4 Mathematical Appendix

$$dY = c'(1-\tau)dY + c'd(M/P) + c''dv - hdr + c'm_r dr + h''dv + h'''de + xde - \frac{x'Y*}{Y^2}dY + x''dv \tag{1}$$

$$(1 - c'(1-\tau) + \frac{x'Y^*}{Y^2})dY + (h - c'm_r)dr - (h'''+x)de = c'd(\frac{M}{P}) + (c''+h''+x'')dv \tag{2}$$

$$d(\frac{M}{P}) = m_Y dY + m_r dr + m_v dv \tag{3}$$

$$m_Y dY + m_r dr = d(\frac{M}{P}) - m_v dv \tag{4}$$

$$Q_\varphi dr + Q_v dv + Q_{q^*} de + xde + \frac{x'Y^*}{Y^2} dY + x'' dv = 0 \tag{5}$$

$$\frac{x'Y^*}{Y^2} dY + Q_\varphi dr + (Q_{q^*} + x)de = -(Q_v + x'')dv \tag{6}$$

The equation system in matrix notation is:

$$\begin{pmatrix} 1-c'(1-\tau)+\frac{x'Y^*}{Y^2} & h-c'm_r & -(h'''+x) \\ m_Y & m_r & 0 \\ \frac{x'Y^*}{Y^2} & Q_\varphi & Q_{q^*}+x \end{pmatrix} \begin{pmatrix} dY \\ dr \\ de \end{pmatrix} = \begin{pmatrix} c' & c''+h''+x'' \\ 1 & -m_v \\ 0 & -(Q_v + x'') \end{pmatrix} \begin{pmatrix} d(\frac{M}{P}) \\ dv \end{pmatrix} \tag{7}$$

Define $a = 1 - c'(1-\tau) + \frac{x'Y^*}{Y^2}$, then we have the system determinant:

$$|A| = \{am_r(Q_{q^*} + x) - (h - c'm_r)m_Y(Q_{q^*} + x)\} + [-(h'''+x)(m_Y Q_\varphi - m_r \frac{x'Y^*}{Y^2})] \tag{8}$$

If {…} exceeds […]: $|A| < 0$; if Q_φ and $|m_r|$ are sufficiently small, then $|A| < 0$.

$$\frac{de}{dv} = \frac{1}{|A|} \begin{vmatrix} a & h-c'm_r & c''+h''+x'' \\ m_Y & m_r & -m_v \\ \frac{x''Y^*}{Y^2} & Q_\varphi & -(Q_v + x'') \end{vmatrix} = \frac{1}{|A|} \tag{9}$$

$$\{a[m_r(-Q_v - x'') + m_v Q_\varphi] - (h - c'm_r)m_Y[-m_Y(Q_v + x'') + \frac{x'Y^*}{Y^2} m_v] + b'(m_Y Q_\varphi - m_r \frac{x'Y^*}{Y^2})\} < 0 \tag{10}$$

Whereas $b' = c'' + h'' + x''$.

For Y* > critical Y_0* (home country is relatively small), second term in squared brackets then is positive.

$$\frac{dY}{dv} = \frac{1}{|A|} \begin{vmatrix} c''+h''+x'' & h-c'm_r & -(h'''+x) \\ -m_v & m_r & 0 \\ -(Q_v+x'') & Q_\varphi & Q_{q^\cdot}+x \end{vmatrix} \tag{11}$$

$$= \frac{1}{|A|}((c''+h''+x'')m_r(Q_{q^\cdot}+x) + hm_v(Q_{q^\cdot}+x) + (h'''+x)(m_v Q_\varphi - m_r(Q_v+x'')))$$

Sufficient condition for $\frac{dY}{dv} > 0$ is that $|m_r Q_v - m_v Q_\varphi| > |m_r x''|$.

$$\frac{dr}{dv} = \frac{1}{|A|} \begin{vmatrix} a & c''+h''+x'' & -(h'''+x) \\ m_y & -m_v & 0 \\ \frac{x'y^*}{y^2} & -Q_v-x'' & Q_{q^*}+x \end{vmatrix} \tag{12}$$

$$= [-am_v(Q_{q^\cdot}+x) - bm_Y(Q_{q^*}+x) + (h'''+x)[m_Y(Q_v+x'') - m_v(x''+\frac{x'Y^*}{Y^2})]$$

Appendix 5 On EU Eastern Enlargement

Eight transition countries have joined the EU on May 1, 2004. The population of the EU has increased by 1/5, national income of the EU by some 5% (of EU-15 GDP) at face value and by about 10% if purchasing power standards, which take into account the fact that the prices of nontradables are still relatively lower in accession countries compared to EU-15, are used. The accession countries have benefited from pre-accession EU transfers and also from asymmetric trade liberalization in Europe. The Commission has estimated that the growth rates of the accession countries will be in the range of 4.5% to 6% in the period from 2005 to 2009, which is clearly above the estimated 3% growth projected in a simulation without accession (Solbes, 2004). EU accession countries will benefit from adopting the EU legal system – the acquis communautaire – which makes investment less risky but some business ventures also more complex to organize. EU accession countries of Eastern Europe are former socialist countries which adopted a very broad range of new institutions and policy patterns in the transformation decade of the 1990s when they also opened up to the world economy and reoriented trade strongly towards Western Europe. Accession countries will benefit from EU transfers for decades which go particularly to regions with per capita income below 75% of EU average (at purchasing power parity), with the average per capita income level of accession countries of Eastern Europe in 2004 close to 45%.

With eastern enlargement, there will be ten new countries in the EU – eight from Eastern Europe – plus Malta and Cyprus, whereby the latter is a Mediterranean island divided between a Greek population in the West and a majority of

Turkish people in the East. Cyprus is difficult political turf, but it also is the home of Russia's largest expatriate banking community. The 1990s were a period of massive capital flight from Russia and the echo effect particularly found root in the dynamic banking scene in Cyprus and massive "Cyprian" (read: Russian) foreign direct investment in Russia. EU eastern enlargement also brings major changes for the Community and Russia as the latter will suffer from trade diversion. Russia's exports of industrial goods – disregarding oil and gas – will decline, in particular due to the protective nature of EU standards. Moreover, the people of the new Russia face exclusion in the sense that almost all European countries are no longer accessible for Russians without a visa. The situation will become worse after Bulgaria and Romania join the Community in 2007. Russia also feels threatened by Nato enlargement which is organized on the side of Western Europe and the US with utter disregard for Russian interests, creating a feeling of alienation in the new Russia. Nato enlargement is also an eastern enlargement, but while Brussels is the center of gravitation of EU eastern enlargement, it is Washington which is steering Nato enlargement. The Bush administration obviously wants to get Nato involved in many new hot spots, including Iraq where some new Nato members from Eastern Europe are already active. Poland, whose president obviously expected to gain in prestige and political clout from following the Bush administration into Iraq, is one example. Foreign adventure to compensate for social tensions at home is not a new motive in politics. The borrowed prestige is in stark contrast to the weak economy in Poland. EU accession countries might, however, be tempted to follow the US in military adventures in more regions, and this brings Europe back to Africa and Asia in a second wave of quasi-colonial activities, this time under the US umbrella. Germany has so far been hesitant to follow the US, but there is little doubt that a future conservative government might close ranks with the US again.

The enlarged Community is a new mixture of advanced OECD countries and relatively poor countries which are characterized by wage rates that are roughly 1/9 of that in Germany. Certainly, productivity of firms in Germany is higher than those in EU accession countries, but it is clear that there will be a new international division of labor in EU-25. Labor-intensive production and partly capital intensive production as well will be relocated to accession countries which therefore naturally become important markets for German exports of investment goods. As EU enlargement goes along with heavy investment in upgrading infrastructure in accession countries, both eastern European supplier firms and exporters will find faster and cheaper access to EU-15 markets in the future. From an EU-15 perspective, it holds that import competition from EU accession countries will therefore grow. At the same time, firms in high wage countries such as Germany, France, Austria or Sweden will have to specialize more on goods using technology and human capital intensively.

The EU enlargement of 2004 means that the Community population will increase by some 70 million inhabitants, whereby Poland is the largest country with 39 million people. In 2002, per capita income relative to EU-15 was 73.7% for the leading country, Slovenia, followed by 59.8% for the Czech Republic and Hungary with 55.9%. At the bottom level were Poland, Lithuania and Latvia which stood at 39.4%, 39.1% and 35.2%, respectively. Figures for Bulgaria, Romania and Turkey were 24.7, 24.5 and 22.9%, respectively; for 2006 the forecast figures (European Commission, 2003) are 28%, 27.6% and 24.5%, respectively. Except for Slovenia and Hungary with inflation rates of 7.5% and 5.3% in 2002, inflation rates were low in accession countries in 2002 and are expected to remain low in 2006 with the relevant range between 0% and 3%. In line with relatively low per capita income, the consumer price level in Eastern European accession countries in 2002 was around ½ of EU-15, except for Slovenia and Poland where the price level stood at 70 and 61, respectively. The unemployment rate was very high in Poland in 2002/03, namely close to 20%; in the Slovak Republic and in Lithuania it reached about 18% and 14%, respectively. At the same time, Poland had the highest participation rate, namely 76%.

Current account imbalances are not a major problem for accession countries, except for Estonia and Poland. If Poland's current account deficit should grow over time, the country might face a major depreciation and a confidence crisis associated with sudden capital outflows and hence rising interest rates. One-third of Poland's government debt is foreign debt. If Poland should face a major crisis in the future, both Germany and the Euroland will have to find an answer to the question addressing the extent to which a problem of a major neighbouring country is considered a common interest worth solving. If such a problem should emerge, neither the German government nor the ECB is likely to be very forthcoming with financial and political support to stabilize the country; there is no pretext with respect to this. However, as much as the US has always helped its neighbouring country, Mexico, through a financial crisis, there are good reasons why Germany and the EU should not treat Polish problems with a benign neglect attitude.

From the perspective of EU-15 countries and Germany, current account deficits in accession countries are rather welcome if they remain manageable for the respective countries; the mirror position of EU-15 countries are net exports of goods and services which stimulate the rise of national output. If EU accession countries' import growth would mainly reflect higher imports of investment goods, a current account deficit would be only a temporary problem since one may assume that rising production potential will contribute to higher production and exports in the future.

The EU will face quickly massive internal problems if serious financial market problems in accession countries should emerge in a period of slow growth in EU-15 core countries. Germany together with Italy is the weak core of the EU in the first decade of the 21st century. Both countries are aging rapidly and both countries have serious problems in their political systems for adopting adequate political reforms. What the North-South divide is for Italy is more or less the East-West divide of Germany. Moreover, the fact that Germany's per capita income (at figures based on purchasing power parity) fell below the EU average in 2003 is shocking news for the largest EU economy. The longer slow growth continues, the more EU partner countries in Western and Eastern Europe will suffer from this.

	Gross domestic product				Consumer price levels		Consumer price inflation		Current account balance		General government debt			Labour markets			
	average annual real growth rate		GDP/capita (PPP, in % of EU average)		(in % of EU-15)		(annual % change)		(in % of GDP)		total debt (in % of GDP)		foreign debt (in % of total debt)	Unemployment rate[2]		Participation rate[3]	
	1998-2002	2003-2006*	2002	2006*	2002	2006*	2002	2006	2002	2006	2002	2006	2002	2002	2006	2002	2006
Cyprus	4,2	3,8	72,3	77,3	90	92	2,8	2,0	-5,3	-1,4	59,7	56,1	22,9	3,2	3,0	70,0	70,0
Czech Republic	1,5	3,0	59,8	62,0	47	47	1,8	2,5	-6,5	-6,2	26,9	39,4	2,3	7,3	7,5	71,1	70,9
Estonia	4,7	5,5	41,7	47,6	52	54	3,6	3,2	-12,3	-9,0	5,8	4,6	93,0	10,3	9,2	62,3	62,5
Hungary	4,3	4,0	55,9	60,2	50	55	5,3	3,0	-4,0	-5,0	56,3	54,0	n.a.	5,8	5,8	59,7	61,5
Latvia	5,7	6,2	35,2	41,2	52	54	1,9	3,0	-7,8	-7,6	14,6	17,4	61,5[1]	12,0	10,1	68,8	68,8
Lithuania	4,5	6,4	39,1	46,1	51	51	0,3	2,6	-5,3	-5,6	22,7	23,3	69,9[1]	14,0	10,2	69,3	70,5
Malta	2,8	2,7	n.a.	n.a.	n.a.	n.a.	2,2	2,0	-4,7	-4,4	66,6	68,4	n.a.	5,2	4,9	56,8	58,0
Poland	5,4	4,7	39,4	43,5	61	61	1,9	2,9	-3,5	-5,1	41,8	49,1	33,1[1]	19,7	n.a.[5]	76,4	76,1
Slovak Republic	3,0	4,3	47,3	51,6	42	50	3,3	3,0	-8,2	-3,3	44,3	48,5	n.a.	18,5	16,1	70,0	70,3
Slovenia	3,9	3,9	73,7	79,0	70	77	7,5	3,7	1,7	1,1	27,8	25,9	41,1	6,4	5,0	67,8	68,3
Bulgaria	4,1	5,3	24,7	28,0	41	43	5,8	3,9	-4,4	-3,8	56,2	39,0	88,4	17,8	14,0	53,3	54,4
Romania	1,4	5,2	24,5	27,6	49	67	22,5	6,0	-3,4	-4,6	22,7	25,1	55,0	8,4	6,8	47,1	46,4
Turkey	1,2	5,2	22,9	24,5	71	n.a.	45,0	6,2	-0,8	-1,2	102,5	83,2	47,0	10,3	9,6	49,6	50,8
EU	2,4	:	100,0	100,0	100	100	2,1	:	-0,2	:	63,1	:	:	8,2	:	:	:

* Without demographic effects; candidate countries growth rates 2003-2006: PEPs; EU growth rates 2003-2006: Spring 2003 COM forecast; EU growth rates 2005-2006: 2,4 %; Inflation rates: PEPs; EU: 2 % const. nominal exchange rates

a) Estimation not reliable

1 Central government
2 According ILO definition
3 Age 15-64
4 Population aged 15 years and older
5 Rates based on registered unemployed: 2002: 18,1

Fig. 8. Selected Macroeconomic Indicators for EU Accession Countries and Turkey

Source: European Commission, 2003 Pre-Accession Economic Programme of the Acceding and Other Candidate Countries: Overview and Assessment.

Poland is the largest accession country with close to 40 million people. However, the country is weak in economic terms with its unemployment rate reaching 20% in 2004. This is not intended to overshadow the considerable growth rate of 3-4% p.a. in recent years. However, for a poor country which reaches less than 50% of EU-15 per capita income, one should indeed expect high growth rates in the context of economic and technological catching-up. The Polish economy made enormous progress after a bold comprehensive transformation in the early 1990s. Successive governments have been slow to modernize infrastructure, however, where for instance building a highway between Warsaw and Berlin is moving forward at a snail's pace. On the positive side, one should emphasize that the inflation rate is very low and the trade balance deficit does not present a serious problem. Rather Poland has recorded a surplus vis-à-vis Germany in 2003 for the first time in a decade. At the same time it is true that Poland is facing rising social tensions as its society is divided in young dynamic strata with rising real incomes and a large number of poor – and often – unemployed people. The creation of more firms is of utmost importance for Poland, but indigenous entrepreneurial dynamics are likely to suffer in the context of EU accession as regulations will become more complex and costly. In addition, access to bank loans could become more difficult as Polish banks will have to obey the stricter rules of Basel II principles of prudential supervision. Warsaw is a very dynamic city with many students in private and public universities with many foreign students, including a minority from Arab countries (and it has been stated that for years Palestinian students attended Polish universities, in most cases studying seriously, however in certain cases students came simply to recover from "action" in the Middle East). On both sides of the German-Polish border, unemployment rates are very high, namely close to 20%.

It is not only Poland which is having problems stimulating growth and employment. There are indeed similar problems in eastern Germany where productivity levels in 1991 stood at 1/3 of western Germany, but at 2/3 in 1999. Since then the productivity gap has not closed. There has been some industrial revival in 2003/04 in eastern Germany, but East Germany suffers from a lack of entrepreneurs, a declining population – there is continuing East-West migration within Germany – and insufficient government spending on public investment and promotion of innovation. At the same time, East Germany is spending too much on civil servants, as there is overstaffing in parts of the government bureaucracy.

EU accession countries have adopted very low corporate tax rates (e.g., 15% in the Slovak Republic) which in turn forced Austria to reduce its corporate tax rate to 20% in 2003. A major weakness of EU eastern enlargement is that the EU-15 has not imposed a minimum corporate tax rate which would be binding for all accession countries after a transition period. Indeed, it is strange that German taxpayers contribute heavily to the EU budget which in effect means that accession countries – getting EU structural funds of up to 4% of gross domestic product – use German taxes to artificially reduce corporate tax rates. As a consequence, there will be accelerated relocation of industry from EU-15 to accession countries. With corporate tax rates effectively reduced to below 20% in the Community, the implication is that mainly workers of EU-15 countries finance tax reductions for corporations with their tax payments. Worse yet, strange tax competition in the EU leads to a weakening of growth and employment in EU-15 which must not be the ultimate goal of EU enlargement. If the strange tax competition would allow accession countries – representing roughly 1/10 of EU GDP – to raise output growth by one percentage point while the growth rate in EU-15 would be reduced by 1/5 of a percentage point the net effect for the community would clearly be negative. To avoid any misunderstanding: countries which are not obtaining major EU transfers should be free to have low corporate tax rates, but it is inappropriate for countries obtaining massive transfers to adopt low rates.

Germany and other EU countries – including those of Eastern Europe – could benefit from a certain growth acceleration effect associated with the expansion of information and communication technology (Welfens, 2003; Van Ark/ Piatkowski, 2004). In Germany, the government has adopted several initiatives including a private public partnership project (D21) which has stimulated reforms. It is noteworthy that the head of the advisory committee, Chancellor Schröder, has participated in all sessions of the committee which is a clear signal the he takes this field quite seriously. At the bottom line, Germany has adopted many new reforms, but only a few of them really meet the challenges ahead – setting adequate priorities has not been a hallmark of government. EU eastern enlargement will bring new pressure to accelerate reforms. However, short-sighted politicians are not very likely to adopt those reforms which are most necessary. Germany is unlikely to record high growth in the coming years unless the government adopts a more professional and consistent set of policy elements.

If Germany should continue to face rising unemployment and slow growth over many years as well as the prospect of EU membership for Turkey, one should not rule out the possibility of debate about a reunited Germany leaving the enlarged community. One can only warn against illusory policy as supported by EU Commissioner Verheugen, who would support Turkey's quick accession into the Community. Neither Germany, the EU-25 nor Turkey are in good shape, and international politics have become quite complicated not least of which is due to the problems of terrorism. Responsible policymakers interested in preserving a stable and dynamic Community should first successfully digest EU eastern enlargement before embarking upon new enlargement dreams. The enlargement of the Federal Republic of Germany, that is German unification, has shown everybody how difficult the merger of two very different countries really is. With Turkey the situation is even much more difficult, not least because the Turkish population is growing by about 1 million p.a.; the country will have some 120 million inhabitants by 2050. Germany alone can be expected to attract some 5 mill Turkish immigrants in the period 2020-2050 (assuming that Turkey were to become a full EU member by 2020). Mr. Verheugen's view that full EU membership of Turkey could be combined with restrictions on labor mobility in the EU is illusory since the European Court of Justice has stated in its rulings that restrictions on labor mobility can only be temporary for EU member countries.

References

Artus, P. (1989), Macroéconomie, Paris: PUF.

Balassa B. (1964), "The Purchasing Power Parity Doctrine: A Reappraisal" , Journal of Political Economy, Vol.72, No.6, pp.584-596.

BorbélyY, D. (2004). EU Export Specialization Patterns in Selected Accession Countries. EIIW Discussion Paper No.116, Wuppertal.

European Commission. (2003), Enlargement Paper No. 20.

Froot, K. A., Stein, J.C. (1991), "Exchange Rates and Foreign Direct Investment: An Imperfect Capital Markets Approach", Quarterly Journal of Economics, November, 1191-1217.

Solbes, P. (2004), The European Union: Economic prospects, structural reforms and enlargement, International Economics and Economic Policy, Vol. 1, 105-110.

Van Ark, B.; Piatkowski, M. (2004), Productivity, Innovation and ICT in Old and New Europe, in: International Economics and Economic Policy, Vol. 2&3 (special issue edited by D. Audretsch, L. Bretschger and P.J.J. Welfens), 105-110.

Welfens, P.J.J. (2003), Interneteconomics.net, Heidelberg and New York: Springer.

Sustainability of Growth and Development of Financial System in Russia

Evgeny Gavrilenkov

1 Introduction

According to the State Statistics Committee (Goskomstat), the GDP grew quickly in 2003 (by 7.3 percent), as did industry (by 7.0 percent). This eclipses the much slower rate in 2002 of 4.7 percent for the GDP (which the State Statistics Committee recently raised from 4.3 percent after yet again, revising its historical data), and 3.7 percent for industry. On the basis of these figures, GDP growth in the post-crisis years (1999-2003) comes to 38 percent, or an average of 6.7 percent annually. In the first half of 2004 growth was also high, so that the GDP grew 7.4 percent y-o-y basis. Therefore, Russia continues to demonstrate a healthier macroeconomic performance than many other countries. Equally important is Russia financed this growth mainly from its own sources, that is, without any massive inflow of FDI or external borrowing (albeit, the latter did increase in 2003).

For decades, Russia exported capital. Capital flight was not a phenomenon of the 1990s, it took place in previous decades, too. For differing reasons and channels, from the macroeconomic point of view, continuous support of the communist regimes all over the world can be treated as capital flight legitimized by the government. It also means that once Russia starts attracting more FDI, which will finance particular projects, growth rates may be high even in the case of a lack of domestic financing. With that, the well-known task of doubling the GDP in 10 years, as was suggested by the Russian president in 2003, in principle, looks achievable. Obviously, higher volumes of FDI cannot be considered as the only sufficient condition for sustainable and higher growth rates. Some of the well-known structural impediments should be removed. In particular, one may point out the need for restructuring the financial system, the issue discussed in the paper.

The growth numbers looked impressive not only in 2003, but for early 2004. More important, some structural changes became more visible. The macroeconomic performance in 2002 clearly indicated the country could no longer rely on the advantages of "easy" growth, and a repeat of the same growth pattern which emerged after the 1998 crisis, would be impossible (Gavrilenkov 2003a). In recent years, a rapid rise in incomes shifted consumer demand toward higher-quality goods that could not yet be produced in Russia (Gavrilenkov 2003b). Domestic manufacturers throughout the market therefore, realized to compete with imports, a need to offer better (and possibly more expensive) products, meant they should invest in new productive capacities. Thus, increased investment activity was one of the major growth drivers most recently.

Various factors caused the growth acceleration in 2003: higher oil prices, which caused the money supply to surge, low interest rates, and a rapid increase in domestic demand. The latter was largely driven by greater investment activity, which was needed to resuscitate the exhausted growth mechanism that had emerged from the 1998 crisis, and was based on increased capacity utilization.

Due to the changing growth model, investment activity in 2003 rose not only in the oil and gas sector, as had always been the case, but across the board. Moreover, medium-sized companies oriented toward the domestic consumer market, set goals for more aggressive growth. On the backside of the liquidity surge in the financial system and low real interest rates, these companies sought to raise funds by issuing ruble corporate bonds and borrowing directly from domestic banks. According to the Central Bank, the broad monetary base in 2003 expanded by more than 55 percent (growth of the money supply also exceeded 50 percent). Meanwhile, nominal lending rates in 2H03 dropped to around 12 percent, the level of inflation reported for the year (and the upper limit of the government's target). Thanks to the zero real interest rates, bank loans to the private sector swelled by around 45 percent, and the ruble corporate bond market by over 90 percent.

Bigger companies with access to global financial markets raised funds there. In 2003, domestic non-financial institutions borrowed some \$14.8 billion on the world markets, versus the financial sector's \$10.6 billion. As a result, Russia's foreign debt in that period rose by \$28.9 billion to \$182.1 billion. This pushed up the country's total debt by nearly 18.9 percent (in dollar terms), which is still no real cause for concern given the dollar's global weakness and appreciated ruble. Due to the economic growth and ruble appreciation, Russia's foreign debt to the GDP ratio decreased from 44.3 percent in 2002 to 42 percent in 2003.

Overall, investment grew by 12.9 percent in 2003. Meanwhile, high oil prices and increased physical volumes of exports bumped up the current account to \$35.8 billion, versus \$29.1 billion a year earlier. This enabled the Central Bank to collect around \$26 billion in international reserves and expand the money supply considerably. As a result, the monetization of the economy exceeded 25 percent, versus only 22 percent in 2002. The same pattern of economic development can be expected in 2004 and beyond (this issue will be discussed more thoroughly below).

When the oil price faltered in early 2003 and the economy faced a lack of liquidity flow; the burden was partly taken up by the above-referenced increase in foreign borrowing, which contributed to growth in investment in 1H03, a time of political stability for Russia, until it was somehow undermined by the YUKOS affair and forthcoming parliamentary elections. All in all, the YUKOS affair seems to have undermined investor confidence, at least temporarily. This again, brings up Russia's dependence on the oil price, apparently still acute, which is an important issue in view of President Putin's suggestion that Russia should aim to double its GDP.

Due to increased foreign borrowing and certain structural changes, Russia's dependence on the oil price has been slipping since the end of 2002 (Gavrilenkov 2003b), but is still strong (see Fig. 1 and it will remain strong in the future as well. Henceforth, it can be expected that energy exports will remain vital for the country for some years to come. It would certainly take massive investment in the non-energy sector to bring about more change in the structure of Russia's exports and economy in general. This has not happened yet on a large scale and growth rates appear still closely tied to the oil price, that is, the higher the price for liquid hydrocarbons, the greater the investment by oil exporters, and the more money absorbed by domestic manufacturing, leading to higher growth.

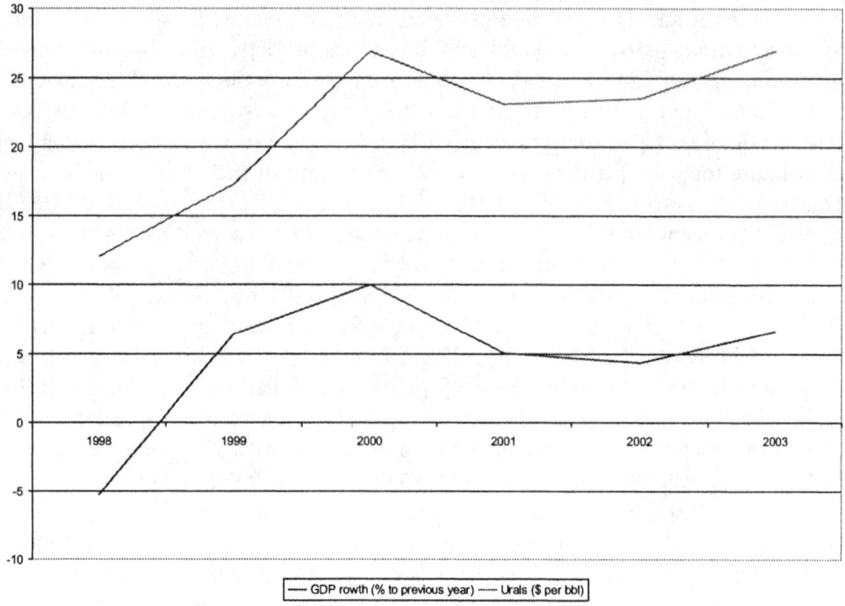

Fig. 1. Growth rates closely tied to oil price

As previously mentioned, some positive structural changes took place in 2003. One important feature of industrial growth in 2003 is it did not originate from increased activity in the export-oriented sectors only. Both the manufacturing and the construction materials sectors grew more rapidly than the oil and gas industry, thanks largely to increased investment demand. In addition, despite the temporary slowdown of both industrial growth and investment activity caused by the start of the YUKOS affair in mid 2003, the aggregate output continued to rise. This indicates that the YUKOS affair had less of an effect on the service sector. Demand for market services continued to rise in line with the steady growth in real incomes that high oil prices brought about. As a result, the sector's share in the GDP has increased (see Table 1).

The rapid expansion of the market services sector (around 7.5 percent in 2003) reflects the ongoing structural changes in the domestic economy, which could be linked to the changes listed above, in consumer demand. On the back of rapid growth in real incomes, consumer demand shifted not only toward higher quality goods (as pointed above), but services. Another sign of change seen in 2003 was the development of small business. According the State Statistics Committee, the output of small enterprises grew by 50 percent in nominal terms, which means rapid expansion in real terms, since inflation in 2003 was only 12 percent. These figures however, should not necessarily be attributed to actual growth, as they may reflect the legalization of business. Nonetheless, this in itself is a very positive change. Moreover, 2003 saw total employment fall by 0.3 million (0.5 percent), while the number of small business employees rose roughly by the same amount: 255,000 (or by 3.2 percent).

Table 1. The structure of GDP (percent)

	1998	1999	2000	2001	2002	2003
GDP at basic prices	100	100	100	100	100	100
Goods	43,8	45,2	45,0	43,1	40,6	40,2
of which:						
Industry	30,0	31,1	31,4	28,3	27,0	27,0
Agriculture	5,6	7,3	6,4	6,6	5,7	5,2
Construction	7,4	6,1	6,6	7,4	7,0	7,2
Services	56,2	54,8	55,0	56,9	59,4	59,8
of which:						
Market services	44,4	46,0	46,6	47,6	48,4	49,0
Non-market services	11,8	8,9	8,4	9,3	11,0	10,8

Given the uncertain future of Russia's oligarchs, it remains to be seen whether large companies will see an increase in investment in 2004 and later. So, mid-sized and state-controlled enterprises might be fairly active, as the recent reduction of the tax on issuing securities has brought down placement costs significantly. Moreover, high money market liquidity, low interest rates, rapid growth of the money supply, and domestic credit may encourage all companies to borrow and make fixed capital investments. So, again investment-driven growth can be expected in the medium term, unless economic policy changes substantially to slow reform or stop it in certain areas.

2 Slow Reforms Will Negatively Affect Growth Stability

Clearly, Russia's economic growth of recent years was stimulated mainly by natural market forces. From that, the country has benefited from an extremely favorable external environment. To support growth and economic restructuring, further reforms are required, especially in the financial sector. This issue will be discussed in the next chapter in more detail, from the macroeconomic perspectives. Long-term developments will depend on political stability and consistency of economic policy. The only way for Russia to deliver high growth rates is to increase its productivity, making the pace and direction of economic reform a matter of increasing importance in the years to come.

Higher productivity has contributed to high growth rates over the past few years. After the 1998 crisis, it rose through the use of existing but idle capacities. As was said, this alley has now been exhausted. Productivity has also been helped through corporate-level restructuring and improved management. In 2003, for instance, industrial output grew by 7 percent while employment in industry fell by nearly 6 percent. The inherited excessive labor force was an obvious target in the search for lower costs. Once again however, this road can be taken only so far. Building new production capacity and installing more efficient technology is the only way to raise productivity and to secure high economic growth. Apart from political stability, a prerequisite for growth, economic reform will play a central role in stimulating further restructuring and creating the incentives for more investment.

A number of reforms were launched during Putin's first term, but little was accomplished. The Russian Parliament, the Duma, adopted thousands of bills, but appear to have had no radical effect on the business climate, outside of some relative improvements. In the year 2000, the government prepared an ambitious plan covering a broad range of problem areas, among them, the natural monopolies and the fiscal, banking and judicial systems.

Most of the reforms were launched, but did not guarantee a significant impact on Russia's economy. As discussed, growth remains heavily dependent on the oil price, while the impact of reform on economic growth is less obvious. According to EBRD (EBRD 2003), Russia continues to stay far behind many East European countries with respect to the implementation of reform (the EBRD's transition index which runs from 1 to 4 and measures how reforms have progressed in a country was 2.95 for Russia in 2003). There is also an obvious correlation between progress on reform and the S&P's credit rating. If Russia wants to see more positive changes in how it is viewed abroad, more fundamental reforms are needed.

Some reforms have gone awry. It is, for example, generally accepted that pension reform has largely failed; the system will remain largely under state control and little will find its way into the State Pension Fund.

Meanwhile, reform of the natural monopolies has slowly begun. The restructuring of UES began in 2003 and will be a gradual process, assuming that it is not canceled, given prevailing sentiment in favor of greater state control of the economy and society. A big question remains regarding Gazprom's restructuring. Reform of the railroads is now under way but could well result in nothing more than a new state monopoly within rail transportation.

Banking sector reform is another area which needs more efforts from the government. Meanwhile, some of the actions of the authorities in mid 2004 aimed at cleaning up the banking system fueled some sort of mini-banking crisis. Moreover, this crisis was largely manufactured. In brief, the chain of events was as follows. In mid May 2004, the Central Bank revoked Sodbisnesbank's license amid allegations of money laundering, which was probably the right move. That said, the timing was extremely inappropriate given the nervous tension already gripping the money market due to the liquidity shortage and soaring interest rates of the previous two months. What is more, after revoking the license, the authorities made no reassuring comments, only several fairly aggressive statements about the possible closure of other unnamed banks. Hearsay about who was next in the firing line began circulating and banks stopped crediting each other and money markets collapsed.

There were no fundamental macroeconomic reasons for the crisis. Quite the opposite in fact, in mid March 2004, after two months of capital outflow, the international reserves began growing again, thus helping to boost the money supply (Fig. 2).

Despite interest rates soaring again after the Sodbiznesbank case, the Central Bank continued to neglect the situation on the money markets. Only a few weeks later did it reduce the mandatory reserve requirements on foreign currency and corporate ruble deposits from 9 percent to 7 percent, thus handing back around R38.5 billion ($1.5 billion) to commercial banks. It also lowered the refinancing rate from 14 percent to 13 percent, although this was evidently insufficient to calm the situation. In fact, the latter move had no effect at all, as the refinancing mechanism in Russia does not work. Meanwhile, the rumors about existing suspects gathered pace and the list of names being bandied about increased.

Unsurprisingly, a run on some banks ensued (for example, Alfa Bank, Dialog-Optim Bank and Guta Bank). Only in July did the situation stabilize. Liquidity came from two sources: the ongoing growth of the money supply and the further reduction of the mandatory reserve requirement (from 7 percent to 3.5 percent), which alone injected more than R100 billion into the money market. As a result, interest rates dropped to around 2 percent. The Duma also stepped in, rushing through a law enabling the Central Bank to guarantee deposits in those banks excluded from the deposit insurance system. The bill flew through all three readings in only one day.

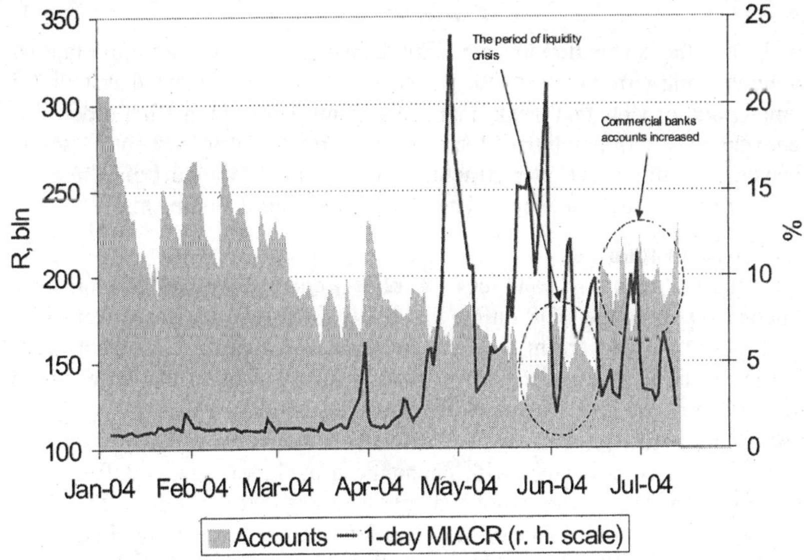

Fig. 2. Correspondent accounts of commercial banks with the CBR were falling and interest rates growing on the back of capital outflow

In early July 2004 the Central Bank confirmed that it would lend the state-owned Vneshtorgbank (VTB) $700 million to finance the purchase of Guta Bank, the worst affected by the run. Guta Bank was acquired for R1 million (around

$34,000) and had capital of some $158 million at the end 1Q04. All in all, the purchase reassured depositors and helped Guta Bank to resume normal operations (at least for now). It is important to mention that the Guta Bank was not granted the stabilization credit by the Central Bank. Because of those actions, the private banking sector lost clients and assets, while the state owned Sberbank and VTB obviously gained from the instability. More than likely, this is not the way in which the banking sector reform should proceed.

With regard to banking sector reform, the Central Bank needs more transparent as well as clearer policies. Restructuring is inevitable and hundreds of banks are likely to disappear, either by being closed or merging with other institutions. It is of note that 1,000 out of 1,300 Russian banks hold only 6 percent of the sector's assets. Given that Russians have already experienced several crises in the past decade, they are quite sensitive to rumors and speculation. Information about the Central Bank's actions and clear explanations of reform plans are therefore, extremely important if the population and business community are to be kept at ease and further crises averted.

3 Peculiarities of the Financial System in the Low Monetized Economy

This chapter draws attention to several fundamental issues that are important when gauging the long-term prospects for Russia's economy and financial system. It is a common point of view that weak financial systems, banks in the first order, should be considered as an impediment for economic growth, or at least for its stability. However, not only a lack of restructuring efforts long awaited from the government is a result of such weakness. There are some other impediments:

- **Low monetization**
  The Russian economy continues to suffer from a low level of monetization (money supply to the GDP ratio). The M2 to GDP ratio increased from 14 percent in 1999 to 23 percent in 2002, and exceeded slightly 25 percent in 2004, but even this is substantially lower than in most emerging market economies, and far below the levels found in developed economies.
- **Higher monetization cannot be artificially induced**
  Monetization is associated with economic growth, earnings, confidence, and incentives to save. Cross-country analysis shows that the higher the GDP per capita, the higher the degree of monetization (the existence of the links between economic development and the level of financial intermediation were mentioned long ago by Goldsmith (1969)).
- **Market performance, or performance of the financial system in a broader sense, should be compared with real money supply**
  In economies with a low level of monetization, it is better to compare equity market performance indicators, such as the stock market index or the market's capitalization, with the M2 money supply rather than the GDP. In developed

economies, there is little difference between the two. The same is relevant to the analysis of the banking system, insurance business, and other segments of financial markets.

- **Market should grow with money supply**
  In a similar vein, one may assume that the capitalization of the Russian market should, in the long run, increase alongside growth in the real money supply (Fig. 3 demonstrates such dependence for the period from 2001 to mid 2004). It should be emphasized that the above statement is true "in the long run." The market is far more volatile than the overall economy and can grow quickly on the back of strong fundamentals and speculation. Similarly, it can fall swiftly if the news flow is bad (however strong the macroclimate). The bigger the gap between the market's capitalization and real capital circulating in the economy, the less likely the market is to grow. This does not necessarily mean a correction, but at least a pause until the gap diminishes (Fig. 4).

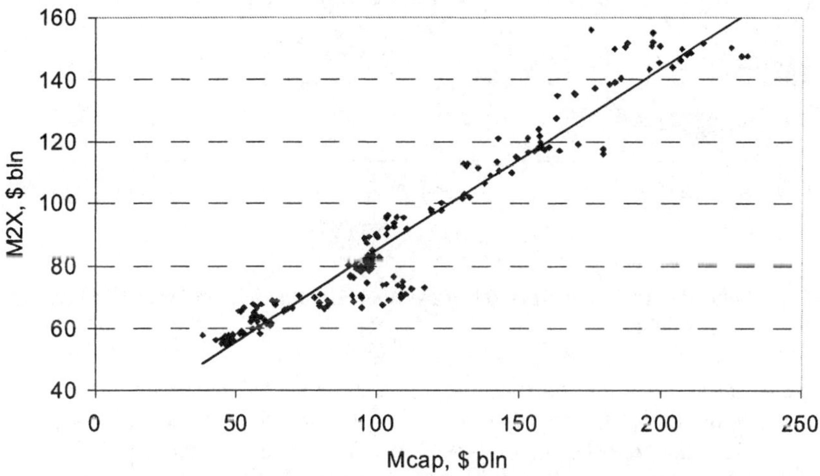

Fig. 3. Money supply and market capitalization since 2001 (weekly data)

These lead to a number of interesting conclusions. The first two imply that the expected long-term economic growth (assuming that the economic reforms continue) will mean growth in monetization, which means the money supply should grow faster than the GDP. In combination with the last premise, this means the market can, in the long run, be expected to grow as fast as the money supply. Therefore, economic growth and the ongoing re-monetization of the economy will prompt Russia's stock market to grow much faster than the GDP. Moreover, this is exactly what has happened over the past few years (as Fig. 4 shows). In addition, fast growth in the market means sustainable long-term growth, albeit substantial short-term fluctuations are likely at any given moment. Financial markets may become an important element of the financial system, which can support economic growth in Russia in the long run. Seriously underdeveloped banking systems will be unable to satisfy growing appetites in the corporate sector, which is targeting growth. The fundamental controversy which arises from the fact that the Russian economy is still dominated by big corporations (which to some extent should be considered as a heritage of a Soviet system) while in the banking sector, one may still find over 1,300 undercapitalized banks: only the 25 largest Russian banks hold over $1 billion in assets.

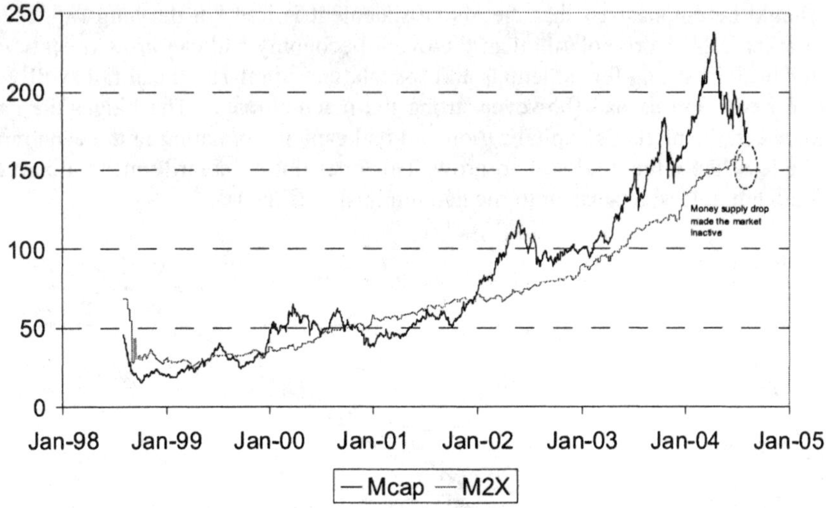

Fig. 4. "Mind the gap" if the market grows too fast: Russian market capitalization and money supply, $ billion

Thus, if the economic reforms continue, Russia's GDP can be expected to grow faster than the global figure and Russia's market should grow considerably faster. This implies that returns on long-term investment in Russian equities may be higher than in many other countries, although the short-term risks of a downward correction of the type seen after the 1998 crisis, in the second half of 2003, at the end 2003 and in mid 2004, remain high. In 2H02, the 'adjustment' was probably triggered by the change in the growth model, as the growth mechanism that developed after the 1998 crisis, based largely on higher capacity utilization, came to the end of its useful life, prompting a slowdown in the economy (as mentioned in the introduction). Downward corrections in 2003 and 2004 were triggered by the developments in the YUKOS affair.

Russia's fundamental long-term macroeconomic risks may, in fact, be lower than in many emerging market economies, since unlike them, Russia's current account should remain strong in the years ahead, largely because of the structure of its economy. The floating exchange rate regime and government commitments to run the budget without a deficit should avert the danger of a repeat of the 1998 crisis. Even in the worst-case scenario, if the oil price dips low for a prolonged period, any devaluation of the ruble will be gradual. However, short-term volatility will remain high due to higher political risks and inconsistent policies.

Thus, it is relatively easy to make long-term projections, but it is practically impossible to predict how a stock market will perform during periods of short-term fluctuation. The system is too complicated to be accurately described in terms of the mathematical models available for practical analysis and this goes for other segments of the financial markets as well. Markets can be affected by any number of factors, many of which cannot be pinned down per se, let alone measured. The issue is further complicated by the combination. This introduces non-linearities and can lead to the existence of multiple areas of equilibrium, which the system can suddenly leap between. In general, similar issues were discussed in Ormerod (1998).

As previously mentioned, positive corporate or political news can rouse the market into growing more rapidly than liquidity, but not for a prolonged period. The bigger the gap between money supply and market growth, the greater the chances of a market correction. Investors need to be aware of this and constantly "mind the gap" between the two curves, represented as liquidity plotted against dollar market capitalization, for example. In November 2003 such a correction looked possible and happened, following the arrest of Mikhail Khodorkovsky, although the market quickly recovered on the back of rapid growth in the money supply, opening up the gap once more.

It makes no difference whether to take the stock market index or market capitalization as an indicator of the stock market performance. Really, the RTS index and Russia's total market capitalization are, of course, closely correlated (Fig. 5). However, the fact that the same scale can be used makes market capitalization the more convenient of the two for comparison with the money supply.

Fig. 5. RTS index vs Russia's total market capitalization

Russia's market performance is thus being driven (and will continue to be driven) by a number of macroeconomic factors. One of these is growth in liquidity within the system, i.e. the money supply. On the basis of this, one can conclude that the risk of a correction increases if (1) the gap between market cap and money supply reaches a critical level, and (2) liquidity stops growing.

A closer look at the trend in Russia's market capitalization and money supply in March 2004 and early April 2004, shows that the latter had practically stopped growing and the gap between the two had widened significantly. This was the warning sign of the correction to come. A wide gap and deceleration in liquidity therefore, tends to make a market jittery and sensitive to hearsay.

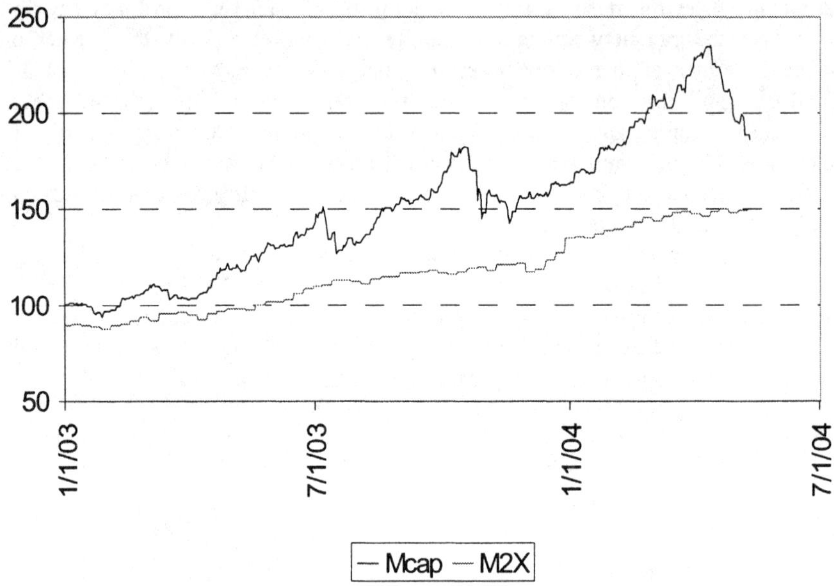

Fig. 6. Early warning of the correction to come

The more formal empirical rule for anticipating a correction can be derived from calculating the difference between market capitalization and broad money (both of them in dollars), divided by the latter.

$$\delta(t)=(MCap(t)-M2X(t))/M2X(t)$$

Empirical evidence suggests that the risk of a market correction increases as $\delta(t)$ exceeds 0.3, i.e. as market cap exceeds the total money supply by more than a third. As $\delta(t)$ climbs above 0.5, a correction becomes even more likely. It should be stressed that this in itself, doesn't make a correction inevitable. The market may simply remain flat, waiting for an increase in the money supply to bring $\delta(t)$ back down. $\delta(t)$ can be thus treated as some sort of the bubble metric index (BMI).

This simple empirical rule does not pretend to predict the exact moment when a market is about to drop, a futile task given the number of factors at play. What it does demonstrate is that a market becomes increasingly sensitive to negative rumors and speculation as δ(t) increases. What is more, the higher the δ(t), the deeper the likely correction will be (if one does take place). As the graph above shows, the arrests of Lebedev (early July 2003) and Khodorkovsky (late October 2003) did not provoke corrections as deep as the latest, although the psychological effect of the arrests was surely stronger than that being felt at present.

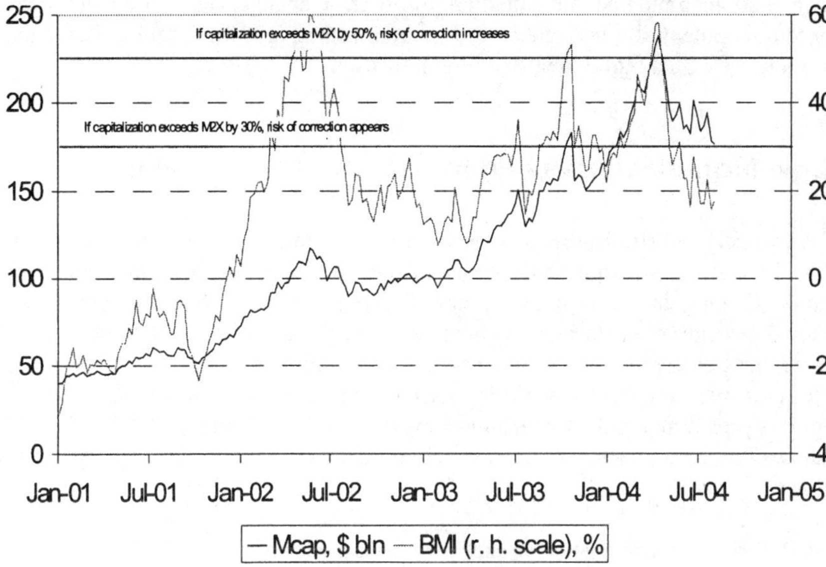

Fig. 7. Bubble metric index

A high δ(t) means that the total value of all of Russia's listed companies substantially exceeds the total cash in circulation, which begs the question: is the market for traded stocks really fairly priced if the economy lacks capital in circulation (for savings in particular). These periods clearly call for more sophisticated analysis.

The single greatest problem however, is that the system (be it the Russian market or the economy as a whole) is never in equilibrium: substantial qualitative changes can occur over a relatively short period. Some of these which can be statistically captured for a past period will, therefore, not necessarily hold true in the future. And the threat of being misguided by spurious regressions is ever present.

Bifurcation theory, the study of structurally unstable dynamical systems (see Medio (1992) or Puu (1997)), provides a more complex tool for analyzing the market. In the case above regarding the Russian market, it is possible to imagine a system of two non-linear differential equations involving two variables: the money supply and market capitalization. Cases clearly arise whereby a minor change (gradually growing market and money supply) can suddenly prompt a change in the entire system (rapid downward correction). Solving these equations is by no means a small task. And changes in market capitalization and liquidity can be described in a similar way: a system gradually accumulating the potential for sudden change.

Instead of attempting to find and solve these equations, we will instead introduce a number of empirical rules, which can help in recognizing the conditions of a market correction. Thus the BMI index, defined as the difference between market capitalization and the money supply, divided by the latter, shows whether the system has accumulated the potential for such a change. Thus, low monetized economy is potentially less stable and is more sensitive toward capital flows than the economy with a higher degree of monetization.

4 Low Monetization as an Impediment for Growth

As previously stated, Russia's dependence on commodities exports clearly remains strong and will not abate much in the foreseeable future, although it has been weakening in the past two years. This dependence, which developed and gathered strength over decades, will not go away overnight. To break it, massive and efficient investment in non-energy sectors is required. Russia has not yet seen such investment on a large scale for all the 12.9 percent growth in fixed investment last year. The breakdown of investment by source of finance for 2003 (Table 2) shows that enterprises continued to rely on their own funds, even though a little less heavily than before.

Table 2. Sources of investment financing: own funds predominate

	2003	2002	2001
Total	100.0 percent	100.0 percent	100.0 percent
Own funds	45.6 percent	45.0 percent	49.4 percent
Bank loans	5.3 percent	5.9 percent	4.4 percent
Loans from other enterprises	9.2 percent	6.5 percent	4.9 percent
Budget	18.7 percent	19.9 percent	20.4 percent
Off-budget funds	1.1 percent	2.4 percent	2.6 percent
Other	20.1 percent	20.3 percent	28.3 percent

Source: State Statistical Committee.

That "own funds" were the single biggest source of fixed investment in 2003 means that money stayed mostly in those sectors where it was generated, contributing little to economic diversification. The share of borrowing (bank loans and loans from other enterprises), although increasing (especially in 2003), remains relatively low. Generally, the higher this share, the greater the economy's opportunities for diversification (provided that the borrowings are allocated to non-energy sectors). It is expected that the share of borrowed money will increase further, although borrowings can scarcely be expected to make a much higher share of Russian investment at present. Cash flows are concentrated in a few export-oriented industries, while the financial system is too weak to reallocate capital to other sectors. Its "weakness" however, does not stem only from the inadequacy of financial institutions themselves. There are other macroeconomic reasons, such as a low monetization rate.

Because of this, low monetization constrains growth, endangers stability and limits the choice of economic policies. As mentioned, monetization cannot be raised artificially but must be fuelled by growing confidence in economic policies, an improving investment climate and higher economic growth, as well as by stronger incentives to save money domestically rather than off shore. Fig. 8 illustrates this point. Real money supply expanded much faster than the GDP when the economy grew (1997 and from 1999 onward), and contracted much faster than the GDP during the 1998 crisis on the back of high inflation. It is also expected that if the Russian economy keeps growing, in the long run, its re-monetization will continue.

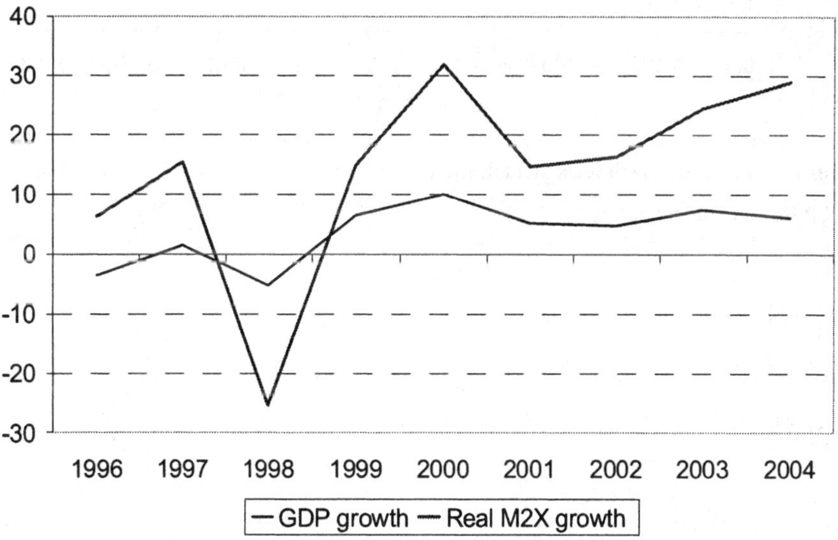

Fig. 8. Real money supply grows faster than economy (percent)

Fig. 9 highlights the link between monetization and economic growth in a different way. Since Russian economic growth resumed in the late 1990s, PPP (purchasing power parity)-based GDP per capita has risen from about $6,000 to $8,000, and monetization has increased from 14 percent to approximately 25 percent of the GDP. This trend is expected to continue into 2004 and beyond, with monetization growing by about 2 percent of the GDP annually, for some years to come. Finally, there are the conclusions of cross-country analysis: the richer the country, the higher its monetization rate.

Increasing monetization is good for the economy. First, it translates into higher capitalization of the banking sector, which in turn, facilitates loan issuance. Fig. 10 shows that in real terms, credits outstanding have been growing as fast as the monetization rate, with deposits also keeping up much the same pace.

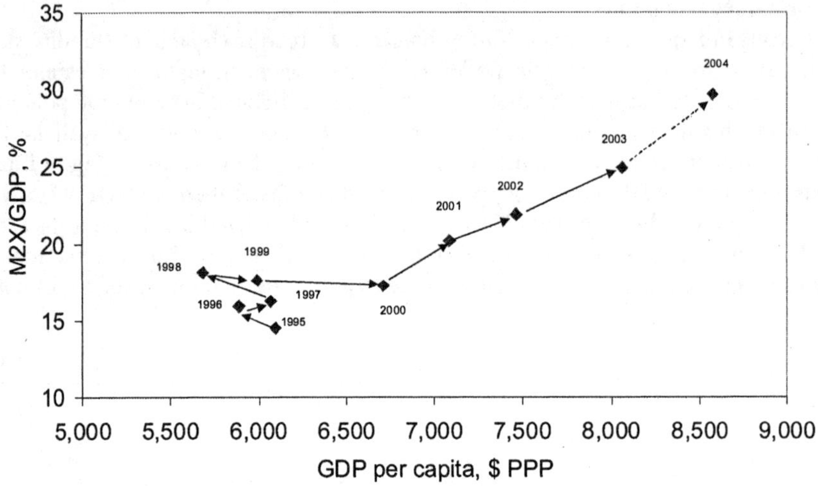

Fig. 9. Economic growth fuels monetization

PPP-based GDP per capita, $

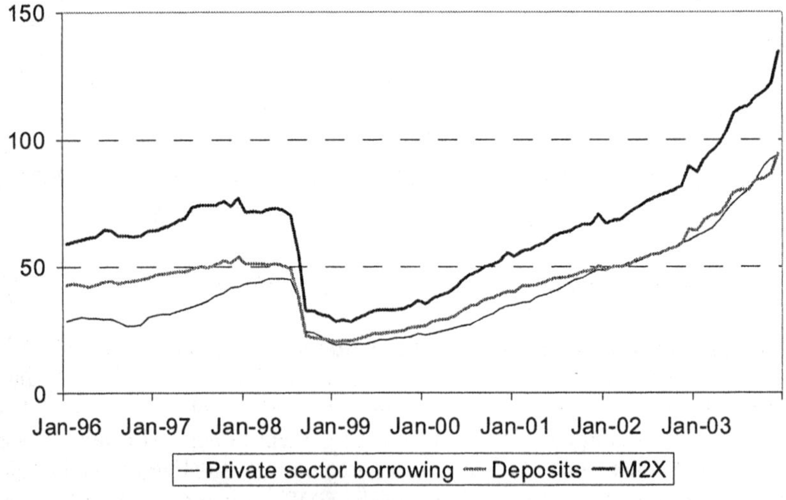

Fig. 10. Credits and deposits outstanding increase in line with money supply, $ billion

Importantly, the lending boom has been fueled by "cheap money" (Fig. 11), with a steady inflow of foreign exchange into the Russian economy causing real lending rates to drop almost to zero, while deposit rates have been on average, negative in real terms. Most likely, credits and deposits outstanding will continue growing in pace with monetization.

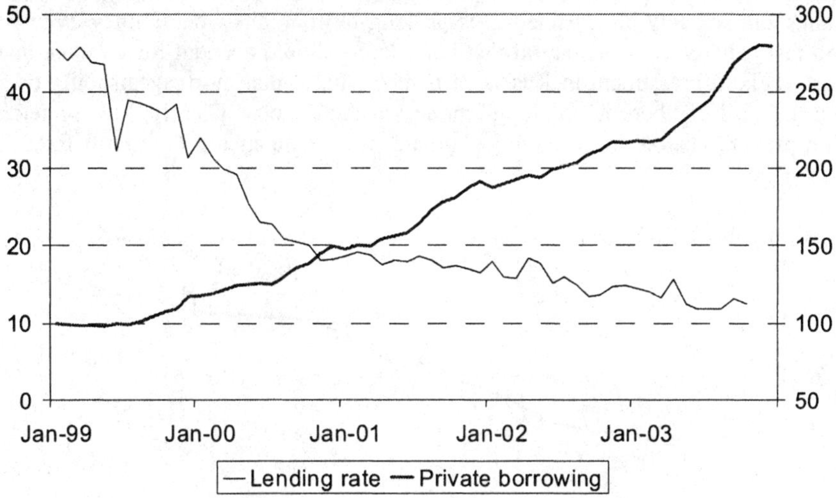

Fig. 11. Interest rates (percent, l.h.s.) plummet as credits outstanding soar in real terms (R billion)

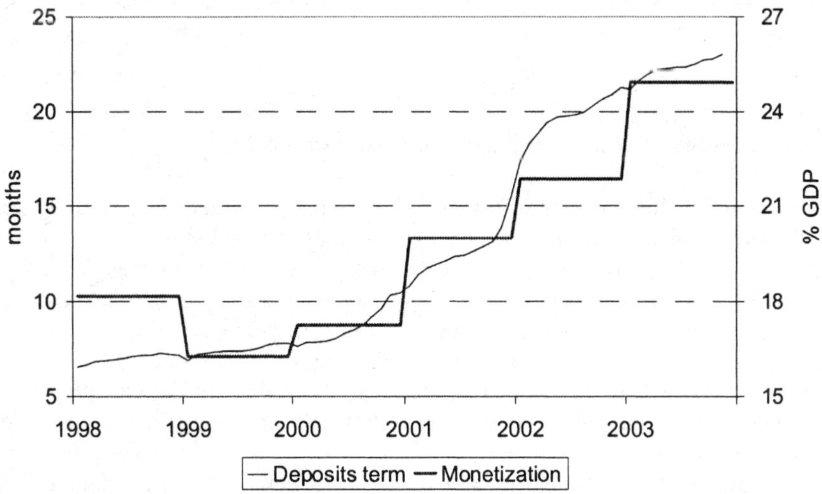

Fig. 12. As deposit maturity grows, monetization mounts

However, it is not only the total volume of credits and deposits that matters, but also maturity. Fig. 12 suggests that the weighted average maturity of deposits has grown in recent years in pace with monetization.

Fig. 13 shows that loan maturity lengthened in the last two years to reach 11 months at the end of 2003. It is still very short, but par for the course in an under monetized environment, as low monetization means high velocity of money, and banks can scarcely be expected to issue long-term credits when money circulates too fast. Therefore, it is natural that bank loans should account for a rather small part of fixed investment in Russia. It is also natural that mortgages should be all but unheard-of: there is no "long" money in the country. Clearly, low monetization prevents banks from playing a greater role in financing long-term fixed investments.

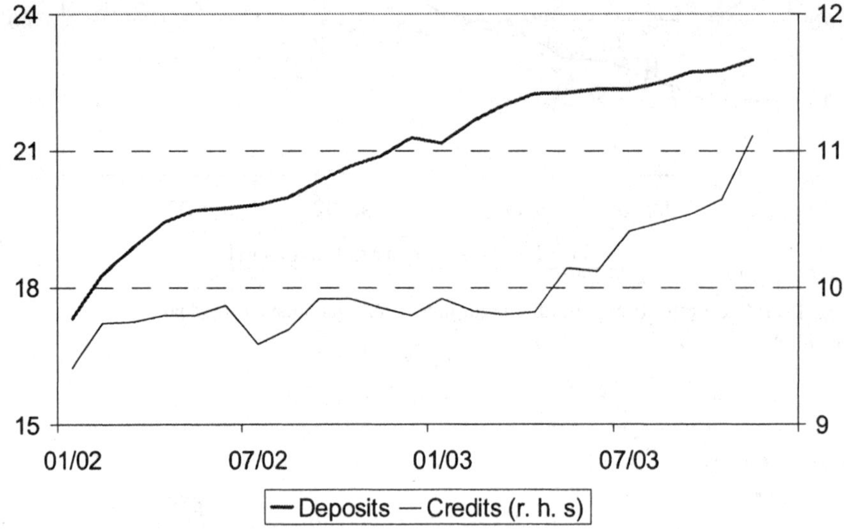

Fig. 13. Deposit and credit maturities are lengthening (months)

It is a widely held view that Russia has been flooded with excess liquidity since 2003. The implication is that banks do have money to lend but no one to lend it to. This may be true, but only up to a point. The point is that this excess liquidity is short-term, so how can banks issue, for instance, five-year loans? Consequently, there is a shortage of long-term money to finance investment.

It can be expected that maturities of credits and deposits to continue growing gradually on the back of rising monetization. Therefore, banks will play an increasingly important role as intermediaries channeling savings into fixed investment. However, until this happens, that is, until monetization reaches a reasonable level, many Russian companies will continue to borrow abroad, either through Eurobonds or directly from international banks. Naturally, this applies only to companies that have access to global capital markets.

Borrowing from domestic banks is clearly impracticable. Commercial banks did not exist in the Soviet Union. Thus, Russia's commercial banking system is barely a decade old. Small wonder that all Russian banks except Sberbank are very small, as they have not had time to accumulate enough assets. On the other hand, Russia has inherited from the Soviet Union, an economy dominated by giant enterprises. This highlights one of Russia's fundamental mismatches: it has big corporations that need a lot of money and small banks that have too little money to offer.

Companies that aim for growth but cannot borrow internationally will have to place ruble bonds. Thus, they will be able to raise long-term capital piecemeal from several lenders when they cannot borrow it in one chunk from a single bank (banks being too small). For this reason the ruble corporate bond market, which has been booming in recent years (Fig. 14), will continue expanding rapidly in the medium term. Of course, all projections will hold only if no major economic upheaval is triggered by an internal or external event, such as a collapse of the oil price (currently a relatively remote possibility).

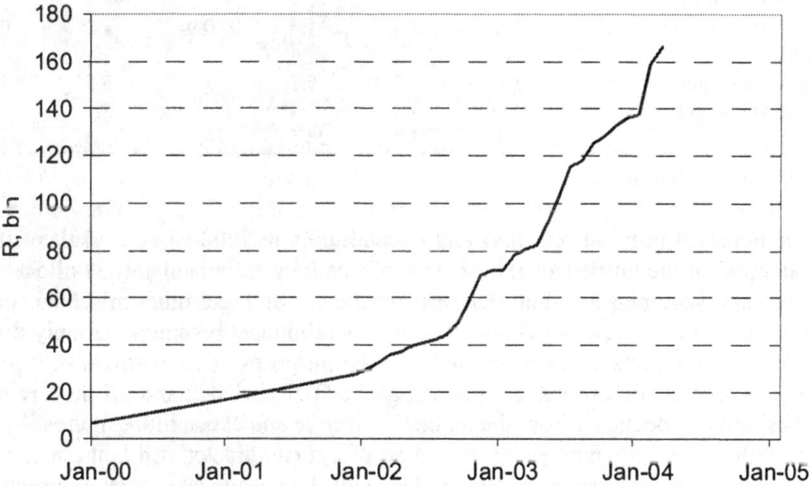

Fig. 14. Ruble corporate bond market is booming on the back of low monetization, R billion

5 Efficiency of the Government Spending is Under Question

The budget of an enlarged government should be considered as a segment of the financial system, which reallocates capital. A gradual reduction in the tax burden was one of the priorities of the long-term economic strategy, developed by the government in 2000. This has not come about, in fact, revenues from taxes have even risen (table 3) quite substantially, over the last few years (largely due to higher taxation of the oil companies), while spending has grown a little (and is still lower than it was before the 1998 crisis).

Table 3. Consolidated (federal and local) budget revenues, percent of GDP

	1998	1999	2000	2001	2002	2003
Tax revenues	20.7	20.8	23.4	26.1	25.8	25.2
Profit tax	3.7	4.6	5.5	5.7	4.3	4.0
Personal income tax	2.7	2.4	2.4	2.9	3.3	3.4
VAT	6.0	5.9	6.3	7.2	6.9	6.6
Excises	2.6	2.2	2.3	2.7	2.4	2.6
Sales tax	0.0	0.4	0.5	0.5	0.5	0.4
Property taxes	1.8	1.1	0.9	1.0	1.1	1.0
Natural resource payments	0.8	0.9	1.1	1.4	3.1	3.0
Tax on foreign trade and operations	1.4	1.8	3.1	3.7	3.0	3.4
Other taxes, fees and tariffs	1.8	1.4	1.4	0.9	1.2	0.8
Non-tax revenues	3.1	4.0	5.1	3.8	3.5	3.1
Unified social tax	-	-	-	-	3.1	2.7
Total	23.8	24.8	28.5	29.9	32.4	31.1

Source: Finance Ministry.

The apparent jump in revenues and expenditures in 2002-03 is a result of the introduction of the unified social tax. Part of this levy is immediately re-allocated between the state pension fund, medical insurance fund and other miscellaneous social funds, but the rest is included among federal budget revenues and only then transferred on to the state pension fund. For the purposes of comparison with previous years, these allocations (3.1 percent of the GDP for 2002 and 2.7 percent for 2003) should be deducted from the budget's revenue and expenditure figures.

Growth in total government spending is, of course, greater still if these extra-budgetary social funds are lumped together with the consolidated budget, producing the so-called "enlarged government budget." However, this "enlarged government budget" has been falling as a share of the GDP in recent years (it is now around 36 percent) and is likely to continue to do so; the revenues and expenditures are growing in real terms, just at a lower rate than the GDP itself (Fig. 15).

Table 4. Consolidated budget expenditures, percent of GDP

	1998	1999	2000	2001	2002	2003
State administration	1.1	1.0	1.0	1.2	1.4	1.4
Judiciary	0.1	0.1	0.1	0.1	0.2	0.2
International activity	0.3	1.2	0.3	0.3	0.3	0.2
Defense	2.2	2.4	2.6	2.8	2.7	2.7
Law-enforcement and security	1.6	1.5	1.8	2.1	2.2	2.3
Basic research and science	0.2	0.2	0.3	0.3	0.3	0.3
Industry, energy and construction	0.8	0.6	0.8	1.8	2.0	2.5
Agriculture and fisheries	0.7	0.7	0.7	0.8	0.6	0.5
Transport, roads service, communication	0.7	0.5	0.5	1.1	1.2	1.2
Housing and utilities	3.6	2.6	2.7	2.6	2.4	1.9
Emergencies	0.3	0.2	0.2	0.1	0.1	0.3
Social Items	9.1	7.6	7.3	8.3	9.5	8.8
Debt servicing	4.1	3.4	2.6	2.7	2.2	1.8
Replenishment of state reserves	0.0	0.0	0.0	0.0	0.0	0.2
Targeted budgetary fund expenditures	1.5	1.9	3.0	1.6	1.6	1.2
Transfer to state pension fund	-	-	-	-	3.1	2.7
Other	2.1	1.9	1.6	1.1	1.2	1.5
Total	28.5	25.9	25.6	26.9	31.0	29.7

Source: Finance Ministry.

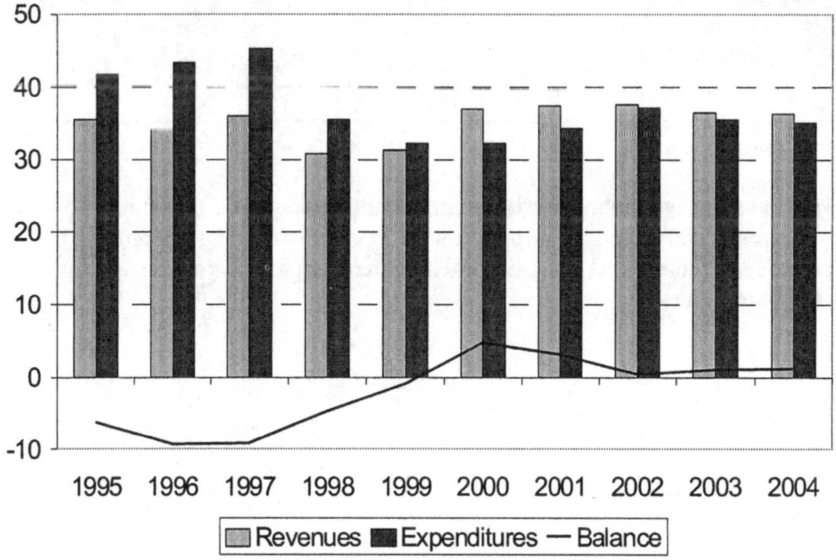

Fig. 15. Government expenditures remain relatively stable after the 1998 crisis

A different trend is observed in the case of the federal budget (table 5). As a percentage of the GDP, this has grown substantially since launch of the tax reform in 2001. One of the consequences of this reform was the large-scale reallocation of revenues from local to federal budgets, although federal budget spending grew to a lesser extent that year. The resulting fiscal surplus, which appeared in 2000 and increased in 2001, suggests that the government was successful in eliminating inefficient spending from local budgets at an early stage of the reform. Since those cuts were made, the economy has continued to grow relatively rapidly.

The composition of revenues in the federal and consolidated budgets also illustrates other aspects of the tax reform. The government always intended, for example, to collect more from the various mining industries, particularly oil, and has succeeded in this. Natural resource payments (a sort of mining tax) increased from less than 1 percent of the GDP in 1998, to more than 3 percent in 2003. This has prompted further discussion of a shift in the tax burden from manufacturing to oil companies, something that government plans support.

Table 5. Federal budget revenues, percent of GDP

	1998	1999	2000	2001	2002	2003	2004E
Profit tax	1.3	1.7	2.4	2.4	1.6	1.3	1.1
VAT	4.0	4.6	5.1	7.1	6.9	6.6	6.5
Excises	2.0	1.7	1.8	2.3	2.0	1.9	0.6
Natural resource payments	0.1	0.2	0.3	0.6	2.0	1.9	1.8
Taxes on foreign trade and operations	1.4	1.8	3.1	3.7	3.0	3.4	3.5
Revenues from targeted budgetary funds	0.9	1.1	1.3	0.2	0.1	0.1	0.1
Unified social tax	-	-	-	-	3.1	2.7	2.9
Other	0.5	1.4	1.5	1.6	1.6	1.5	1.5
Total	10.3	12.6	15.4	17.8	20.3	19.4	17.9

Source: Finance Ministry.

However, the government has promised not to squeeze companies too hard, only “expropriate” a modest proportion of their profits and then only if the oil price exceeds $25 p/bbl (Urals), all of which hardly spells major concern for companies’ bottom lines.

Table 6. Federal budget expenditures, percent of GDP

	1998	1999	2000	2001	2002	2003	2004E
State administration	0.4	0.3	0.3	0.5	0.5	0.5	0.5
Judiciary	0.1	0.1	0.1	0.1	0.2	0.2	0.2
International activity	0.3	1.2	0.3	0.3	0.3	0.2	0.3
Defense	2.2	2.4	2.6	2.8	2.7	2.7	2.7
Law enforcement and security	1.2	1.1	1.4	1.7	1.8	1.9	2.0
Basic research and science	0.2	0.2	0.2	0.3	0.3	0.3	0.3
Industry, energy and construction	0.4	0.4	0.5	0.5	0.6	0.5	0.4
Agriculture and fisheries	0.1	0.2	0.2	0.3	0.3	0.2	0.2
Environmental protection, meteorology and cartography	0.1	0.1	0.1	0.1	0.1	0.1	0.1
Social items	2.2	1.8	1.8	2.3	2.6	2.3	2.3
Debt servicing	4.1	3.4	2.4	2.6	2.1	1.7	1.9
Financial aid to other government levels	1.6	1.3	1.4	2.6	2.9	3.2	2.4
Transfer to pension fund	-	-	-	-	3.1	2.7	2.9
Targeted budgetary fund expenditures	0.9	1.1	1.3	0.2	0.1	0.1	0.1
Other	0.9	0.2	0.4	0.8	0.9	1.1	1.1
Total	14.6	13.8	13.1	14.8	18.5	17.7	17.4

Source: Finance Ministry.

Higher taxation of the mining companies will be compensated by lower taxes in the rest of the economy. The general principles of the final stage of the tax reform were unveiled two years ago in the government's medium-term fiscal strategy, which in fact was confirmed by high-ranking government officials in 2004. The plan, as announced, was to reduce the social tax further in 2005 and VAT in 2006. Given the tightness of the budget, this would inevitably mean a drop in public spending. At the same time, official policy is for a "greater emphasis" on the social sphere, including education, health, housing and social insurance. This will involve a more selective approach in allocating subsidies to individuals and a reduction in the government's role. The plan suggests that the free market should step in and take over from the government in some areas, such as health care. This would mean the introduction of private insurance schemes. Regional budgets currently bare the brunt of the costs of social spending, but also benefit from federal government support (financial aid to the regions accounted for 18 percent of total federal spending in 2003 – table 7). All levels of the consolidated budget should therefore, benefit.

The social sphere is obviously a very delicate issue from a political standpoint. However, imbalances have built up over the years and have not been redressed by reform. These could become a real burden in the long term, particularly if windfall profits in the oil industry start to slow down. Most likely the budgets for 2005 and 2006 could see more radical changes than before (accompanied by at least some restructuring of the social sector).

Table 7. Structure of federal budget revenues, percent

	1998	1999	2000	2001	2002	2003	2004E
Profit tax	12.9	13.3	15.8	13.5	7.8	6.6	6.0
VAT	38.8	36.4	33.0	40.2	34.2	34.2	36.1
Excises	19.4	13.8	11.6	12.8	9.8	9.8	3.4
Natural resource payments	1.2	1.7	1.7	3.1	9.7	9.7	10.2
Taxes on foreign trade and operations	13.5	14.2	20.3	20.8	14.7	17.5	19.4
Revenues from targeted budgetary funds	8.8	9.1	8.2	0.9	0.7	0.6	0.5
Unified social tax	-	-	-	-	15.4	14.1	16.0
Other	5.3	11.5	9.4	8.7	7.7	7.6	8.3

Source: Finance Ministry.

Table 8. Structure of federal budget expenditures, percent

	1998	1999	2000	2001	2002	2003	2004E
State administration	2.5	2.2	2.6	3.2	2.8	2.8	2.9
Judiciary	0.6	0.8	0.9	0.9	1.0	1.1	1.3
International activity	2.2	8.7	2.4	2.2	1.6	1.2	1.7
Defense	14.8	17.5	20.0	18.6	14.7	15.1	15.5
Law enforcement and security	8.0	8.3	11.0	11.2	9.5	10.5	11.7
Basic research and science	1.3	1.7	1.8	1.8	1.5	1.8	1.7
Industry, energy and construction	2.9	2.5	3.7	3.3	3.3	2.9	2.4
Agriculture and fisheries	0.8	1.4	1.4	1.8	1.4	1.3	1.2
Environmental protection, meteorology and cartography	0.5	0.4	0.4	0.4	0.5	0.5	0.5
Social items	14.9	12.8	13.9	15.4	13.9	12.9	13.4
Debt servicing	27.7	24.5	18.0	17.4	11.2	9.4	10.9
Financial aid to other government levels	11.2	9.3	10.6	17.3	15.9	18.3	13.9
Transfer to pension fund	-	-	-	-	16.9	15.5	16.5
Targeted budgetary fund expenditures	6.1	8.3	10.2	1.1	0.8	0.6	0.5
Other	6.3	1.5	3.0	5.3	5.1	6.0	6.1

Source: Finance Ministry.

Meanwhile, there have already been a number of remarkable changes. First and foremost has been a substantial drop in debt servicing, from 4.1 percent of the GDP in 1998 to 1.7 percent in 2003. This was due to rapid economic growth and real appreciation of the ruble.

Another remarkable change has been rapid growth in spending on law enforcement and national security, albeit this appears to have not yet yielded any real change in their effectiveness. Regular terrorist attacks across Russia, the ongoing war in Chechnya, and the arrest of two Russian agents in Qatar in February, who left a trail of evidence incriminating them in the local murder of a Chechen warlord, all go to show that the professional level of Russia's Secret Service is falling at an inverse proportion to growing demand for money. The same can be said of the army.

Real reform of the military and secret services is urgently needed. Spending on the two accounted for 5 percent of the GDP in 2003, against a figure for 1998, of just 3.8 percent (and the GDP has in itself, grown since then by nearly 40 percent). But the average Russian feels no more secure as a result. In fact, a paradoxical situation exists: the government has been unceasing in its squeeze on the oligarchs, the proceeds from which are used largely to finance a machine consisting of bureaucracy (spending on the state administration and judiciary have also increased), off-force structures and judiciary, which continues to weigh down the oligarchs (still Russia's major tax payers), and yet talks of the need to improve social policy. As seen from the above tables, social spending has, in fact, not grown that much. Indeed, as a percentage of the GDP, it even contracted from 1998-2003. The government could certainly have gained higher moral ground if the additional revenues received from oil companies had been spent on social items.

As can be seen from the budget plan for 2004, this same allocation of resources will remain unchanged. If the oligarchs are to be squeezed again, by higher taxation in 2005, and the proceeds merely poured into the bureaucracy and "power structures," this should be seen as a further decline in the economic efficiency of public spending in Russia-to put it mildly.

6 Conclusion

Growth mechanism started to change in 2003 so that investments became the catalyst of economic growth. The Russian producers realized that the repeat of the same growth patterns as was in the early post-crisis period, is impossible due to a lack of spare capacities and shifts in consumer demand. At the same time dependence on oil prices is still strong and will remain so in the foreseeable future.

Investment in recent years was financed from retained earnings. The role of the financial system in financing investments in productive capacities was low, although started to grow recently. Low monetization of the economy is a fundamental constraint for a greater role of the financial system in financing growth. Remonetization of the Russian economy will take place in the coming years, although it will be a very gradual process associated with growing confidence in economic policies, better investment climate, economic growth, higher incomes and higher incentives to save money domestically.

Money is short in the low monetized economy: both with respect to deposit and loan maturity. Loan and deposit maturity will grow on the back of growing monetization. Meanwhile, growing monetization means that the real money supply will grow faster than real GDP. It means that financial system performance (banks, financial markets) will outstrip the real economy. Strong fundamentals will drive the markets up while politics may shape the markets. A low monetized economy is sensitive toward capital flows, thus market volatility will remain strong.

The share of the government as a percentage of the GDP decreased after the 1998 crisis, which was followed by its modest growth later on. However, in recent years this growth has stopped which should be viewed as a positive development given low efficiency of government spending. Given that there are no plans to increase the role of the budget in reallocating financial resources, the private financial sector will be playing a greater role in the years to come, which should contribute to higher efficiency in the system.

References

EBRD (2003): Transition report 2003.

Gavrilenkov, E. (2003a): Macroeconomic Situation in Russia: Growth, Investment, and Capital Flows, in: E. Gavrilenkov, P. J.J. Welfens, R. Wiegert (editors), Economic Opening Up and Growth in Russia, Springer 2003.

Gavrilenkov, E. (2003b): Diversification of the Russian Economy and Growth, paper presented at the International Conference, Slavic Research Center, Sapporo.

Goldsmith, R. (1969): Financial Structure and Development, Yale University Press.

Medio, A. (1992): Chaotic Dynamics – Theory and Applications to Economics, Cambridge University Press.

Ormerod, P. (1998): Butterfly Economics, Faber and Faber.

Puu, T. (1997): Nonlinear Economic Dynamics, Springer.

The Transmission of Economic Fluctuations Between Russia, Europe, Asia and North America

Hans Gerhard Strohe and Noer Azam Achsani[1]

[1] The authors would like thankfully acknowledge helpful comments and suggestions by Andre Jungmittag from Wuppertal and constructive criticism by Alexandr Sonin from Moscow.

1 Introduction

Business cycles within individual countries have been studied for almost a century (Schumpeter, 1927). Particularly since the late 1960s, sophisticated statistical methods for detecting and measuring business cycles have been developed, such as spectral analysis of economic time series (Granger/ Hatanaka, 1964), Hodrick-Prescott filtering (Hodrick/ Prescott, 1997), and many others. Most of these studies focused on the U.S. and developed European economies. Later, the progressively growing Asian countries became topical for exploring business cycles. Links among emerging economies have been comparatively less explored, and therefore, a need for more research in this area exists. During the last two decades the question for the transmission of cycles among economies has been moved to the center of interest. Globalized economies are becoming increasingly integrated. The U.S. is dominant and influences other economies. Useful econometric tools for the purpose of analyzing these relationships proved cross correlation analysis, cross-spectral analysis and vector autoregressive models (Gjerde/ Saettem, 1999). The extension of the European Union to Central/Eastern Europe has caused initiatives for studying the transmission of business cycles into transition countries (Tamla, 2003). Growing economic links create faster transmission channels such as foreign trade, foreign direct investment and financial markets.

Our first intention was to analyze the transmission of business cycles from Europe and North America to Russia. But soon we found that the time series available from Russia was not suitable for detecting more or less regular business cycles. The time span only 9 years because after the dissolution of the Soviet Union not only the output collapsed but so did the statistical and monetary system for measuring it (Strohe/ Faber, 2000). Furthermore, they are affected by the singular event of the financial crisis in 1998 that exceeded any possible developing cycle.

Therefore, this paper examines only the dynamic links among the output of some economies of international importance, including Russia between 1995 and 2003, using correlation analysis, Granger causality and VAR models. The primary focus is on the phenomenology of the transmission of shocks from one economy to another. The main methods used for this purpose are the forecast error variance decomposition and the impulse response function. These methods have reached their limits of applicability with data from six countries in only nine years.

Chapter 2 is concerned with the definition and presentation of the data used, its transformation and description. As the first results of a preliminary analysis, we present their descriptive statistics. Chapter 3 explains the theoretical framework and provides a short introduction to the methods used for later analyzing the data. Chapter 4 explains the results of the econometric analysis. The dynamic interactions among GDP growth rates will be examined by the use of estimated vector autoregressive models. Therefore, it includes a number of diagrams and tables, such as those of the impulse response functions that will be interpreted as conditional answers to the question of how rapidly shocks in a single economy are transmitted, particularly to Central/East European countries.

2 Variables and Data

The data to be analyzed in this study was compiled from the IMF online data service (International Monetary Fond, 2004). Figure 1 depicts output paths for the Russian Federation (RU), the United States of America (US), the United Kingdom (UK), Germany (DE), Japan (JP) and the Czech Republic (CZ). These data are indices of real Gross Domestic Product measured quarterly in local currency terms from the first quarter of 1995 to the forth quarter 2003, with the base period 1995. For the purpose of price adjustment the consumer price index was used as deflator.

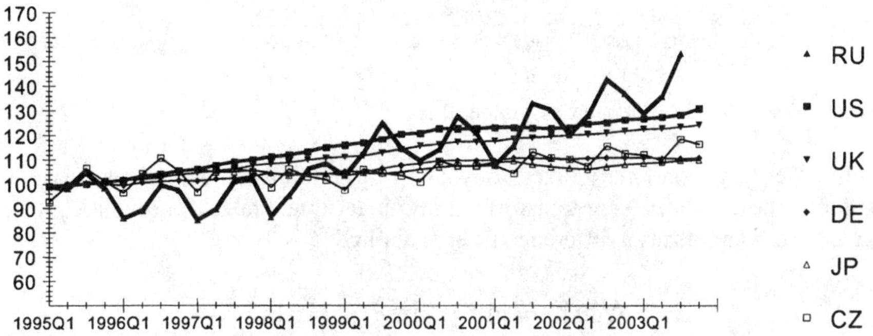

Fig. 1. GDP index for six countries

The quarterly series span only 9 years. Because of the very short time the number of countries could not be further extended according to the limitations set by the methods used. Earlier studies by the authors concerning the transmission of finance market shocks to Russia included more countries due to the abundance of data available from stock markets (Achsani/ Strohe, 2003).

Here Russia and the Czech Republic represent different parts of the transitional countries in Central/Eastern Europe. The UK and Germany represent the "old Europe" while the USA and Japan stand for North America and the developed part of Asia, respectively. Figure 1 unveils a totally different pattern of GDP development in Russia compared to the other countries.

In order to enlarge the picture for the less volatile economies figure 2 depicts the same time series except for Russia. With the exception of seasonal fluctuations in the GDP of the Czech Republic all other countries present a comparatively smooth graph of GDP.

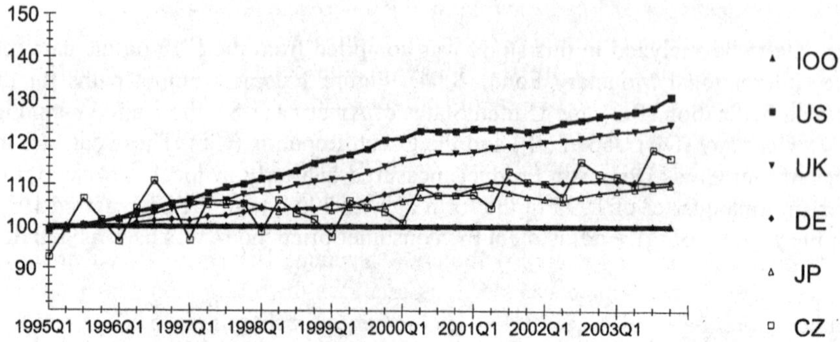

Fig. 2. GDP index for the countries without Russia

In order to get stationary time series, that is, to eliminate the trend and seasonal patterns, these indices were transformed into logarithmic rates of growth $R^4_{j,t}$ over 4 quarters. That means a difference filter is applied:

$$R^4_{j,t} = \Delta^4 \ln Y_{jt} = \ln Y_{jt} - \ln Y_{jt-4} = \ln \frac{Y_{j,t}}{Y_{j,t-4}}$$

where $Y_{j,t}$ is the value of Y of the j-th economy at time t (here quarterly). This is a first order approximation to the quarterly growth rate over one year of the GDP:

$$\frac{\Delta^4 Y_{j,t}}{Y_{j,t-4}} = \frac{Y_{j,t} - Y_{j,t-4}}{Y_{j,t-4}}$$

Table 1. Descriptive Statistics of the GDP 4-Quarter Growth Rate 1995Q1 - 2003Q4

Country	RU	US	UK	DE	JP	CZ
Maximum	0,2334	0,0473	0,0421	0,0440	0,0411	0,0642
Minimum	-0,4762	-0,0004	0,0143	-0,0030	-0,0313	-0,0468
Mean	-0,0277	0,0303	0,0261	0,0131	0,0118	0,0210
Std. Dev.	0,1545	0,0144	0,0074	0,0108	0,0181	0,0284
Coef of Var.	5,5820	0,4757	0,2821	0,8292	1,5337	1,3510

Table 1 presents the main descriptive indicators of the logarithmic rates of growth $R^4_{j,t}$. All average rates were positive. The United Kingdom only had positive values, thereby resulting in a minimum standard deviation. Russia shows the largest range of growth rates, an extremely high negative "growth" and consistently, the highest standard deviation.

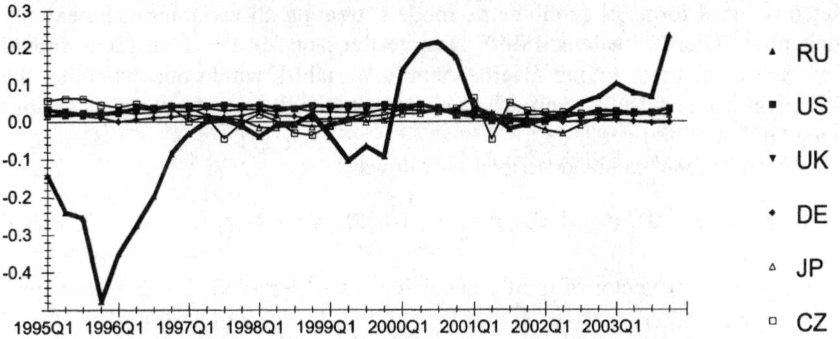

Fig. 3. GDP 4-quarter growth rate for the six countries including Russia

In figure 3 the extreme volatility of Russian GDP growth rate is seen. It sharply declined in the mid-1990s and recovered until 1997. However, the chart shows a sharp upward pique a couple of quarters after the 1998 currency crisis. This reflects the impact of the ruble depreciation and afterward, the stabilization on GDP despite the price adjustment of the data. As early as 2001, the path returned to a normal long term trend as seen before the crisis.

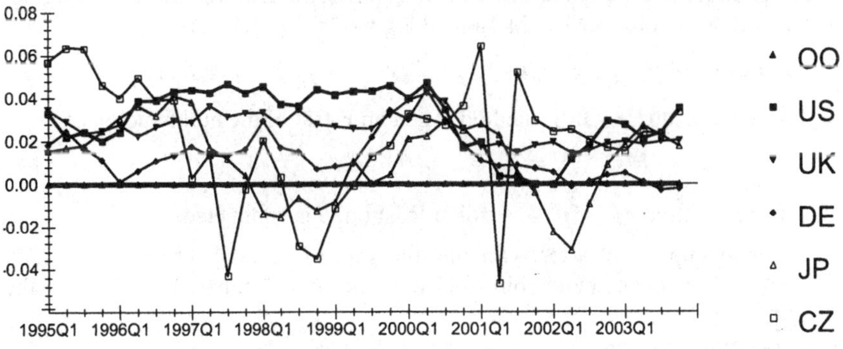

Fig. 4. GDP growth rates for the countries without Russia

3 Methods of Analysis

The multivariate vector autoregressive method is a useful alternative to the conventional structural modeling procedure. The VAR analysis works with unrestricted reduced forms of econometric models, treating all variables as potentially endogenous (Gjerde/Saettem, 1999). Despite the fact that the main focus should be on causal relations among macroeconomic variables within one economy, the VAR technique is a useful approach to investigate the degree of international links among GDP growth rates.

A VAR(p) model can be described as follows:

$$x_t = a + \Phi_1 x_{t-1} + \Phi_2 x_{t-2} + \ldots + \Phi_p x_{t-p} + \varepsilon_t \tag{1}$$

where x_t is an $m\times 1$ vector of jointly dependent variables $x_1, x_2, \ldots, x_m$. **a** is an $m\times 1$ vector of constant terms, Φ_i $m\times m$ matrices of coefficients and ε_t an $m\times 1$ vector of white noise errors independently and normally distributed with zero mean. The order p of the VAR denotes the maximum lag of the x-variables.

The method requires the time series analyzed to be stationary. The unit root test based on the augmented Dickey-Fuller test procedure (ADF) was employed to achieve this. The order of VAR, p, can be selected using maximum Akaike Information Criterion or Schwarz Bayes Criterion.

One of the key questions that can be addressed with VAR is how useful some variables are for forecasting others, which is answered by the notion of Granger causality. This paper deals only with bivariate and not block Granger causality.

The question investigated by the bivariate Granger causality test is whether a lagged variable y can help forecast a variable x. If it cannot, than we say that y does not Granger cause x. Here, we assume a particular autoregressive lag length p and estimate the autoregressive distributed lag model (ARDL (p))

$$x_t = c_t + \alpha_1 x_{t-1} + \alpha_2 x_{t-2} + \ldots + \alpha_p x_{t-p} + \beta_1 y_{t-1} + \beta_2 y_{t-2} + \ldots + \beta_p y_{t-p} + u_t \tag{2}$$

by ordinary least square (OLS) method. Then an F-test of the null hypothesis

$$H_o: \ \beta_1 = \beta_2 = \ldots = \beta_p = 0 \tag{3}$$

versus the alternative $H_1: \ \beta_i \neq 0$ for at least one i is conducted.

In order to implement a test variable, the sum of squared residuals from (2), $RSS_1 = \sum_{\forall t} \hat{u}_t^2$, is calculated and compared with the sum of squared residuals of the univariate autoregression for x_t, $RSS_0 = \sum_{\forall t} \hat{e}_t^2$, where

$$x_t = c_0 + \gamma_1 x_{t-1} + \gamma_2 x_{t-2} + \ldots + \gamma_p x_{t-p} + e_t \tag{4}$$

is also estimated by OLS. If the test statistic

$$S = \frac{(RSS_0 - RSS_1)/p}{RSS_1/(T-2p-1)} \tag{5}$$

is higher than (1-α) quarter of an F(p, T-$2p$-1) distribution the null hypothesis that y does *not* Granger cause x is rejected. That means, if S is sufficiently large, we can conclude that y does Granger cause x. For more details see e.g. Hamilton (1994).

Using the VAR method makes it possible to analyze the dynamic responses to shocks in the system. Using impulse response analysis, it is possible to analyze the effect of a unit shock in a variable, to the changes in other variables in successive future periods. To analyze the dynamics of the system, the VAR model in equation [1] can be transformed into its infinite moving average (MA) representation as follows:

$$x_t = \sum_{k=0}^{\infty} M_k \varepsilon_{t-k} \tag{6}$$

If the elements of the error vector ε_t are orthogonal the element $[M_k]_{i,j}$ of the matrix M_k expresses the response of the i-th variable to a shock in the j-th variable after k periods. If they are correlated, the error term can be transformed by a suitable triangular matrix Q:

$$\varepsilon = Q^{-1}v \qquad \text{with } QQ' = \sum$$

so that the then orthogonalised innovations **v** can be incorporated in the above MA model

$$y_t = \sum_{k=0}^{\infty} P_k v_{t-k} \tag{7}$$

where $P_k = M_k Q$ (for details see Eun/Shim, 1989). The element $[P_k]_{i,j}$ of the matrix P_k is the impulse response of the i-th variable in the period k to a shock in the j-th variable. Usually, this shock is given in terms of a standard error.

The VAR also provides the possibility of the decomposition of forecast error variance of one individual variable corresponding to each of all variables:

$$\Theta_{ij,K} = \frac{\sum_{k=0}^{K} [M_k Q]_{ij}}{\sum_{k=0}^{K} [M_k \Sigma M_k']_{ij}} \tag{8}$$

where the square brackets refer to the indicated element of the corresponding matrix. $\Theta_{ij,K}$ gives the proportion of the contribution of the variable j to the whole K-step forecast error variance of a variable i. This way the shares of each variable at the variance of another variable can be interpreted as the relative importance of that variable in generating the variation in this individual variable.

4 Empirical Results

This chapter analyzes the numerical output of the application of the above methods on the time series of GDP growth rates of the six economies under consideration.

4.1 Correlation Analysis

Table 2 presents the contemporaneous linear correlation coefficients between the rates of GDP increase of the economies under consideration.

Table 2. The linear correlation coefficients between rates of growth

r_{ij}	RU	US	UK	DE	JP	CZ
RU	1,0000	0,0278	0,0423	0,0875	-0,1474	-0,2849
US		1,0000	0,7090	0,4618	0,1664	-0,2630
UK			1,0000	0,7812	0,1866	-0,1290
DE				1,0000	0,1036	0,0810
JP					1,0000	0,3393
CZ						1,0000

Bold entries are statistically significant at 5% level.

The Russian rate is comparatively high but negative and not significantly correlated with the Czech rate. Significantly higher than this coefficient and rather natural are the interdependencies within the block Great Britain, America and Germany, i.e. among the great Western economic powers. Seemingly, the United States contributed negatively but not significantly to growth in the Czech Republic. Because of the widespread existence of indirect and spurious correlation, the explanation power of these co-variabilities is limited. Due to the autocorrelation of the growth rates the correlation coefficients estimated can be biased. The sophisticated procedure of pre-whitening the data because the results of simple correlation analysis seem quite reasonable has been skipped.

4.2 Results of Granger Causality and VAR Analysis

a) Granger Causality

Table 3 presents results of the bivariate Granger causality analysis. We learn from the tests that the United States and Germany are significantly causal for each other and the U.S. for the UK, and *this* for Russia. This means the past data of these countries would contribute to a forecast of the growth rate in the other country.

Table 3. Bivariate-Granger-Causality Test to find the importance of GDP-growth in the first row in predicting the GDP-growth in the first column

S	RU	US	UK	DE	JP	CZ
RU		0,28632	2,93885	1,84882	0,57625	0,81729
US	2,64049		2,85355	4,65085	0,41226	0,38483
UK	1,61119	7,11565		1,88611	0,12419	0,16292
DE	2,46446	2,96910	1,17116		0,50113	1,63216
JP	1,35378	0,81414	0,14077	0,15232		2,31497
CZ	0,34982	1,58121	0,10723	0,32416	0,20653	

Bold entries are statistically significant at 5% level.

Concerning block Granger causality, we have tested whether one country would contribute to the forecast of the growth of the block of all others. The results have been equally surprising and disappointing: each economy has proved causal to all others. The numeric results of block Granger causality test are not to be displayed here because, despite the fact that a general causal climate in an increasingly integrated world is reflected, the figures would not provide any detailed information.

b) The VAR model

The VAR model assumes the time series data to be stationary. In order to check this assumption the augmented Dickey-Fuller test (ADF) of up to 12 lags was applied. The tests for all series of growth rates can reject the hypothesis of non-stationarity on the 5-percent level, except for Russia, where the test statistic is beyond to the critical value.

Table 4 describes the selection of the order p of the VAR model [1]. Equally, Akaike Information Criterion and Schwarz Bayesian Criterion propose order 4 for the VAR model, due to its maximum values.

Table 4. Choice Criteria for Selecting the Order of the VAR Model

Based on 31 observations from 1996Q1 to 2003Q3.
Order of VAR = 4

Order	LL	AIC	SBC
4	898 ,0981	748 ,0981	638 ,1679
3	760 ,9334	646 ,9334	563 ,3865
2	675 ,5750	597 ,5750	540 ,4113
1	625 ,8677	583 ,8677	553 ,0872
0	509 ,8085	503 ,8085	499 ,4113

LL=Loglikelihood
AIC=Akaike Information Criterion
SBC=Schwarz Bayesian Criterion

Presented here is the estimation results for the VAR(4) model of the GDP growth rates of the six countries. In order to keep them visible at one glance, only the estimated coefficients are printed in Table 5. The full results contain additional data and test statistics concerning each equation and the corresponding residuals, as well as the model *as a whole.*

Each column of table 5 corresponds to one equation of the model. The coefficients measure the contribution of the lagged values of growth in all countries, to the model value of the growth in one country (top row) under the assumption of six simultaneous linear equations explaining mutual dependency.

Russia, the UK, Germany and Japan are significantly influenced by their past, which is less stunning than *the opposite case in the other countries.*

Concerning the value of the corresponding coefficient, the UK seems to positively contribute to Russian growth, particularly with lags of one or three quarters. But these coefficients are comparatively high only because the growth rate of Russia is much more volatile then those of the UK and the countries and therefore, in a way, the contributions of all countries must be multiplied in order to have any effect. Russia's rates a couple of years ago show a negative influence on British and German growth, respectively.

Here, the absolute values of the coefficients are low for the same reason but with the opposite conclusion, as mentioned above. Furthermore, the equation for Britain contains three significant coefficients for the lagged American and Japanese growth rates while the Czech GDP growth does not show any interrelationship.

Table 5. Coefficient of VAR(4) Model for all countries

Regressors are		Equation	for GDP	Growth		in	
Growths	(lag) in	RU	US	UK	DE	JP	CZ
RU	(-1)	0,8169	0,0132	-0,0217	0,0371	0,0084	0,0012
	(-2)	0,0456	-0,0487	0,0084	-0,1112	-0,0547	-0,2339
	(-3)	-0,0102	0,0335	-0,0023	0,0678	0,0592	0,1739
	(-4)	0,0171	-0,0208	-0,0013	-0,0175	-0,0147	-0,0443
US	(-1)	-0,1037	0,6839	0,5831	1,3431	1,1201	-3,2226
	(-2)	-9,0037	0,3784	0,7211	-1,1499	1,1938	-3,0231
	(-3)	3,0768	0,1049	-0,0183	-1,1085	-0,3000	-1,1678
	(-4)	4,2819	0,1182	0,0466	-0,0260	-0,7383	0,3940
UK	(-1)	7,7453	0,2607	-0,6682	-1,0082	-1,3584	0,6997
	(-2)	-1,1507	-0,3180	-0,9641	-0,6328	-1,3319	7,2763
	(-3)	6,4322	-0,1555	-1,1656	1,4074	-0,9231	6,1032
	(-4)	-0,7011	-0,3712	-0,8169	0,3711	-0,3338	0,1075
DE	(-1)	2,1321	-0,2986	0,1416	0,8967	0,1524	3,5423
	(-2)	0,0520	-0,5364	0,3837	1,0992	-0,0240	-1,8566
	(-3)	-8,8736	0,6492	0,7713	0,6155	1,8474	-3,0043
	(-4)	-3,1586	-0,1914	0,4817	-1,0593	0,4266	-3,1825
JP	(-1)	2,1984	-0,1229	-0,0925	0,5318	0,3596	1,9295
	(-2)	-3,3371	-0,0225	0,0055	0,2215	-0,1286	-0,0922
	(-3)	1,3176	-0,1524	-0,0874	-0,0213	0,6543	-0,3974
	(-4)	-1,4599	0,1550	0,3201	0,1026	-0,4755	-0,9346
CZ	(-1)	-0,0506	0,0643	0,0507	-0,1817	0,1647	-0,6380
	(-2)	0,7711	0,0105	-0,0146	-0,3514	0,0710	-0,3253
	(-3)	1,0111	0,0496	-0,0316	-0,1586	0,0719	0,1093
	(-4)	0,2005	-0,0444	-0,0246	-0,1742	0,0127	0,0545

Bold entries are statistically significant at 5% level.

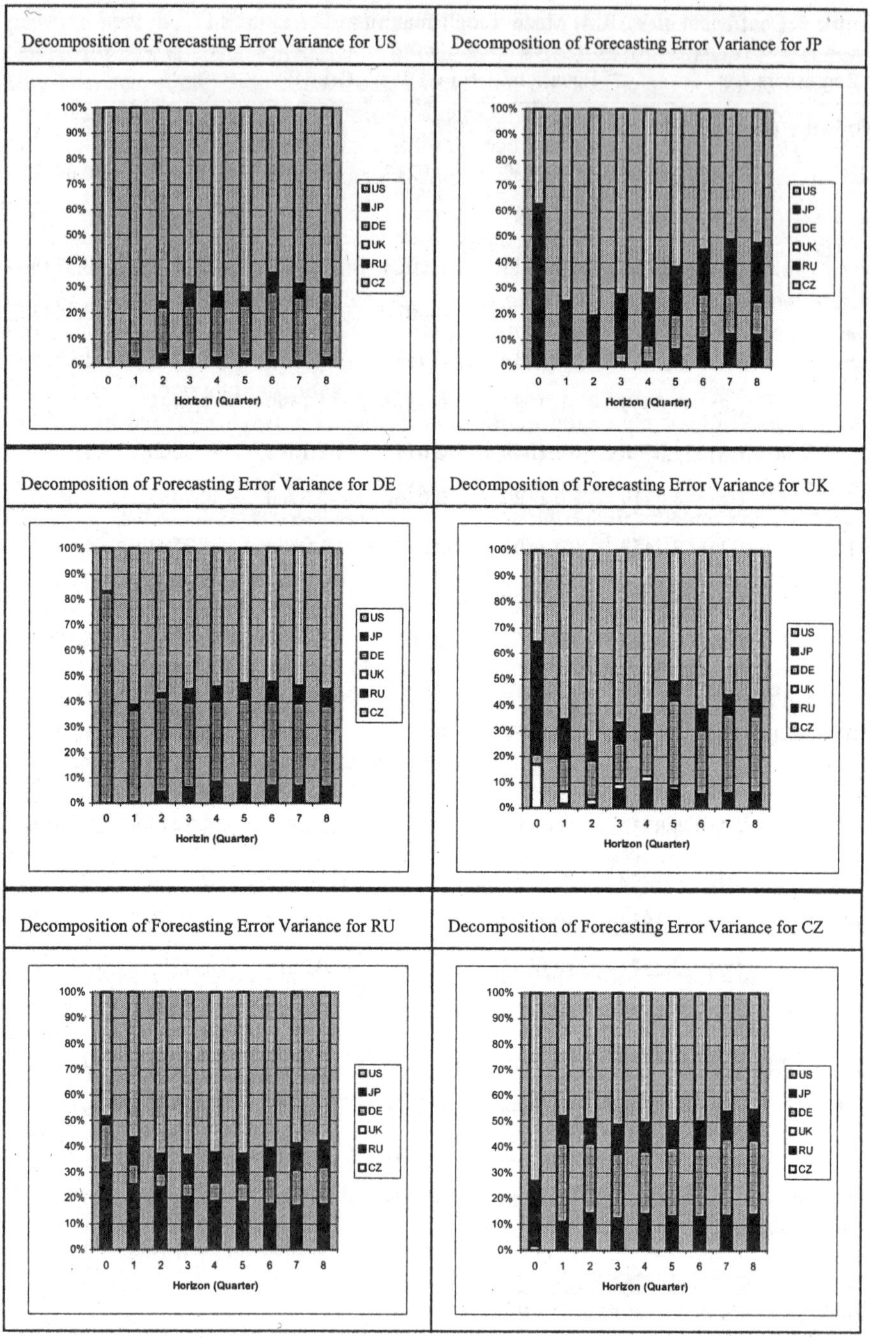

Fig. 5. Orthogonalised decomposition of forecasting error variance in each VAR equation

c) Decomposition of Forecasting Error Variance

Another view of interdependence will be enlightened by forecast error variance decomposition. Here the squared residuals, i.e. the errors of the model, are in the center of interest, not the model equations. If the model equations with their coefficients cover the linear part of the relationships, the growth rate at the error variance of another growth rate is a sort of nonlinear influence. Preference toward to the orthogonalised decomposition of forecasting error variance instead of the generalized one despite the effect of variables order in the model, is used in this area (Pesaran/ Pesaran, 1997). In the generalized system, a tiny economy such as the Czech Republic obtained a totally unrealistic share in the variance of powerful economies.

The domestic share of the United States at its own error variance is the biggest one in the entire set of countries, and it declines eventually. It is followed by Germany and Japan which means, when concerning the origin of errors, American, German and Japanese economies develop comparatively independently from the others. In contrast to these countries, the *national parts* of Russia barely exceed 30 percent. The strongest foreign contribution to the variability of the Russian and other growth rates comes from the U.S., with a minimum influence from Britain, possibly as a side effect of orthogonalisation and ordering of the variables.

d) Impulse Response Analysis

The extent and delay to which output shocks are transmitted from one country to another is interesting in the analysis of international integration. Again, the use of the orthogonalised instead of the generalized impulse response analysis, as explained in a previous section, is the preferred method. Figure 4 depicts the impulse response functions derived from the VAR(4) representation. On the horizontal axis the time unit in plotted quarters. On the vertical axis the impact of a shock of one standard deviation of the residuals of the corresponding equation in the VAR system is shown.

Tendencies in Western countries and Japan cannot be analyzed sophisticatedly due to their responses being hidden behind an overwhelming response in Russia after half a year on average. This is a result of the high variability of the Russian growth rate interpreted by the algorithm as a response to slight shocks in the West while the smoother Western rates react to each other with more moderate responses. The diagram below shows shocks in Russia do not seem to be transmitted to other countries as intensively. If a shock transmission exists from Russia it would be transmitted to the Czech Republic and induce a certain negative response after two quarters. This can be explained by the close economic relationships and common parts of the political history between the two countries.

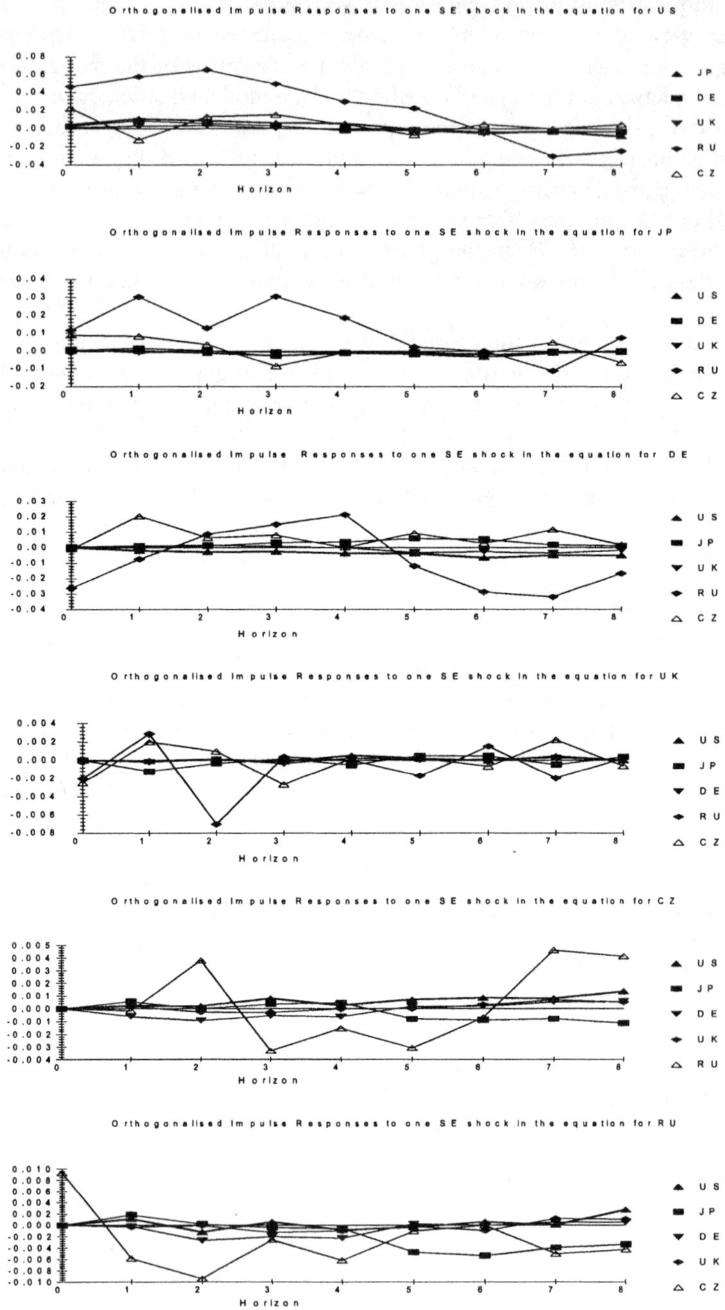

Fig. 6. Impulse response of all GDP growth rates to one standard error shock in an individual rate

Perhaps the picture is immensely biased by the two huge shocks in Russia during the observation period, that is, the sharp decline of the Russian GDP in 1995, and the steep growth in 2000, after the currency crisis of 1998. In this case, any measurable arbitrary relationship of these singular and extreme shocks to any minor shock in another country would be overrated compared to the transmission of regular shocks. With reservation as to this bias we can learn from the diagrams in Fig. 6. that Russia responds positively on GDP unit shocks in America, the UK, Germany, Japan and the Czech Republic, after one to four quarters. Later, this effect dies out.

As shown earlier (Achsani/ Strohe, 2004), shocks in the international stock markets have been rapidly transmitted in the same day to Russia. By way of contrast, the transmission of shocks in GDP growth takes up to one year.

5 Conclusion

In this paper, causal relationships between Central/East European countries and four other powerful economies in the world have been explored using correlation analysis, Granger causality, vector autoregressive models, forecast variance decomposition and impulse response analysis. The main conclusions are as follows: A detailed analysis of multinational GDP dynamics has been provided. Some of the methods used in this study generally give qualitatively similar results varying only in their extent and the special point of view, but other methods deliver totally different results. More specifically, Russia's growth is not significantly correlated with any other country. But more than 70 percent of the forecast error variance for Russia is caused by shocks in other economies. The UK has the minimum share at the Russian forecast error, but it significantly influences GDP growth in Russia in the Granger meaning. These different answers by different methods are not necessarily contradictory. Seemingly inconsistent results obtained can correspond to different views expressed by these methods.

For a deeper understanding of the mutual growth dynamics with the countries under or after transition, the mentioned surprising effect is to be further investigated, especially the question whether this is a direct impact of the Russian GDP or a rather secondary effect of close connection with third economies. Of course it was desirable to separate the real economic dynamics from the influence of the ruble depreciation during the currency crisis in 1998. But with the crisis eliminated, would it now be the real dynamics? Therefore, it would be worthwhile to more deeply examine the importance of this crisis for the structure of the international dynamic causal relationships between Russia, the other countries under transition, and the Western industrial powers.

There are further reasons why the results of these estimations must be interpreted cautiously. Taken into account, the Czech Republic, and the relative importance of this small country in the system, should be questioned. The results connected with it are in a way, suspect to be spurious, but can easily bias the others because this minor economy has the same weight in the system as the United States.

In the near future, the results obtained so far are to be completed by the examination of the influence of singular political and economical events on the relationships between the countries under consideration, and by the investigation of the more detailed mechanism of causal dependencies.

With a longer time series available in the future and covering a longer post-crisis period, the approach presented in this paper can be refined in order to obtain more stable and sustainable patterns of multinational growth dynamics and the transmission of business cycles to Eastern Europe.

References

Achsani, N. A. and Strohe, H. G. (2004): *Dynamic Causal Links Between the Russian Stock Exchange and Selected International Stock Markets.* In Gavrilenkov, Welfens, Wiegert (eds.): Economic Opening Up and Growth in Russia. Springer Berlin, Heidelberg, 91-120.

Eun, S.C. and Shim, S. (1989). *International Transmission of Stock Market Movements.* J. of Financial and Quantitative Analysis, 24, 241-256.

Granger, CWJ and Hatanaka, M. (1964): *Spectral Analysis of Economic Time Series.* Princeton.

Gjerde, O. and Saettem, F. (1999). *Causal relations among stock markets returns and macroeconomic variables in small, open economy.* J. of International Financial Markets, Institutions and Money 9, 61-74.

Hamilton, J.D (1994): *Time Series Analysis.* Princeton University Press.

Hodrick, R.J. and Prescott, E.C. (1997): *Post-war U.S Business Cycles: an Empirical Investigation.* In: Journal of Money, Credit and Banking, 29,1-16.

International Monetary Fond (2004): IMF's International Financial Statistics site, http://imfStatistics.org

Pesaran, M. H. and Pesaran, B. (1997): *Working with Microfit 4.0: Interactive Econometric Analysis.* Oxford University Press.

Strohe, H.G./ Faber, C. (2000): *Official Statistics in Russia and the Measurement of the Crisis.* In: Welfens, P.J.J. / Gavrilenkov, E. (Eds.): Restructuring, Stabilizing and Modernizing the New Russia: Economic and Institutional Issues Springer, Berlin, Heidelberg, 471-475.

Schumpeter (1927): *The Explanation of the Business Cycles*, in: Economica, Vol. VII, pp 286-311.

Tamla, K. (2003):*Business Cycles in Transition Countries*, Kroon & Economy No 2, 2003.

U.S.-Russian and U.S.-Ukrainian Trade Relations and Foreign Direct Investment Effect

Olga Nosova

1 Introduction

International trade contributes significantly to a country's development through the full utilization of domestic resources; expansion of market size; the transfer of new ideas, technologies, and skills; and stimulation of capital transfer. The elimination of trade barriers, reduction of transportation costs, and the upsurge in telecommunication upsurge all promote trade benefits. The level of internal conditions in the state affects a country's economic performance. The stability and prosperity of Eastern Europe would significantly affect global development. Successful economic reforms, continued opening-up, and the liberalization of policy will all enhance competition and export growth by positively affecting intratrade growth.

The broad debate between free trade economists and their opponents emphasizes the weak and strong points of free trade development. The existence of two points of view in trade policy results in two concepts: free trade, which purports that trading nations will enjoy privileged benefits, and protectionist, which argues that countries will have gains and loses based on a game theory approach. Global free trade enhances the further opening up of international markets, trade benefits in the long-run, and enforces international institutional settings.

The traditional trade theory provides static and irrelevant analysis to the countries' interchange of commodities. Ohlin (1967, p. 309) pointed out that a good many factors do not exist at all in developing countries, and the quality of others differs from factors in the industrialized countries. This is the explanation for why a simple method of analysis – such as the factor proportions model which does not take this into account – is to some extent unrealistic. Statist theory is itself flawed, because it has no theory of the politics of foreign policy choices (Cowhey, 1993, p. 225).

Neoclassical trade theory is based on conditions related to bounds of relevancy and credibility. Scientists argue on the one hand that assumptions exist by which all nations have homogeneous production functions and the same level of economic development, and, on the other hand that obvious asymmetries in the comparative levels of technology and development exist between the United States and its Mexican neighbor (Brinkman, 2004, p. 117).

The huge variety of approaches explains the different scientific methods applied to new trade theories. Scientists make attempts to resolve this complexity through methodological rationalism, economic rationality factors, profit maximization, and the creation of a complex model. The successful transformation of East European countries to market economies is based on efficient foreign trade policy and the application of a complex trade theories approach. Transition countries need to provide policy changes in the pattern of trade and the development of further international economic relations in order to increase trade and foreign capital movement benefits.

2 Theoretical Foundations of New Trade Theory Investigations

The rapid growth of world trade and merchandise trade at the end of 20th century and global economic slow down at the beginning of 21st century forced many scientists to find new theoretical explanations for the factor proportions of international trade, intra-industry trade in bilateral exchanges of the same good, and state policy in stimulating competitiveness in specific trade sectors.

Generalizing global economic changes and theoretical new trade approaches, Czinkota, Roikainan, Moffet, Moykihan (2001, p. 97) emphasize the basic two works in new trade theory: the work of Paul Krugman at MIT in analyzing trade for real world economies – economies that do not possess perfect competition, free trade or unregulated markets – and the work of Michael Porter at Harvard who attempted to examine the competitiveness of industries on a global basis rather then relying on country-specific factors to determine their competitive advantages.

Under free trade, Meier (1998) agues that comparative advantages dictate what a country can produce most efficiently in comparison to those good which others can produce most efficiently. Even in the event a country has absolute advantages in commodity production, it would gain by specializing and using comparative advantages. Free trade theory assumptions include the absence of government intervention in foreign exchange markets, market determinants of exchange rates. The company's strategic behavior is based on local market demand, labor productivity, and other costs. The protectionist approach is based on the application of national advantages. They suggest the strategic directions of trade policy, including infant industry protection, country's sufficient market power improvement in terms of trade through rising export prices relative to import prices. The existence of factor endowment in trade with less-developed countries affects skilled labor scarcity in developed countries through increased wages and makes unskilled labor effectively more abundant thereby reducing wage. Protectionist policies cause a loss of jobs and the reallocation of the labor force abroad.

Factor endowment and increasing returns also affect trade patterns. Product variety differs horizontally with respect to the production of techniques vertically with regard to the quality of product improvement, including higher capital and labor ratios. Caves, Frankel, Jones (1996) argue that in spite of the role of fixed costs, economies of scale, and a love for variety all conspire to explain intra-industry trade among countries producing roughly comparable quality products. Nevertheless, factor endowments, including human capital and production technology, are crucial in explaining trade in low-, medium-, or high-quality products.

Some economists consider the crucial role of scale economies argument. To a large extent, export competitiveness in the SME sector could be increased through cluster formation, especially in traditional and mature industries (UNCTAD, 2003). The promotion of clusters has to stimulate the generation of common externalities and the provision of innovative, value-added services, and also creates the foundation for economic growth.

The development of new information and communication technologies influences national competitiveness. It affects traditional trade relations, stimulates trade turnover growth, and decreases trade costs. European governments spend about 1 percent of GDP on R&D, the same proportion as the United States, yet the USA registers almost twice as many patents per research as Europe. Private R&D expenditures amount to 2 percent of GDP in the United States, compared with only 1 percent in Europe (Bennhold, 2004, p. W1). Clarke, Wallstein (2004) find that higher internet penetration in developing countries is correlated with greater exports to developed countries, but not with trade between developing countries or with exports from developed countries.

Wilson, Mann, Otsuki (2004) estimated the relationship between trade facilitation, trade flows, and capacity buildings across 75 countries. The following four indicators of trade facilitation were used: port efficiency, the customs environment, regulatory environment, and service sector infrastructure in the gravity model of international trade flows to modeling bilateral flows. The authors suggested that the scope and benefit of unilateral trade facilitation reforms are very large and that gains are seen disproportionately in exports.

The most recent theory of international trade and geography applies to the interdisciplinary approach. Venables argues that "the Dixit-Stiglitz model of monopolistic competition transformed international trade theory, as it did other fields of economics, and provided one of the key building blocks for the new economic geography literature that developed in 1990s" (Venables, 2003, p. 501). The analysis of the welfare economics of product selection shows that in a case of symmetric constant elasticity of the substitution utility function and an equilibrium identical to the allocation in which welfare is maximized, there are increasing returns to scale within the firm, but there are also increasing returns to scale with groups of firms. This approach is directed to provide analysis of clustering and of the cumulative causation process of regional and international development.

Summarizing the above-mentioned approaches, Husted, Melvin (2000) conclude that some economists have reacted to the results of empirical tests of traditional models by seeking to reconcile the evidence within these theories, while others have set out to develop and explore new theories of trade.

The analysis of existing new trade models demonstrates such diverse approaches, which explains the variation theories in terms of foreign trade. Modeling gives the methods of estimation as well as the construction of the model. Specific model application for transition countries is aimed at the elaboration of trade policy measures. Effective national commodity market and capital market functioning aims at providing country gains from commodity and capital movement. The restricted mobility of factors between various occupations, reallocation possibilities, asymmetry information, trade barriers, growing imbalances between countries, and the existence of technological gaps rouse the necessity for further scientific research and explanations for new trade models in transition.

3 U.S.-Russian and U.S.-Ukrainian Trade Performance and Structure

Rapid globalization affects the ability of a country's policy makers to effectively create domestic policy. It causes trade gains, improvement in national productivity and compatibility, and stimulates domestic growth.

Kindleberger (1968, p. 84) points out two conditions which prevent trade development in lesser-developed countries: growth in developed countries with antitrade-biased demand and antitrade-biased factor growth and technological change. Conditions in developing countries, their capacity to take advantage of the opportunities for growth presented by trade, is restricted by limited possibilities of shifting resources where they can earn the highest rate of return. As a consequence of these global circumstances and within developing countries, many of the latter actively seek to substitute domestic production for imports. They misallocate resources for wasteful purposes.

Ohlin (1967, p. 184) emphasized the comparative advantages for labor in the United States. The USA had incentives to invest in labor-saving machinery in a high wage country, resulting in an unusual supply of highly-efficient technical labor. The presence of specialists producing finished manufactured products helped in sustaining the mechnical superiority of the USA.

Modern U.S. trade policy is influenced by the rise of the world's major trade actors including European Union, Japan, and China. Scientists consider there a need to develop "new" theories of trade to serve as a basis for the formulation of a rational trade policy relevant to the current economic problems that America faces. "The problem facing America is basic cultural lag. There is a need for fundamental institutional adjustment manifest in a new trade policy. We need to re-emphasize dynamic comparative advantage to serve as a basis for a rational trade policy. Dynamic comparative advantage requires the rebuilding of industrial strength in connecting trade to the dynamics of economic and cultural evolution," Brinkman points out (2004, pp. 133-134). According to econometric estimations, the total gain in trade flow in manufacturing goods from trade facilitation improvements in 75 countries is estimated to be $377 billion, with all regions gaining in imports and exports. (Wilson, Mann, Otsuki, 2004). The USA had a positive trade balance and international creditor positions based upon absolute advantages achieved via technological advantages and scale economy until the 1980s.

Today's discussion concerns whether the American industry is losing its international competitive position and raises questions concerning the American government's promotion of its export industries and the type of trade policy used to shift profits from foreign firms to domestic firms. Total U.S. foreign trades grew by 33 percent in 2000 over 1999, with imports from all countries at nearly 11 percent and export growing by 25 percent.

The growing import of unskilled labor-intensive goods from lesser-developed countries into the USA results in protectionist policy for the American industry. The protectionists offer two arguments against free trade (The Economist, 1988, p. 75). The first suggests the need to account for the role of externalities and external benefits on the rest of economy. The second argument assumes that a protected domestic market can promote exports and raise national income. Lowett (1998, p. 138) suggests three strategies for the United States in resolving its external imbalance predicament. They include substantial dollar devaluation, a new reciprocity-based U.S. trade policy that emphasizes bilateral and regional relationships and enforces reasonable balance in the U.S. trading as well as the comprehensive renewal of U.S. technology, manufacturing, and export expansion.

Economists have scaled back their forecasts of US economic growth which are mainly above 4.5 percent for 2004 compared with more than 3 percent last year (Morrison, 2004). US imports of crude and oil products, including gasoline, rose by 12 percent to $ 1.41 billion in January, one-quarter of the record monthly trade deficit and equivalent to an annualized $136 billion in 2004. The latest rise in oil prices differs from previous ones in that it is being driven by demand rather than a shortage of supply. Inflated energy costs have depressed the U.S. GDP and those of other oil-importing countries by 15 to 30 percent. Restoration of market energy prices could alone boost economic growth by one percent a year (Bergsten, 2004). According to the US Department of Energy, natural gas demand will grow by more than 50 percent by 2025.

Today, the United States suffers from both trade deficits and current account deficits. Bergsten points out that the U.S. economy and U.S. foreign policy are thus put at serious risk by the prospect of an outbreak of trade protectionism and a foreign unwillingness to finance the $4 billion needed daily to balance U.S. currency held abroad. Sharp declines in demand have weakened prospects in certain high-technology industries in the U.S. Business debt has risen since 1999, and business insolvencies in Japan and Germany have escalated (World Development Report, 2003).

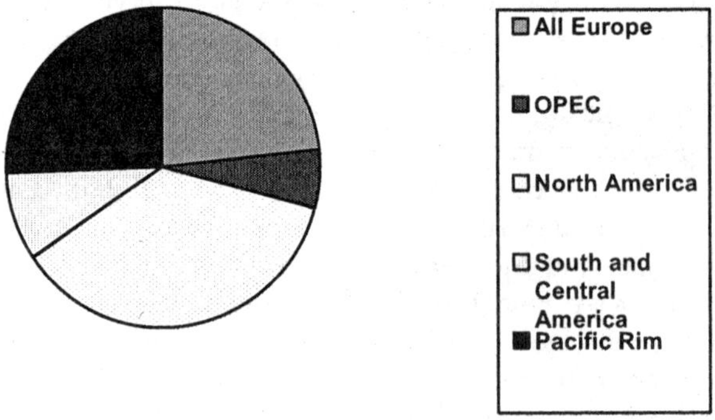

Fig. 1. Global Shares of U.S. Me Merchandise Exports in 2002 (in US $ Billions)

Source: Gordon (2003), A High-Risk Trade Policy, Foreign Affairs, July/August, p. 111.

The share of trade in U.S. GDP has tripled to about 30 percent over the past decade. On the financial side, foreign willingness to invest more than $500 billion a year in the United States funds massive trade deficits and makes up for low domestic savings rates. In all, the reduction of trade barriers over the past 50 years has raised the annual income of the average family by $2000 (Bergsten, 2004).

In 2002, the sum of merchandise exports of all countries had increased to 19 percent of world output. For the United States, the sum of merchandise exports and imports rose from 7 percent to 18 percent of its GDP over the same period. Total U.S. foreign trade continued growing in 2003 (see Figure 1). Almost 90 percent of U.S. exports are directed to the three main regions of North America, East Asia, and the EU. The U.S has a record export distribution rate in comparison to other countries (Gordon, 2003, p. 111). The trade balance (net exports) added 0.19 percentage point to GDP growth in the fourth quarter after adding 0.80 percentage point in the third. Exports increased more than in the third quarter, but it was less compared with that of imports (Survey of Current Business, 2004, 2, p. 223). The United States ran merchandise trade deficits totaling $549 billion with the rest of the world in 2003, equivalent to 7.6 percent of all world trade in goods (Williams, 2004, 7). The goods and services deficit made up $43.1 billion in January 2004, $0.4 billion more than the $42.7 billion observed in December based on data from the U.S. Census Bureau and the U.S. Bureau of Economic Analysis. U.S. international trade in goods and services with Eastern Europe is characterized with the predominance of U.S. imports (see Figure 2).

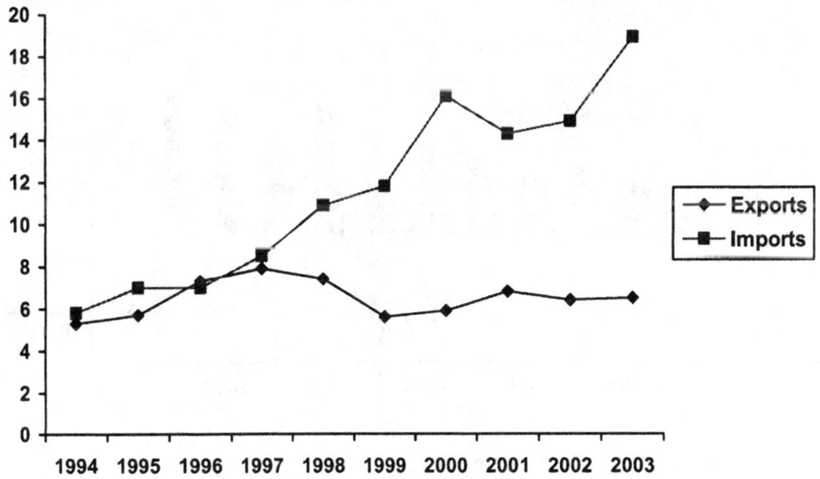

Fig. 2. U.S. International Trade in Goods with Eastern Europe (in US $ Billions)

Source: Economic Report of the President Transmitted to the Congress February 2004 Together with the Annual Report of the Council of Economic Advisers, United States Government, Printing Office, Washington, 2004, p. 405.

Total Russian foreign trade contracted by 11 percent in 1999 compared to 1998. Russia's current account balance reached a record high of US $46.3 in 2000, before decreasing to US $35 billion in 2001. It rose once again to US $36.4 billion by mid-2003. The surplus of Russia's balance of trade amounted to US $60.5 billion based on the State Statistics Committee of the Russian Federation in 2003. Russia's foreign trade turnover rose by 25.3 percent to $210.8 billion in 2003 in comparison with 2002. Russia exported 53 percent of crude oil it extracted last year. The low level of value-added production share has increased in the total volume of exported goods. Crude oil brought in 30 percent of export earnings, with natural gas and oil products making up 15 and 10 percent, respectively. Altogether, energy accounted for 56 percent of export earnings. The share of machinery and equipment rose to 37 percent of all imports. Passenger car imports and a boom in cellular phone imports increased by 50 percent (Bofit, 2004). Total bilateral trade between the United States and Russia expanded 32 percent in 2000 over 1999 to more then $ 10 billion, recovering from an 18 percent decline in 1999 compared to 1998. The U.S. trade deficit with Russia continues to climb. The U.S. trade deficit with Russia reached $5.5 billion in 2000. It was more than five times that seen in 1997 (see Figure 3). The last year during which the U.S. experienced a trade surplus with Russia was in 1993 (more than $ 1 billion). The U.S-Russian trade deficit is considered to be the result of existing price products differentials inside the country and abroad as well as higher domestic prices compared with lower prices in foreign country because of the non-profitability of goods export abroad.

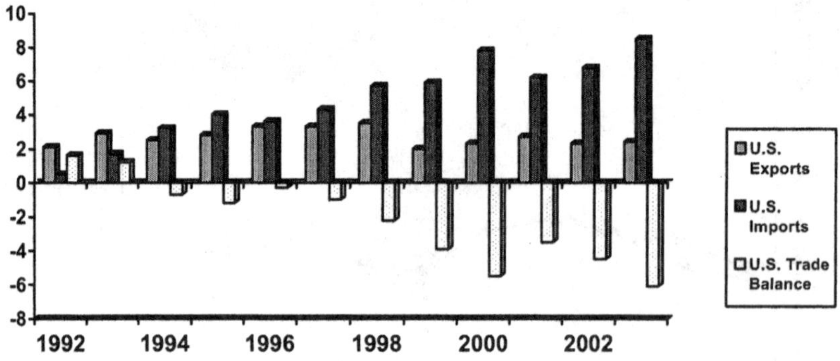

Fig. 3. U.S. -Russian Foreign Trade (in US $ Billions)

Source: Constructed on the data of U.S. Census Bureau, Foreign Trade Division, Washington D.C.

U.S. free trade policy is concentrated on benefits from goods produced more cheaply abroad, encouraging country-specific specialization and raising company competition in the country. Russia accounts for only 0.5 percent of U.S. imports and 0.4 of U.S. exports. In 2000, U.S. trade accounted for 7.6% of Russian exports and 5.4% of Russian imports (International Monetary Fund, 2001).

Russia's treatment under the U.S. trade law of "Normal trade relations" (NTR) status and classification as a "non-market economy (NME)" under U.S. trade remedies laws prevail U.S.-Russian trade development. Under U.S. antidumping laws, "fair prices" for imports from nonmarket economies are calculated differently than prices on imports from other economies. The methodology used to make these calculations leads to higher antidumping margins and places imports from Russia at a competitive disadvantage vis-à-vis other imports or U.S. domestic production (Commerce to Review Russia's Status, 2001).

The imposition of import restrictions on Russian steel into the United States and an existing ban on exports of U.S. poultry meat to Russia affected trade turnover. U.S. exports to Russia include poultry, machinery and equipment, high technology products, and meat and grains. Russian exports to the U.S. consist primarily of raw materials, including precious stones, inorganic chemicals, mineral fuels, aluminum, iron and steel, and fish. Russia ranks 39th place worldwide as a recipient of U.S. exports and 28th place as a supplier of U.S. imports. Russia's trade share accounts for less than 1 per cent of total U.S. trade worldwide. Russia provides high tariffs on some U.S. goods, including passenger cars, sports utility vehicles, and aircraft.

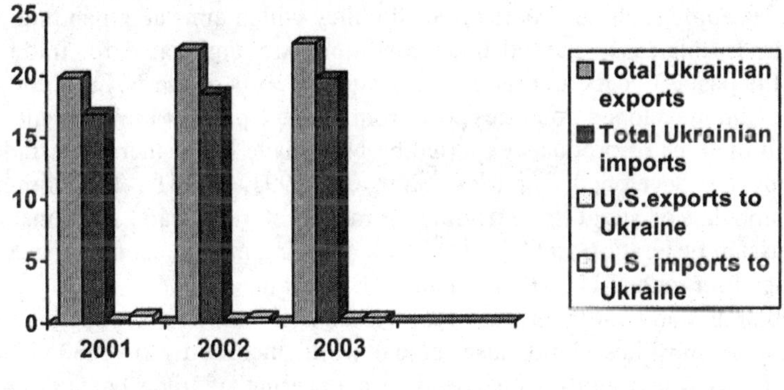

Fig. 4. Cumulative Ukrainian Exports, Imports, U.S. –Ukrainian Exports, U.S.-Ukrainian Imports (in US $ Millions)

Source: Ukraine Country Commercial Guide FY 2004 (2003).

In 2002, exports totaled $22.3 billion and imports $18.5 billion, providing trade surplus in the Ukraine (see Figure 4). In 2002, the exports volume relative to GDP amounted to 56.3 percent. The share of raw materials, semi-manufactures and finished products with an insignificant value-added in the structure of Ukrainian exports amounted to more than 70 percent. Energy products account for 38.6% of Ukrainian imports. Export growth, a reduction in capital flight, and development in oil refining, retail trade, and food processing affect economic performance improvement. Ukraine's current account surplus exceeded 3 percent of GDP in 2003. The privatization of six electricity distribution companies (oblenergos) in 2001 included two purchases by a U.S. investor. The lack of clear regulatory control impedes the privatization process in strategic sectors in the Ukraine. U.S. restrictions on the Ukrainian export of the steel production and compact discs shorten trade turnover between the two countries.

An analysis of Russian and Ukrainian exports confirms the need for export diversification, including export diversification of primary goods and, at a later date, that of industrial goods. Primary commodity processing has traditionally been related to the basic sector from which export diversification started. Free market access relates to the precondition of export diversification and commodity-based development. Institutional environment formation includes the elaboration of new forms, types of institutional behavior, the creation of new institutions, and the influence of diversification. Export diversification contributes to a reduction in the economic vulnerability of commodity-dependent developing countries and increases value-added generated and retained in the country (UNCTAD, 2003).

Russia and Ukraine have a dilemma as to which kind of import substitution or export oriented policy they should give preference. During the 1950s and 1960s, the developed nations used the import substitution policy. This kind of policy was considered to be more beneficial in early developmental stages. The emergence of inefficient industries, high capital intensity and low labor absorption challenge developed countries to turn to an export-oriented policy. The majority of transition countries apply such an export-oriented policy which aims at expanding country's exports. In this case, internal trade conditions are aggravated for trade partners. Over the past 20 years, the ratio of industrial exports of the NICs to the total imports of the developed countries rose from about 1 percent to 6 percent. The timing and the type of products exported by NICs have led to increased trade restrictions by the developed countries (Salvatore, 1993, p. 341). The elimination of trade imbalances suggests extending permanent normal trade relations status for the Russian Federation and Ukraine and that giving market economy status will be beneficial for mutual U.S.-Russian and U.S.-Ukrainian trade.

Research study estimates that removal of tariff barriers, production subsidies, and export subsidies could raise annual world income by over $355 billion by 2015. Successful rounds which lead to a lowering of trade barriers around the world could raise the level of U.S. GDP by $144 billion each year (Economic Report of the President, 2004).

Trade expansion will lead to a change in U.S. trade balance. Trade deficit reduction causes trade surplus growth. A rise in productivity and an in the country's competitiveness affect domestic policy and influence foreign trade balance improvement. Diversification of export in Russia and the Ukraine includes the diversification of both primary goods and industrial goods. It reduces economic vulnerability of commodity developed countries, raises value-added commodities, and stimulates trade. Extending US permanent normal trade relations status to Russia and the Ukraine will be directed at providing price advantages and stimulating reciprocal trade policy. The elimination of trade barriers, including government policy, financial markets, infrastructure, and knowledge constraints stimulates the development of mutual bilateral trade. Macro-level operational goals and changes in performance standards are directed at implementing reciprocal trade policy among countries and stimulating mutual beneficial cooperation. Trade monitoring relates to the important issue of effective trade policy organization. It includes current reporting on foreign trade policy, the removal of existing trade imbalances, and direct policy mechanisms for the achievement of specific goals.

4 U.S.-Russian and U.S.-Ukrainian Foreign Direct Investment Flows

Global FDI inflows made up $651 billion or just half the peak in 2000. Central and Eastern European FDI inflows rose by 15 percent, although flows to 10 countries in the region fell. Both manufacturing and services were hard hit, while FDI flows to the primary sector rose (World Investment Report, 2003, p. 3). The major factor of this decline is considered developments in the business cycle. Between 1989 and 2003, cumulative inflows in FDI into the Central and Eastern Europe amounted to $117 billion (Wolf, 2004, p. 11). An increasing number of financial market participants contribute to rising uncertainty about the macroeconomic outlook and the future course of monetary policy. The feeling of uncertainty was further exacerbated in the first months of 2003 by the unsettled international political and security environment (OECD, 2003).

The U.S. current account deficit – the combined balances on trade in goods and services, income, and net unilateral current transfers – increased to $541.8 billion in 2003 from $480.9 billion in 2002 (see Table 1). An increase in the deficit on goods more than accounted for this rise in addition to an increase in net flows for unilateral current transfers and a decrease in the surplus on services. In contrast, the balance on income shifted to a surplus in 2003. (U.S. International Transactions, 2004, p. 3). The IMF warned that the U.S. budget and current account deficit was a principal risk to strong global growth (World Economic Outlook, 2004). The US current account deficit was caused by the increase in imports of foreign goods. The tendency of the US current account deficit is estimated to grow in the medium term (Williams, 2004).

Current account restoration and the consolidation of international financial position are considered two ways to cut external deficits through an increase in private savings. The policy involving decreases in foreign borrowing will provide current account and capital account restoration and sustainability. Effects on FDI inflow raises productivity of foreign affiliates and provides spillover effects through technology transfer, trade growth, labor and management training, and the improvement of quality of public administration in transition economies.

In order to explain the present situation in capital markets, one can consider the modern theoretical approaches for FDI. Graham, Krugman (1995) argue that FDI is essentially best seen as a means to extend control for reasons of corporate strategy rather than as a channel for shifting resources from one country to another.

Table 1. Current and Financial Account (Percent of GDP)

Accounts	1990	2000	2002	2003: Q1-Q3
Current account balance	-1.4	-4.2	-4.6	-5.1
Trade balance in goods	-1.9	-4.6	-4.6	-5.0
Exports	6.7	7.9	6.5	6.4
Imports	-8.6	-12.5	-11.1	-11.5
Service (net)	0.5	0.8	0.6	0.5
Other (net)	0	-0.4	-0.6	-0.6
Net capital flows	0.9	4.6	5.0	5.0
Financial account balance	1.0	4.6	5.0	5.1
Direct investment (net)	0.2	1.7	-0.9	-0.5
Portfolio (net)	-0.1	3.0	4.2	3.7
Equity securities (net)	-0.4	0.9	0.3	-0.8
Debt securities (net)	0.3	2.2	3.8	4.5
Other	1.0	0	1.8	1.8
Capital account balance	-0.1	0	0	0
Memo:				
Foreign purchases of U.S. Government securities	0.5	-0.5	1.6	2.6

Source: Department of Commerce (Bureau of Economic Analysis).

Bedi, Cieslik (2002) examine the effect of FDI on wages in Poland and find that workers in industries with a higher presence of joint venture foreign investments enjoy higher wages. The magnitude of the foreign presence increases over time, confirming that workers in industries with greater foreign participation have faster wage growth. Forslid, Haaland, Knarvik, Maestad (2002) draw attention more to short-term adjustment problems rather than to long-term possibilities. The analysis of possible long-run outcomes on productivity growth and investment show that the consideration of transition in the former Soviet Union in addition to the transition of Eastern European has a negligible effect on all regions other than the Former Soviet Union itself, which experienced a strong real income effect. The region's insignificant trade in manufacturing goods draws attention to the main reason for this. Corden (1974) analyses the relationship between protection and foreign investment in models of the pure theory of international trade and considers if protection leads to an increase inward foreign capital flows, while lowering outward foreign capital flows. In case of relatively capital-intensive industries, general protection through import tariffs induces foreign capital inflows if import commodities on the whole are capital-intensive. Graham (2000, 83) maintains that outward US FDI leads to wage differentiations in foreign and domestic firms, and creates job opportunities for workers. In general, outward direct investment helps rather hurts US workers.

The definition of foreign direct investment in the United States is determined by ownership or control, directly or indirectly, by one foreign resident of 10 percent or more of the voting securities of an incorporated U.S. business enterprise or the equivalent interest in incorporated U.S. business U.S. business enterprise (Survey of Current Business, 2003, p. 45). U.S. net capital flow grew from about 1 percent of GDP in 1990 to over 4.5 percent of GDP in 2000. As a result, foreign purchases of debt securities, equity securities, and direct investment increased roughly by the same amount (Economic Report of the President, 2004). Inflows into the United States in 2002 stood at US $30 billion, which represented a decline of 77 percent in comparison to 2001. This reduced the U.S. to the status of fourth-largest FDI recipient after having dominated the league table for a decade. FDI outflows from the United States reached US $123.5 billion in 2002, down by only US $4 billion from the previous year (OECD, 2003, 2). As a result, the U.S. earned the status of net exporter of FDI (see Figure 5). In their study, Graham, Wada (2000) made use the gravity model for trade and investment activities between the United States and the rest of the world. The data encompass 58 countries engaged in significant trade or investment with the United States in the years from 1983 to 1996. The results of their empirical research of the relationship between foreign direct investment and trade (exports and imports) confirms that US exports and US direct investment abroad are net complements in each income category. There is no statistically significant relationship (again) between US direct investment abroad and US imports.

FDI outflows declined by 27 percent in 2001 and increased by 15 percent in 2002, while gross domestic private investment fell by 3 percent in each year (World Investment Report, 2003, p. 15). The fall in the share of domestic M&A in developed countries reflected the decline of the value of stocks. This resulted in a slowdown in corporate restructuring and international resource reallocation in profit maximization.

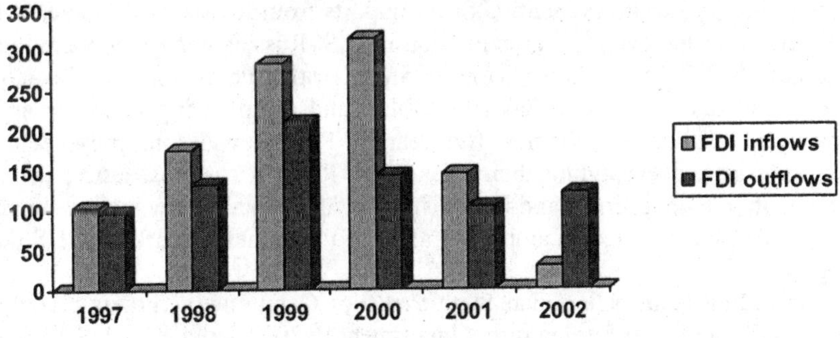

Fig. 5. FDI inflows and outflows in the USA, by home region and economy (Billions US $)

Source: UNCTAD. Constructed on the data of World Investment Report 2003 (2003), pp. 249, 253.

Since the mid-1990s, Russia has tended to attract FDI to the tune of $2 to 3 billion per year, a trend seen once again in 2002 (OECD, 2003, p. 7). The success of attracting such FDI inflow depends on the use of competitive advantages. They include huge natural resources, an abundance of a highly-qualified labor force, unused industrial potential, and large markets in both Russia and the Ukraine. FDI in Russia has both natural resource and market-seeking motives. More than half of the respondents indicated that promising potential for the domestic market was a motive with the proximity to regional markets being a second (World Investment Report, 2003, p. 63). According to the Russian State Statistics Committee, capital investments in Russia were 13.7 percent more in January 2004 than in December 2003 (see Figure 7).

The United States is a leading foreign direct investor in Russia, accounting for nearly 35 percent of all cumulative U.S. FDI within Russia. The cumulative FDI inflow made up $5.49 billion in 2003 (Bisnis, 2003). The branches which are deemed of priority for foreign investment include transportation, fuel, communications, and engineering. Cyprus invested $3.2 billion in Russia. Germany's cumulative FDI in Russia made up $1.3 billion. Regional foreign capital distribution demonstrates investment concentration in the capital, Moscow, and in the biggest Russian cities. Cumulative foreign investment amounted to $13 billion in the capitol itself. Market-seeking investments have been directed to food and telecommunication industries in the capital and Russia's biggest cities. Improvement in the investment environment in pharmaceuticals and the determination of property rights will additionally affect capital inflow. Northwest Russia (Leningrad Oblast and Novgorod Oblast) had attracted about $1.4 billion in U.S. FDI, with Sverdlovsk region accounting for $ 1.3 billion in U.S. foreign investment in 2001 (Russia Country Commercial Guide, 2003). U.S.-Russian foreign investment relations are based on the Bilateral Investment Treaty guaranteeing non-discriminatory treatment for U.S. investments and operations in Russia. The Treaty for avoiding the double taxation of income reduces or eliminates tax liability at its source, thus supporting greater investment. U.S. oil imports from Russia could increase by up 10 percent in the event of an expansion in U.S.-Russian energy cooperation over the next 5 to 7 years. Exxon Mobile, Shell, British Petroleum and Texaco have had organized business in Sakhalin Oblast and are planning to invest approximately $13 billion over the next five years. U.S. firms with long-presence in Russia have started expanding their operations. Russian customs duties, increasing competition among firms, and inconsistent governmental policy are considered the major obstacles for access and penetration of the domestic market by US companies.

According to the Ukrainian State Statistics Committee, Ukraine received US $531 million in total foreign direct investment in 2002 and a mere US $5.6 billion since its independence (see Figure 6). The Ukraine has signed the Bilateral Investment Treaty with more than 50 countries. U.S. FDI has reached almost US $1 billion, making up 17.5 percent of total cumulative direct investment within the Ukraine; this is considered the largest source of FDI in the country. U.S. companies have remained at the top of the list of foreign direct investors in the Ukraine. Russian total cumulative FDI to Ukraine is equivalent to US $334 million, making up 6 percent of the cumulative volume of FDI inflow within the Ukraine since 1992.

Oil refining, trade, food, processing, and agriculture received the bulk of all foreign investment. The most attractive spheres for foreign investment are informational technologies and telecommunications, food processing and packing, pharmaceuticals, medical equipment, building materials, automotive parts, and agricultural machinery (see Figure 7). U.S. companies such as Coca-Cola, Kraft-Jacobs-Suchard, Mars, PepsiCo, Procter & Gamble, McDonalds and the like develop the distribution networks in the Ukraine.

Outward FDI from Russia was lower than its inward FDI in 2002 (see Figure 6). High outward FDI from Russia demonstrates that government policy does not offer sufficient financial incentives for capital to stay inside the country and thus leads investors to move to more profitable sectors in other countries. Outflows exceeded registered inflows at a relatively low GDP per capita. Russia's 7 percent share in projects worldwide in 2003 made it the third most important global location after China and the United States (World Investment Report, 2003). Russia attracted more technology-based, efficiency–type projects in its automobile industry. Liberalization of FDI laws, the stability of the economy, and the provision of targeted incentives make up the main factors for the improvement of the business environment. As a result, natural resource-seeking FDI could lead to an increase in inflows of potential foreign capital in Russia. The geography for attracting natural resource-seeking projects in Russia depicts that the Far Eastern Sakhalin region is the second largest recipient of FDI (14 percent) behind the greater Moscow area (44 percent) (UNCTAD, 2003). Production sharing agreements offer access to natural resources regions for foreign investors in its framework and are confirmed by laws dealing specifically with ownership and oil extraction. The industry composition of inward FDI stock demonstrates the predominance of investments in transport, telecommunications, fuel, and petrochemicals. The most debated question by foreign investors relates to the openness of Russia's natural resources for foreign investment.

In accordance with the cost-capital approach, it has been suggested that the growth of FDI in the United States is tied to the same factors that have led to a growth in US indebtedness (Graham, Krugman, 1995, p. 35). FDI has a long-term tendency for growth within the United States (see Figure 5, 8).

Some scientists point to potential US economic losses to its innovative positions in the product life cycle and advantages in the production of high technology products. Price increase of foreign stock and dollar appreciation make US assets cheaper in comparison to foreign assets. Moran (2002) argues that instead of encouraging backward linkages and creating vibrant and competitive industries, domestic-content and joint-venture requirements yield inefficient, high-cost operations that utilize technologies well behind the cutting edge of international markets in developing countries. Plants subject to such requirements seldom acquire economies of scale and dynamic learning that are required to propel them from the position of infant industries to full competitive status.

In contrast to the above-mentioned approach, the Economist Intelligence Unit report points out that the 0.4 percent increase in the difference between average annual growth of GDP per capita in European countries and the U.S. was caused by lower use of information and communications technology by European countries (Crooks, 2004, p. 4). Preferential or association agreements for trade between non-accession countries and EU may affect market size, one of the key determinants of FDI (World Investment Report, 2003, p. 66).

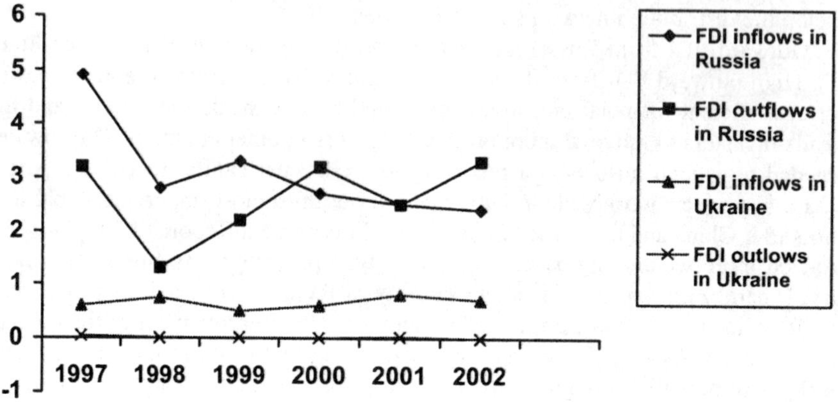

Fig. 6. FDI inflows and FDI outflows in Russian Federation, Ukraine, by home region and economy (in Billions US $)

Source: UNCTAD. Constructed on the data of World Investment Report 2003 (2003), pp. 252, 256.

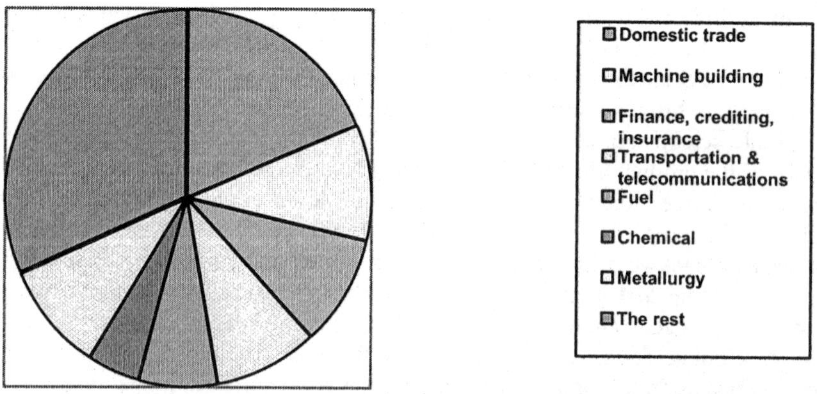

Fig. 7. Foreign Direct Investment by Industry Sector Destination in Ukraine (Percentage)

Source: Ukrainian Country Commercial Guide FY 2004 (2003).

By 2002, the concentration of FDI within the Triad (EU, Japan and the U.S.) represented approximately 80 percent for the world's outward stock and 50 to 60 percent for the world's inward stock (see Figure 8). The United States became the largest net exporter of foreign capital in the world.

The share of machinery and equipment is insignificant in the total inward foreign investment structure in Russia (see Figure 9). The share of transport and telecommunications makes up 25%; fuel and petrochemicals 19%; food, beverages and tobacco 15%, machinery and equipment 4%; other services 20%; and miscellaneous industries 17 % of inward stock in Russia in 2002. (UNCTAD, 2003, p. 64).

Institutional factors relate to the basic problem with the market seeking strategies of foreign investors. Poor institutional development, high levels of corruption, and uncertainty could be accompanied with the accumulation of high levels of debt through purchases of unproductive assets. One approach to limiting these risks is to restrict foreign capital flows. Another approach suggests which minimizes the risks associated with opening-up to capital movements involves careful timing, or sequencing, of policies designed to "liberalize" financial markets (Economic Report of the President, 2004).

The further development of financial institutions, the adoption of international economic relations, and the establishment of new international organizations require a certain period of time in Russia and Ukraine. The privatization of 3000 state-owned enterprises with assets estimated at US $2.2 billion in Russia could enhance FDI inflow into the country (World Investment Report, 2003, p. 28). Foreign investor participation in privatization is limited to 30 percent in TV and radio broadcasting and publishing companies in the Ukraine. The liberalization of FDI law includes openness, transparency, transfertibility, and property rights protection. U.S. restrictions on interstate banking hamper interregional regulation with the European Union and an important policy issue affecting foreign-control operations.

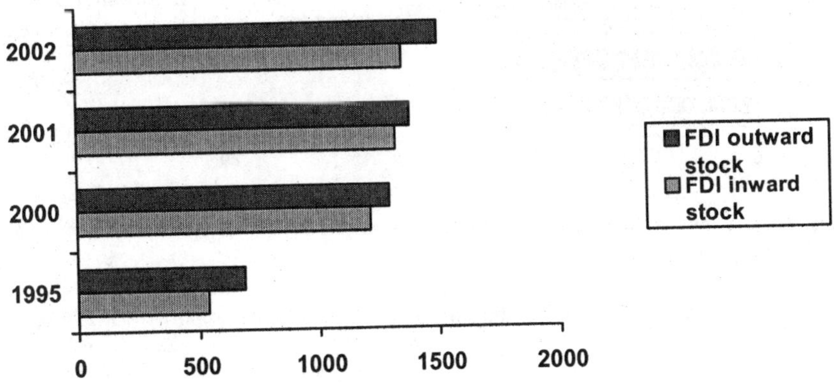

Fig. 8. U.S. FDI inward stock and FDI outward stock, by home region and economy (in Billions US $)

Source: UNCTAD. Constructed on the data of World Investment Report 2003 (2003), pp. 257, 262.

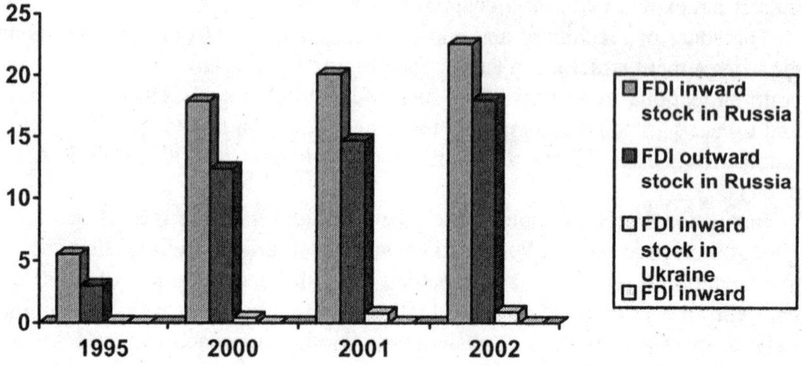

Fig. 9. Russian, Ukrainian FDI inward stock and FDI outward stock, by home region and economy (in Billions US $)

Source: UNCTAD. Constructed on the data of World Investment Report 2003 (2003), pp. 260, 265.

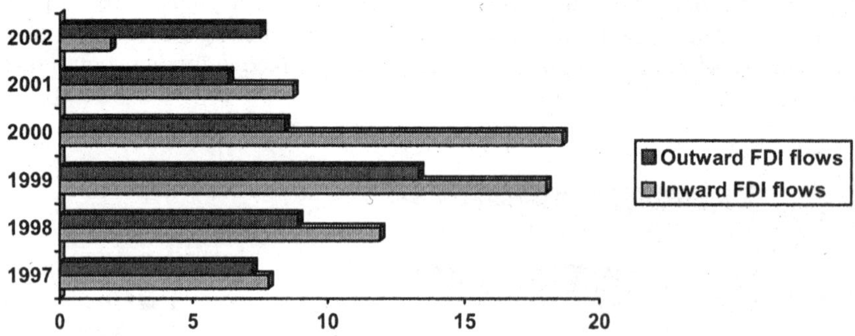

Fig. 10. U.S. inward and outward FDI flows as a percentage of gross capital formation, by region and economy (Percentage)

Source: UNCTAD. Constructed on the data of World Investment Report 2003 (2003), p. 268.

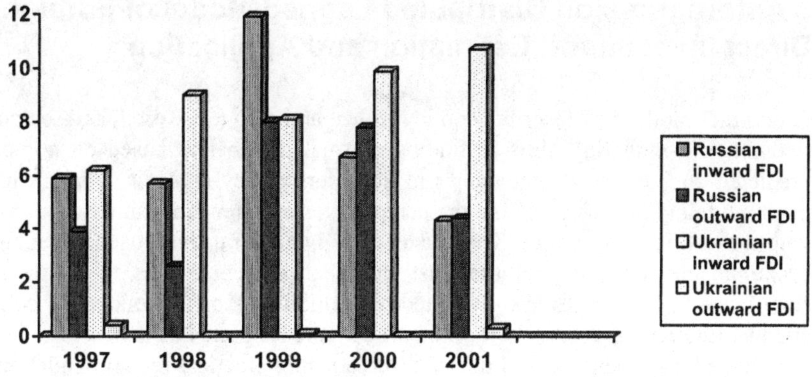

Fig. 11. Russian and Ukrainian inward and outward FDI flows as a percentage of gross capital formation, by region and economy (Percentage)

Source: UNCTAD. Constructed on the data of World Investment Report 2003 (2003), p. 277.

Table 2. Inward and outward FDI stocks as a percentage of Gross Domestic Product, by region and economy (Percentage)

Region/economy	1995	2000	2001	2001
United States				
inward	7.3	12.4	13.1	12.9
outward	9.5	13.2	13.7	14.4
Russian Federation				
inward	1.6	6.9	6.5	6.5
outward	0.9	4.8	4.8	5.2
Ukraine				
inward	2.5	12.4	12.3	12.9
outward	0.3	0,5	0.4	0.4

Source: UNCTAD. Constructed on the data of World Investment Report 2003 (2003), pp. 279, 288.

FDI growth provides for the effective allocation of resources as well as technological and managerial spillovers effects to the transition countries. Low levels of FDI inflows and FDI outflows in addition to FDI outward stocks and FDI inward stocks in Russia and the Ukraine demonstrate the necessity of further developing an attractive investment environment within these countries. The liberalization of FDI policies and regulations in Russia and the Ukraine will help to decrease barriers to free capital movement, thereby stimulating lower production costs in the countries. Favorable foreign investment policy will increase competition, improve management and firm profitability, stimulate the creation of jobs, and increase foreign capital inflows into the countries.

5 Autoregression Distributed Lagged Model of Foreign Direct Investment: Estimation and Application

Economic modeling describes policy rules and suggests predicted outcomes. Econometric modeling aims at finding optimal parameters based on comparing predicted and observed outcomes and considers policy analysis. Foreign investment modeling is used to define the perspectives and trends in future development within transition economies. The existence of huge parameters used for analyzing economic characteristics in the East European system makes modeling rather complicated. Researches are interested in including as many economic, political, and institutional parameters within their econometric model as is possible. Estimation of such parameters could be used for choosing practical recommendations for macroeconomic and political priorities as well as the elaboration of theoretical foundations in the field of foreign trade policy in transition countries.

The large number of theoretical and empirical works in foreign direct investment modeling demonstrates the broad interest of economists in explaining the complexity of transition periods in East European countries. The majority of research works reflects a variety econometric approaches for FDI.

Scientists consider investment, with its emphasis on uncertainty and non-convexity, a ripe area for the application of dynamic programming techniques. Adda, Cooper (2003) analyze a general dynamic optimization problem and focus on special cases of convex and non-convex adjustment costs. Using the techniques of the estimation of dynamic programming models, they present evidence on the nature of adjustment costs. Barro, Sala-I-Martin (2004) pay attention to some aspects of foreign investment and intellectual property rights in the process of technological diffusion. The honoring of intellectual property rights across international borders helps to provide the proper incentive for discoveries of new goods and techniques in the leading economies. The institutionalization of these rights tends to raise long-term growth rates in leading and following economies. Carstensen, Toubal (2004, 17) suggest that EU enlargement will have considerable effects on FDI flows to CEECs, because the market potential of the entrants will lead to an increase in their GDPs and a simultaneous reduction in the economically-relevant distance to the EU (i.e., transportation costs). Decreasing trade costs should also be reflected in CEEC tariffs, reducing thereby the unit labor cost.

Nevertheless, a large number of publications on the following topic argue that a whole number of unexplained problems and unsolved questions exist. The majority of publications include the estimation and determination of significant variables in econometric modeling. The optimal econometric model is based on high reliability and stability of obtained results. It provides effective methods of system functioning for the defined period of time.

Autoregression econometric models study the influence of independent variables in past periods on dependent variables at present. The autoregression distributed lagged model (ARDL) of foreign direct investment in the Ukraine uses a series of factor variables (lagged), changed to one or more time series. The data used in this analysis are from the quarterly Ukrainian balance of payments published by the National Bank of Ukraine, Information Bulletin of Ukrainian State Statistic Committee, quarterly TACIS (UEPLAC) reports, the World Investment Report (UNCTAD), and Euromoney from 1992 to 2001. The tested hypothesis includes multiple correlation estimation for FDI inflow and a variety of macroeconomic variables in the estimated period of time for the Ukraine.

The general equation of multiple regression model is:

$$FDI_i = f(GDP, ER, TRBAL, CR, MU, IO, BD, RIR) \tag{1}$$

Where there is endogenous variable:
FDI_i – foreign direct investment inflow in the Ukraine in the i period of time (in US $).
The exogenous variables are:
GDP – real Gross Domestic Product (in US $);
ER – real exchange rate (UAH/US$);
TRBAL – trade balance (in US $);
CR – country risk integral index, estimated by "Euromoney". Country risk integral index includes political risk, economic perspectives, foreign debt index, default and restructuring debt, credit rating, access to bank resources, access to short financial resources, access to capital markets, and access to forfeiting services. The maximum score is 100;
MU – money supply (in US $);
IO – industrial output (in US $);
BD – budget deficit (in US $);
RIR – real interest rate on credits (in per cent).

Econometric ARDL modeling of FDI inflow for macroeconomic variables reveals FDI inflow of the dependent variable at present correlated from its value in the past. The coefficient is significant at 5 % level according to the t-value statictic. The estimated results are shown in the equation 2:

$$\begin{aligned} FDI_i = & -\underset{(89,3)}{239{,}6} - \underset{(0,16)}{0{,}37}\,FDI(-1) - \underset{(0,17)}{0{,}11}\,FDI(-2) + \underset{(0,15)}{0{,}01}\,FDI(-3) \\ & - \underset{(0,14)}{0{,}09}\,FDI(-4) - \underset{(0,17)}{0{,}85}\,FDI(-5) + \underset{(0,01)}{0{,}03}\,GDP(-1) - \underset{(0,01)}{0{,}01}\,GDP(-2) \\ & + \underset{(0,01)}{0{,}04}\,GDP(-3) - \underset{(0,01)}{0{,}02}\,GDP(-4) + \underset{(0,01)}{0{,}04}\,GDP(-5) + \underset{15,8}{62{,}9}\,ER \\ & - \underset{0,01}{0{,}02}\,TRBAL - \underset{5,9}{17{,}6}\,CR + \underset{0,23}{0{,}06}\,MU \end{aligned} \tag{2}$$

$$R^2 = 0{,}77; DW = 2{,}61$$

Further ARDL modeling of FDI was conducted to exclude insignificant variables from equation 2. The estimated results can be seen in equation 3. The estimated regression coefficients characterize a climate of investment in the Ukraine. The short-term multiplicator is equal to 0.67. This means that an increase in FDI inflow within the Ukraine by USD $1 million is not accompanied by investment capitalization at present. The negative value in front of the coefficient signifies the short-term characteristic of foreign investment. High uncertainty and investment risk are the factors of low foreign capital inflow into the country. FDI inflow first increased by \$0.26 million after an increase in GDP of USD \$1 million in the previous quarter.

$$FDI_i = -\underset{(69,6)}{31,4} - \underset{(0,19)}{0,67}\,FDI(-5) + \underset{(0,01)}{0,26}\,GDP(-1) + \underset{(0,01)}{0,02}\,GDP(-3) \quad (3)$$

$$+ \underset{(0,01)}{0,02}\,GDP(-5) - \underset{(17,0)}{51,8}\,ER - \underset{(6,47)}{16,9}\,CR,$$

$$R^2 = 0,52; DW = 2,6$$

An increase of FDI inflow by 83% brings with it a corresponding growth in GDP, and is caused by changes in the previous period of time. An increase FDI inflow of 8% stimulates changes in the third quarter and an increase of 7% was seen in the fourth quarter. The average lag of the model is one-half of a quarter. The short lag period confirms that investors make investment decisions based on lagged volume FDI and estimation in changes to the GDP over the short run. Total FDI inflow in the Ukraine depends on lagged FDI inflow during the 5th quarter and lagged GDP in the 1st, 3rd and 5th quarters. The real exchange rate and country risk index correspond to significant variables and the influence of FDI inflows into the Ukraine. Absolute change in FDI inflow correlates with time series (lagged) GDP in the Ukraine in case of a finite period of lag. The lag change per one relative GDP unit causes a cumulative FDI change.

The results from the econometric ARDL FDI estimation confirm that GDP per capita is the main FDI attracting factor for the country. GDP estimation is comprised of economic, technological, institutional, and cultural development levels in the country. FDI inflow per capita in 2000 was equivalent to US \$500 in the Czech Republic, US \$320 in Croatia, and US \$200 in Hungary (Hunya, 2000). In accordance with the data of Economic Intelligence Unit, FDI inflow per capita in the same period was equal to US \$160 in Russia and US \$117 in the Ukraine. Annual FDI inflow in Ukraine's neighbor, Poland, was nearly 10 times higher at that time. The increase in GDP per capita is related to the important factor of foreign capital attractiveness. Domestic production improvement and GDP value per capita are considered the basic factors influencing foreign investor's decision making process for market-seeking investment.

ARDL modeling of FDI confirms the investment development path theory of J. Dunning and R. Narula (Dunning, Narula, 1996). In accordance with this theory, a country's investment development includes five stages from FDI net-importers to FDI net-exporters. Small FDI inflows within a country and an insignificant amount of legal outflow confirm that the Ukraine is on the first stage of the investment development path; the country has the position of FDI net importer.

Instable financial policy, high financial risk, and frequent exchange rate fluctuations affect financial market performance and aggravate the investment climate in the country. Financial and political stability are both reasons for foreign capital attractiveness.

Recent studies of Russia's and Ukraine's economies demonstrate the predominance of strategic goals related to foreign investor behavior. They are interested in free access to the significant market share (especially in the strategic sector). The number of indirect duties and commercial risks influence the pricing policy in the Ukraine. Foreign investors wish to have guarantees as to the security of their investments over the long-run.

Stable development of the financial sector, budget deficit restriction, foreign debt cutting, and industrial development are related to the urgent tasks of industrial policy in transition. The period of reform is limited in transition due to the urgency of solutions to problems in development. The allocation of effective branches stimulates structural reform. Competition between domestic and foreign firms affect fixed capital renovation, the creation of optimal industrial structure, and the need for capital inflow into the country.

6 Foreign Trade Policy Conclusions

Trade and capital liberalization provide huge benefits to the countries, while also stimulating the creation of new opportunities, including access to new markets and stimulated economic growth. East European integration into the international division of labor and the world economy depends on micro, macro, and institutional factors. EU enlargement poses challenges with respect to economic policy decisions in non-accession countries. Extending permanent normal trade relations status between the United States and Russia and the Ukraine would provide specific price advantages and stimulate reciprocal trade policy.

The analysis of U.S.-Russian and U.S.-Ukrainian foreign trade and FDI confirms the necessity for introducing new changes aimed at the liberalization of bilateral investment treaties (BIT) and double taxation treaties (DTT). The elimination of trade barriers would be directed to the improvement of U.S.-Russian and U.S.-Ukrainian trade balance. Concluding results of trade policy and FDI analysis could be summarized in the following suggestions:

- to continue export structure diversification in Russia and the Ukraine;
- to adjust foreign trade policy to the demands of the world market;
- to eliminate trade imbalances and elaborate on policy measures directed at defining achievements in policy goals;
- to adopt foreign trade policy measures directed at guaranteeing transparency and predictability of the foreign direct investment system in Russia and the Ukraine;
- to establish a monitoring system and transparency for foreign trade and FDI relations;
- to provide further liberalization of national banking laws;
- to use institutional mechanisms for providing negotiations with trade partners on the abrogation of export limitations on a mutually-beneficial basis;
- to stimulate the effectiveness of U.S., Russian and Ukrainian bilateral and multilateral cooperation within international organizations for improvement in international trade policy;
- to increase GDP value per capita for FDI inflows in Russia and the Ukraine.

– to increase GDP value per capita for FDI inflows in Russia and the Ukraine.

Appendix

Table 3. A Russia's Macroeconomic Indicators

	GDP, %	Industrial production, %	Fixed investments	Unemployment, %	Exports, $ billion	Imports, $ billion	Current account, $ billion
1996	-3,6	-4,5	-18,0	9,3	89,7	68,1	10,8
1997	1,4	2,0	-5,0	9,0	86,9	72,0	-0,1
1998	-5,3	-5,2	-12,0	11,8	74,4	58,0	0,2
1999	6,4	11,0	5,3	11,7	75,6	39,5	24,6
2000	10,0	11,9	17,4	10,2	105,0	44,9	46,8
2001	5,1	4,9	10,0	9,0	101,9	53,8	35,0
2002	4,7	3,7	2,6	7,1	107,2	61,0	32,8
2003	7,3	3,7	12,5	8,9	134,4	74,8	39,1
2004		8,1	13,4	8,1	35,8	18,8	11,0

Source: GOSKOMSTAT, CBR.

Table 4. Leading U.S. Exports to Russia in 2000

Product	2000 (Mln)	As compared to 1999 (1990=100%)
Poultry	335	190
Aircraft	197	150
Oil/gas	173	110
Uranium	132	-
Corn and Wheat	109	50
Computers and Components	91	130
Beef and Pork	167	200
Telecom Equipment	62,3	120
Electrical Machinery	76,5	150
Other Machinery	283	Small decline

Source: U.S. – Russian Trade Summary (2000).

Table 5. Leading U.S. Imports from Russia in 2000

Product	2000 (Bln)	As compared to 1999 (1999=100%)
Platinum	2,25	132
Aluminum	1,3	11
Uranium	0,94	160
Oil	0,82	158
Crab	0,15	107
Fish Filets	0,08	64
Iron/Steel	0,48	-
Clothing	0,26	200
Nickel	0,15	-
Copper	0,11	-
Paintings	0,09	90

Source: U.S. – Russian Trade Summary (2000).

Table 6. Key Greenfield FDI Projects started in Russian Federation, January-April 2003

Investor	Home country	Value ($Mln)	Main motivation
Royal Dutch Shell	Netherlands/United Kingdom	5500	Natural resources
TotalFinalElf	France	2500	Natural resources
Pfleiderer	Germany	647	Efficiency/exports
Segura Consulting Assoc., Ferrovial and Caixa Bank	Spain	319	Market seeking
Renault	France	250	Market seeking/efficiency
Phillip Morris	United States	240	Market seeking
Baltic Beverages seeking	Denmark	50	Exports/market
Krka	Slovenia	20	Strategic assets
Tex Development	United Kingdom	12	Efficient/exports
Outocoumpu	Finland	4,5	Efficient/exports
Bank Austria	Austria	. .	Strategic assets
Nuclea Solutions	United States	. .	Strategic assets

Source: LOCOmonitor, OCO Consulting.

Table 7. Catching up – Inward FDI stock as a percentage of GDP in CEE

Country/region	1995	2001
Estonia	14,4	65,9
Czech Republic	14,1	64,3
Moldova	6,5	45,0
Slovakia	4.4	43,2
Hungary	26,7	38,2
Latvia	12,5	32,4
Lithuania	5,8	28,9
Croatia	2,5	28,4
Bulgaria	3,4	25,0
Poland	6,2	24,0
TFYR Macedonia	0,8	23,9
Slovenia	9,4	23,1
Albania	8,3	21,0
Romania	2,3	20,5
Serbia and Montenegro	2,7	20,1
Bosnia and Herzegovina	1,1	15,8
Ukraine	2,5	12,9
Belarus	0,5	8,7
Russian Federation	1,6	6,5
Memorandum:		
Central and Eastern Europe	5,3	20,9
World	10,3	22,5

Source: UNCTAD, FDI/TNC database.

References

Adda, J., Cooper, R. (2003), Dynamic Economics, Quantitative Methods and Applications, The MIT Press, Cambridge.

Barro, R., Sala-i-Martin, X. (2004), Economic Growth, The MIT Press, Cambridge.

Bedi, A.S., Cieslik, A. (2002), Wages and Wage Growth in Poland. The role of Foreign Direct Investment, Economics of Transition, Vol. 10(1), P.1-27.

Bennhold, K.(2004), Paris Looks Inward on Jobs Industry, The New York Times, May 5, p. W 1,7.

Brinkman, R.L. (2004), Free Trade: Static Comparative Advantage, in: Lovett, W.A., Eckes, A.E., Brinkman, R.L., U.S. Trade Policy. History, Theory and the WTO, M.E. Sharpe, Inc., p. 106 – 118.

Bergsten C., F. (2004), Foreign Economic Policy for the Next President, Essay in Foreign Affairs, March/April 2004, Institute for International Economics, http://www.iie.com/publications/papers/bergsten0304.htm

BISNIS. (2000), U.S. – Russia Trade Highlights http://www.bisnis.doc.gov/bisnis/country/USRStrade_2000.htm

BISNIS. (2001), Commercial Overview – Russia http://www.bisnis.doc.gov/bisnis/country/rus_overview_3.htm

Carstensen, K., Toubal, F. (2004), Foreign Direct Investment in Central and Eastern European Countries: a Dynamic Panel Analysis, Journal of Comparative Economics, Vol. 32, NO 1, p. 3-22.

Caves, R.E., Franke,l J.A., Jones R.W. (1996), World Trade and Payments. An Introduction, Harper Collins College Publishers, 7th Edition.

Clarke, G.R., Wallsten, S.J. (2004), Has Internet Increased Trade? Evidence from Industrial and Developing Countries? World Bank Policy Research Working Paper 3215, February.

Commerce To Review Russia's Status as a Non-Market Economy (2001), Inside U.S. Trade. October 5.

Corden W.M. Trade Policy and Economic Welfare (1974): Clarendon Press, Oxford.

Crooks, E. (2004), Europe 'to lag behind US', Financial Times, April 26, p.4.

Czinkota, M.R., Ronkainan, I.A., Moffet M.H., Moynihan O. (2001), Global Business, South-Western, Thomson Learning, 3rd Edition.

Dunning, J. H., Narula, R. (1996), Developing Countries Versus Multinationals in a Globalizing World: the dangers of falling behind, Maastricht, Merit, Maastricht Economic Research Institute on Innovation and Technology.

Economic Report of the President (2004), Transmitted to the Congress February 2004 together with the Annual Report of the Council of Economic Advisers, United States Government, Printing Office, Washington, 2004.

Foreign Direct Investment in the United States. (2003), Detail for Historical-Cost Position and Related Capital and Income Flows, Survey of Current Business, September.

Gordon, B. (2003), A High –Risk Trade Policy, Foreign Affairs, July/August, p.111.

Graham, E. M., Krugman P.R. (1995), Foreign Direct Investment in The United States, Institute for International Economics, Washington D.C., January, Third Edition.

Graham, E. M. (2000), Fighting Wrong Enemy. Antiglobal Activists and Multinational Enterprises, Institute for International Economics, Washington D.C.

Hunya, G. (2000), Recent FDI Trends, Policies and Challenges in South-East European Countries, The Vienna Institute for International Economic Studies (WIIW), NO 273, December.

Husted, S., Melvin M. (2000), International Economics, Addison Wesley, Fifth Edition.

International Monetary Fund (2001), Direction of Trade Statistics, Yearbook.

Kindleberger, C.P. (1968), International Economics, Richard D. IRWIN, INC, Homewood, Illinois, 4th Edition.

Lovett, W., A. (1999): Rebalancing U.S. Trade, in: Lovett, W.A., Eckes, A.E., Brinkman, R.L., U.S. Trade Policy. History, Theory and the WTO, M.E. Sharpe, Inc., p. 136 – 182.

Meier, M. G. (1998), The International Environment of Business. Competition and Governance in the Global Economy, Oxford University Press, New York.

Moran, T.H. (2002): Beyond Sweatshops, Brookings Institution Press, Washington D.C., 196 p.

Morrison, K. (2004), Senate Oil Move Renews Fears over Price Rise, Financial Times, March 15, p. 17.

OECD (2003), Trends and Recent Development in Foreign Direct Investment, June.

Ohlin, B. (1967), Interregional and International Trade, Harvard University Press, Cambridge, Massachusetts, Revised Edition.

Protectionism gets clever (1988), The Economist, November, p.75.

Salvatore, D. (1993), International Economics, MACMILLAN, New York, Fourth Edition.

Survey of Current Business (2004), U.S. Department of Commerce, Washington D.C., Vol. 84, No 2.

Ukraine Country Commercial Guide FY 2004 (2003), http://www.bisnis.doc.gov/bisnis/bisdoc/

Venabled, A.J. (2003), Trade, Geography, and Monopolistic Competition: Theory and Application to Spatial Inequalities in Developing Countries, in: Arnott, R., Greenuald, B., Kaubur, R. and Nalebuff, B., eds., Economics for Imperfect World., The MIT PRESS, Cambridge, p. 501-518.

UNCTAD, World Investment Report (2003), FDI Policies for Development: National and International Perspectives, United Nations, New York and Geneva.

UNCTAD, Improving the Competitiveness of SMEs through Enhancing Productive Capacity (2003), Report by the UNCTAD secretariat, Geneva, 24-28 February.

U.S. International Transactions: Fourth Quarter and Year 2003 (2004), News Release, BEA News, http://www.bea.gov/bea/newsrel/transnewsrelease.htm

U.S. – Russian Trade Summary (2000), http://www.bisnis.doc.gov/bisnis/country

Wada, E., Graham, E. (2000), Is Foreign Direct Investment a Complement to Trade, in: Graham E., M., Fighting Wrong Enemy. Antiglobal Activists and Multinational Enterprises, Institute for International Economics, Washington D.C., p.207 -212.

Williams, F. (2004), Trade in Goods Forecast to Grow 7.5%, Financial Times, April 6, p. 7.

Wilson, J.S., Mann C.L., Otsuki T. (2004), Assessing the Potential Benefit of Trade Facilitation: A Global Perspective, World Bank Policy Research Working Paper 3224, http://econ.worldbank.org.htm

Wolf, M. (2004), Coming Together: a Small Step for Europe's Economy but a Giant Leap for the Continent, Financial Times, April 26, p. 11.

Inflation in the New Russia

Irina Eliseeva

1 Introduction

The liberalization of prices in January 1992 under conditions of state control of the economy (during this period of time), led to uncontrolled inflation across a broad spectrum of industries. In December of 1992 the composite price index increased by roughly 2609%, while wholesale prices increased 34 times over.

Based on initial impressions, the reason behind the price liberalization was the government's inability to support its level using the budget.

This is confirmed by the budget deficit (-12%) and by a rapid decrease of the state's external debt payments (17% of planned payments). Nevertheless, the most pertinent reason behind the liberalization move was not the budget deficit, but rather future transition from state holding to privatization of capital and imminent voucher privatization. According to Keynes, "there is no more cunning, more certain way (means) to overturn principles, than disbalance of the monetary system. This process directs all the hidden forces of the economic system aside of distraction of this system, so, nobody of us can find out the root of the evil".

Because the balance values of fixed assets stayed at the same level in 1992, entrepreneurs could pay lower prices for the shares of firms than the true price. Inflation depreciated the price of privatization cheques, when purchased from individuals. There was also a deprecation of the credits that were borrowed from banks preceding 1992, and a decrease of demand for fuel resources allowed to increase its export. Therefore, the economic agencies were interested in such rapid changes in the prices.

The history of inflation in new Russia was very dramatic as is clearly seen in the following data:

Table 1. Official price indices in Russia,%

Year	CPI	Food	Non-Food	Services
1991	260.4	236.1	310.7	178.8
1992	2608.8	2626.2	2673.4	2220.5
1993	933.9	904.9	741.8	2411.2
1994	315.1	314.1	269	622.4
1995	231.3	223.4	216.3	332.2
1996	121.8	117.7	117.8	148.4
1997	111	109.1	108.1	122.5
1998	184.4	196.0	199.5	118.3
1999	136.5	135.9	139.2	134
2000	120.2	117.9	118.5	133.7
2001	118.6	117.1	112.7	136.9
2003 (11 month)	110.8	108.6	108.6	121.2

The independence of the fuel-energy complex on the domestic market led to it taking the first place in price expansion and to close power-consuming industry's prices food industry moving in 2000 according total 1991 – 2001 price increasing from the 8th to 2nd place in explaining with steady demand on its merchandise and wide import raw material use. In total the change of the industry structure of price expansion during these years performs their dependence of taking part in global economy association and lowering demand on mechanical engineering products.

Since 1997 the total consumer price increase background balance values of fixed assets has begun to fall, that points (reflects) a break off thus simple reproduction and may be used in bankruptcy as a form of property redivision.

If production industry price liberalization led to payment crisis/ emission increasing in 1992 was only 1635%/ to working asset's savings loss and company's, consequently it turned to the break of the fixed assets reproduction, to debts, barter and rapid production decrease. However in the social sphere price liberalization led to the loss of personal savings and decrease of the living standards of the population. The cost of the consumer basket in SPb, for example, calculated to cover 58 items, has grown 40 times over.

Beginning in 1995, price rates gained constant size and expand roughly 30% annually. In 1998 under the influence of declining world prices for energy resources, the fall of the financial pyramid GKO began and the price leaf was about 184.4%. However in 1999 rates were stabilized. The stability of inflation rates is determined by the financial policy of the authorities, the constancy of international raw materials market and energetic raw materials stocks in the territory of Russian federation.

Thus the problem of inflation is still very current for Russia. Inflation is deemed to be responsible for bringing uncertainty, destabilising the economy, preventing economic growth (though the link is debatable for industrialised countries, it seems to be true for the transition economies) and acting as a self-fuelling phenomena, making it difficult to stop.

The aims of this paper are:

- the evaluation of methods for measuring the inflation effect;
- the clarification of inflation tendencies in Russia.

2 What is Core Inflation and Why Worry About it

All these negative factors associated with inflation has made fighting it one of the priorities of economic policy conduct. Most of the Central Banks during the last 10-20 years have adopted inflation or price level targeting. However, methods of measuring inflation are far from perfect, and this makes it difficult to use conventional measures of inflation as indicators for monetary policy actions. In particular, it is commonly stressed, that the most wide-spread inflation measure – Consumption Price Index (CPI) – is comprised of very different product categories, some of which are subject to seasonal high volatility (food prices), others are subject to administrative regulations (electricity, transport and housing services, etc.). The first group of products has highly volatile prices due to substantial changes of supply over relatively short periods, the second group of products is characterised by unpredictable timing of price changes, it is also dependent on the supply-side of the economy. Pricing of these two groups illustrates the problem Central Banks run into when trying to control inflation. Should monetary policy change in response to seasonal increase of prices of vegetables and fruits in winter? As the mainstream economics view is that "monetary policy works primarily through its influence over demand pressures in the economy", the answer is clearly "no". This poses the question for the Central Banks: how to distinguish between the essentially temporary influence of supply-side inflation shocks and long-run drift of prices caused by demand phenomena. These considerations led to the introduction of the concept of core inflation (or underlying or trend inflation). If the trend inflation is growing, the core inflation index will be more than CPI and vice versa.

In the literature there exist two different approaches to defining core inflation: one introduced by Eckstein, and the other defined by Quah and Vahey. Eckstein determined core inflation as systematic increases in the costs of factors of industrial production or "the sate of price increases that would occur along the economy's long-term growth path". Quah and Vahey defined core inflation "as that component of measured inflation that has no medium- to long-run impact on real output" (Quah, Vahey, 1995). The two definitions are not identical, as is mentioned in (Makarova et al, 2002). The first definition presupposes that only unexpected price increases result in changes of real output. However in principle it is possible that price changes are expected and anticipated, but do lead to changes in real output. In this sense the definition of Quah and Vahey is a stronger one, as it excludes all price changes leading to changes in output in the middle- and the long-run. Therefore in Makarova et al. (2002) it was suggested to term core inflation corresponding to Eckstein's definition as weak core inflation (further denoted as $\pi_t^{(1)}$), and the core inflation corresponding to the definition of Quah and Vahey as strong core inflation (further denoted as $\pi_t^{(2)}$).

Decomposition of measured inflation accounting for the above reasoning is the following:

$$\pi_t = \pi_t^{(2)} + (\pi_t^{(1)} - \pi_t^{(2)} + \upsilon_t) \tag{1}$$

In (1) υ_t accounts for the unpredictable .part of inflation in time t, and $\varpi_t = \pi_t^{(1)} - \pi_t^{(2)} + \upsilon_t$ accounts for that part of inflation at time t, which has impact on real output in the long-run.

Knowing only weak core inflation $\pi_t^{(1)}$ (or, more precisely, the difference between actual and weak core inflation), one is able to estimate inflation impact on real output when it is unknown which part of expected inflation is output-neutral. At the same time weak core inflation is easier to forecast and is a better instrument for forecasting of future inflation. On the other hand, it is better to know the estimate for $\pi_t^{(2)}$since it allows to estimate ϖ_t as a good indicator of consequences of the proposed economic policy.

3 Evaluation of Monetary Policy Effectiveness

In order to estimate potential monetary policy effectiveness the index called *MIRE* (Measuring Inflation Real Effect) was introduced:

$$MIRE_t = \pi_t^{(1)} - \pi_t^{(2)} \tag{2}$$

In the case that *MIRE* > 0, expansive monetary policy is more appropriate[1]. To illustrate this, let us consider an example. Let weak core inflation be 10%, and strong core inflation be 8%. In the case where expansive monetary policy (reduction of interest rates) is planned, we can assume that together with a positive effect on aggregate output, inflation will rise up to 15%. In a case in which monetary policy is restrictive, inflation will fall by up to 5%. It can be seen that the effect on total inflation is symmetrical to the weak core inflation. If we also assume that real GDP changes proportionally to that part of changes in inflation that lead to changes in output, expansive and restrictive monetary policy will result in symmetric changes in real output and total inflation only if string core inflation equals weak core inflation. In a case in which strong core inflation is less than weak (let us say 8%), restrictive monetary policy is evidently less effective, as the decrease in real output will be equal to the difference between strong core inflation and total inflation, i.e. 3%, while for the expansionary monetary policy the effect on real output will be 7%. Accordingly, in case *MIRE* < 0, restrictive monetary policy will have more effect (negative) on real output. However under positive *MIRE* monetary policy can be considered as more effective than under negative *MIRE* in the sense that expansionary policy brings a larger increase in output and contractionary policy is less costly in terms of output foregone.

However, MIRE in its present form is subject to some criticism, and some possible improvements of MIRE measures have been suggested.

Mechanistic

$$MIRES_t \frac{(2k+1)(\pi_t^{(1)} - \pi_t^{(2)}}{\sum_{2-k}^{k}(\pi_{t+i}^{(1)} - \pi_{t+i}^{(2)}} \tag{3}$$

[1] S.B. Makarova, W.W. Charemza, W. Parkhomenko, "Core inflation: methods of estimation and forecasting", in "Economic research: theory and applications", Vol.2, St. Petersburg, 2002

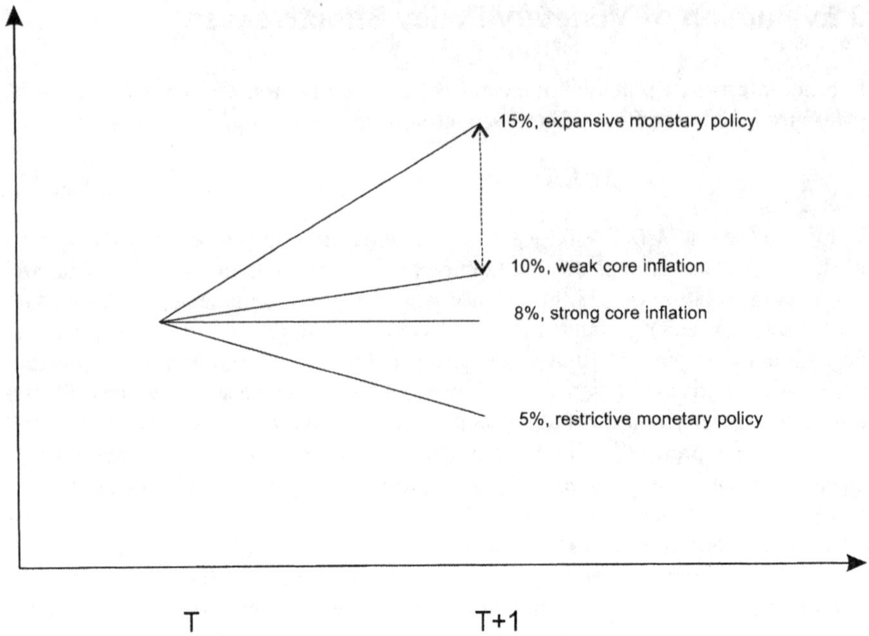

Fig. 1. Monetary policy effectiveness under positive MIRE

With the Use of the Concept of Neutral Interest Rate

The neutral interest rate is defined as the level of market interest rates for which expansionary and restrictive monetary policies are least effective. If we denote the neutral interest rate as r^n, and current interest rate as r_t, when $r_t > r^n$, there exists a natural tendency for the market to expand, and if $r_t < r^n$, there is a tendency to contract. Accordingly, the *MIRE* concept is changed to incorporate the neutral interest rate:

$$MIRER_t = \frac{(\pi_t^{(1)} - \pi_t^{(2)})}{r_t - r^n} \tag{4}$$

If *MIRE*, is positive ($\pi_t^{(1)} - \pi_t^{(2)} > 0$), and the market exhibits a tendency to contract ($r_t < r^n$), monetary policy should be contractionary. If $MIRE_t$ is positive, and the market has a tendency to expand ($r_t > r^n$, monetary policy should be expansionary.

The introduction of the concept of neutral interest rates poses a new question as to how neutral interest rates should be computed. Several alternatives have been suggested:

1. to formulate a two-equation *VAR* model for changes in real GDP (Δy_t) and level of real interest rate (r_t), and to perform impulse response decomposition of real interest rate r_t into the two components: $r_t = r_t^a + r_t^n$, where the item r_t^n is chosen so that its real effect (impact on changes in real GDP) is close to zero;

2. to formulate an *ADL* model for the real interest rate of the form:

$$r_t = \alpha_0 + \sum_{i=1}^{k} a_i r_{t-1} + \sum_{i=-\upsilon}^{\upsilon} \beta_i \Delta y_{t-i} + \varepsilon_t \tag{5}$$

and then to approximate the neutral interest rate by averaging:

$$r_t^n \cong \hat{\alpha}_0 + \sum_{i=1}^{k} \hat{\alpha}_i r_{t-i} + \sum_{i=0}^{\upsilon} \hat{\beta}_i \Delta v_{t-i} \tag{6}$$

3. to compute a moving average of the real interest rate r_t and to check for its structural breaks and stability (to ensure it is a long-term indicator).

Accounting for Autocorrelation

Since the *MIRE* concept is evaluated for the purpose of policy effectiveness evaluation, it should take into account possible time autocorrelations of *MIRE* measure to allow for a lagged influence of previous policy conditions:

$$MIREAR_t = MIRE_t + \sum \rho_i MIRE_{t-i} \tag{7}$$

where $\rho_i = \text{corr}(\text{MIRE}_t, \text{MIRE}_{t-i})$.

Combination of Methods Taking Into Account Neutral Interest Rate and Accounting for Autocorrelation

Since the MIRER measure is not certain to be free from autocorrelation, and thus policy conditions in the past may influence present and future policy conditions, a measure accounting for autocorrelation in MIRE and for the concept of neutral interest rates may be constructed:

$$\frac{MIREAR_t}{MIRERAR_t} = r_t - r_n \tag{8}$$

Since several different modifications of *MIRE* were suggested, the next logical step is to define the one that is most suitable for the purposes of advising on monetary policy actions. The rationale for *MIRE* can be verified with the help of simple *ADL* analysis of changes in real GDP:

$$\Delta y_t = \alpha_0 + \sum_{i=1}^{k} \alpha_j \Delta y_{t-i} + \sum_{i=1}^{\upsilon} \beta_i MIRE_{t-i} + \varepsilon_i \tag{9}$$

Then for every modification of *MIRE* after evaluation of such an ADL model, we can apply the Granger causality test to test whether coefficients β_i are jointly statistically not different from zero, i.e. the corresponding MIRE index captures only the part of output-neutral inflation, and cannot be efficiently used for estimation of monetary policy effectiveness in terms of real output impact.

4 Methods to Evaluate Weak Core Inflation

Weak core inflation is easier to estimate statistically, as the methods involved are relatively simple. There are two general sets of methods for weak core inflation estimation. The first group (smoothing methods) includes those that require only standard CPI statistics over the period of time under study, the second group (limited influence estimators) involves more detailed disaggregated data about individual price indices and weights for separate components of CPI.

Smoothing Methods

This group of methods is based on the idea of finding an easy to forecast statistical process for which time series of differences between CPI and values of the process at time t has no autocorrelation and minimal possible variance. For this purpose the variety methods of time series smoothing are used:

- moving average processes (MA),
- autoregressive processes (AR),
- autoregressive moving average models (ARMA),
- exponential smoothing,
- Hodrick-Prescott, Holt and Kalman filters.

In the last few years the suggestion has appeared with the Morana method of fractal cointegration between the growth rate of money and inflation.

However simple, these methods have a common disadvantage in that they do not provide policy makers with timely measures of core inflation needed for policy planning. Besides, most of these methods assume symmetry and normality of an underlying process distribution, which is often not the case.

Limited Influence Estimators

Major methods used in the framework of this group are:

- *Means with exclusion.* This method involves removing certain categories of goods and services from the CPI index. Usually excluded categories are all or almost all food-related categories, energy and electricity aggregates (for industrialised countries) and categories of goods and services with administratively controlled prices (relevant for developing countries and countries in transition). The rationale for exclusion of these categories stems from the fact that prices of these categories are, usually, the most volatile, and have much more to do with supply-side shocks, transitory in their nature, than with the state of demand in the economy. This method is very appealing and easy to use, but it is subject to voluntary decisions regarding the choice of excluded categories. And whether permanent exclusion of some categories can be justified is also a question.
- *Trimmed means.* This method is based on systematic exclusion of extreme price movements regardless of the CPI category these prices belong to. Thus, k-% trimmed mean is obtained by dropping (or 0-weighting) k-% highest and k-% lowest price movements during the period under study. Percentage here refers to basket weights, not the number of categories. A special case of trimmed

mean is a median price (50-% trimmed mean), and the CPI index itself (0-% trimmed mean).

- *Percentile means.* The k-percentile measure of core inflation is defined as the kth percentile of a weighted distribution of price changes over the given horizon. The 50th percentile is median. The major difference of this method from the trimmed means is that the percentile method does utilise all available observations in the sample, but in a different way from simple averaging.

5 Methods to Measure Strong Core Inflation

Strong core inflation refers to that part of total inflation that does not cause changes in industrial output over the medium- and long-run periods. As one possible method of measuring strong core inflation the *method of exclusions* is suggested, so as not to account, for example, for the prices under administrative regulation, which will not change timely in response to changes in factor prices. As was already mentioned, the method is subject to certain criticism, and it would be methodologically more correct to define core inflation with the help of econometric models relating output changes to inflation.

In their seminal paper, Quah and Vahey (1995) mention that "standard approaches to definition of core inflation have little economic interpretation" and "proposed a measure of core inflation [termed here as strong core inflation] consistent with a vertical long-run Phillips curve". In their work, core inflation was estimated from a VAR-model under the assumption that observed changes in the observable inflation measure (CPI) are produced by two types of disturbances. The first type (strong core inflation) of disturbances have no impact on the real output over the medium- to long-run period, while the second type of disturbances may well influence real production. By doing impulse response analysis of the resulting VAR-model. the estimate of core inflation was produced.

According to this approach, the *VAR*-model should be constructed, including inflation as one of the dependent variables, and some indicator of changes in production as another dependent variable. Then by decomposition of disturbances in output changes, one can produce an estimation of strong core inflation. It should be mentioned that in case some estimation of weak core inflation was done in advance, then it can be used in the *VAR*-model instead of total inflation observed, as it is expected that strong core inflation will be statistically estimated more effectively. The major problem with this method is choosing the proper measure of real output. Usually the index of industrial output in constant prices is taken as a proxy of real output. Further approaches to generalise the concepts of weak and strong core inflation:

- general equilibrium model and VAR (Folkertsma, Hubrich, 2002);
- regional panel data VAR model with simultaneous usage of exclusion means (Rechlin, 2002).

6 Inflation in Russia in 1994 – 2002

After the liberalization of prices in January 1992, inflation was several hundred percent per month. The existence of the rouble zone until the autumn of 1993 did not allow Russia to pursue truly independent monetary policy and to try to fight inflation. After the rouble zone was finally cancelled in the first months of 1994, inflation in Russia was brought to a single-digit level per month (between March and September 1994 monthly inflation was from 4.7% to 8.5%). However, in the last quarter of the year, the downward trend was again reversed due to the first large currency crisis ("Black Tuesday". October 11. 1994, inflation in October 1994 was 15%). And it was not until March 1995 that inflation fell below 10% again (8.9%). A sustainable downward trend in inflation was, however, set only after August 1995 with the introduction of the exchange rate band. The stabilisation of the exchange rate seemed to be successful for fighting inflation, as in July 1998 the monthly inflation rate (compared to the previous month) was about 0.2%.

The financial crisis of August 17th, 1998 was a second large currency crisis with severe inflationary consequences. Thus, alone in September 1998, prices rose by up to 38%. The reason for such a drastic increase was the increase in prices of imported products (mostly food), and also speculative demand and further expectations of price increases. The increasing trend of inflation prevailed until February 1999, and after that inflation started to decrease and oscillate around average monthly inflation of 1.4%[2] (the period March 1999 – September 2003). After the rouble started its nominal appreciation in January 2003, inflation set on a decreasing trend with average monthly inflation of 0.7% (February – September 2003).

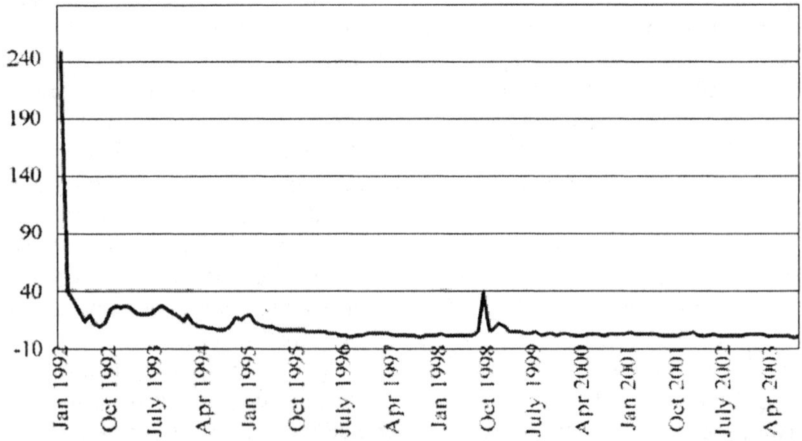

Fig. 2. Monthly inflation rate in Russia, January 1992 – September 2003.

Source: Bank of Russia, http://www.cbr.ru

[2] Since inflation is high in Russia, it is customary to measure it on month-to-month basis rather than on a yearly basis.

Major periods of inflation developments accounting for institutional arrangements and macroeconomic background:[3]

1. January 1992 – June 1995; high inflation: starting from 245% in January 1992 after price liberalization, it decreased to 10–30% in 1992–1993, then declined to less than 10% per month in the first half of 1994, and after the first currency crisis ("Black Tuesday", October 11, 1994) it increased again up to about 15% per month (see Fig. 2); freely floating rouble; vague monetary and fiscal policy;
2. June 1995 – August 1998; crawling band exchange regime; steady decreasing inflation trend; sharp decline of interest rates on the inter-bank market gave way to highly volatile interest rates closely tacking the tendency of changes in GKO yield (see Fig. 3); serious problems in fiscal policy (see *Monetary policy* section for more details);
3. August 1998 – February 1999; floating rouble with Bank of Russia interventions, depreciation of rouble by 70%, high inflation (increasing trend); sharp increase and following sharp decrease in interest rates on the inter-bank market; monetary expansion in response to fiscal problems;
4. March 1999 – January 2003; stable exchange rate (slightly depreciating rouble) under interventions of the Bank of Russia, decreasing inflation trend; relatively stable interest rates on the inter-bank market, tacking the tendency of changes in inflation rather than changes in GKO yield (see Fig. 3); ightened fiscal policy, high rate of monetary expansion due to increase in net foreign assets (favourable oil prices);
5. January 2003 – September 2003; nominal appreciation of rouble/US dollar exchange rate (Bank of Russia interventions), decreasing trend of inflation, strong fiscal surplus, monetary expansion due to increase in net foreign assets (favourable oil prices) and credit to private sector.

[3] Following T.J.T. Balino (1998) and M. Dabrowski, W. Paczynski, L. Rawdanowicz (2001).

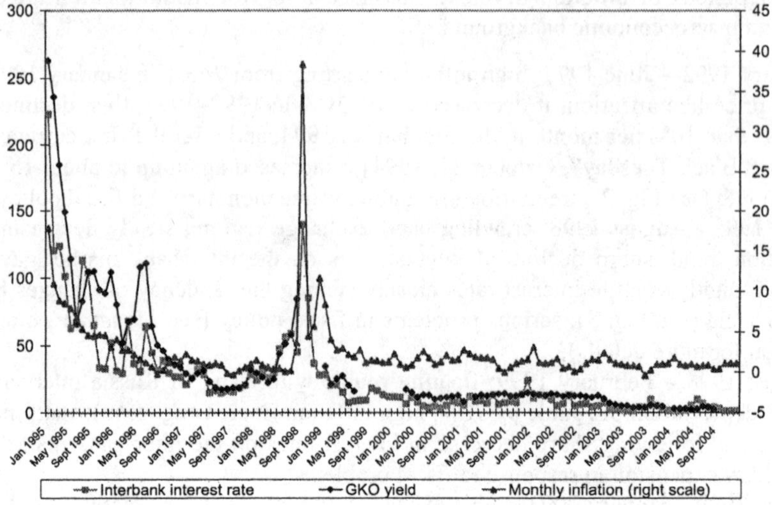

Fig. 3. Dynamics of inter-bank interest rates, GKO yield and monthly inflation in January 1995 – December 2004.

Source: Bank of Russia, http://www.cbr.ru

7 Monetary Policy in Russia in 1994 – 2002

After the abolition of the Soviet Union, all newly independent states (except for the Baltic States) continued to use the rouble as their currency. They were largely interested in using a common currency, but preferably without giving the conduct of monetary policy solely to the Bank of Russia or some form of cross-national monetary authority. This resulted in the well-known "tragedy of commons": every newly independent state tried to pursue its own monetary and fiscal policies, usually expansionary, partly shifting the burden of resulting inflation onto other states using the same currency. This evidently led to huge inflation rates in all countries in question, and to speedy depreciation of rouble.

The Rouble area had been disappearing very slowly, with the Bank of Russia gradually taking control of first credit money, and later, cash. The process of disintegration of the Rouble zone lasted from mid 1992 till the end of 1993, when the Bank of Russia was finally able to pursue its own independent (from other countries) monetary policy, with the first task of fighting inflation.

As the fiscal policy in the early period of transition was very vague and the Federal Government of Russia experienced a severe budget deficit, monetary aggregates expanded at a high rate due to huge credits to government. In April 1995 the new Law on the Central Bank of Russia was approved, it declared that the Bank of Russia should be independent in its formulation of monetary policy, and direct lending to the government was prohibited. These legal changes allowed the

Bank of Russia to introduce the exchange rate band in July 1995. It should be stressed however, that independence of the Bank of Russia has been more declarative in nature, since in the same Law on the Central Bank of Russia it is stated that one of its main tasks is "to elaborate and pursue in collaboration with the Government of the Russian Federation a single state monetary policy" (article 4, Federal Law #86). Fiscal policy was also tightened, and this led to the reduction of the rate of growth of credit to government in 1995 – 1998. Still, it this component that was the major driving force for increases in M2.

Taking into account the wide-spread practice of arrears (including on tax liabilities) and mutual nonpayment in the Russian economy of the period, and the declining rate of growth of direct credit to the government from the Bank of Russia, it is evident, that the Russian government financed its expenditures primarily by the issuance of new treasury bills. Treasury bills (GKO and OFZ) were considered attractive assets both by domestic and foreign investors. In order to make every following issue of bills more attractive, more yield was promised on treasury bonds: the GKO yield was systematically over the inflation rate, and "risk-free" securities offered 16 – 245% (see Fig. 3). Commercial banks, though obliged to place a certain share of their assets into safe treasury bills, ended up more interested in investing into treasury bills than the real economy, which later resulted in a severe banking crisis. The world outlook on the Russian economy at the time was quite favourable, and in the period between November 1996 and December 1997 Russia successfully issued Eurobonds on 4,5 billion USD[4].

The Asian crisis changed the disposition of investors, and in late 1997 the Bank of Russia had to fight with capital outflows in order to protect the band. The operation was successful for the time being, but it led to a loss of about two-thirds (3,6 billion USD[5]) of total liquid assets held by the Bank of Russia by that time. Besides, the Bank of Russia was involved in financing the government again. As direct credit to the government was prohibited, it was redeeming maturing treasury bills instead on behalf of the government. Net credit to the government from monetary authorities was expended by 14,7% during the last quarter of 1997. The Bank of Russia also tried to support commercial banks in substantially weakened positions due to excessive involvement in treasury bills speculative operations.

The next wave of capital outflows occurred in May 1998, resulting in a decline in the reserves of the Bank of Russia by 2,3 billion USD in two months. At the same time (May 1998) the Bank of Russia increased rates on refinancing operations (twice within this month) from 30% to 150%. At the end of May Lombard auctions were resumed. Commercial banks needed additional liquidity as they were apparently playing on the GKO market with the credit to the non-financial sector of the economy being about the size of credit to the governmental authorities (275,7 mln RUR to the non-financial sector and 215,4 mln RUR to the authorities in May 1998). At the beginning of June the rate of refinancing was lowered to 60%.

4 Data of M. Dabrowski, W. Paczynski, L. Rawdanowicz (2001).
5 Data of M. Dabrowski, W. Paczynski, L. Rawdanowicz (2001).

On August 1998, facing a large-scale financial crisis, monetary authorities attempted to introduce emergency measures. They devalued the rouble by half, widening the band by up to 9 roubles per US dollar. This measure was not able to stop the process of devaluation due to the loss of credibility in the system, and the Bank of Russia first closed the trading sessions on the foreign exchange market, then to introduce on the 2nd of September 1998 a floating exchange rate regime. In theory, the floating regime has been in operation since then, but in practice the Bank of Russia intervenes regularly to prevent serious changes in the exchange rate, and the exchange rate regime might be better termed a dirty float.

At the same time (August 1998) the Bank of Russia tried to prevent a liquidity crisis in the system of commercial banks and to escape legal procedures leading to bankruptcy of major commercial banks. In particular, on the 24th of August 1998 it lowered its rate of obligatory reserves from 11% to 10% for all commercial banks, and to 7% for Sberbank. In a week (September 1st, 1998) the rate of reserves was decreased to 5% for Sberbank and commercial banks with more than 40% of assets invested in GKO, and to 7,5% for commercial banks with 20–40% of assets in GKO. Two months later (December 1st, 1998) the rate of reserves was unified to 5% for all commercial banks.

However, the measures taken did not really help, and the problem still largely unresolved, was seen in the collapse of the banking system following the financial crisis of 1998. As a result of the financial crisis, most banks became illiquid and were either forced to close or to restructure. The crisis hit mostly the big banks, as they were far more involved in treasury bills speculation. Loss of liquidity of the banking system resulted in big and some medium-sized banks leaving the system. The banking system as a result was represented by medium and small banks with no real capacity for providing credit to the real sector of economy. This fact, combined with credit constraints on banks is deemed to be responsible for the loss of potential growth of the real sector. After devaluation, the Russian industrial sector became more competitive than the foreign one, however the resources to expand in reply to growing demand were soon exhausted, as bank credit appeared to be inaccessible to most enterprises.

Immediately following the crisis, the monetary policy of the Bank of Russia was to monetise government debt and to support commercial banks with losses of liquidity. In the period from the second quarter of 1998 to the third quarter, net credit to the government was about the size of the entire monetary base: 257.1M RUR credit to the government, 186.4M RUR money base (end of September 1998), and in the next quarter credit to the government expanded by approximately 80% (465M RUR at the end of December versus 257.1M RUR at the end of September 1998), and by credit to the banking system increased by 68% (37M RUR at the end of December versus 22M RUR at the end of September 1998).

In 1999 monetary policy was tightened, and the growth rate of net credit to government was reduced (525.3M RUR in January 1999 versus 465M RUR in December 1998). But in the same period net credit to commercial banks increased by appr. 100% relative to the end of 1998 (76M RUR in January 1999, and 37M RUR in December 1998). The IMF stressed (2000) that after the crisis, the Bank of Russia was reluctant to use market-based instruments of monetary policy (interest rate management on different types of refinancing operations. Bank of Russia bonds etc.) to ensure the liquidity position of the banking system, and relied instead on the reserve requirements rate, which was increased on four occasions by mid 2000 (from 5% to 10% as the highest). After the collapse of the treasury bills system, commercial banks were reluctant to choose any other market instruments to invest in, and preferred to deposit their excessive funds with the Bank of Russia. Since the end of the crisis, the banking system has not experienced liquidity loss, leading to the failure of Bank of Russia Lombard auctions in 2000 – 2003.

By 2000 the growth rate of net credit to the government was decreasing and the major contribution to the monetary expansion came from growth in net foreign assets resulting from favourable oil prices and the mandatory sell of parts of foreign export currency receipts.

The current account balance of Russia has sufficiently improved in 2000 with 46.4 billion USD surplus. This situation, though usually viewed as favourable, put the Bank of Russia in a very difficult position, as on the one hand it had to prevent the nominal appreciation of rouble in order to support development of the real sector of the economy, while on the other hand it had to struggle with monetary expansion being the consequence of current account surplus. The latter introduced inflationary pressure into the economy, and pushed the rouble to real appreciation.

The main aim of the Bank of Russia's monetary policy after the financial crisis of 1998 (since 1999) is the consecutive decreasing of inflation. In the official statement in the "Basic directions of the state monetary policy" (1999 – 2003) the Bank of Russia stresses that inflation from year to year should be lower, and to achieve this the Bank of Russia uses monetary methods so as not to prevent a balanced combination of economic growth, increase in real income, and investment consumption. The disinflation process "is chosen to be led in a very smooth way, as analysis of disinflation practices of other countries suggests that only smooth and consistent disinflation policies gives the best results"[6].

Such views on the aims of monetary policy and disinflation are closely consistent with the concept of MIRE, namely, to perform disinflation measures, the Bank of Russia needs a timely and reliable indicator of the desirability of certain policy developments. Accounting for this, the Bank of Russia announced in 2003 that it has estimated core inflation since the beginning of 2002 by the method of exclusions, not accounting for prices under administrative regulation and highly volatile prices (including those with seasonal volatility)[7].

Up till now the disinflation policy of the Bank of Russia was not successful when judged in terms of the target and real inflation indicators (see Table 2).

---

[6] CBR: "Basic directions of the state monetary policy on 2003", http://ww.cbr.ru

[7] Ibid.

Table 2. Inflation target and real inflation

Year	Inflation target*	Real inflation**
2000	18%	20,2%
2001	12-14%	18,6%
2002	12-14%	15,1%
2003	10-12%	12%
2004	8-10%	

* Source: "Basic directions of the state monetary policy on 2000, 2001, 2002, 2003, 2004".
** Source: State Statistical Committee of Russia (www.gks.ru).

Core inflation measured since the beginning of 2002 was below 1% per month through most of the period (see Fig. 4). October of 2003 is a remarkable month in the sense of core inflation, since the latter peaked in October up to 1,4%, mostly due to increase in prices of food products (with the exception of seasonal increase in prices of vegetables and fruit). This tendency is explained by the increase in wholesale prices of agricultural products (mostly of corn). Taking this into account, it is doubtful that the Bank of Russia's inflation target of a maximum 12% for 2003 will be realised.

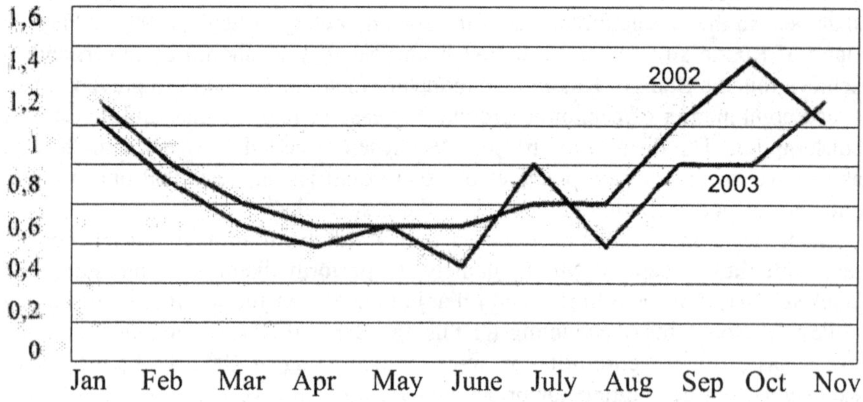

Fig. 4. Core inflation as measured by the Bank of Russia in January 2002 – November 2003

Source: Data of the Bank of Russia, http://www.cbr.ru

Apart from its main aim, the Bank of Russia also sets each year as an intermediate goal of monetary policy, a certain percentage increase in the M2 aggregate. At the same time, in its "Basic directions ... 2003" the Bank of Russia mentions that even though its intermediate goal is to control M2 growth, the effectiveness of this control in relation to the main aim is diminishing, as along with decreasing inflation the short-term statistical inter-relation between inflation and M2 weakens. Mostly the problem is seen in an almost unpredictable statistical path of change of velocity of money. Besides, the M2 target is also referred to as an indicative target without commitment to achieve it.

As its operational goal, the Bank of Russia sets a growth rate of monetary base, since the parameter is almost totally under control of the Bank of Russia. As was already mentioned, monetary growth was mostly due to the increase of the money base, rather than other monetary aggregates. The Bank of Russia attributes the situation to a substantially lower money multiplier than existed before the crisis. Accordingly, the Bank of Russia mentions as a desired outcome of its policy, monetary growth as a result of increase in the money multiplier, not the money base. Taking into account that the money base forms about ½ of M2 aggregate (see Fig. 5), control over the money base allows the Bank of Russia to manage the M2 aggregate (intermediate goal) efficiently, though again it does not help to manage inflation (primary goal).

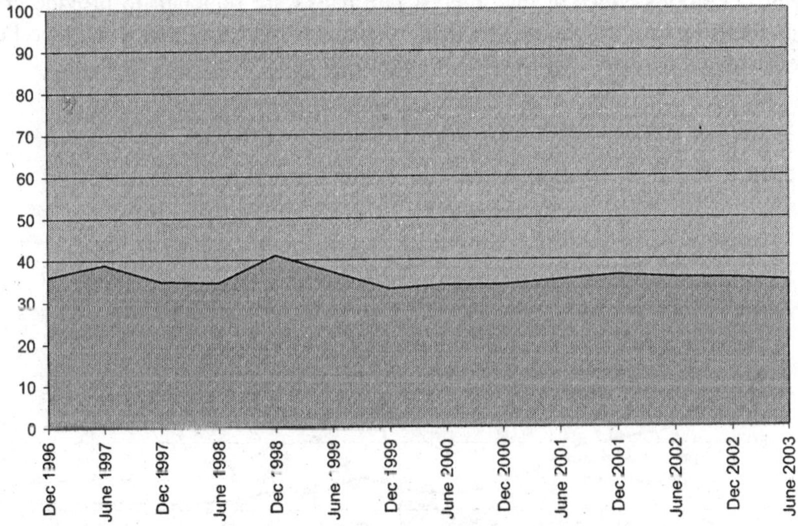

Fig. 5. Balance between M0 and M2 monetary aggregates in Russia in December 1996 – November 2003

Source: Bank of Russia, http://www.cbr.ru

As was already mentioned, the IMF (2000) and other experts noticed that the Bank of Russia was somewhat reluctant to use monetary policy instruments other than reserve requirements. Another popular instrument of monetary policy was the rate of refinance, which was lowered from 60% to 25% at the end of 2000, and further to 18% by the beginning of 2003 alongside nominal rouble appreciation. In the new version of the Law regarding the Bank of Russia (July 10, 2002) the two norms concerning reserve requirements were postulated: the required reserve ratio may not exceed 20% of a credit institution's obligations, and it may not be changed by more than 5 points at a time (article 38). These two norms stress that the banking system has largely recovered according to the Bank of Russia, and the devotion of the latter to gradual policy measures.

The decrease in the refinance rate was the consequence of a general lowering of interest rates in the economy and a decreasing inflation rate. On the one hand, the Bank of Russia tried to push commercial banks towards the development of credit schemes for the real sector of economy. On the other hand, it had developed a number of requirements oriented towards control over liquidity and solvency of commercial banks. In particular, commercial banks cannot draw on credit to one organisation in a sum over 5% of the equity capital of the commercial bank; it is prohibited to use more than 25% of equity capital for buying shares of stocks of one company, to draw on the credit to its shareholders over 20% of equity capital, etc.[8] The operating rules of accounting, state that any percentage allocations above the interest rate of "refinance rate + 3%". This also exerted a negative impact on credit operations, since at this interest rate banks are reluctant to provide credit, and enterprises are reluctant to accept credit rates over the mentioned (sec Fig. 6 for credit and deposit interest rates dynamics).

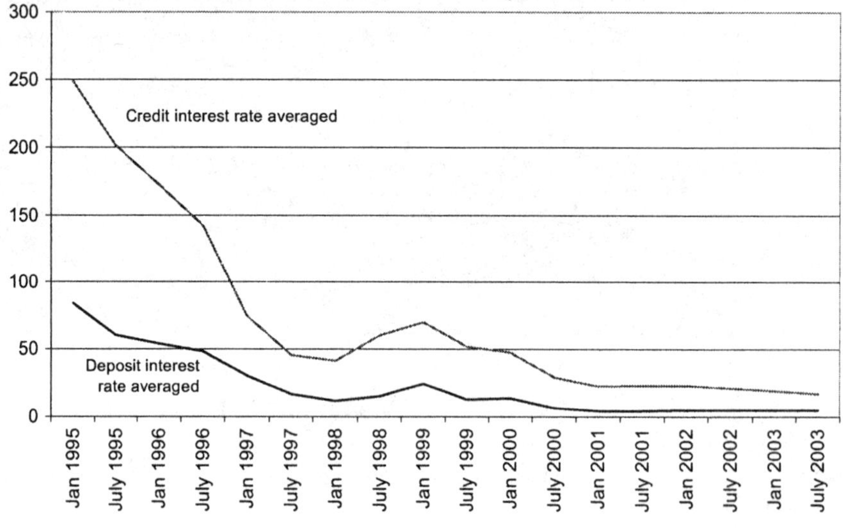

Fig. 6. Averaged interest rates on deposits and credits in banking system of Russia in January 1995 – July 2003

Source: Bank of Russia, http://www.cbr.ru

Since mostly small- and medium-size banks had survived after the crisis, these measures, coupled with cautious credit policies of commercial banks, prevented the development of real sector credit programmes. It is the modest share of credit operations that explains why the refinance mechanism has not been working for

[8] Federal Law on the Bank of Russia, №65-ФЗ (from 12.07.99), art. 66, 69, 72.

the years following the crisis, as in the absence of credit, the banking system was characterized by excessive liquidity throughout the period. However, credit to the non-financial and private sector has been gradually increasing, in particular since mid-2000, when it reached pre-crisis levels (see Fig. 7). It should be stressed that most credit expansion is due to foreign currency denominated credits, with the total sum of credit in roubles accounting for the national determination of M2 aggregate (2674 min RUR of credit and 2740 min RUR of M2 in November 2003). The reserves of commercial banks peaked in December 2000 with 13% of the overall balance, being otherwise about 9–10%.

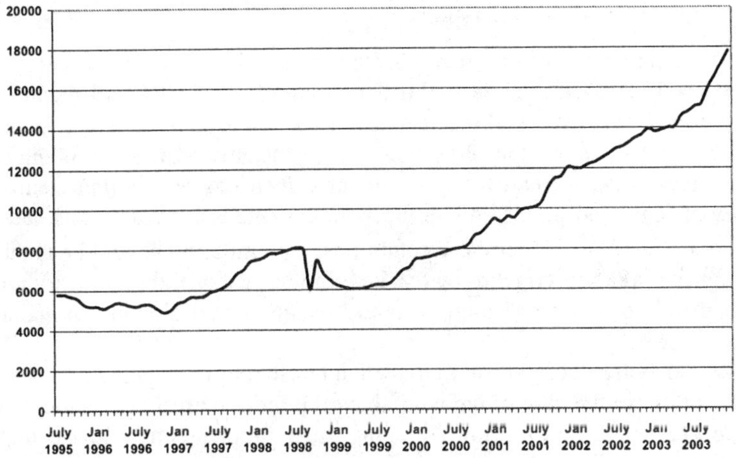

Fig. 7. Credit to non-financial enterprises and private sector in comparable prices (Dec. 2000=100%)

Source: Bank of Russia, http://www.cbr.ru

8 Monetary Policy for 2004

For 2004 the Bank of Russia plans the following basic components of its policy:

1. **to preserve the dirty floating exchange rate regime**; the appreciation of Rouble is forecasted to be 3–5% per year; the limit of appreciation is settled to be 7%, that does not lead to significant loss of competitiveness of Russian enterprises according to the estimations of the Bank of Russia;
2. **management of interest rates will be directed to (a) regulate capital flows in order to balance currency market; and (b) to regulate money and credit supply in the economy.** In case the worldwide oil prices decrease, the Bank or Russia plans to increase interest rates in order to prevent capital outflows, but so as to make credit accessible for borrowers from the real sector. In case the world-wide oil prices are relatively high, interest rates will be kept at low level

so as to prevent speculative capital inflows and to leave Bank of Russia able to sterilise excessive liquidity;

3. **money supply will be formed on the basis of increase of official currency reserves**. In case money demand will exceed money supply based on official currency reserves, additional money supply will be provided by changes of net credit to federal government. As the extreme measure of money supply control, changes of obligatory reserves ratio are left;
4. **further perfection of refinancing and sterilising instruments is expected**. Bank of Russia plans to continue issuing its own bonds (OBR), to introduce backward currency swap operations, and to widen the range of pawning tools under Lombard crediting operations.

The "Basic directions of the state monetary policy for 2004" are subject to certain criticism. First of all, the desired inflation targets of 8-10% will require tight monetary policy, that may well result in lower economic growth, which is subject to tight scrutiny due to the President's announcement of a "non-ambitious budget". Taking into account the government's decisions concerning changes in the prices of regulated goods and services, prices increases due to this category may be up to 19–22%[9]. Under these conditions, core inflation should be about 6% in order for the inflation target to be reached. In the case of tight monetary policy, money demand could exceed money supply resulting in a slowing of economic growth.

The second policy component – that of interest rate management – deserves special attention. In the case of unfavourable oil prices, interest rates should be increased to prevent capital outflow. Keeping them simultaneously low enough in order to provide credit to the real sector appears impossible. For the largest part of the industrial sector in Russia, the ceiling of credit rates is 12–13%[10], representing the current level of credit interest rates. In the case that interest rates on credit are increased, most industrial enterprises will lose access to this credit. Thus it appears that the priority for the Bank of Russia is to prevent capital outflows with possible negative consequences for economic growth. This stresses the importance of timely and competent interest rate management.

References

Quah, D., S.P. Vahey "Measuring core inflation", The Economic Journal, 1995, pp. 1130-1144

Balino, T.J.T., "Monetary policy in Russia", Finance development, quarterly magazine of the IMF, December 1998, Vol. 35, #4

Dabrowski, M., Paszynski, W., Rawdanowicz, L., "Inflation and monetary policy in Russia: transition experience and future recommendations", WP of RECEP, July 2001

[9] Data of Centre for Macroeconomic Analysis and Short-Term Forecasting; http://www.forecast.ru

[10] Ibid.

Makarova, S.B., Charemza, W.W., Parkhomenko, W., "Core inflation: methods of estimation and forecasting", in "Economic research: theory and applications", Vol. 2, St. Petersburg, 2002

IMF, "Russian Federation: Selected Issues", IMF Staff Country Report, #00/15, Nov. 2000

Buchs, T.D., "Financial crisis in the Russian Federation", Economics of Transition, Vol. 7, 1999, pp. 687-715

Balino, T.J.T., Hoelscher, D.S., Hoeder, J., "Evolution of monetary policy instruments in Russia", IMF Working Paper, 180/97, 1997

"Basic directions of the state monetary policy on 1999, 2000, 2001, 2002, 2003, 2004"; Bank of Russia, http ://www.cbr.ru

Bank of Russia, official data statistics, http://www.cbr.ru

State Statistical Committee, official data statistics, http://www.gks.ru

Center for Macroeconomic Analysis and Short-term Forecasting, http: //www. forecast. ru

Russian Fuel and Energy Sector: Dynamics and Prospects

Ruslan Grinberg

1 Introduction

Russia's fuel and energy complex has always played an important role in the country's economy. Its role has further increased during the reforms, in connection with an abrupt decrease in production in other economic sectors. Over the recent decade, Russia's fuel and energy sector did meet its basic requirements in fuel and energy, thus maintaining the country's energy independence. At present, this sector is one of Russia's economic sectors showing stable performance and determining the present state and prospects of the national economy, accounting for around one-quarter of its GDP, one-third of industrial production and revenues of Russia's consolidated budget, and around one-half of exports and currency revenue.

Table 1. Russian Fuel and Energy Complex: Basic Indices

Production	1990	2000	2003
Oil (mln tons)	516	324	408 (111.1% against 2002)
Gas (bln cubic meters)	641	584	581 (103.4% against 2002)
Coal (mln tons)	395	258	275 (176% against 2002)
Electric energy (bln kW/h)	1082	878	915 (102.6% against 2002)

Source: The Energy Strategy of Russia for the Period of up to 2020. Ministry of Energy of the RF, Moscow, 2003, p. 64.

The major factors impeding the development of Russian fuel and energy complex are as follows:

- lag of the development and objective growth of costs for developing prospective raw materials base for hydrocarbons production, especially regarding the gas industry;
- in all the branches of the fuel and energy complex putting new production facilities into operation decreased twofold to sixfold over the 1990s;
- a high degree of wear of the main funds (over 50%);
- the practice of prolongation of the equipment's term of service is fraught with the future production inefficiency. As a consequence an accident rate is high;
- lag of the productive potential of fuel and energy complex from the world science and technology level. The shares of both oil extraction using modern methods and oil processing with the help of technologies that increase the quality of production are low;
- deformation of price ratio regarding the interchangeable energy sources resulted in the absence of competition between them and led to a demand structure characterized by excessive orientation toward gas and reduction of coal share. In the long term the policy of maintaining the relatively low prices for gas and electric energy may lead to an increase in the deficit of corresponding

energy resources due to lack of economic preconditions for investments in their production and outstripping growth in demand;
- lack of the market infrastructure and of civilized energy market. Necessary transparency of economic activities of natural monopolies agents is not secured, which adversely influences both the quality of state control over their activities and development of competition;
- remaining shortage of investment resources in the fuel and energy sectors (except for the oil industry) and their misallocation. With the high investment potential of fuel and energy complex industries, the influx of foreign investments is less than 13% from financing of all the capital investments. At the same time 95% of these investments are accounted for in the oil industry. In the gas and electric energy industries no preconditions are created for the required investment growth, which can make these branches impede the economic growth that has started.

2 The Russian Government's Energy Strategy

In August 2003, the Government of the Russian Federation issued *The Energy Strategy of Russia for the Period of up to 2020* (approved by the Decree No.1234-p of August 28, 2003), containing the basic indices of the long-term development of Russian fuel and energy complex.

Such a document should be of special importance for Russia, since it is a large energy exporter, the share of energy resources in the country's exports being about 50%. In this connection the country's energy strategy should be considered in a broader context – not only as a task of supplying the national economy with energy but as one of the key issues of the structural economic policy.

The main problem those who developed *The Energy Strategy of Russia* faced was the lack of clear notions and aims of Russia's economic development for the period of up to 2020.

At present there are a number of documents determining medium- and long-term prospects of the Russian economic development. Both the (unapproved) Strategy of National Economic Development for the Period of up to 2010 (developed in 2001 by the Centre for Strategic Research headed by German Gref) as well as The Indices of the Medium-Term National Economic Development for 2004-2007, approved by the Government as a basis for the draft federal budget for 2004, exist.

However, the goals set in these documents do not correspond to those proclaimed in May 2003 in the President's annual Address to the Federal Assembly, namely doubling GDP during the next decade (by 2014). To solve this task over the ten years to come, the minimum annual GDP growth in Russia should amount to 7.2%.

It is to be noted that the necessity to increase the economic dynamics, repeatedly emphasized by the RF President, has intelligible quality reference points. An increased growth rate would allow approaching the level of economic development (per capita GDP) of the advanced European countries in the course of 20 years.

The Energy Strategy of Russia is based on four scenarios of the country's social and economic development (The Energy Strategy of Russia, 2003, pp. 14-19):

- optimistic scenario foresees the 3.3-fold growth of GDP by 2020 comparing to the level of the year 2000 (average annual GDP growth – 6.2 %);
- favourable scenario is characterized by the 2.6-fold growth of GDP by 2020 (average annual GDP growth – 5.0-5.1%);
- moderate scenario foresees the 2.3-fold growth of GDP (average annual GDP growth – 4.3%);
- critical scenario is characterized by the average annual GDP growth of 2.5-3%.

At the same time it is to be mentioned that from the point of view of quality differences (the influence of the factors taken into consideration and the contents of possible scenario conditions of the economic policy), all the scenarios presented in *The Strategy* are not concrete enough – the only difference between them being related to the dynamics of the world prices for energy resources – and contain quite abstract statements concerning the degree of intensity of economic reforms implemented in Russia.

The moderate scenario can be regarded as the inertia scenario, which can be realized within the framework of the present economic policy.

At the same time even the optimistic scenario of *The Strategy* does not go as far as the aims of Russia's economic growth set by President V. Putin in his Address to the Federal Assembly in May 2003.

I suspect that the energy strategy (projected indices of the main energy resources production) is aimed at the realization of the optimistic scenario, being implemented in favourable external conditions – with the high world prices for the Russian oil (up to $30 per barrel in 2020) and gas ($138 per thousand cubic meters), intense economic restructuring and accelerated liberalization of prices and rates for natural monopolies' production and services, which will decrease the power/GDP ration by 26-27% by 2010 and by 45-55% by the end of the period concerned. Up to 50% of the foreseen economic growth must be achieved without energy consumption growing. More than 20% of the growth should be achieved through technological energy saving; only about one-third of the GDP growth will require an increase in energy consumption. As a result the level of energy consumption efficiency is estimated at 0.42, which means that every percent of Russia's GDP growth should be provided for by the growth of energy consumption by a maximum of 0.42%. According to *The Energy Strategy*, this level of energy consumption efficiency is characteristic of the most economically advanced European countries.

It is quite understandable that to achieve these extremely desirable indices it is necessary to radically modernize the whole production apparatus of the national economy on the basis of energy-saving technologies. For the time being the country lacks foundations for such a strategy of structural industrial policy. Moreover, until recently the Russian cabinet was dominated by the point of view according to which an active structural policy as such is inexpedient. An increase in domestic prices for energy resources is considered the main and sufficient stimulus for developing the energy savings.

With all the above taken into consideration, according to the optimistic scenario the consumption of primary fuel and energy resources should grow from 904 mln tons of oil and gas equivalent in 2000 up to 1270 mln tons of oil and gas equivalent (the 1.4-fold growth).

According to the same scenario, export of Russian energy resources should grow from 514 mln tons of oil and gas equivalent up to 725 mln tons of oil and gas equivalent by 2010 and up to 760 mln tons of oil and gas equivalent by 2020 (the 1.48-fold growth).

Provided the optimistic scenario is realized, the total production of Russian energy resources will thus grow from 1418 mln tons of oil and gas equivalent up to 1820 mln tons of oil and gas equivalent by 2010 and up to 2030 mln tons of oil and gas equivalent by 2020 (the 1.43-fold growth) (The Energy Strategy of Russia, 2003, pp. 39-42). The dynamics of oil, gas, coal and electric energy production is shown in Table 2.

Table 2. The Dynamics of Oil, Gas, Coal and Electric Energy Production in Russia (2000-2020)

	Production				
	2000	2010		2020	
		Moderate scenario	Optimistic scenario	Moderate scenario	Optimistic scenario
Oil (mln tons)	324	445	490	450	520
Gas (bln cubic meters)	584	635	665	680	730
Coal (mln tons)	258	310	330	375	430
Electric energy (bln kW/h)	878	1015	1070	1215	1365

If we consider the export potential of the Russian energy sector, oil and natural gas will remain the main component of its exports. The estimates of export volume of these products are presented in Table 3.

Table 3. The Dynamics of Oil, Gas, Coal and Electric Energy Exports in Russia (2000-2020)

	Export				
	2000	2010		2020	
		Moderate scenario	Optimistic scenario	Moderate scenario	Optimistic scenario
Oil (mln tons)	205	305	340	305	350
Gas (bln cubic meters)	185	250	265	270	280
Coal (mln tons)	45	45	50	45	50
Electric energy (bln kW/h)	-	20	35	30	75

In other words, *The Strategy* proceeds from the possibility of 1.48-1.65-fold growth of the total export of Russian oil (including that to the CIS countries) by 2010 with the ensuing stagnation of the export volume.

Russia's oil resources are estimated at 44 bln tons, of which 10 bln tons are situated on shelves. And the explored reserves of oil amount to 12-20 bln tons. At the same time, the scale of geological exploration does not guarantee the reproduction of the raw materials base for the oil industry. The structure of the explored oil reserves keeps deteriorating. Reserves difficult to extract account for more than half of the country's explored reserves (The Energy Strategy of Russia, 2003, pp. 71-74).

Oil production will be realized and developed in the traditional regions of Russia such as Western Siberia, North Caucasus, Volga region as well as in the new oil and gas provinces: on the European North (Timan-Pechora region), in the Eastern Siberia and on the Far East and the south of Russia (North-Caspian province). The main oil base of the country for the regarded period of time will be the Western-Siberian oil and gas province. According to all scenarios, oil extraction in this region will grow through 2010 to 2015, after which it will somewhat decrease to a level of 290-315 mln tons in 2020.

Under favourable conditions of the economic development, new centres of oil production will be formed in the Eastern Siberia, in the republic Sakha (Yakutia), on the Sakhalin Island shelf, on the Barents Sea shelf. Provided the geological prospecting/exploration is intensive, the raw materials base will allow for an increase in oil extraction in the Eastern Siberia and Yakutia up to 50-80 mln tons and on the Sakhalin shelf up to 25 mln tons by 2020, which is desirable also from the point of view of regional development.

However, we consider it difficult to raise the oil export volume up to this level by 2010, because the transport infrastructure will impede it. Evidently, if price competition is favourable, the level of 300 thousand tons will be reached closer to 2015. The markets are expected to expand mainly eastward toward China and South-East Asia through a new pipeline Angarsk-Nakhodka. In the near future Russian oil will be transported to China by rail.

The majority of experts are quite skeptical about the possibility of increasing the shipment of Russian oil to the USA through Murmansk. There is no port there suitable for supertankers. (Double transshipment is constantly mentioned in the scheme, which is at the limit of profitability even with the present high level of oil prices. Should the scheme be realized, it will be necessary to construct a special pipeline the Yamal peninsula-Murmansk.) For this reason for the next 20 years, the EU countries will continue be the main markets for the Russian energy resources, accounting for up to one-half of oil exported by Russia (160 mln tons) and for up to 60% of gas (165 bln cubic meters). Moreover, Russian oil and gas will continue to be exported to the European CIS countries and China (gas from Yakutia), and Sakhalin gas will be shipped to the Asia-Pacific region, first and foremost to Japan.

3 Fuelled Economic Growth

At the same time, if we adhere to the economic growth rate declared in the RF President's Address, GDP should increase 3.8 times its size in 2000 (the base year of *The Strategy*) and 3.3 times in 2003 size by 2020.

Such economic growth will provide for a 2.3-fold increase compared to the year 2000. In its turn this means that by 2020, according to the level of efficiency of domestic energy consumption approved by *The Strategy*, consumption will grow by a minimum of 1.6 times compared to the level seen in the year 2000 of up to 1490 mln tons of oil and gas equivalent, which is 220 mln tons of oil and gas equivalent more than *The Strategy* projects.

In this case, the export volume of energy resources being in accordance with that foreseen by the optimistic scenario of *The Strategy* (760 mln tons of oil and gas equivalent), by 2020 the total energy resources production in Russia will increase to 2030 mln tons of oil and gas equivalent, which is 11% more than is foreseen by the optimistic scenario.

In the event that the total energy resources production foreseen by *The Strategy* is 2030 mln tons of oil and gas equivalent and their domestic consumption grows in order to provide for the higher economic growth rate declared by the RF President by 2020, the volume of export of Russian energy resources can make about 70% of that foreseen by the optimistic scenario of *The Strategy*.

In connection to this, the situation with the Russian natural gas deserves special attention (The Energy Strategy of Russia, 2003, pp. 81-86). First, gas will continue to be the basis of the country's energy balance, though a certain decrease of its share is forecasted. Secondly, from the point of view of export development, the necessity to develop the pipeline system currently being considered, it is the most capital consuming product. It is due to this circumstance that Russia develops its gas export on the basis of long-term contracts and tries to secure the stability of markets.

According to *The Strategy*, the share of gas in the total energy resources consumption (including the cost of electric energy and heat production) in the country's future energy balance will decrease from a current level of 50% to 48% by 2010 and to 45-46% by 2020.

With the economic growth rate specified in the RF President's Address and the structure of fuel balance foreseen by *The Strategy*, domestic consumption of natural gas in Russia will grow from 400 bln cm to almost 640 bln cm by 2020 (160% up against the level of the year 2000). Correspondingly, by 2015 the natural gas domestic consumption can grow by 140%, reaching 560 bln cm. In reality, the demand may turn out to be markedly lower due to a considerably lower rate of growth in natural gas consumption in the communal sector. Taking this factor into consideration, the total domestic demand for gas can be estimated at 560 bln cm by 2020 and 480 bln cm by 2015. In this case, export resources of Russian gas would not reach the figure determined by *The Strategy*, make up about 170-180 bln cm by 2015 with an ensuing stagnation at this level. Up to 30 bln cm of this volume can flow to the markets of China and other countries of the Asia-Pacific region.

4 Scenarios for Expanded Gas Extraction

Analysis of the resource base of Russia's gas industry shows that the explored gas reserves (46.9 trillion cubic meters, categories A, B, C1) can provide for an annual volume of gas extraction at the level of 700-750 bln cm. To maintain this volume of extraction in the long term, it is necessary to increase the gas reserves by about 30 trillion cubic meters up to 56 trillion cubic meters.

The joint-stock company, Gazprom, has taken 530 bln cm as a basic volume of natural gas extraction in the European part of Russia and Western Siberia for the period of up to 2020. It is to be noted, however, that depending on the amount of investments this volume may change from 470 bln to 590 bln cm.

The further strategy of Gazprom is based on developing new gas fields to maintain the annual gas extraction at the level of minimum 560 bln cm. The rest of an increase (160-180 bln cm) should be provided for by independent oil and gas extracting companies.

Priority directions of expanding the raw base are as follows:

1. Timan-Pechora region;
2. the shelf of Barents and Pechora seas;
3. the Urals and Volga regions (Devonian clastic play of Astrakhan arch);
4. Western Siberia (the Yamal field, the Achimovskoe formation in the Yarainerskoe oilfield, Obskaya and Tazovskaya inlets, Gydan region);
5. Eastern Siberia and Far East (Evenk Autonomous Area, Irkutsk region, Sakha Republic (Yakutia));
6. the shelf of the Okhotsk Sea and the Sakhalin island.

The extraction from the new fields is expected to make 23.4% (124.3 bln cm) and 38.5% (204.1 bln cm) of the total extraction in 2015 and 2020, respectively.

According to expert estimates, gas extraction in Eastern Siberia and the Far East will reach 55-60 bln cmpy by 2020, including 15 bln cmpy extracted on the Sakhalin shelf. In this connection, the major part of gas extracted by independent companies should be delivered to the Unified Gas Supply System in Western Siberia and Timan-Pechora region.

Due to its resource base, the Yamal peninsula is regarded as Russia's strategic oil and gas region. In January 2001, its gas reserves (18 gas and gas condensate fields) were reported to make 10.5 trillion cubic meters (categories A, B, C1) and 341 trillion cubic meters (category C2). Oil extraction will amount to 292 million tons (categories A, B, C1) and gas condensate extraction to 228 million tons.

Priyamal shelf of the Karsk Sea, where some unique fields (Rusanovskoe, Leningradskoe) are found, is regarded as very perspective. By 2030, it is feasible to increase the extraction on this shelf by 9 trillion cubic meters of gas, and on the Yamal peninsula as a whole by 11.7 trillion cubic meters of gas and 600 billion tons of liquid carbohydrates. With that taken into consideration, the 'Yamal scenario' was taken by Gazprom as a basis for developing new fields.

This scenario foresees maintaining gas extraction until 2007 by developing new fields in Nadym region. Gas extraction will amount to 13.5 bln cm in 2006, 16 bln cm in 2007, 20 bln cm in 2008, 21.2 bln cm in 2009 and 24 bln cm in 2010.

Developing new fields will require the following investment:

- $6.5 bln in 2002-2005 (including $5.6 bln for Nadym region and $0.9 bln for the Yamal peninsula);
- $8.8 bln in 2006-2010 (including $4 bln for Nadym region and $4.8 bln for the Yamal peninsula).

The total investment in 2002-2010 will amount to $15.3 bln (including $9.6 bln for Nadym region and $4.8 bln for the Yamal peninsula), $0.3 bln for drilling 160 wells and $5.4 bln for developing them.

The estimated total extraction potential of the Yamal's three natural gas fields to be developed first (Bovanenkovskoe, Kharasaveyskoe, Kruzenshternovskoe) is 147 bln cmpy (reserves of the gas of categories A, B and C1 are 5.6 bln cm, of category C2 0.91 bln cm) and that of the whole Yamal peninsula is up to 240 bln cmpy of natural gas. Construction costs for the three-thread system of gas pipelines to Yamburg are estimated at $5.7 bln. Estimated cumulative capital investment into development of Bovanenkovskoe and Kharasaveyskoe gas fields (with the volume of extraction equal to 178 bln cm of natural gas and about 4 mln tons of stable condensate per year) amounts to $15.6 bln. Total capital investment into the Yamal scenario is estimated at $41 bln, including that into pipelines to Ukhta ($31.8 bln). It is evident that with the existing tax rates and domestic prices for gas the development of the Yamal natural gas fields will be unprofitable.

Another serious problem the Russian gas industry may face during the period concerned is a considerable rise in gas extraction costs in the newly developed regions. These costs turned out to be higher than the average costs of production on the fields already being developed (five- to twentyfold difference on the Yamburg field, six- to tenfold on the Urengoy field, threefold in Orenburg region). The costs of extraction on the fields both new and being developed are almost equal to that in the North Caucasus and in the Timan-Pechora region.

Thus, more and more gas fields will get into the category of the so-called medium- and low-effective fields. As a result, the so-called 'commercial or commodity reserves' of natural gas (the volume of gas that can be profitably sold on the gas market) may decrease with time, with the physical gas reserves growing simultaneously.

This situation will inevitably lead to an increase in domestic prices for gas as well as to a decrease in its extraction's investment appeal compared to that in Northern Africa and Central Asia. This factor is essential for attracting foreign investment to the Russian gas industry.

5 What Will This Situation Means for Europe

For the period up to 2015, the average annual growth of the European countries' demand for natural gas is estimated at 1.5%, which I consider to be quite realistic from the point of view of the region's total economic growth. In this case by 2015 gas consumption in the European countries may increase 1.23 times, reaching 610 bln cmpy.

According to the scenario proposed by the Cambridge Energy Research Association, natural gas extraction in the European Union may grow by 3% annually through to 2005. Afterwards there will be a period of stagnation and from 2010 to 2015, gas extraction will decrease significantly (3.2% per year), mostly due to its reduction in Great Britain and the Netherlands. By 2015, the total volume of extraction will stabilize at a level of 245-270 bln cm.

This will mean that the EU's import demand for natural gas may reach 340 bln cm. At the same time the estimated import demand for natural gas of Ukraine, Belarus and Moldova is about 90 bln cm and that of Transcaucasian countries and Turkey is about 25 billion cubic meters, which together comprises about 115 bln cm.

Taking into account the projected growth of liquefied gas import (from 12 bln to 20 bln cm), the total volume of gas imported into Europe from other regions (first of all from Northern Africa) may amount to 120 bln cm. In this case an additional demand of European countries for natural gas by 2015 is estimated at 220 bln cm, and if we take into account former European Soviet republics and Turkey, it will be as much as 330 bln cm. The major suppliers of such amounts of gas to the Eurasian gas market may be Russia and Central Asian republics.

Iran, disposing of the second largest natural gas reserves in the world (26 trillion cubic meters), has considerable resources for increasing its gas production and export, though there is no reliable information about a projected increase in extraction. Projected total economic growth being taken into consideration, the growth of the country's domestic consumption of natural gas by 2015 is estimated at 80 bln cm. However, it is hardly probable that the Iranian gas will enter the

European market. Iran is most likely to develop its gas export in the Eastern direction.

As mentioned above, Russia's export potential (minimum estimate) is 170-180 bln cm (including exports from the Far East regions). Despite the ambitious projects of Central Asian republics for increasing gas extraction, it will grow by about 5% annually by 2015 up to 260 bln cm (110 bln cm in Turkmenistan, 100 bln cm in Uzbekistan, and 60 bln cm in Kazakhstan).

In this case, the growth of domestic demand (up to 100 bln cm) being taken into consideration, by 2015 export reserves of Central Asian countries may reach 160 bln cm, which, together with the Russian gas export, will allow Europe's forecasted demand for natural gas to be met.[1]

There are two factors threatening this scenario's realization. The first one is the possibility of directing a part of Central Asian resources to China. The second factor (a political one) is an unstable situation in the region. To implement the scheme of gas delivery from Central Asia, stability in Uzbekistan is of great importance (the Turkmen gas also passes through this country on its way to Europe).

Natural gas can be delivered from Central Asia to the European gas market using two routes, one going through Azerbaijan, Georgia, Turkey and further on through the Mediterranean Sea to Italy and Austria (the southern corridor), the other through Russia to the Ukraine, Belarus, and the EU.

Russia is interested in implementing the latter scheme of gas transportation from Central Asia, because it allows for a maximal use of the available transport infrastructure to actively apply the scheme of substitution of Siberian gas to increase total exports to Europe. It is possible to ship gas from Central Asia through the pipeline Central Asia-Centre now under reconstruction (its capacity is to be raised from 48 bln up to 70 bln cmpy). Besides that, 30-50 bln cm can be transported through the southern route (Baku-Jeyhan corridor).

Thus with respect to the single energy system of the EU and Russia, it is important to enhance the coordination of activities aimed at determining the most rational (efficient) schemes and routes for meeting the demand of the EU, Russia and energy-lacking former USSR republics for energy resources.

6 Conclusion

In conclusion I'd like to say a few words about reforming the Russian gas industry. This issue has also been under discussion for more than one year. It is essential not only from the point of view of the so-called systemic transformation (overcoming the monopoly of Gazprom) but also in the context of creating conditions for increasing oil and gas extraction by independent companies. As was said above, *The Strategy* expects this group of producers to increase the volume of natural gas extraction 2.5-fold, from 70 bln cm up to 170-180 bln cm. They do not

---

[1] Estimated by the experts of the Institute for International Economic and Political Studies, Russian Academy of Sciences.

export gas but enjoy the right to set their own prices when selling gas on the domestic market. Gazprom would also like to sell a part of its gas at arbitrarily-set prices, while independent producers are willing to have access to export shipments.

Gas consumers in other industries, as well as in households, would like the price of gas to remain low. Differing interests find their reflection in different approaches to reforming the gas industry.

The Ministry for Economic Development and Trade adheres to a liberal approach, involving Gazprom's division in the way RAO 'UES of Russia' (Russian joint-stock company 'Unified Energy System of Russia') is divided: with formation of several extracting companies, making a transportation company a separate juridical person, transition over to free price-setting by 2007.

From the point of view of liberal market ideology it is the most acceptable project. The availability of several Russian gas suppliers allows for strengthening competition, reducing prices and making life easier. Yet this is an unrealistic project. In reality, it would involve the division of Gazprom's not only active assets but also external obligations ($13 bln). How long this 'noble deed' will take and how it will affect the volume of gas extraction, no one can say for sure. As a result of this, the volume of Russian gas exports to Europe might well drop (thus the opposite market effect might be obtained). Furthermore, who other than Gazprom could coordinate large-scale projects of developing gas fields in the North of Russia and transporting gas to Europe? Who else if not Gazprom can effectively cooperate with the state gas companies of Central Asian republics when implementing schemes of gas extraction and transportation? Not that Russian private companies succeed in it.

As for the price for Russian gas, the regulated price for gas in the European part of the country last year was $23 per thousand cubic meters. It is to be taken into consideration that the average per capita income in Russia is significantly (five- to sixfold) lower than that in Western Europe. Under these circumstances transition over to world gas prices is both unreasonable and unrealistic. According to the Ministry for Economic Development and Trade, gas price can be increased to $40 to $45 (which is planned over the next several years) without aggravating the problem of non-payments.

On the other hand, all the forecasts agree in that even by 2020, Gazprom's share in gas extraction will still be 75%, which means it will actually remain a monopolist. Gas rates should be controlled by the state.

Liberalization of the market is possible, though the share of gas being sold through commodity exchange cannot exceed 50% of domestic consumption, since the budget sector and households, which account for the other 50%, buy it at a fixed price. Beginning in 2003, gas is being sold through the electronic commodity exchange. Though the volume of trade is insignificant, it is undoubtedly very useful, since it improves sales technologies.

A problem of transparency and reasonableness of regulated rates exists from the point of view of both extraction costs and transport tariffs. Gazprom authorities have promised to secure the transparency of costs of transportation and storage of natural gas, which will increase the transparency of all the costs of the main stages of technological process.

There is also a problem of equal access to the pipe, although equal access was established by the Law on Pipeline Transport. But in practice, problems do exist and the technology of access as such offers advantages for Gazprom. Technology needs to be significantly advanced on the basis of establishing economic responsibilities for the infringement of agreements on gas shipment. More problems are connected with the coordination of gas extraction projects and the development of the transport system as well as with attracting investment for pipeline construction.

References

The Energy Strategy of Russia for the Period of up to 2020 (2003), Ministry of Energy of the RF, Moscow.

Russia's Energy Strategy and the Energy Supply of Europe

Roland Götz

1 The Russian Energy Strategy for the Period Until 2020

In discussing the energy relations between Europe and Russia, the forecasts of the EU as well as the Russian energy strategy may well serve as starting points. The Russian energy strategy for the period until 2020, approved by the Russian government in 2003, is replacing an analogous document from 1995.[1] The preparatory work on the "guidelines" for the new version began in 2000, but it took three more years until a document could be presented which the ministries involved, in particular, the Ministries of Energy and Economy, could agree upon. The new energy strategy is more than just a perpetuation of trends. It is meant to set the course for Russia's energy policy and to serve as a guideline of the administration's energy policy, although it does not have a binding character. This was made clear a few weeks after the strategy was passed, when the Russian government refrained from presenting the Kyoto Protocol to the State Duma for ratification, in spite of the energy strategy providing for this.

According to the energy strategy, the primary strategic goal of the Russian national energy policy is security in the fields of energy and ecology as well as energetic and budgetary efficiency. A threat to energetic security is seen in a deficiency of the energy supply in remote regions, while ecologic security appears to be highly threatened by environmental pollution, more specifically, with regard to oil production. Additionally, the dangers of exploiting the oil and gas deposits in arctic regions are pointed out. In order to reach energetic efficiency, the energy strategy sets the goal to reduce the high energy input in production and to make greater efforts to conserve energy. Budgetary efficiency aims at producing a greater contribution of the energy sector to the state budget. All these strategic goals refer to an important circle of internal problems. However, searching for substantial statements concerning the strategies toward external parties involved, such as the CIS or the EU, would be in vain. It is astonishing that the energy dialogue with the European Union, which on the governmental level is given a high priority, is mentioned only in very short and general terms with respect to energy strategy.[2] Yet what the Russian side has in mind can implicitly be derived from what it says about transport routes and the envisaged export volumes.

As a means of governmental energy policy, the energy strategy mentions the regulation of prices and tariffs, tax, customs and anti-monopoly policy as well as the control of state-owned mineral resources and other state property in the energy sector. In addition to the Ministries of Economy and Energy, the government has the Ministries of Nuclear Energy and Natural Resources, and other administrative bodies, which is more than adequate to regulate the so-called "fuel and energy

---

[1] Energeticheskaya strategiya Rossii. A short description of the energy strategy in English by Alexey Mastepanov is based on the temporary version: <http://europa.eu.int/comm/energy_transport/russia/energy-strategy2020_en.pdf>.

[2] For the relations EU-Russia see: <http://europa.eu.int/comm/external_relations/russia/intro/index.htm>. For the energy dialogue EU-Russia see: <http://www.europarl.eu.int/meetdocs/delegations/russ/20030707%20Moscou/10.pdf>.

complex."[3] Given the multitude of authorities involved, an overall conception, such as the energy strategy, is all the more important.

The strategy proceeds on certain assumptions concerning the general economic development until 2020, and the development of the Russian economy during that period. An "optimistic" scenario presumes that, due to far reaching reforms and a favorable external economic environment, and in particular, to a growth of the world economy of 3.5 percent per year, the Gross Domestic Product of Russia will triple by the year 2020, compared to that in the year 2000. According to this, investment in the energy sector will increase by seven times at the end of the period, and prices for oil and natural gas will be high ($30 per barrel or $138 per 1000 cubic meters). A moderate scenario presumes a growth of the world economy of 2.5 percent per year, and doubling of the Russian GDP in the period from 2000 to 2020, whereby investments will increase short of four times. This scenario assumes lower prices for oil and gas ($18 per barrel or $118 per 1000 cubic meters).

For principal considerations with regard to Russian growth potential, the presumption of an annual economic growth of 6.2 percent, underlying the optimistic scenario, seems to be too high.[4] However, the presumptions concerning the prices of energy sources are more convincing in an optimistic scenario than in a moderate one.

The following analysis is based on the optimistic scenario of the Russian energy strategy.[5] It implies a relatively large amount of production of energy sources and correspondingly large exports. This outlines the maximum contribution of the Russian energy sector to the long-term energy supply of Europe. From the European point of view these figures can serve as a basis to calculate the volume of further diversification of energy imports. Finally, it turns out that Russia will remain the main energy supplier to Europe, but in time, more energy imports must come from other supplier countries.

---

[3] In Russia, the energetic economy is referred to as the "fuel and energy complex" (toplivno-energeticheskiy kompleks). This term goes back to the era of planned economy, when the entire economy was subdivided into "complexes".

[4] Götz, R. (2002/1), pp. 329-331). The main reason for this scepticism is the Russian investment rate which at the beginning of the new decade is less than 20 percent, i.e. only about half of what is necessary for a sustainable growth of 5-6 percent. The Russian energy strategy presupposes that the investment rate will not rise substantially until 2010 and by the end of the prognosis period 2020 will reach only 25 percent of the GNP. Underlying is the expectation of an economic growth without an investment boom.

[5] For reasons of space it is not possible to discuss here the transport infrastructure in particular. An elaboration by the author on this subject will appear in Osteuropa (2004) 8.

2 The Oil Sector of the Economy

2.1 Resources, Production, Investment

By the end of 2001, the Russian oil reserves – referring to the deposits that can be produced under the current economic conditions – had a volume of 9.7 billion tons or 6.4 percent of the worldwide reserves. Thus, Russia is seventh place behind the leading OPEC countries (Saudi-Arabia, Iraq, United Arab Emirates, Venezuela). However, as to the resources, that is, deposits which for economic or technical reasons, are not producible at the moment, or are only assumed, Russia is in first place with 14 percent.[6] Three quarters of the oil reserves are concentrated in the northern part of Western Siberia.

After the crash of the system of planned economy, oil production decreased from its high in the 1980s (550 million tons per year) to approximately 300 million tons. This was due to the closure of existing oil fields and a dramatic decline of new explorations, both of which happened in the context of the restructuring process of the branch, but also as a late consequence of Soviet mismanagement which, ruthlessly exploiting the oil fields under the pressure of the plan, was unable to counterbalance the exhaustion of the large fields by opening up newly discovered fields. Western Siberia became prematurely an "old oil region," where many oil wells were closed without properly removing the oil, because further exploitation would have required great efforts to inject water and gas under pressure.[7]

Two factors were responsible for the rise of the Russian oil sector after 1999: The tripling of oil prices between January 1999 and September 2000, as well as the devaluation of the ruble, saved the Russian oil companies from insolvency, because the higher oil prices produced higher profits from oil exports, while the expenses for production, material and staff, which were calculated in dollars, sank. Secondly, a new generation of oil managers, such as Mikhail Khodorkovsky (Yukos) and Yevgeni Shvidler (Sibillioneft), went on co-operation with foreign oil companies like Halliburton and Schlumberger, whose specialists made a great number of closed oil wells fit for production again.

While in 1999, investments in the Russian oil sector amounted to only $2.6 billion, but reached almost $8 billion in 2001, which, accordingly, brought positive results.[8] The overall requirement of investment in the oil sector for the period from 2000 to 2020, is estimated in the Russian energy strategy to be $230-240 billion or approximately, $12 billion a year. Because the Russian oil sector seems to be quite attractive for Western investors, as the increased activity of BP has demonstrated, this considerable investment volume may, at least approximately, be reached, if the great international oil companies get involved accordingly.

---

[6] Bundesanstalt für Geowissenschaften und Rohstoffe (BGR), (2003), Tab. 2–6, p. 316.

[7] Ziener G. (2003), pp. 62ff.

[8] Calculated on the basis of data in the Russian Statistical Yearbook 2002, p. 578. The prices in rubles are converted at the average Dollar rate.

The Russian energy strategy presumes a second maximum of production for the year 2020, which will nearly reach the Soviet peak volume of the 1980s: about 550 million tons (see table 1). The forecasts of Russian oil companies are even more optimistic than those of the energy strategy in its optimistic version. Yukos is expecting a volume of 550 million tons for 2010, while the energy strategy presumes only 490 million tons.[9] The forecasts of the oil companies are based on presumptions concerning oil fields in Eastern Siberia which are known, but so far unexploited, as well as anticipated new discoveries.[10] Which of the forecasts will come true, the energy strategy or the oil companies, will depend upon the extension of pump capacities outside Russia and also upon the development of the oil price.

2.2 Domestic Consumption

According to the Russian energy strategy, the domestic consumption of crude oil will rise only slightly, from 185 million tons in 2000 to 235 million tons in 2020, which means an annual rise of 1.2 percent, while in the optimistic scenario an average economic growth of 6.2 percent is anticipated. This means that the annual growth of the domestic oil consumption is expected to be 4 percent less than the growth of the GNP, which would be a considerable energy saving effect. It is, however, doubtful that such a reduction of consumption can in fact, be reached. But a continuous economic growth of more than 6 percent per year over a period of almost 20 years, seems rather unlikely. But if an average growth of 3 to 4 percent per year is assumed, an increase in the domestic consumption of somewhat more than 1 percent per year seems to be a realistic presumption.

The domestic consumption of oil depends on the oil price on the Russian domestic market which, unlike gas prices, is not state controlled. Although no details are known, the Ministry of Economy has required the oil industry to an obligatory supply.

2.3 Foreign Trade

According to the Russian energy strategy for 2003, the volume of oil exports, which was 145 million tons in the year 2000, will increase to more than 300 million tons in 2020. Compared with the calculated average annual growth rate of production of 2.4 percent, this means an over proportional increase of 3.8 percent annually. However, exports to Europe will increase in the period 2000-2020, by a little more than 30 million tons from 127.5 million to 160 million tons, or 1.1 percent per year. An increase of the same scope is expected for the exports to the CIS countries, whereas oil exports to other countries like the USA and China, which have been low so far, will rise to about 100 million tons in 2010. Thus, the in-

[9] Stinemetz D. (2003), p. 20–30 (22).

[10] See also Laherrere, J. (2002), pp. 29–35.

crease of oil exports will clearly shift from the West to East. Accordingly, the energy strategy expects the highest increases of oil exports to be from Eastern Siberia.

According to the forecasts of the American Energy Information and the European Commission, the European requirement for oil imports in the period 2000-2020, will increase by about 180 million tons under the premise of a moderate growth of oil consumption, because European oil *consumption* will increase while its *production* in Europe decreases.[11] According to current plans and forecasts, Russia will contribute less than 20 percent to this. Consequently, more than 80 percent of additional import requirements of Europe must be covered from other world regions.[12]

Table 1. Russian Oil on the European Market

	2000	2020	Increase 2000-2020
Net imports of EU-30 (million t)	428	>600	~180
among this,			
imports from Russia (million t)	128	160	~30
Russian share (percent)	30	27	17

Sources of the primary dates: Energy Information Administration (EIA), International Energy Outlook 2003, May 2003; European Commission, Directorate-General for Energy and Transport, European Energy and Transport Trends to 2030, Paris 2003.

However, for Europe (EU-30)[13], Russia will remain the most important individual oil supplier, though its share will slightly decrease from 30 to 27 percent.[14]

[11] The American Energy Information Administration (EIA), an independent statistical department within the US Department of Energy, is regularly publishing data about domestic energy consumption in world regions and individual states in its International Energy Outlook, the May 2003 issue of which is here referred to; see <http://www.eia.doe.gov/oiaf/ ieo/index.html>. In the reference case of an average growth of production and energy consumption in the EU-30 area, the requirement of additional oil imports ist 179 million tons, in the case of low economic growth 75 million tons, and in the case of high growth 324 million tons. By order of the European Commission, a working group under I. Mantzos has presented a new version of the Energy and Transport Trends, which arrived at similar results; see European Commission, Directorate-General for Energy and Transport, European Energy and Transport Trends 2030, Paris 2003, Appendix 2, p. 152, <http://europa.eu.int/comm/dgs/energy_transport/figures/trends_2030/index_en.htm>.

[12] For the prognosticated international trade streams 2025 see EIA, International Energy Outlook 2003, Tab. 14, p. 42, <http://www.eia.doe.gov/oiaf/ieo/index.html>.

[13] Europe is here defined as the whole of Europe, i.e. the European Union extended to about 30 members, including the ten states joining the Union in 2004, plus the South East European candidate countries and Turkey (EU-30), but excluding the CIS countries – notwithstanding the discussion of Russia's position in Europe; for details see the contributions in the special issue of the journal Osteuropa (2003) 9-10.

While in 2000, 88 percent of the Russian oil exports went to Europe (EU-30), this share will, according to the forecast of the energy strategy, be reduced by the year 2020, to approximately 50 percent. In contrast, the share the U.S, and the far East, which in 2000, amounted to no more than 3 percent, will be 1/3 or more by 2020.[15] Thus, the Russian energy strategy expects a diversification of the Russian oil exports, which, from the Russian point of view, will contribute to reducing the dependence on a small number of importing countries.

3 The Natural Gas Sector of the Economy

3.1 Resources, Production, Investment

Having 47.6 trillion cubic meters of natural gas by the end of 2001, Russia disposes of the largest reserves worldwide, followed by Iran (26 trillion cubic meters) and Qatar (14.4 trillion cubic meters).[16] Its share of the overall world reserves is about 30 percent, those of Iran and Qatar 16 percent and 9 percent, respectively. As far as the potentially produceable reserves are concerned, Russia is even more ahead. The main regions of Russian gas production are extending from the Caspian depression northward, covering areas north of the Caspian Sea near Astrakhan, in the Volga-Ural Basin near Orenburg, in the Timan-Pechora Basin on the Western side of the Northern Urals, in the West Siberian Basin East of the Northern Urals, on Yamal Peninsula, in the Kara Sea and in the Russian part of the Barents Sea. Other areas of gas production are by the upper and lower course of the Lena River, and in the northern part of Sakhalin Island. As the costs for the construction of pipelines for natural gas, unless liquified, are higher, in terms of the specific energy content of the transported energy carrier, than those for oil pipelines, it is only profitable to exploit large gas fields in a maximum distance of 4000-5000 km from the consumers.[17]

For the natural gas supply of Western Europe the fields in Western Siberia will remain crucial. Beginning at the latest in 2015, there will be a noticeable decrease of production in these fields, and this will be at the same time that Europe will have an increasing demand on gas imports, because the three West Siberian "giant fields" Urengoy, Yamburg and Medvezhye, which in 2000, supplied 85 percent of the Russian natural gas, are exhausted by 50 percent, 26 percent and 68 percent respectively.[18] The decrease of production will be compensated at best by 2020 by

---

[14] The share of 30 percent or 27 percent respectively refers to the case of an average growth of consumption in EU-30 and, moreover, to the optimistic scenario of the Russian energy strategy.

[15] The share of the CIS countries in Russian oil exports is likely to be approximately 10 percent in the period 2000-2020.

[16] Bundesanstalt für Geowissenschaften und Rohstoffe (BGR), (2003), Tab. 3–4, p. 350.

[17] Ibid., pp. 133-134.

[18] Ibid., p. 368.

the continental Russian giant field Zapolyarnoe, which exploitation of it began in 2001.[19]

Increasing the production of gas would require exploitation on the greater deposits on the Yamal Peninsula and in the Barents Sea (Shtokman Field), which have not been opened yet. This would be a great challenge in terms of extreme climatic conditions and technical feasibility.[20]

The costs for opening up the two arctic offshore gas fields will be tens of billions of U.S. dollars, which is far beyond the financial capacity of Gazprom.[21] When and whether foreign gas companies will be ready to engage in the two regions will depend on whether the planned *Production Sharing Agreements* will meet the interests of all parties involved.[22]

The gas producing capacities of the Russian oil companies, which so far have not been granted access to the pipeline network run by Gazprom, seem to not be properly considered in the energy strategy.[23] About 30 billion cubic meters every year of associated gas from oil production, which so far is either used for heating or is just being flared because of lacking transportation capacities, could be used more efficiently. Moreover, the well-funded Russian oil companies could replace the financially weak Gazprom in exploiting the 500 minor gas deposits which are not opened. In spite of lower daily output and higher running costs compared with the large "old" fields, the exploitation of these fields requires much less investment. While in 2003, the output of the independent companies was about 70 billion cubic meters, the companies say that they could produce 170-250 billion cu-

[19] Zapolyarnoe is to supply 100 bn cubic meters of gas per annum for 15 years (beginning in 2005); see the statements of Gazprom director Aleksandr Ananenkov in his interview with Rustem Tell in: Tribuna, 25.6.2003. For a less pessimistic assessment of the volume of gas production on the three giant fields of Western Siberia see International Energy Agency (IEA)(2002), p. 113–114, <http://library.iea.org/dbtw-wpd/Textbase/nppdf/stud/02/russia2002.pdf>.

[20] For Shtokman see the presentation on the Rosneft homepage , <http://www.rosneft.ru/projects/stockmanovskoye.html>. There it is said that the deposit will be opened up with investments of 18 bn US-$ and that a "plateau production" of 60 bn cubic meters is to be expected.

[21] Götz, R. (2002/2).

[22] In a Production Sharing Agreement (PSA) the division of profits between the foreign investor and the state is agreed on for the entire term of the project, which guarantees that future changes in the tax legislation will have no effect. The Russian government fears that this would give foreign companies unjustified privileges, therefore they prefer open tenders. The State Duma has not approved the majority of planned PSA's in the last few years. See Pravosudov, S. (2003); and Anonymous, Russia Sees No Future for Production Sharing Practices, <http://www.gasandoil.com/goc/company/cnr31842.htm>. The 1999 act on PSA has been substantially improved in 1999 by fixing the priority of PSA regulations over the act on natural resources. In addition, the reservation of export limitation for the investor was abolished.

[23] Only in 2003 Gazprom began to buy natural gas from Lukoil, although at a low price of 22.5 US-$ per 1000 cubic meters; see Gazovyj torg [Gas Deal], in: Ekspert, 27.10.2003.

bic meters if the price would be raised to $50-55 per 1000 cubic meters,[24] provided the independent companies and/or the gas-producing Russian oil companies would be granted access to the pipelines ran by Gazprom on fair conditions. This has been promised by Gazprom, however, there is good reason for skepticism, as the current practice is already a discrimination of the independent producers, delivering them at the mercy of Gazprom.

Investments in the branch of natural gas increased in the 1999-2001 period, from somewhere less than $1 billion to more than $2 billion per year.[25] According to the energy strategy, it will rise until the year 2020, to an average of $10 billion per year, amounting to a total of $170-200 billion. Such investment activity can be reached only if the gas sector will be made more attractive to foreign investors than it is now. As long as there is no greater attractibility for investors, for which there are no indications so far, it must be considered that the amounts of gas production envisaged in the energy strategy cannot be reached.

3.2 Domestic Consumption

In Russia, a great deal of energy-natural gas and electric power which are relatively cheap, are wasted in all phases of production, transportation and consumption, due to outdated and poorly serviced production and transport equipment, as well as inadequate isolation of buildings. A particularly negative impact on the technological evolution of the gas sector has the low domestic price of natural gas.[26] There is no incentive to save gas by means of modernization of the production and processing plants and gas power stations. In Russia, the loss of energy in the production of electric and thermal power from natural gas accounts for as much as 60 percent, while in Western Europe a maximum of 20 percent is tolerable. Technical innovation would enable Russia to save 40-100 billion cubic meters of natural gas per year.[27] It must be doubted that such technical improvement would be feasible on a large scale without raising the domestic price of natural gas.

Whether coal and nuclear power will be able to raise the production of energy until 2020, as envisaged in the Russian energy strategy, will largely depend on the

---

[24] Grivach, A. (2003).

[25] In 1999 they were 22.8 bn Rubles or .9 bn US-$, and in 2001 they had risen to 64.5 bn Rubles or 2.2 bn US-$, underlying an average Ruble/Dollar exchange rate. The Ruble data are taken from the Russian Statistical Yearbook 2002, p. 578.

[26] In 2003, the Russian domestic price for natural gas was approximately 24 US-$ per 1000 cubic meters. The "market price" was noted as 30-35 US-$ per 1000 cubic meters, although there is no such thing as a developed domestic market. The export price on the Russian border was in the same period well over 100 US-$ per 1000 cubic meters, which, however, includes the higher transportation costs compared with the domestic market; see e.g. Reznik, I. (2003).

[27] Report of a meeting of representatives of the regions with Gazprom: Tsena severnogo gaza [The Price of Northern Gas], in: Gazovaya promyshlennost, 30.4.2002.

domestic price policy. The low gas price has so far been keeping coal and nuclear power out of the domestic market while stabilizing the share of natural gas. The Russian domestic price of natural gas is only 1/5 of what is paid for its export on the Western borders of Russia, and it is half of the price of gas delivered to Kazakhstan and, dependent on the season, three to five times cheaper than heavy oil which is used in thermal power plants.[28] According to the planning of the Russian government, the domestic gas price, which was $24 dollars in 2003, will rise to $31 in 2005, and $45 in 2010. Only in 2013, will it reach the level of $55, which in CIS countries, was reached in the year 2003.[29]

It is true that a significant rise in the price of gas would have an effect on the general level of prices, but contrary to the public opinion, higher prices would not affect the population. In 2002, only 13 percent of the gas sold in Russia was supplied directly to the population. As much as 40 percent of the domestic sales went into the generation of electric power, 33 percent to industrial branches such as metallurgy, artificial fertilizer production and chemical industry, and 14 percent was consumed by the housing sector and municipal institutions.[30] While low gas prices for the population are maintained for social reasons, it seems possible to raise them for the industry, and this would not have a serious effect on the general price level. The domestic price of natural gas is a key value of the Russian energy policy: A sufficiently high price provides profits on the domestic market which can be used for financing investments in the increase of the production and export potential without claiming means from the state budget. Moreover, reduced domestic consumption as a result of higher prices helps although it does not reduce scarcely profitable areas of production. Nevertheless, it thereby helps in delaying investments in problematical areas of production. Thus, an adequately higher price for natural gas serves the "rational exploitation of natural resources," which the Russian leadership fails to appreciate.[31]

3.3 Foreign Trade

The rapidly increasing demand of natural gas in Europe is due to the intention to substitute coal and oil by the "clean" natural gas for ecological reasons (emissions of carbon dioxide), and to the progressing "gasification" of European border areas.

---

[28] Materials of the Forum "Russia's Gas in 2003", in: Neftegazovaya vertikal, 9.6.2003; according to a statement of the deputy chairman of the Federal Energy Commission Oleg Zhilin.

[29] Ryazanov, A. (2003).

[30] Ibid.

[31] Prime Minister Kasyanov in a widely noted interview (Vedomosti, 12.1.2004) gave the reasons for a low price of natural gas, stating that a "rational exploitation of natural resources" helps to save investments for the opening up of new gas fields which is unnecessary in the case of a moderate increase of production. By this statement he ignored the fact that a low gas price causes high demand and thus gives incentives for an extension of the production.

While European oil imports are likely to increase in the period between 2000 and 2020, by approximately 40 percent, the demand of gas imports of EU-30, according to the EIA standard forecast, will increase in the case of medium economic growth by more than 200 percent and in the case of low economic growth still by 150 percent.

The multiplication of West European gas imports which is to be expected for the period 2000-2020, is a result of both an increase of consumption by 50-75 percent and a stagnation of Europe's own gas production. This drastic widening gap between increasing consumption and decreasing production of gas makes the European demand on gas imports increase by approximately 300 billion cubic meters and thus, to an extent that exceeds Russia's intentions and potential.

But what are the Russian plans for the gas supply of the European market?[32] While the overall volume of Russian gas exports is to increase between the years 2000 and 2020, by 87 billion cubic meters (= 45 percent), exports to the extended European Union will rise by only 31 billion cubic meters (= 23 percent). Thus, according to the Russian energy strategy, the intended increase of Russian gas production will be predominantly for export into regions outside of Europe. This corresponds to the fact that the increase of gas production is expected not in Western Russia, but in Eastern Siberia and the Far East, from where the gas can be transported either overland or, in the form of liquid gas, by ship to Southeast Asia and the USA. An analogous shift to the East is also to be expected in the increase of oil production.

Table 2. Russian Natural Gas on the European Market

	2000	2020	Increase 2000-2020
Net imports of EU-30, total (billion cubic meters)	200	500	~300
among this, imports from Russia (billion cubic meters)	134	165	~30
Russian share (percent)	67	33	10

Sources of the primary dates: Energy Information Administration (EIA), International Energy Outlook 2003, May 2003; European Commission, Directorate-General for Energy and Transport, European Energy and Transport Trends to 2030, Paris 2003.

While in 2000, about 70 percent of the European (EU-30) gas imports came from Russia, this share will be only 50 percent in 2010 and less than 30 percent in 2020. The remaining deficit of 70 percent will then have to be covered by a multitude of supplier countries, whereby for the time after 2010, no exact forecast is possible. Europe will find itself compelled to increasingly import gas, partly in the form of liquid gas, from countries like Algeria, Libya, Egypt, Nigeria, Iran, Iraq, Qatar and Central Asia.

---

32 It is planned to deliver in 2020 to the CIS countries about 10 bn cubic meters less than in 2000. One should, however, be not too strict with these figures, because the energy strategy gives only an orientation.

In Europe, there seems to be little awareness of this necessity to find new sources for gas. While the slight decrease of the share of Russian oil in European imports is not a cause for concern, the foreseeable decrease of the share of Russian natural gas in European imports raises some questions: How to satisfy Europe's future demand for natural gas? A part from deliveries of liquid gas, suppliers can only be from North Africa, the Middle East and the Caspian region, because for geographical reasons, gas pipelines are economically efficient only at a maximum length of 4000-5000 km.[33] Algeria, next to Russia, is the main supplier for Europe, and will probably be able to raise its deliveries until 2020, from approximately 60 to 120 billion cubic meters, provided that new fields like the Salah region in the Sahara, are opened and new export pipelines to Europe are built. In this case, Algeria could reach an increase of its gas deliveries to Europe which is twice as much as Russia had envisaged in its energy strategy. Libya, too, will be able to raise its so far petty exports from one billion cubic meters to a possible volume of 30-40 billion cubic meters by using the new Green Stream pipeline. Future gas exports from Egypt to Europe will go via the Jordan pipeline to Turkey and in addition, will be realized by liquid natural gas (LNG) projects, thus reaching a possible volume of 30 billion cubic meters in 2020. Nigerian gas deliveries to Europe will be realized only in the form of LNG, because transportation via Algeria is too expensive. Other supplies, which are by now still insignificant but will increase in the future, will come to Europe from Trinidad and Venezuela, and from the Middle East, excluding Iran. Iran will presumably become, next to Algeria, a main supplier of gas when its "super giant field", South Pars, will be connected to the European gas infrastructure, which will be the case only after 2015. Beginning in 2020, 60-100 billion cubic meters can be delivered from Iran to Europe, and from 2025, approximately 150 billion cubic meters. According to these presumptions, gas supplies to Europe from these regions by 2020, will have increased by approximately 250 billion cubic meters, compared with the year 2000, which means that North Africa, the Middle East and the Caspian region will deliver more natural gas to Europe than Russia.

The contracts concluded with Russia providing delivery of natural gas from the Caspian region to Europe almost exclusively through the Gazprom pipeline net. An alternative would be the connection of this region to the pipelines leading from Iran to Europe.

[33] Seeliger, A. (2003); Jens Perner, Die langfristige Erdgasversorgung Europas. Analysen und Simulationen mit dem Angebotsmodell EUGAS, Munich 2002 (Schriften des Energiewirtschaftlichen Instituts, Bd. 60); Perner, J. (2002), pp. 87–103. See also the maps in: Hafner, M. (2002/1); Hafner, M. (2002/2).

Table 3. Gas Exports to Europe (EU-30) from North Africa, the Middle East and the Caspian Region 2000-2020 (billion cubic meters)

	2000	2010	2020	Difference 2000-2020
Algeria	60	85	120	60
Azerbaijan		15	30	30
Egypt		26	31	31
Iran		10	30	30
Iraq		10	20	20
Libya	1	11	27	26
Nigeria	1	15	20	19
Qatar/UAE/Yemen	2	9	16	14
Trinidad	1	5	10	9
Turkmenistan			10	10
Total	65	186	314	249

Sources: Seeliger, A. (2003); Perner, J. (2002); Hafner, M. (2002/1); Robert Schuman Centre/Observatoire Méditerranéen del l'Energie/Sonatrach, Medsupply. Developments of Energy Supplies to Europe from the Southern and Eastern Mediterranean Countries, June 2003, <http://serveur.ome.org/ftpmedsup/>.

Turkey will presumably become an important transit country for natural gas from the Middle East, Iran and the Caspian region.[34] Apart from the pipelines which will have to be combined to a network, it will be necessary to build storage stations and gas liquefaction plants in various places of the extra-European gas compound network.

If deliveries from North Africa and the Middle East, including Iran, indeed increase as described above, a shortage of gas in Europe is not likely to emerge. But this presupposes political stability in the respective regions. It would be helpful if the extra-European suppliers, and Russia as well, could be included in the European energy dialogue.

4 Russia and the Energy Supply of Europe

According to its energy strategy, Russia will continue to increase its energy exports to Europe in the period until 2020. However, this goal can be reached only if there will be considerable investments in the energy sector which include not only new regions of production, but also existing ones. Moreover, a great deal of the entire transportation system must be restored and improved.

To mobilize the necessary amount of domestic and foreign investment capital, there must be favorable conditions of investment. In the first place, there must be confidence in the stability of ownership rights. Investors must be given evidence

[34] See Conference on Natural Gas Transit and Storage in Southeast Europe – An Opportunity to Diversity European Gas Supply?, Istanbul, 31.5. bis 1.6.2002, <http://www. iea.org/about/gas.htm>.

that the state wants its share of the profits of energy enterprises, but does not claim principal ownership and is not confiscating private property.

Moreover, the increase and regional orientation of energy exports, as prognosticated in the energy strategy, requires an adequate business policy on the side of the large oil and gas producing companies. While the Russian state, due to its ownership of *Gazprom*, is able to exert great influence on the business policy in the gas sector, it is much less able to do so in the oil sector, where *Rosneft* is the only company which is still state owned. Nevertheless, by disposing of the production licenses and control of the oil pipelines through *Transneft*, the state also has in this sector, some mechanisms left to give effect to its interests.[35] But which are the interests of the state?

In the energy strategy there are indications of a distinct interest in the control of increased oil and gas exports from the West to East or, in other words, to the world market outside of Europe. Apart from the fact that this is aimed at the future growing energy markets, it can help to promote the envisaged "strategic partnerships" with China/Japan and the USA.

However, relatively modest increases of energy exports to the West (Europe) require strategic decisions, e.g., the improvement of the transport infrastructure. As far as the gas sector is concerned, there are several alternatives: The Yamal-Europe pipeline which goes through Poland can be extended, and/or it is possible to build the Baltic Sea pipeline from Russia to Germany and Great Britain. The option of a southern route from Iran via Turkey to Europe is still beyond Russian planning. In particular, it must be clear whether the projects of extending the Yamal-Europe gas pipeline or the construction of the Baltic Sea gas pipeline are to be pursued simultaneously or in succession and in which order.

Given the fact that Russia is able to satisfy the prognosticated European demand of oil and gas imports only sub-proportionally, deliveries from other countries must increase proportionally. For the oil sector this has little effect, and, in addition, because of the world market character of oil supply there will be no distinct regional center of gravity. In the gas sector, in contrast, the Russian share will decrease relatively distinctly and (as long as LNG will not get a dominant position), due to the dependence on pipelines, is restricted to regions closer to Europe, therefore, a new orientation of the additional supply of Europe toward the south will occur, i.e., to North Africa, the Middle East and the Caspian region. This implies that the mentioned southern route Iran-Europe, will have to be included in the energy dialogue between the EU and Russia.

[35] The nuclear energy industry is completely under control of the Russian state, whereas the coal industry has been almost completely transferred into private property. Because of its little significance for the energy supply of Europe in the forseeable future, the Russian policy in these two fields is not to be discussed here in particular.

Annex

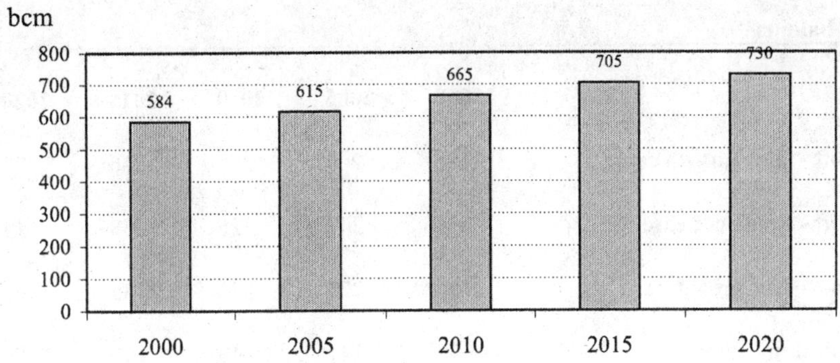

Fig. 1. Russia: Gas production 2000-2020 (optimistic scenario)

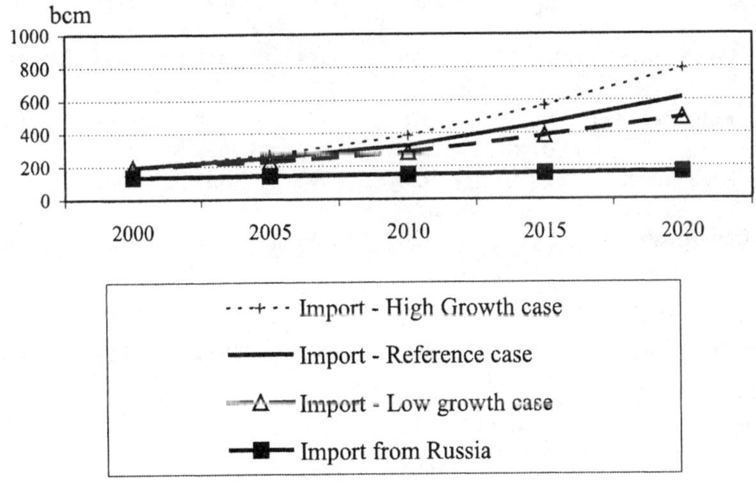

Fig. 2. EU30 Gas import 2000-2020

Table 4. International Energy Outlook

Gas balance					
EU30	**2000**	**2005**	**2010**	**2015**	**2020**
Import - High growth case	196	269	385	566	792
Import - Reference case	196	249	326	458	614
Import - Low growth case	196	227	283	385	495
Import from Russia	134	141	149	157	165
Oil balance					
EU30	**2000**	**2005**	**2010**	**2015**	**2020**
Import - Low growth	428	453	458	483	503
Import - Reference case	428	473	508	568	608
Import - High growth	428	498	563	662	752
Import from Russia	128	135	143	151	160
Gas Bcm bn cm	**2000**	**2005**	**2010**	**2015**	**2020**
Production	584	615	665	705	730
Oil Mt Mio. t	**2000**	**2005**	**2010**	**2015**	**2020**
Production	324	447	490	506	520

Energetičeskaja strategija Rossii na period do 2020 goda [Energiestrategie Rußlands bis 2020], http://www.mte.gov.ru/files/103/1354.strategy.pdf>.

Energy Information Administration (EIA), International Energy Outlook, Mai 2003, <http://www.eia.doe.gov/ oiaf/ieo/index.html>.

Natural Resources and Economic Growth: From Dependence to Diversification

Thorvaldur Gylfason[1]

[1] This chapter, under a slightly different heading, was presented at an international workshop on "Sustainable Economic Liberalization and Integration Policy: Options for Eastern Europe and Russia," organized by European Institute for International Economic Relations (EIIW), University of Wuppertal, Germany, and held in Brussels on April 24-26, 2004.

1 Introduction

This chapter reviews some aspects of the experience of natural-resource-rich countries around the world since the 1960s. The discussion will emphasize five main channels through which natural resource intensity appears to have inhibited economic growth across countries. By natural resource intensity is meant the extent to which a country depends on its natural resources. Resource abundance *per se* need not do any harm: many countries have abundant natural resources and have managed to outgrow their dependence on them by diversifying their economic activity. An important challenge to policy makers in many developing countries with abundant natural resources is to find ways to reduce their dependence on these resources, through successful diversification of economic activity. The chapter offers some suggestions along these lines. As we proceed, an attempt will be made to provide a glimpse of some of the empirical results that have emerged in recent years from studies of the cross-country relationships between natural resource dependence and economic growth and various key determinants of growth across the world. Even if the evidence reviewed below is exclusively cross-sectional, it reflects a general pattern that accords well with a number of historical case studies of individual resource-rich countries.[2] This broad review is followed by a brief discussion of the disappointing economic growth record of the OPEC countries, and then by a brief discussion also of the lessons that may be drawn from Norway's singularly successful management of its oil wealth.

2 Five Channels: Theory and Evidence

The structure of recent models of the relationship between natural resource intensity and economic growth is nearly always the same. An abundance of or heavy dependence on natural resources is taken to influence some variable or mechanism "X" which impedes growth. An important challenge for economic growth theorists and empirical workers in the field is to identify and map these intermediate variables and mechanisms. This chapter is an attempt in this direction.

To date, five main channels of transmission from natural resource abundance to slow economic growth have been suggested in the literature.[3] As we shall see, these channels can be described in terms of crowding out: a heavy dependence on natural capital, it will be argued, tends to crowd out other types of capital and thereby inhibit economic growth. Let us now consider the five channels one by one.

---

[2] For a number of such case studies, see Auty (2001).

[3] This discussion draws on and extends Gylfason and Zoega (2001).

2.1 Channel 1: The Dutch Disease and Foreign Capital

An overvalued currency was the first symptom associated with the Dutch disease following the discovery of natural gas deposits within the jurisdiction of the Netherlands in the North Sea in the late 1950s and early 1960s, but subsequently several other symptoms came to light. Natural resource dependence is, as a rule, accompanied by booms and busts: the prices of raw materials fluctuate a great deal in world markets, and so do supplies. The resulting fluctuations in export earnings trigger exchange rate volatility, perhaps no less so under fixed exchange rates than under floating rates. Unstable exchange rates create uncertainty that can be harmful to exports and other trade, including foreign investment. Further, the Dutch disease can strike even in countries that do not have their own national currency. In this case, the natural-resource-based industry is able to pay higher wages and also higher interest rates than other export and import-competing industries, thus making it difficult for the latter to remain competitive at world market prices. This problem can become particularly acute in countries with centralized wage bargaining (or with oligopolistic banking systems, for that matter) where the natural-resource-based industries set the tone in nation-wide wage negotiations and dictate wage settlements and banking arrangements that other industries can ill afford.[4]

In one or all of these ways, the Dutch disease tends to reduce the level of total exports or bias the composition of exports away from those kinds of high-tech or high-value-added manufacturing and service exports that may be particularly good for growth over time. Exports of capital – i.e., inward foreign direct investment (FDI) – may also suffer in the same way. The mechanism is essentially the same. In other words, natural capital tends to crowd out foreign capital, broadly speaking.

These linkages seem to accord well with the experience of the Arab world, a natural place to start an empirical overview of the macroeconomic consequences of abundant natural resources. Figure 1 presents relevant empirical evidence for two groups of Arab countries, a group of six countries that do not belong to the Organization of Petroleum Exporting Countries, OPEC (Egypt, Jordan, Morocco, Sudan, Syria, and Tunisia) and a group of six OPEC countries (Algeria, Iran, Kuwait, Libya, Saudi Arabia, and United Arab Emirates).[5] Figure 1a shows that the nonoil-producing countries have achieved, on average, a significant increase in their total exports relative to GDP since 1960. Meanwhile, the total exports of the oil-producing countries have declined as a proportion of GDP. Hence, oil exports appear to have crowded out nonoil exports.

[4] Greenland, which uses the Danish krone, is a case in point (Paldam, 1997). Greenland's fishing industry dominates the national economy to the virtual exclusion of other manufacturing.

[5] Some of the countries in the first group, especially Egypt and Tunisia, produce and export oil, but they do so on a smaller scale than OPEC countries in the second group.

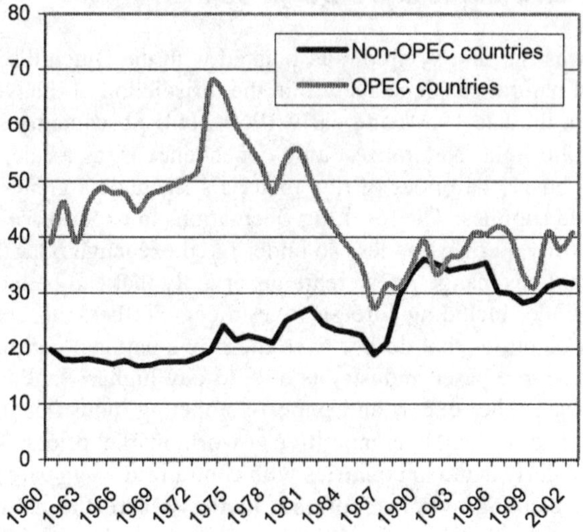

Fig. 1a. Arab Countries: Exports of Goods and Services 1960-2002 (% of GDP)

Figure 1b tells a similar story about FDI, but here the pattern is less clear. In the nonoil-producing Arab countries, gross FDI hovered around one percent of GDP until the late 1990s, and then increased to two to three percent of GDP. In the oil-producing countries, foreign investment relative to GDP exhibited a similar pattern until the late 1990s (except for the boom in FDI in Saudi Arabia following the first oil price hike in 1973-1974), and then fell below one percent of GDP.

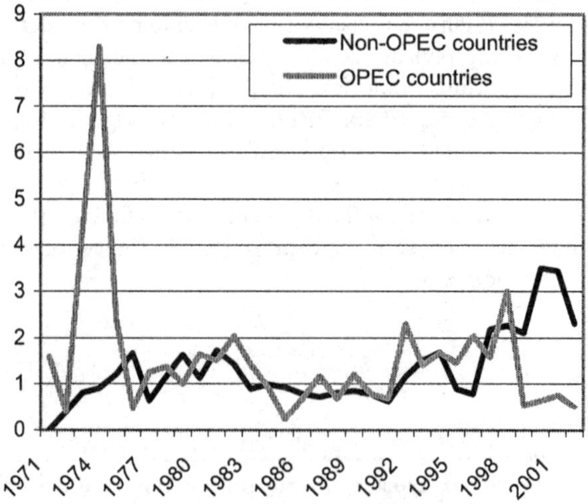

Fig. 1b. Arab Countries: Gross Foreign Direct Investment 1971-2002 (% in GDP)

Figure 1c shows that the share of manufacturing exports in total merchandise exports in the nonoil-producing Arab countries increased from about ten percent in the 1960s to 40-50 percent in the 1990s, while the same ratio has hovered around ten percent in the oil-producing Arab countries without showing a strong tendency to rise over time. These things matter because exports and foreign investment are good for growth (Frankel and Romer, 1999). Openness to trade and investment stimulates imports of goods and services, capital, technology, ideas, and know-how. Furthermore, too much primary-export dependence and too little manufacturing may hurt economic growth over the long haul. The upshot of this is that the Dutch disease is a matter of concern mainly because of its potentially deleterious consequences for economic growth.

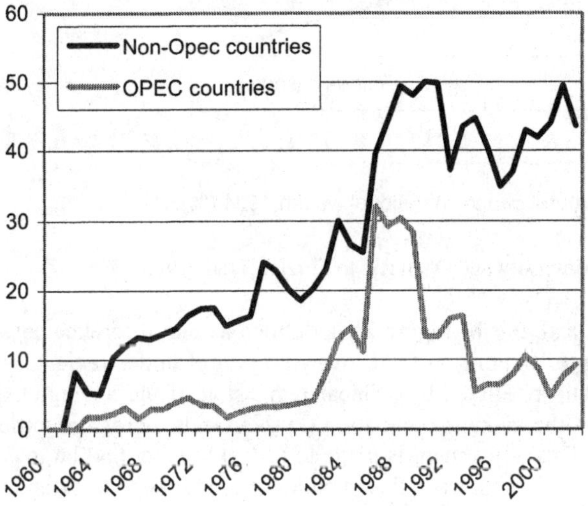

Fig. 1c. Arab Countries: Manufacturing Exports 1962-2002 (% of Total Exports)

What is the empirical evidence from other parts of the world? Figure 2a shows a scatterplot of natural resource intensity and openness to external trade around the world. The figure covers 85 countries. Natural resource intensity, which is measured along the horizontal axis, is measured by the share of natural capital in national wealth in 1994 – i.e., the share of natural capital in total capital, which comprises physical, human, and natural capital (but not social or financial capital; see World Bank, 1997). The natural capital share used here is close to the source: it is intended to come closer to a direct measurement of the intensity of natural resources across countries than the various proxies that have been used in earlier studies, mainly the share of primary (i.e., nonmanufacturing) exports in total exports or in gross domestic product (GDP) and the share of the primary sector in employment or the labor force.[6] The latter proxies may be prone to bias due to product and labor market distortions.

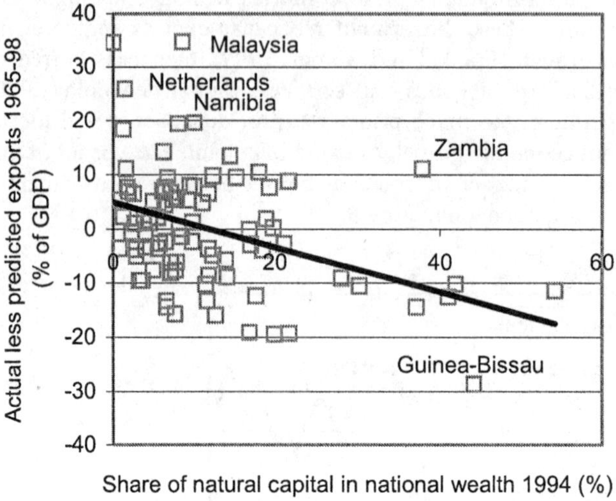

Fig. 2a. Natural Resource Intensity and Openness to Foreign Trade 1965-1998

Openness on the vertical axis of Figure 2a is defined as the difference between the actual average ratio of exports to GDP over the period under review, 1965-1998, and the export ratio predicted by a linear regression of the average export ratio on the logarithm of the average population (in thousands) across countries to adjust for country size. This adjustment is made to reflect the fact that large countries are less dependent on foreign trade than smaller ones that need to extend their home markets beyond their national borders to make up for their small size. This indicator of openness is larger than zero for countries that are more open to trade than their size predicts, and smaller than zero for countries that are less open to trade than their size predicts. The 85 countries in the sample are represented by one observation each for each variable under study.

The regression line through the scatterplot in Figure 2a suggests that an increase of ten percentage points in the natural capital share from one country to an-

---

[6] The year 1994 is the only year for which the World Bank has as yet produced data on natural capital, for 92 countries. In most cases, however, natural capital in 1994 is probably a pretty good proxy for natural resource abundance or intensity in the period under review, 1965-1998. There are some exceptions, true, but even so all the empirical results reported in this chapter can be reproduced without significant deviations by using the average share of primary exports in total exports or GDP or the average share of the primary sector in total employment during 1965-1998 rather than natural capital in 1994 as a proxy for natural resource abundance, and also by measuring growth in terms of GNP per worker rather than GNP per capita.

other is associated with a decrease in the openness indicator by about four percent of GDP on average. The relationship is economically as well as statistically significant; Spearman's rank correlation is -0.31.[7] Given existing evidence that foreign trade is good for growth, Figure 2a suggests that natural resource intensity may hurt growth by harming trade.

It needs to be emphasized that no conclusions are being drawn here as to cause and effect. Figure 2a is only intended to display the data in a way that accords with the results of multivariate regression analyses that can help account for more potential determinants of exports and openness to trade (Gylfason, 1999), and where an attempt was made to distinguish cause from effect. The same disclaimer applies to all the figures that follow. Even so, the study of bivariate cross-sectional relationships has many shortcomings. For one thing, such studies bypass the diversity of individual country experiences. For another, they do not account for economic developments over time, as panel studies are designed to do.

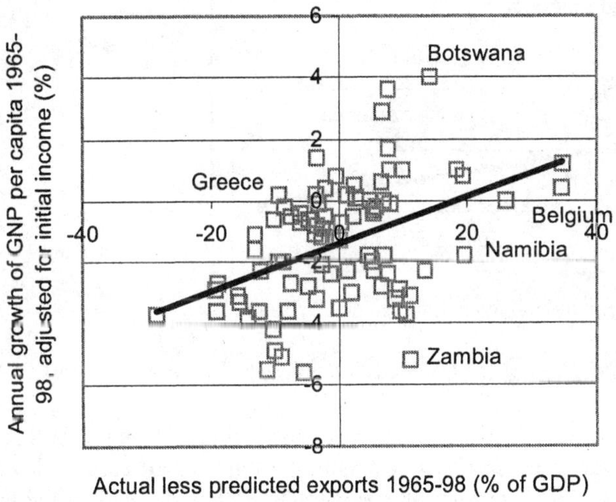

Fig. 2b. Openness to Foreign Trade and Economic Growth 1965-1998

Figure 2b shows a scatterplot of openness as defined above and economic growth per capita from 1965 to 1998. The figure covers the same 85 countries as before. The growth rate has been adjusted for initial income: the variable on the vertical axis is that part of economic growth that is not explained by the country's initial stage of development, obtained from a regression of growth during 1965-1998 on the logarithm of initial GNP per capita (i.e., in 1965) as well as natural capital. The regression line through the scatterplot in Figure 2b suggests that an increase of 14 percentage points in the openness indicator from one country to an-

[7] Because it is based on ranks rather than on actual values, the Spearman correlation is less sensitive to outliers than is the more commonly used Pearson correlation.

other is associated with an increase in per capita growth by one percentage point per year on average. The relationship is thus economically as well as statistically significant; Spearman's rank correlation is 0.40. The data thus seem to support the time-honored view that openness to foreign trade is good for growth.

Taking Figures 2a and 2b together, we see that an increase in the natural capital share by ten percentage points goes along with a four point decrease in the index of openness to foreign trade which, in turn, goes hand in hand with a decrease in annual per capita growth by about 0.3 percentage points.

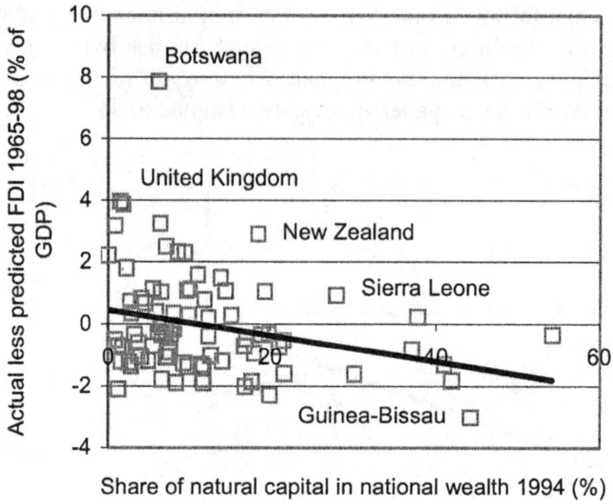

Fig. 2c. Natural Resource Intensity and Openness to Foreign Investment 1965-1998

How about openness to foreign direct investment? Figure 2c suggests that the natural capital share varies inversely with openness to gross FDI across the same 85 countries as before. The indicator of openness to FDI is defined in the same way as the corresponding indicator of openness to foreign trade, i.e., as the as the difference between the actual average ratio of gross FDI to GDP over the period under review, 1965-1998, and the FDI ratio predicted by a linear regression of the average FDI ratio on the logarithm of the average population (in thousands) across countries to adjust for country size. The relationship between natural resource intensity and openness to FDI is not very strong, true, but it is nonetheless economically as well as statistically significant. Notice that no country with a natural capital share above 20 percent as an FDI index above one percent of GDP. The slope of the regression line through the scatterplot suggests that an increase in the natural capital share by ten percentage points goes along with a decrease in the FDI index by 0.4 percent of GDP; the rank correlation is -0.24.

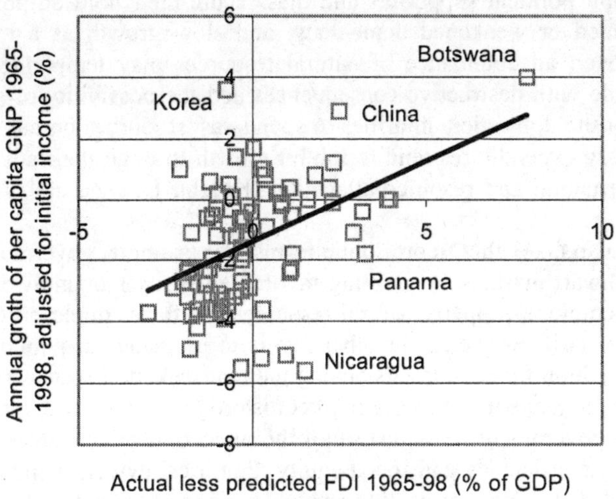

Fig. 2d. Openness to Foreign Investment and Economic Growth 1965-1998

Figure 2d shows the relationship between openness to FDI and per capita growth from 1965 to 1998. Specifically, an increase in gross FDI by two percent of GDP goes along with an increase in per capita growth by one percentage point. The rank correlation is 0.44. Adding Figures 2c and 2d together, we see that an increase in the natural capital share by ten percentage points goes along with a decrease in the FDI index by 0.4 percent of GDP which, in turn, entails a decrease in annual per capita growth by about 0.2 percentage points.

In sum, then, since openness to foreign trade and investment is good for growth by Figures 2b and 2d, Figures 2a and 2c suggests that natural resource dependence may hurt growth by harming foreign trade and investment.

2.2 Channel 2: Rent Seeking and Social Capital

In second place, huge natural resource rents, especially in conjunction with ill-defined property rights, imperfect or missing markets, and lax legal structures in many developing countries and emerging market economies, may lead to rampant rent-seeking behavior on the part of producers, thus diverting resources away from more socially fruitful economic activity (Auty, 2001; Gelb, 1988). The combination of abundant natural resources, missing markets, and weak institutions may have quite destructive consequences. In extreme cases, civil wars break out – such as Africa's diamond wars – which not only divert factors of production from socially productive uses but also destroy societal institutions and the rule of law. In other, less extreme cases, the struggle for huge resource rents may lead to a concentration of economic and political power in the hands of elites that, once in power, use the rent to skew the distribution of income and wealth in their favor as well as to placate their political supporters and thus secure their hold on power, with inequality, stunted or weakened democracy, and slow growth as a result (Karl, 1997). Moreover, an abundance of natural resources may tempt foreign governments to invade with destructive consequences and the possibility of such an event may prompt the domestic authorities to spend vast resources on national defense. Large military expenditures tend to inhibit growth through their adverse effects on capital formation and resource allocation (Knight, Loayza, and Villa-neuva, 1996).

Rent seeking can also take other, more subtle forms. For example, governments may be tempted to thwart markets by granting favored enterprises or individuals privileged access to common-property natural resources, as, for example, in Russia, or they may offer tariff protection or other favors to producers at public expense, creating competition for such favors among the rent seekers. Extensive rent seeking – i.e., seeking to make money from market distortions – can breed corruption in business and government, thus distorting the allocation of resources and reducing both economic efficiency and social equity. Empirical evidence and economic theory suggest that import protection (which is often extended to foreign capital as well as goods and services), cronyism, and corruption all tend to impede economic efficiency and growth (Bardhan, 1997; Mauro, 1995).

Furthermore, abundant natural resources may imbue people with a false sense of security and lead governments to lose sight of the need for good and growth-friendly economic management, including free trade, bureaucratic efficiency, and institutional quality (Sachs and Warner, 1999). Put differently, abundant natural capital may crowd out social capital, by which is meant the infrastructure and institutions of a society in a broad sense: its culture, cohesion, law, system of justice, rules and customs and so on, including trust (Woolcock, 1998; Paldam and Svendsen, 2000). Incentives to create wealth through good policies and institutions may wane because of the relatively effortless ability to extract wealth from the soil or the sea. Manna from heaven can be a mixed blessing. The argument can be extended to unconditional foreign aid. There are indications that natural-resource-rich countries are more dependent than others on foreign aid, which may actually exacerbate their economic predicament.

Let us now consider three different aspects of the corrosion of social capital that can follow from rent seeking, starting with corruption. Insofar as natural resource abundance involves public allocation of access to scarce common-property resources to private parties without payment, thereby essentially leaving the resource rent up for grabs, it is only to be expected that resource-rich countries may be more susceptible to corruption than others. What do the data say?

In Figure 3a, the share of natural capital in national wealth is plotted along the horizontal axis as before and the corruption perceptions index for the year 2000 along the vertical axis.[8] The figure covers 55 countries, all the countries from our original sample of 85 for which both data series are available. The corruption perceptions index (from Transparency International, Berlin) is constructed from information obtained from businessmen who are willing to report how often and

[8] Corruption rankings for earlier years (1995-1999) give similar results.

how forcefully bribes and the like are demanded of them in various countries, and how high these are. The index extends from zero, in countries where corruption is greatest, to ten, where corruption is practically nonexistent (as, for example, in Finland and Denmark). The picture shows a clear and statistically significant relationship: corruption, as measured by this index, increases from one country to the next in accordance with the increase in natural resource intensity. When the share of natural capital in national wealth goes up by nine percentage points from one place to another, the corruption perceptions index drops (i.e., corruption increases) by one point per year on the average, for given initial income. This is not a small effect – if it is an effect, that is, as opposed to a mere correlation. The pattern is quite significant; the rank correlation is -0.42.[9]

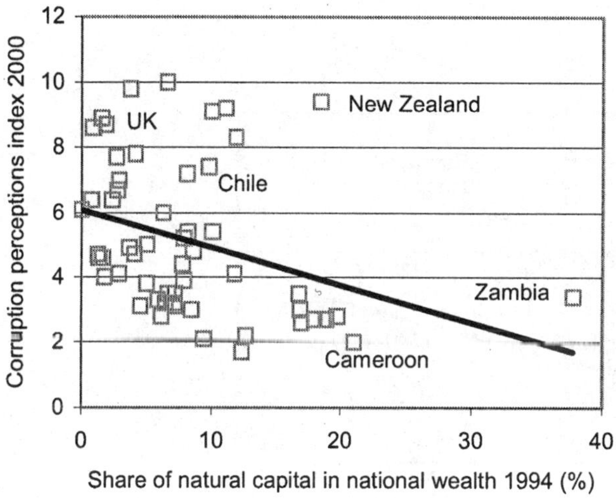

Fig. 3a. Natural Resource Intensity and Corruption 1994-2000

Figure 3b shows the pattern of corruption and economic growth across the same 55 countries as in Figure 3a. We now measure corruption – or rather, honesty – along the horizontal axis and per capita growth along the vertical axis. There is a discernible tendency for honesty to go along with economic growth. The rank correlation is 0.42. A decrease in the corruption perceptions index by four points (i.e., increased corruption), corresponding to the corruption differential between the United States (7.8) and Turkey (3.8), is associated with a decrease in per capita growth by one percentage point. This result is the same as that reported by Mauro (1995) whose econometric evidence also suggests that a decrease in the corruption index by four points from one country to the next is associated with a

[9] When the corruption perceptions index is purged of that part which is caused by initial income, the results remain unchanged.

reduction in per capita growth of one percentage point per year on the average. Corruption does not pay, at least not in a macroeconomic perspective.

Taking Figures 3a and 3b together, we see that an increase in the natural capital share by 36 percentage points goes hand in hand with a decrease in the corruption perceptions index by four points (Figure 3a), which in turn goes along with a decrease in per capita growth by one percentage point per year on the average, for given initial income (Figure 3b). Here we have another possible reason why natural resource intensity appears to inhibit economic growth across countries.

Next, consider income inequality. There are two schools of thought about the relationship between inequality and economic growth. Some claim that inequality is good for growth because too much equality weakens incentives to work, save, and acquire an education. Others think that inequality is bad for growth because too much inequality reduces social cohesion and creates conflict. What do the data say?

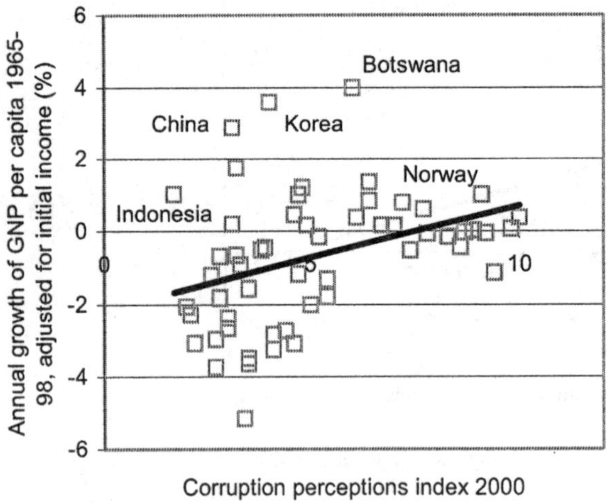

Fig. 3b. Corruption and Economic Growth 1965-1998

Figure 3c shows that the share of natural capital in national wealth is positively correlated with income inequality as measured by the Gini coefficient; the rank correlation is 0.41. The Gini index measures the extent to which income (or, in some cases, consumption) among individuals or households within an economy deviates from a perfectly equal distribution. A Gini index of zero represents perfect equality while a Gini index of 100 means perfect inequality.[10] Notice that no

[10] While Gini coefficients based on net (i.e., after-tax) incomes are preferable in principle as measures of income inequality, the Gini coefficients published by the World Bank are more often than not based on gross (i.e., before-tax) incomes. Hence, the equalizing effects of taxes and transfer schemes on the distribution of income are not fully reflected in

country with a natural capital share above 25 percent has a Gini coefficient below 45.

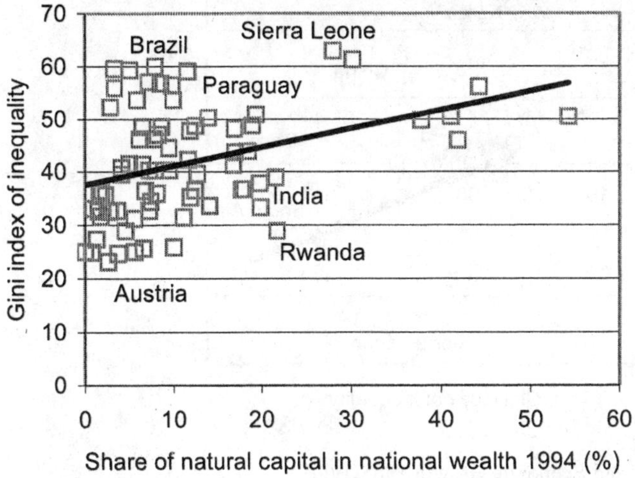

Fig. 3c. Natural Resource Intensity and Inequality 1994-2000

Figure 3d shows a scatterplot of per capita growth as measured before and the inequality of income or consumption as measured by the Gini coefficient (World Bank, 2000, Table 2.8).[11] The figure covers 75 countries, all from our original sample for whom the requisite data are available. Each country is represented by one observation as before. The regression line through the scatterplot suggests that an increase of about 12 points on the Gini scale from one country to another – corresponding to the difference in income distribution between India (Gini = 38) and Zambia (Gini = 50), for example – is associated with a decrease in per capita growth by one percentage point per year on average. The relationship is statistically significant; the rank correlation is -0.50.[12] A reduction in a country's annual per capita growth rate by one percentage point is a serious matter because the (weighted) average rate of per capita growth in the world economy since 1965 has been about 1½ percent per year.

the Gini coefficients used here. The data come from nationally representative household surveys and refer to different years between 1983-85 and 1998-99. See World Bank (2000), Table 2.8.

[11] Our sample does not include any transition economies because, for them, there is no information available on natural capital, which is one of the key determinants of growth in our framework. See Gylfason and Zoega (2001).

[12] See Gylfason and Zoega (2003) for similar cross-country correlations between economic growth and both land inequality (-0.37) and gender inequality (-0.32). In our data, the distribution of income and land is highly correlated (0.57).

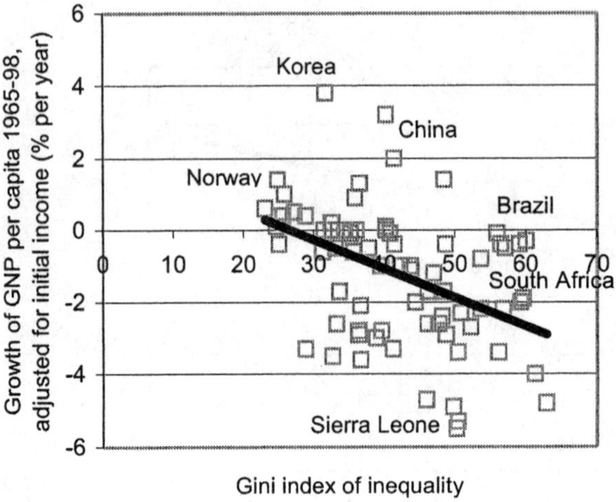

Fig. 3d. Inequality and Economic Growth 1965-1998

We now turn to political liberties, another essential ingredient of social capital. The political liberties index used here is an average for the period 1972-1990 and is taken from Przeworski et al. (2000). The index ranges from one (full political liberties) to seven (negligible political liberties). *A priori*, it is not obvious what to expect from the empirical evidence. One might speculate that natural resource riches seem likely to stifle political liberties by increasing the costs to the powers that be of being removed from power through the political process because their loss of political power would entail also their loss of control over the natural resource rents. If so, abundant resources may tend to go hand in hand with political oppression. After all, none of the oil-rich countries in the Middle East is a full-fledged democracy. On the other hand, it could be argued that natural resource wealth, if well managed, could be used to create conditions for political as well as economic and social progress by fostering political liberalization. Along similar lines, some observers have argued that political liberties are good for growth because they facilitate the peaceful replacement of bad governments by better ones through popular elections. Others have argued that there can be too much of a good thing, i.e., that too much liberty may be misused in the political arena to derail good governance through pressure group activity and such.[13] What do the data say?

[13] Barro (1997, p. 2) puts it as follows: "Another adverse feature of representative democracy is the strong political power of interest groups, such as agriculture, environmental lobbies, defense contractors, and the handicapped."

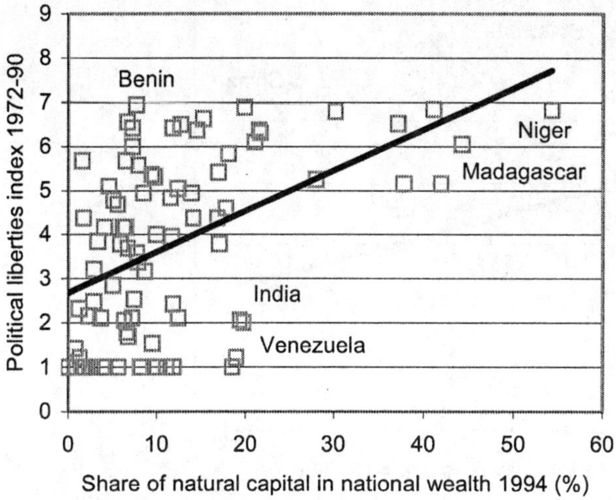

Fig. 3e. Natural Resource Intensity and Political Liberties 1972-1990

Figure 3e shows a tendency for natural resource intensity measured as before to be inversely related to political liberties across countries, all 84 countries for which both series are available (data on political liberties in Namibia are missing). The pattern observed is significant in a statistical sense: the rank correlation is 0.50. An increase in the natural capital share by 11 percentage points goes along with a one point increase in the political liberties index, which means a decrease in liberty corresponding to the difference between India (2.0) and the United Kingdom (1.0), for example. All the countries with a natural capital share above 20 percent or so have limited political liberties. The removal of this cluster of eight countries from the sample does not materially reduce the statistical significance of the correlation shown in Figure 3e. In Figure 3f, we see the pattern of per capita growth and political liberties: an increase in freedom of two points, corresponding roughly to the difference between Thailand (4.2) and Botswana (2.1), is associated with an increase in per capita growth of more than one percentage point per year. The pattern in the figure suggests that political liberties are good for growth, and vice versa. The rank correlation is -0.63.

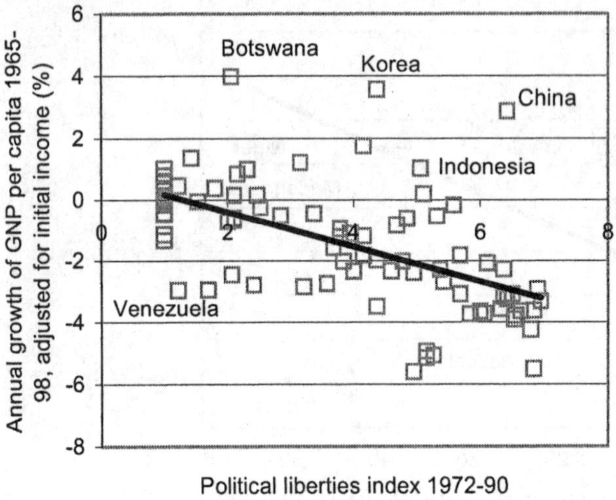

Fig. 3f. Political Liberties and Economic Growth 1965-1998

2.3 Channel 3: Education and Human Capital

Natural resource abundance or intensity may reduce private and public incentives to accumulate human capital due to a high level of non-wage income – e.g., dividends, social spending, low taxes. Awash in cash, natural-resource-rich nations may be tempted to underestimate the long-run value of education. Of course, the rent stream from abundant natural resources may enable nations to give a high priority to education – as in Botswana, for instance, where government expenditure on education relative to national income is among the highest in the world. Even so, empirical evidence shows that, across countries, school enrolment at all levels is inversely related to natural resource abundance or intensity, as measured by the share of the labor force engaged in primary production (Gylfason, Herbertsson, and Zoega, 1999). There is also evidence that, across countries, public expenditures on education relative to national income, expected years of schooling, and school enrolment are all inversely related to natural resource abundance (Gylfason, 2001a; see also Temple, 1999). Once again, abundant natural capital appears to crowd out human capital. This matters because more and better education is good for growth.[14]

As far as economic growth is concerned, however, the supply of education may matter less than demand (Birdsall, 1996). This is relevant here because public expenditure on education tends to be supply-led and of mediocre quality, and may thus fail to foster efficiency, equality, and growth, in contrast to private expenditure on education, which is generally demand-determined and thus, perhaps, likely

[14] For a survey of education and growth in OECD countries, see Temple (2000).

to be of a higher quality and more conducive to growth. For this reason, we use school enrolment rates rather than public expenditures on education as a measure of education in the empirical analysis to follow.

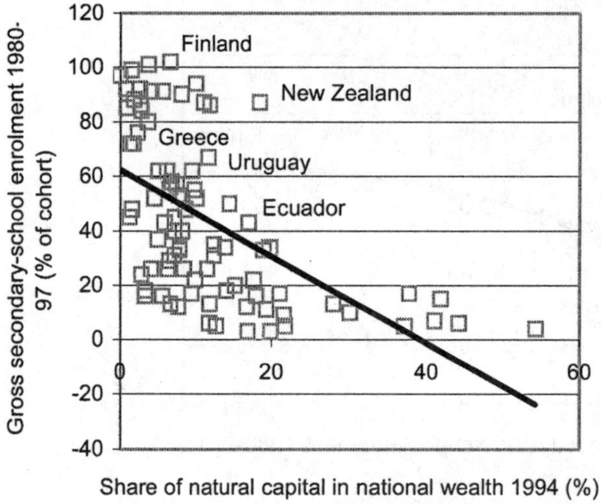

Fig. 4a. Natural Resource Intensity and Secondary Education 1980-1997

Figure 4a shows a scatterplot of secondary-school enrolment as a percentage of each cohort from 1980 to 1997 on the vertical axis and, on the horizontal axis, the natural capital share measured as before. Imperfect though it is, secondary-school enrolment is the most commonly used yardstick for education in the empirical growth literature. Even so, other measures of education such as primary-enrolment rates, tertiary-enrolment rates, public expenditures on education, and years of schooling for girls or boys yield similar results (Gylfason, 2001a). The regression line through the 85 observations suggests that an increase of ten percentage points in the natural capital share from one country to the next is associated with a decrease in secondary-school enrolment by 15 percentage points. The Spearman rank correlation is -0.65.

Figure 4b shows a scatterplot of secondary-school enrolment for both genders from 1980 to 1997 and economic growth. If we fit a straight line through the scatter (not shown), the figure shows that a 25 percentage point increase in secondary-school enrolment goes along with a one percentage point rise in the annual rate of growth of GNP per capita. In fact, the relationship is significantly nonlinear, indicating decreasing returns to education, and it is, moreover, statistically significant (the rank correlation is 0.72). The number of observations is once again 85. It needs to be emphasized that school enrolment reflects, at best, the quantity of education provided rather than the quality of education received. Public expenditure on education is also positively correlated with economic growth across countries in our sample (not shown), but the correlation is not significant in a statistical sense.

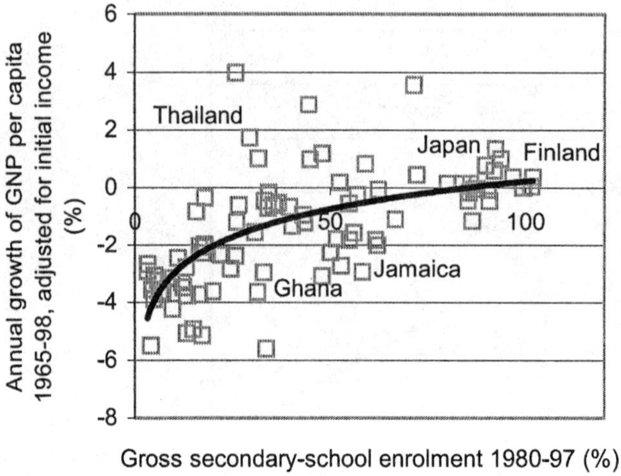

Fig. 4b. Secondary Education and Economic Growth 1965-1998

Taking Figures 4a and 4b together, we see that, across countries, secondary-school enrolment is inversely related to natural resource abundance and directly related to economic growth. Specifically, an increase in the natural capital share by 17 percentage points goes along with a decrease in secondary-school enrolment by 25 percentage points according to Figure 4a, which, in turn, goes along with a decrease in economic growth by one percentage point by Figure 4b. Therefore, high natural resource intensity seems capable of reducing economic growth significantly, not only through the Dutch disease, rent seeking, and overconfidence that tends to reduce the quality of economic policy and structure, but also by weakening public and private incentives to accumulate human capital. If so, the adverse effects of natural resource abundance on economic growth since the 1960s that have been reported in the literature may in part reflect the effect of education on growth.

How can we interpret these results? Natural-resource-based industries as a rule are less high-skill labor intensive and perhaps also less high-quality capital intensive than other industries, and thus confer relatively few external benefits on other industries (Wood, 1999). Moreover, workers released from primary industries, such as agriculture, fisheries, forestry, or mining, often have relatively limited general, labor-market relevant education to offer new employers in other industries. There are exceptions, though, such as in modern agriculture and, indeed, in high-tech oil-drilling operations. But insofar as high-skill labor and high-quality capital are less common in primary production than elsewhere, this may help explain why natural resource abundance and the associated preponderance of primary production and primary exports tend to impede learning by doing, technological advance, and economic growth. This linkage reinforces the case for investment in education and training as an engine of growth: more and better education tends to shift comparative advantage away from primary production towards manufacturing and services, and thus to accelerate learning by doing and growth.

2.4 Channel 4: Saving, Investment, and Physical Capital

Natural resource abundance may blunt private and public incentives to save and invest and thereby impede economic growth. Specifically, when the share of output that accrues to the owners of natural resources rises, the demand for capital falls, and this leads to lower real interest rates and less rapid growth (Gylfason and Zoega, 2001). Moreover, if mature institutions are conducive to an efficient use of resources, including natural resources, and if poorly developed institutions are not, then natural resource abundance may also retard the development of financial institutions in particular and hence discourage saving, investment, and economic growth through that channel as well. As in the case of education, it is not solely the volume of investment that counts because quality – i.e., efficiency – is also of great importance. Unproductive investments – white elephants! – may seem unproblematic to governments or individuals who are flush with cash thanks to nature's bounty.

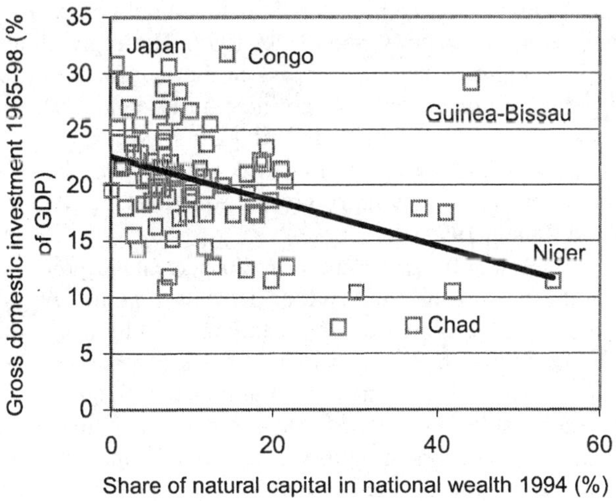

Fig. 5a. Natural Resource Intensity and Investment 1965-1998

Figure 5a shows a scatterplot of the average ratio of gross domestic investment to GDP in 1965-1998 and natural resource abundance or intensity measured as before. The regression line through the 85 observations suggests that an increase of about ten percentage points in the natural capital share from country to country is associated with a decrease in investment by two percent of GDP. The relationship is statistically significant: the rank correlation -0.38.

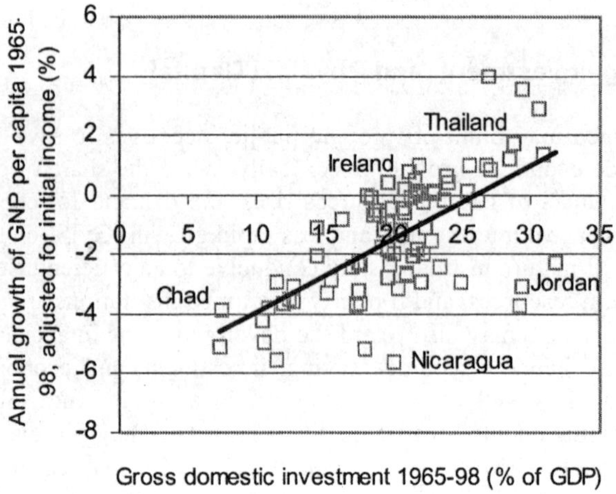

Fig. 5b. Investment and Economic Growth 1965-1998

Figure 5b shows a scatterplot of economic growth as measured before and the average investment ratio over the same period, 1965-1998. The regression line through the 85 observations suggests that an increase in the investment ratio by about four percentage points is associated with an increase in annual economic growth by one percentage point. The relationship is highly significant: the rank correlation is 0.65. The slope of the regression line is consistent with the regression coefficients on investment in cross-country growth equations reported in recent literature (Levine and Renelt, 1992).

In sum, an increase in the natural capital share by 20 percentage points goes along with a decrease in the investment ratio by four percentage points by Figure 5a, which in turn goes along with a decrease in economic growth by one percentage point by Figure 5b. Thus, the empirical evidence seems consistent with the idea that an abundance of or heavy dependence on natural resources may erode or reduce the quality of physical capital as well as foreign, social, and human capital, and thus stand in the way of rapid economic growth on a significant scale. It is a matter of taste and classification whether the some or even all the mechanisms reviewed above are regarded as additional symptoms of the Dutch disease or as separate channels of transmission from resource dependence to slow growth. But we are not done yet.

2.5 Channel 5: Money, Inflation, and Financial Capital

Figure 6a shows a cross-sectional scatterplot of financial development, for which we use the average ratio of braod money (M_2) and GDP in 1965-1998 as a proxy, like King and Levine (1993), and natural resource dependence as measured before. The figure covers the same 85 countries as before. Figure 6a shows a clear negative correlation between natural resource dependence and financial depth (the rank correlation is -0.68).[15] Natural capital seems to crowd out financial capital. Figure 6b relates our measure of financial development to average economic growth per capita over the same period. The relationship is positive and the rank correlation is 0.66. But the question of causality remains. It is possible that heavy dependence on natural resources actually hinders the development of the financial sector and also growth, as appears plausible, but other possibilities also exist; in particular, some unspecified third factor may inhibit both financial development and economic growth. Naturally, the same reservation applies to all the other correlations presented in this chapter.

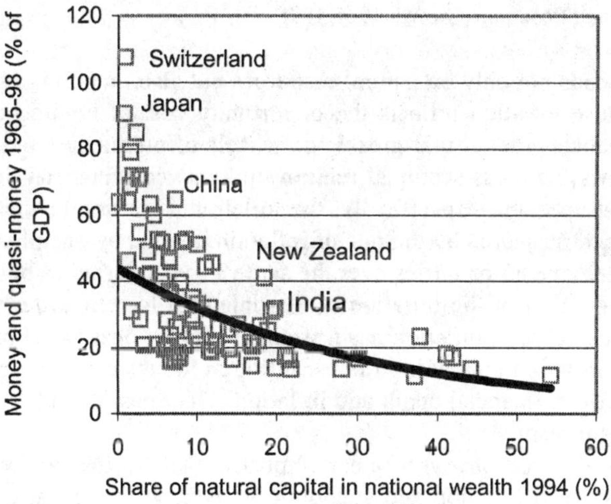

Fig. 6a. Natural Resource Intensity and Financial Depth 1965-1998

[15] The exponential regression curve becomes steeper if the regression is confined to the 77 countries where the natural capital share is below 0.25, but the correlation remains highly significant (-0.61).

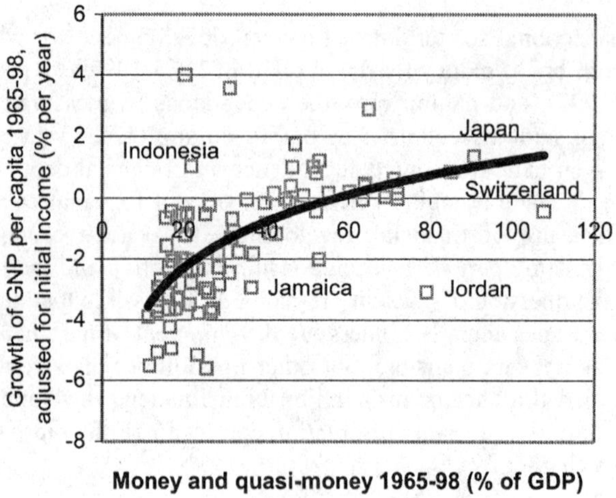

Fig. 6b. Financial Depth and Economic Growth 1965-1998

Financial depth depends not only on natural resources but also, importantly, on inflation. This is because inflation reflects the opportunity cost of holding cash and other forms of financial capital that grease the wheels of production and exchange. Figure 6c shows the cross-sectional relationship between financial depth as measured above and inflation – specifically, the inflation distortion or the implicit rate of inflation tax, measured by the rate of inflation divided by one plus the rate of inflation – in the same 85 countries over the same 33-year period as before. This nonlinear transformation of the inflation rate is intended to reflect the phenomenon that a given decrease in inflation has a stronger proportional effect on liquidity at low rates of inflation than at high rates. In Figure 6c we can see a clear inverse association between financial depth and inflation. The Spearman rank correlation is -0.45 and significant.

Adding Figures 6b and 6c conveys a clear impression of an inverse cross-country relationship between inflation and economic growth, *via* financial depth or maturity. Inflation hurts growth by depriving the economic system of necessary lubrication. There is, however, no clear evidence of a two-dimensional correlation between inflation and growth around the world. The reason is that the relationship between inflation and growth is a complicated one, and involves several factors other than financial maturity, as mentioned before – among them, real interest rates and saving, real exchange rates and trade, and probably also political governance and stability. The relationship between inflation and growth is too complicated to be discernible to the naked eye as a two-dimensional cross-country correlation summarizing the impressions conveyed by Figures 6b and 6c. Even so, the relationship exists as can be ascertained by multiple regression analysis (for a recent survey, see Temple 2000).

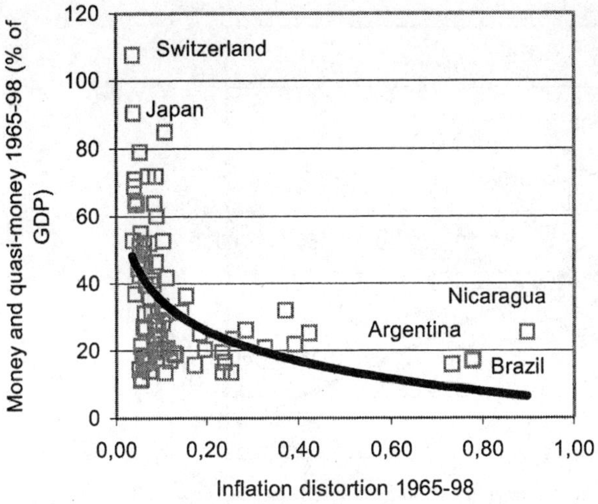

Fig. 6c. Inflation and Financial Depth 1965-1998

2.6 Natural Capital and Economic Growth

To conclude the story, Figure 7a shows a scatterplot of economic growth per capita from 1965 to 1998 and natural resource intensity as we have measured it here. Once more, the figure covers the same 85 countries as before. The growth rate has been adjusted for initial income as before. The regression line through the scatterplot in Figure 7a suggests that an increase of about ten percentage points in the natural capital share from one country to another is associated with a decrease in per capita growth by one percentage point per year on average.[16] The relationship is also significant in a statistical sense (Spearman's rank correlation is -0.64), and conforms to the partial correlations that have been reported in multiple regression analyses where other relevant determinants of growth (investment, education, etc., as well as initial income to account for catch-up and convergence) are taken into account. A relationship of this kind has been reported in a number of recent studies (Sachs and Warner, 1995, 1999; Gylfason and Herbertsson, 2001; Gylfason, Herbertsson, and Zoega, 1999).

[16] There is admittedly an element of statistical bias in Figure 7a in that increased education and investment increase human and physical capital, thereby reducing the share of natural capital in national wealth *and* increasing economic growth. This bias, however, is probably not serious because Figure 7a can be reproduced by using different measures of natural resource abundance, such as the share of the primary sector in the labor force or the share of primary exports in total exports or GDP.

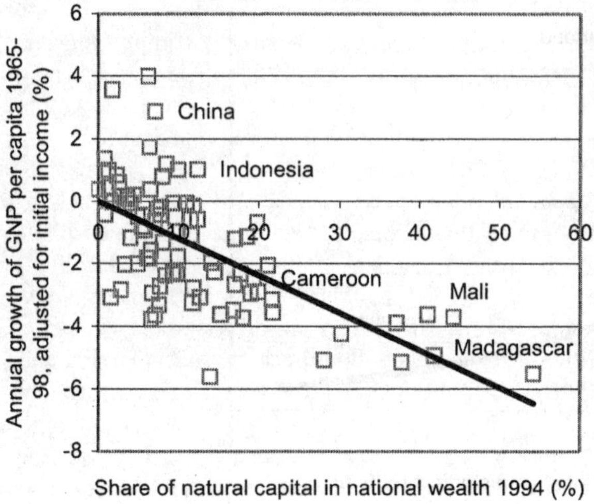

Fig. 7a. Natural Resource Intensity and Economic Growth 1965-1998

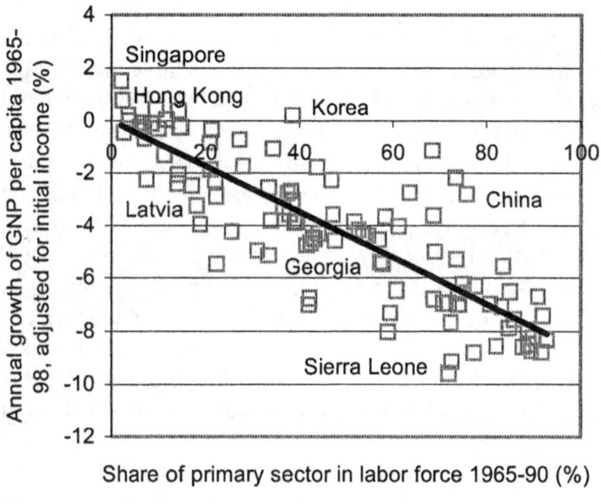

Fig. 7b. Natural Resource Intensity and Economic Growth 1965-1998, again

At last, therefore, Figure 7b shows the relationship between economic growth and natural resource intensity when the latter is measured by the share of the primary sector in total employment.[17] There are now 105 countries in the sample because the primary labor share is available for many more countries than the natural capital share. The relationship is negative, and highly significant. The Spearman correlation is -0.85. The adjustment for initial income entails a speed of convergence of about 2 percent a year (not shown), a common result in empirical growth research. An increase of 11 or 12 percentage points in the primary labor share from one country to the next goes along with a decrease in per capita growth by one percentage point per year on average, for given initial income.

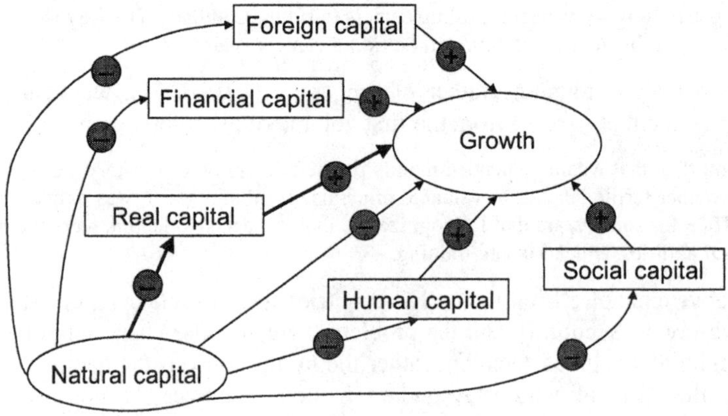

Fig. 8. Determinants of Growth

The punch line of the foregoing argument is summarized in Figure 8, which shows how natural capital affects economic growth directly as well as indirectly by crowding out other types of capital through the five channels of transmission outlined above. Let us now leave the cross-sectional evidence to one side and consider the experience of individual countries.

3 The Experience of the OPEC Countries and Norway

In most countries that are rich in oil, minerals, and other natural resources, economic growth over the long haul tends to be slower than in other countries that are less well endowed. For example, in Nigeria, with all its oil wealth, gross national product (GNP) per capita today is no higher than it was at independence in 1960.

[17] Notice that the growth measures are slightly different than before. The reason is that the adjustment for initial income is based on different measures of natural resource abundance, and the primary labor share in Figure 7b and the natural capital share everywhere else. This difference has no material effect on the patterns displayed in the figures.

Nedadi Usman, Nigeria's economy minister, has said in a newspaper interview: "Oil has made us lazy." And Nigeria is not alone. From 1965 to 1998, the rate of growth of GNP per capita in Iran and Venezuela was on average -1 percent per year, -2 percent in Libya, -3 percent in Iraq and Kuwait, and -6 percent in Qatar (1970-1995), to mention six other OPEC countries (World Bank, 2000). For OPEC as a whole, GNP per capita actually *decreased* by 1.3 percent on average during 1965-1998 compared with 2.2 percent average per capita growth in all lower- and middle-income countries. King Faisal of Saudi Arabia (1964-1975) would hardly have been surprised, for he sized up the situation as follows (quoted from a newspaper interview with his oil minister, Shaikh Yamani):

> In one generation we went from riding camels to riding Cadillacs. The way we are wasting money, I fear the next generation will be riding camels again.

Lee Kwan Yew, founding father of Singapore (1959-1991), would not have been surprised either (quoted from the first volume of his autobiography):

> I thought then that wealth depended mainly on the possession of territory and natural resources, whether fertile land ..., or valuable minerals, or oil and gas. It was only after I had been in office for some years that I recognized ... that the decisive factors were the people, their natural abilities, education and training.

The above examples from the OPEC countries seem to reflect a consistent pattern as we saw in Section II. But the problem there and elsewhere is not the existence of natural wealth as such, but rather the failure to avert the dangers that accompany the gifts of nature. Abundant natural resources do not necessarily prevent the emergence of a dynamic economy. The discovery of natural resources does not necessarily dampen an already developed economy. Natural resources can be a blessing as well as a curse. Norway, indeed, is a case in point.

The world's third largest oil exporter (after Saudi-Arabia and Russia), Norway shows as yet no clear symptoms of the Dutch disease – other, perhaps, than a stagnant ratio of exports to GDP, albeit at a rather high level. Norway and Iceland, historically dependent on its fisheries, are the only industrial countries whose exports of goods and services have grown no more rapidly than their GDP since 1960 (in Iceland's case, the stagnation of exports relative to GDP reaches as far back as the data, to 1870). In Norway, manufacturing exports have fallen sharply in proportion to GDP and total merchandise exports since the mid-1970s: the share of manufacturing in total exports declined from 60 percent in 1974 to 22 percent in 2002. Moreover, Norway has attracted a relatively limited, yet gradually increasing inflow of gross FDI, equivalent to five percent of GDP in 2002, far below the figures for Sweden and Finland next door (13 percent and 15 percent). The lack of interest among a majority of the Norwegians in joining the European Union – a proposition they have rejected in two referenda, in 1972 and 1994 – may well reflect similar forces as Norway's failure to fully open up to foreign trade and investment: many Norwegians consider their country so rich, thanks to their oil wealth, that they have no need for EU membership.

Norway does not show any signs yet of socially damaging rent-seeking behavior even if increasingly loud calls are being voiced for using more of the oil revenue to address domestic social needs rather than continue to build up the government-owned oil fund, which is invested in foreign securities. There are no clear signs either of a false sense of security or of an inadequate commitment to education, on the contrary Growth has thus far remained stubbornly high. Even so, some observers of the Norwegian scene have recently expressed concerns that some deep-seated structural problems in the country's education and health care sectors (government monopoly, insufficient competition, low efficiency, etc.) may be misdiagnosed as financial problems because the money available from the oil fund may blunt the willingness of politicians to undertake difficult structural reforms.

One of the factors that separate Norway's experience from that of OPEC is timing. Norway was already a developed country and a democracy at the time of the oil discoveries in the 1970s. Most importantly, Norway's social institutions were mature and the financial system relatively well developed, although by no means fully liberalized. All of this facilitated judicious and far-sighted management of Norway's oil wealth, at least compared with most other oil producers (Hannesson, 2001). In contrast, full-fledged capitalist development did not take place in most OPEC countries prior to the discovery of their oil resources, or since for that matter (Karl, 1997). While Norway has built up substantial assets abroad, Saudi-Arabia has accumulated debts.

Norway has charted a long-run-oriented, tax-based, and reasonably market-friendly approach to the management of its vast oil resources, estimated at 50-250 percent of GNP depending on oil prices (Thøgersen, 1994). By law, the oil wealth belongs to the State. In principle, all the rent from oil and gas should accrue to the Norwegian people through their government. The State's title to these resources constitutes the legal basis for government regulation of the petroleum sector as well as for its taxation. Exploration and production licenses are awarded for a small fee to domestic and foreign oil companies alike. The Norwegian government expropriates the oil and gas rent through taxes and fees as well as direct involvement in the development of the resources rather than through sales or auctioning of exploration and production rights (OECD, 1999). The State has a direct interest in most offshore oil and gas fields and, like other licensees, receives a corresponding proportion of production and other revenues. Through its direct partnership with other licensees as well as through various taxes and fees, it is estimated that the Norwegian State has managed to absorb about 80 percent of the resource rent since 1980.[18] In 1997, revenues from petroleum activities accounted for more than a fifth of total government revenues and amounted to eight to nine percent of total GNP, including oil. In 2000, the oil sector's contribution rose to more than 25 percent of GNP, but it is envisaged to drop to five percent by 2020. The oil revenue is deposited in the Petroleum Fund, which was established in 1990 and is being built up and invested mostly in foreign securities for the benefit of the current generation of Norwegians when they reach old age as well as for future generations, and also in order to shield the domestic economy from overheating and possible waste – a shrewd strategy, efficient and fair. In 1999, the management of the Petroleum

[18] The main revenue items are corporate tax (28 percent) and a special resource surtax (50 percent), but also royalty (8-16 percent), area fee, and carbon-dioxide tax.

Fund was transferred from the Ministry of Finance to the Bank of Norway in order to distance the fund further from political considerations in view of the central bank's increased freedom from political interference in keeping with recent developments in central banking practices and legislation.

Even so, a variable proportion of each year's net oil-tax revenue is transferred from the Petroleum Fund to the fiscal budget, essentially to cover the nonoil budget deficit. The proportion of net tax revenues from petroleum thus transferred to the government budget is envisaged to drop to less than ten percent in the years ahead. The Norwegians have not chosen to expand their central government beyond reasonable limits, or at least not to extravagant levels, as a result of the oil boom. Decades after discovering their oil, the Norwegians continue to live with smaller central government than Denmark, Finland, and especially Sweden, even if local government has expanded in terms of expenditure and manpower.

Norway's long tradition of democracy and market economy since long before the advent of oil has probably helped immunize the Norwegian people from the ailments that inflict most other oil-rich nations. Large-scale rent seeking has been averted in Norway, investment performance has been adequate, and the country's education record is excellent. For example, the proportion of each cohort attending colleges and universities in Norway rose from 16 percent in 1970 to 70 percent in 2000. It is not certain, however, whether the average quality of college education in Norway has changed in tandem with – or perhaps, as some fear, in inverse proportion to – the huge increase in enrolment since 1970.

Even so, Norway faces challenges. Some (weak) signs of the outbreak of the Dutch disease can be detected, as was indicated above, notably stagnant exports, the absence of a large, vibrant high-tech manufacturing industry (as in Sweden and Finland next door), and sluggish FDI. But perhaps the main challenge is to make sure that the oil fund does not instill a false sense of security, a feeling that anything goes and that difficult decisions can be deferred or avoided. To this end, it may be necessary to find new ways to immunize the fund from political interference, just as other key institutions – the courts, media, central banks – have been depoliticized over the years. The transfer of the fund to the Bank of Norway a few years ago was a step in this direction. Further immunization may require privatization, by, for example, turning the oil fund over to the people in the form of pension savings. It is not certain, however, that such a solution would be perfect, for the private sector is not infallible either. Another, intermediate solution might be to invest the authority to dispose of the oil revenues in a special independent, yet democratically accountable and fully transparent authority in accordance with the spirit of modern central banking legislation in countries that have granted their central banks and financial inspection agencies substantial independence from political interference. This would severe the link between the allocation of oil revenues and monetary policy considerations. Perhaps it would be most advisable to adopt a mixed strategy, with shared public and private responsibility for the disposal of the oil wealth, in order to spread the risks and reconcile different points of view.

4 Concluding Remarks

Natural resources bring risks. This chapter has reviewed the cross-country evidence of the various ways in which a heavy dependence on natural resources may adversely affect economic growth performance. Natural-resource-based activity sometimes drives the real value of the domestic currency up to levels that other export industries and import-competing industries find difficult to cope with, thus reducing the economy's openness to foreign trade and investment. Further, too many people tend to become locked in low-skill intensive natural-resource-based industries, including agriculture, and thus fail through no fault of their own to advance their own or their children's education and earning power. Another related risk is that the authorities and other inhabitants of resource-rich countries become overconfident and therefore tend to underrate or overlook the need for good economic policies and institutions as well as for good education and good investments. Excessive dependence on natural resources can thus weaken various societal institutional arrangements that need to be strong for the economy to grow briskly. The empirical evidence presented in this chapter suggests that a heavy dependence on nature's bounty tends to be directly associated with corruption, inequality, and political oppression, all of which tend to impede economic progress and growth. Moreover, the evidence suggests that high natural resource intensity is inversely associated with financial depth – i.e., with the development of monetary and financial institutions and policies that keep inflation low and the economic system well lubricated, thereby advancing economic growth.

In short, nations that believe that natural capital is their most important asset may develop a false sense of security and become negligent about the accumulation of foreign, social, human, physical, and financial capital. Indeed, resource-rich nations can live well of their natural resources over extended periods, even with poor economic policies and institutions and a weak commitment to education, trade, and investment. Awash in easy cash, they may find that difficult reforms do not pay. Nations without natural resources have a smaller margin for error, and are less likely to make this mistake. In resource-rich countries, awareness of these risks, as well as a conscious effort and ability to contain them, is perhaps the best insurance policy against them. The experience of Norway shows, however, that efficient and far-sighted management of abundant oil wealth is clearly possible.

References

Auty, R. M. (2001) (ed.), *Resource Abundance and Economic Development,* Oxford University Press, Oxford and New York.

Bardhan, P. (1997), "Corruption and Development: A Review of the Issues," *Journal of Economic Literature* 35, September, 1320-1346.

Barro, R. J. (1997), *Getting It Right: Markets and Choices in a Free Society*, MIT Press, Cambridge, Massachusetts.

Birdsall, N. (1996), "Public Spending on Higher Education in Developing Countries: Too Much or Too Little?", *Economics of Education Review* 15, No. 4, 407-419.

Frankel, J. A., and D. Romer (1999), "Does Trade Cause Growth?," *American Economic Review* 89, June, 379-399.

Gelb, A. (1998), *Windfall Gains: Blessing or Curse?*, Oxford University Press, Oxford and New York.

Gylfason, T. (1999), "Exports, Inflation, and Growth," *World Development* 27, June, 1031-1057.

Gylfason, T. (2001a), "Natural Resources, Education, and Economic Development," *European Economic Review* 45, May, 847-859.

Gylfason, T. (2001b), "Nature, Power, and Growth," *Scottish Journal of Political Economy* 48, November, 558-588.

Gylfason, T., and T. T. Herbertsson (2001), "Does Inflation Matter for Growth?," *Japan and the World Economy* 13, December, 405-428.

Gylfason, T., T. T. Herbertsson, and G. Zoega (1999), "A Mixed Blessing: Natural Resources and Economic Growth," *Macroeconomic Dynamics* 3, June, 204-225.

Gylfason, T., and G. Zoega (2001), "Natural Resources and Economic Growth: The Role of Investment," CEPR Discussion Paper No. 2743, March.

Gylfason, T., and G. Zoega (2003), "Inequality and Economic Growth: Do Natural Resources Matter?", Chapter 9 in T. Eicher and S. Turnovsky (eds.), *Growth and Inequality: Theory and Policy Implications*, MIT Press.

Hannesson, R. (2001), *Investing for Sustainability: The Management of Mineral Wealth*, Kluwer Academic Publishers, Dordrecht, the Netherlands.

Karl, T. L. (1997), "The Perils of the Petro-State: Reflections on the Paradox of Plenty," *Journal of International Affairs* 53, Fall, 31-48.

Knight, M., N. Loayza, and D. Villaneuva (1996), "The Peace Dividend: Military Spending and Economic Growth," *IMF Staff Papers* 43, No. 1, 1-37.

Levine, R., and D. Renelt (1992), "A Sensitivity Analysis of Cross-Country Growth Regressions," *American Economic Review* 82, September, 942-963.

Mauro, P. (1995), "Corruption and Growth," *Quarterly Journal of Economics* 110, August, 681-712.

OECD (1999), *Economic Surveys: Norway*, OECD, Paris, Ch. 3.

Paldam, M. (1997), "Dutch Disease and Rent Seeking: The Greenland Model," *European Journal of Political Economy* 13, No. 1, 591-614.

Paldam, M., and G. T. Svendsen (2000), "An Essay on Social Capital: Looking at the Fire behind the Smoke," *European Journal of Political Economy* 16, No. 2, 339-366.

Przeworski, A., M. E. Alvarez, J. A. Cheibub and F. Limongi (2000), *Democracy and Development: Political Institutions and Well-Being in the World, 1950-1990*, Cambridge University Press, Cambridge.

Sachs, J. D., and A. M. Warner (1995, revised 1997, 1999), "Natural Resource Abundance and Economic Growth," NBER Working Paper 5398, Cambridge, Massachusetts.

Sachs, J. D., and A. M. Warner (1999), "Natural Resource Intensity and Economic Growth," Ch. 2 in J. Mayer, B. Chambers, and A. Farooq (eds.), *Development Policies in Natural Resource Economies*, Edward Elgar, Cheltenham, UK, and Northampton, Massachusetts.

Temple, J. (1999), "A Positive Effect of Human Capital on Growth," *Economics Letters* 65, 131-134.

Temple, J. (2000), "Inflation and Growth: Stories Short and Tall," *Journal of Economic Surveys* 14, September, 395-426.

Temple, J. (2000), "Growth Effects of Education and Social Capital in the OECD," ECO Working Papers No. 263, October.

Thøgersen, Ø. (1994), "Economic Policy, Macroeconomic Performance and the Norwegian Petroleum Wealth: A Survey", Stiftelsen for Samfunns- og Næringslivsforskning, Norges Handelshøyskole, Bergen, unpublished manuscript.

Wood, A. J. B. (1999), "Natural Resources, Human Resources and Export Composition: a Cross-country Perspective", Ch. 3 in J. Mayer, B. Chambers, and A. Farooq (eds.), *Development Policies in Natural Resource Economies*, Edward Elgar, Cheltenham, UK, and Northampton, Massachusetts, 1999.

Woolcock, M. (1998), "Social Capital and Economic Development: Toward a Theoretical Synthesis and Policy Framework," *Theory and Society* 27, 151-208.

World Bank (1997), "Expanding the Measure of Wealth: Indicators of Environmentally Sustainable Development," *Environmentally Sustainable Development Studies and Monographs Series* No. 17, World Bank, Washington, D.C.

World Bank, *World Development Indicators 2000*, World Bank, Washington, D.C., 2000.

Corruption and Public Investment Under Political Instability: Theoretical Considerations

Frank Bohn[1]

[1] I am grateful for comments from my former colleagues at Essex University Tatiana Damjanovic, Gordon Kemp, Adrian Masters, Suresh Mutuswami and Sam Wilson. All remaining errors are mine. – Comments most welcome

1 Introduction

Political instability makes governments behave myopically, because beneficial effects of their policies may not accrue to them in the future. This may lead to underinvestment in infrastructure or reluctance in promoting structural change. Political instability may also explain the lack of determination in some governments' fight against corruption, even in cases when those governments do not benefit from corruption themselves.

This paper studies public investment under political instability. The main result is that there is a political instability threshold below which the government is so myopic that it does not want to invest at all. Going above the threshold leads to a strong increase in investment, at first, because additional political stability effectively increases the discount factor for the future. However, the additional investment increments (for more and more political stability) become smaller because marginal investment profitability goes down.

The result is obtained in a parsimonious model framework. The paper investigates a government's optimal choice between (i) public goods spending and (ii) public investment. To keep the revenue side as simple as possible a proportional income tax is modelled. Other sources of revenue could also be incorporated as done in other papers on political instability: seigniorage as in Cukierman, Edwards and Tabellini (1992), domestic debt as in Devereux and Wen (1998), or seigniorage and foreign debt as in Bohn (2000)[2]. However, the idea is to show a fundamental mechanism. The results do not primarily depend on economic, but rather on political (stability) conditions.

Sections 2 and 3 present the intertemporal framework of the theoretical model. Sections 4 and 5 summarize and simplify the government maximization problem. Interior and corner solutions are discussed in sections 6 and 7. Section 8 concludes.

2 Government Preferences and Political Instability

The model captures the intertemporal decision problem of the government. It consists of two periods: period 1 (current period) and period 2 (next period). There are two sectors in the economy: (i) the government and (ii) the private sector. The model is specified in real terms.

Government preferences over periods 1 and 2 are given by the following utility function:

$$W = V_1(C_1) + H_1(G_1, F_1) + E\{\rho(V_2(C_2) + H_2(G_2, F_2))\} \tag{1}$$

The V.(•) functions are concave and twice continuously differentiable utility functions of the government in private sector consumption C. The H.(•) functions

[2] As in this paper, Svensson (1998) also models public investment, but interprets it as property rights investment and studies its impact on private investment.

are the utility functions in the government provision of public goods G and F. E is the expectation operator and $\rho < 1$ is the government's discount factor. Total government utility is additively separable in two senses: first, with respect to periods; and second, with respect to utility derived either from private consumption or from public goods provision.

Assuming two types of governments (i.e. policymakers) political instability comprises two features: (i) the probability of government change and (ii) political polarization. After the first period the incumbent government may loose office to the other set of policymakers with a fixed probability π; it stays in power with probability $(1 - \pi)$[3]. It is assumed that there are two ethnic or social groups. Each one benefits more from one of the two public goods. Each of the two types of government provides both types of public goods, but to differing degrees. Political polarization then depends on the differences of policymakers' preferences with respect to their public good provision. The government utility function H is specified for one type of government (for the other type, α must be replaced by $(1 - \alpha)$):

$$H(G,F) = \frac{1}{\alpha(1-\alpha)} \min\{\alpha G, (1-\alpha)F\} \tag{2}$$

For simplicity, their disagreement in public goods provision is parameterized symmetrically by α which is exogenous. The denominator in equation (2) is a normalization such that

$$H(G,F) = F + G = X \tag{3}$$

and the marginal public goods utility is unity. Without limiting the general validity of the analysis, it is assumed that $1 \leq \alpha \leq ½$. When α equals half, the two types of government have identical preferences; the more distant α is from half, the more they disagree on how much to spend on each of the two public goods. If preferences of both policymaker types are very dissimilar, political polarization is large. Political polarization measured by α contributes to political instability because it accounts for the extend of preference changes given a change in government. For α equals half, the instability effect of a government change is eliminated.

---

[3] Technically, this random change of government at fixed intervals is referred to as Markov switching (or Markov chain). If several time periods were considered and their lengths were fixed, for instance, at six months, some governments would only be in power for half a year, fewer would last for a year, and fewer yet for any longer period of time. This is a simple way of describing government change, but it matches the situation in many developing or transitional countries. In Russia, for instance, there were 5 changes of government in 1998 and 1999 despite the fact that no Duma or presidential elections were held. President Yeltsin alternately replaced representatives of the nomenclature (Chernomyrdin, Primakov, Putin) with so-called reformist Prime Ministers (Chubais, Stepashin) in arbitrary and irregular intervals.

3 Budget Constraints

The government budget constraints for both model periods (1 and 2) are:

$$I + G_1 + F_1 \leq \tau \bar{Y} \tag{4}$$

$$G_2 + F_2 \leq \tau Y(I)$$

Government expenditure consists of two kinds: investment I; and consumptive spending F and G which is spent on the two types of public goods. Government revenue is modeled at a rudimentary level only. As, for instance, in Aghion and Bolton (1990) tax revenues are calculated from constant tax rate τ and income as tax base. The tax rate and first period income $\bar{Y}$ (an endowment) are exogenous, but second period income Y (I) depends on public investment I in the previous period. We assume an increasing function, but decreasing marginal returns: $Y'(I) > 0$, $Y''(I) < 0$. Investment may be interpreted in terms of standard infrastructure investment or investment in any type of structural change leading to more efficiency and hence higher private sector production and income levels. It could, however, also be interpreted as anti-corruption measures with similar effects on production and income.[4]

The private sector budget constraints for both periods are simply:

$$C_1 \leq (1-\tau)\bar{Y} \tag{5}$$

$$C_2 \leq (1-\tau)Y(I)$$

Each period real private consumption depends on real income net of non-distortionary taxes. The model could be interpreted in per capita terms, but the private sector is passive in the sense that it cannot take optimizing decisions on labor, savings or investment. Thus, the two private sector budget constraints are not directly linked intertemporally. In that regard the model is similar to the model in Cukierman, Edwards, and Tabellini (1992). Income growth is only generated by (anti-corruption) investment, not by private sector activity. These assumptions allow us to focus on the government and its decision problem. They may be justified in two ways: first, this is a short run model; and, second, growth in transition and developing countries is not so much determined by the private sector, but more by other factors like structural investment (as modelled here) or foreign direct investment (which is not captured in the model).

[4] The latter interpretation requires the assumption that corruption does always have a negative effect on output as confirmed in convincing empirical studies by Mauro (1995), Méon and Sekkat (2003) and others, but previously contested by Huntington (1968), Lui (1985), Beck and Maher (1986), Lien (1986) and others.

4 Government Maximization Problem

The government has two types of instruments to increase its utility: public investment in period 1 and public spending on each of the two public goods in both periods. Increasing this period's public spending raises contemporaneous public goods utility H. Higher investment this period increases future private sector income (and thereby private sector utility) as well as tax revenues (and thereby public goods spending and utility) in the following period.

The government decision problem is made tractable because of three assumptions: (i), public goods spending F and G does not appear in the private sector budget constraints (5); (ii), government objective function (1) is additively separable; (iii), the functional format of the polarization assumption embedded in equation (2) guarantees H(G, F) = F + G (equation 3). Due to assumptions (i) and (ii) the government optimization problem can be decomposed into two problems: first, the optimal distribution of the total public goods spending between F and G (**distribution problem**); and second, the fundamental revenue and expenditure problem of the government (**fundamental problem**).

The (optimal) distribution problem is not really interesting since its results hinge on specific (though quite sensible) assumptions for public goods utility H (assumption (iii)). Indeed, the mathematical solution of the distribution problem for public goods spending is only required for being able to solve the fundamental revenue and expenditure problem of the government. Due to assumption (iii) the fundamental problem of the government is independent of the actual government in power (see next paragraph). Nonetheless, the fact that there are two potential governments does have crucial implications for any government decision on the total amount of public goods spending as well as on public investment. In fact, the model is constructed that way to allow for the analysis of political instability by itself (as, for instance, in Devereux and Wen (1998) or Svensson (1998)) as opposed to analyzing the effect of different types of government with different objectives (as, for instance, in Aghion and Bolton (1990) or Tabellini and Alesina (1990)).

We proceed as follows. In the next paragraph, the solution for the optimal public goods distribution problem is used to simplify total government utility and, thereby, make the government maximization problem tractable. Then both the interior and the corner solution for the fundamental problem of government revenue and expenditure are discussed.

5 Simplifying Total Government Utility

Assumption (iii), which refers to the functional format of utility function H, has three specific implications. First, the optimal distribution of the total partial interest spending between F and G is crosswise symmetrical for both types, say i and k, of governments (when in power). Second, government utility H derived from type i's choice of F and G (when in power) is equal to government utility derived from type k's choice (when in power):

$$H^i(G^i,F^i) = G^i + F^i = X^i = X = X^k = G^k + F^k \\ = H^k(G^k,F^k) \tag{6}$$

In either case, the marginal utility of public goods spending is unity. Third, the (real) total value of public goods spending H is normalized – for each government – by the sum of its arguments (F + G), when chosen optimally by any incumbent government. For i and k representing different governments and $\alpha > ½$ being assumed (without loss of generality), note, however, that government k's optimal choice for F and G is, of course, suboptimal for government $i: X^i(G^i,F^i) > H^i(G^k,F^k) = \frac{1-\alpha}{\alpha}X^i$.

On this basis, the government utility function (1), can be simplified. For each period separately, utility derived from private consumption and from partial interest spending is considered for the government in power in period 1 only. Superscripts are only used for the other government (marked by k). In period 1, this government's optimal choice for F and G results in H(G1, F1) = X1. Thus first period utility is

$$V(C_1) + H(G_1,F_1) = V(C_1) + X_1 \tag{7}$$

If this government is still in power in period 2 (with probability $(1 - \pi)$), it will choose F and G such that $H(G_2, F_2)=X_2$. If, however, this government looses power in period 2 (with probability π), it has to put up with the public goods spending chosen by the other government, i.e. $H(G_2^k,F_2^k) = \frac{1-\alpha}{\alpha}X_2$. Hence its second period total expected utility is:

$$E\{\rho(V(C_2) + H(G_2,F_2))\} \\ = \rho\left((1-\pi)(V(C_2) + X_2) + \pi(V(C_2) + \frac{1-\alpha}{\alpha}X_2)\right) \\ = \rho(V(C_2) + \beta(\alpha,\pi)X_2) \tag{8}$$

Thus government utility in period 2 depends on three exogenous parameters: discount factor ρ, political polarization α and the probability of loosing power π. The latter two parameters are subsumed under quasi-exogenous parameter β, which is to represent political instability: $0 \le \beta(\alpha,\pi) = (1-\pi) + \pi\frac{1-\alpha}{\alpha} \le 1$. Note that political instability augments the effect of the discount factor: it lowers the valuation for the second period, i.e. it increases government myopia. Obviously, $\beta = 1$ if both governments have identical preferences ($\alpha = ½$) or if the government stays in power with certainty ($\pi = 0$). For $\alpha = 1$ and $\pi = 1$, $\beta = 0$. In other words, β

decreases with more political diversity (polarization $\alpha\uparrow$) and/or more political uncertainty (probability of government change $\pi\uparrow$).

6 Interior Solution

The fundamental revenue and expenditure problem of the government can now be specified on the basis of government preferences as stated in (1) and equations (7) and (8). Government budget constraints (4) and private sector budget constraints (5) can be substituted into equations (7) and (8) for $F_t+G_t=:X_t$ and C_t, t=1,2, respectively. Then the government objective function is:

$$\max_I V((1-\pi)\bar{Y})+\tau\bar{Y}-I+\rho V((1-\tau)Y(I))+\rho\beta(\alpha,\pi)\tau Y(I) \tag{9}$$

The first order condition (FOC) with respect to the (remaining) policy variable I is as follows:

$$-1+\rho V'((1-\tau)Y(I))((1-\tau)Y'(I))+\rho\beta(\alpha,\pi)\tau Y'(I)=0 \tag{10}$$

The FOC requires that the marginal utility of (giving up 1 unit of) public good provision in period 1 (which is unity due to assumption (2) on public goods utility H) must be equal to the (additional) utility derived (i) from (additional) second period consumption (due to the after-tax income effect of increased investment) and (ii) from the (additional) public goods provision in period 2 (due to the tax effect of increased investment). Note that the discounted marginal utilities for (i) and (ii) are different. As for (i), marginal utility V' is discounted by discount factor ρ. As for (ii), unity marginal utility of the public goods provision is discounted by $\rho\beta$.

The FOC is, of course, only a necessary condition. The sufficient condition for a maximum is that the second derivative of (9) must be negative. It can be that this is only true for β above a threshold value, $\beta > \beta^*$, where β^* is the value for which the second derivative equals 0.

We are interested in the effect of political instability β on public investment I. Remember that political instability parameter β introduced in equation (8) represents both the probability of government change π and political polarization α. Remember also that both π and α are negatively related to β, which takes values between 0 (complete instability) and 1 (perfect stability). Assuming now that (9) is a well-defined maximization problem (i.e. $\beta > \beta^*$), applying total differentials leads to

Proposition 1 (Interior Solution)
For $\beta > \beta^*$, the following perturbation results hold at the equilibrium:

(i) $\frac{dI}{d\beta} > 0$ (ii) $\frac{d\frac{dI}{d\beta}}{d\beta} < 0$

Point (i) states that increasing β, i.e. less political instability, leads to more public investment (as long as $\beta > \beta^*$). As the government becomes less myopic, it is optimal to invest more into the future. Additional political stability effectively increases the discount factor for the future. This is intuitive and straightforward. However, point (ii) asserts that the (positive) marginal effect on investment of more political stability decreases. This is so because the marginal investment profitability goes down. Conversely, proposition 1 means that political instability leads to a depletion of public investment which accelerates for more and more instability (up to β^*).

7 Corner Solution

For two reasons, this is not the full story: first, β could be smaller than β^*; and second, public investment cannot be reduced at an ever increasing rate for increasing political instability (β decreased). The rest of the story is simple. For β below β^*, public investment must be zero. To see this consider the government's optimal choice problem for $\beta < \beta^*$. Formally, the government problem becomes a minimization problem as the second order condition turns positive. If, however, public investment is constrained to zero in this two period model, the optimal choice of the government is the corner solution.

Proposition 2 (Corner Solution)
For $\beta < \beta^*$, it is optimal for the government not to invest.

The proposition appears obvious from first inspection of the problem, but can be formally proved by using the Kuhn-Tucker conditions. The intuition is also simple. For small β, the government values the present much more than the future. Given such myopia, the government does not want to move resources from today to tomorrow. Hence there is no investment. In the real world, disinvestment (like the sale of infrastructure, e.g. train coaches) might actually result from large myopia.

The overall solution can be illustrated by two figures which plot optimal I and $\frac{dI}{d\beta}$ as functions of β. Figure 1 shows that there is no public investment for small β. However, from $\beta = \beta^*$ onwards, it is optimal for government to invest more and more for increasing β. That I(β) is non-differentiable at β^*[5] and concave thereafter can be seen from figure 2. $\frac{dI}{d\beta}$ is zero for $\beta < \beta^*$. It becomes infinity at $\beta = \beta^*$ and decreases though still positive thereafter.

---

[5] Note, however, that the level of investment is not necessarily zero at $\beta = \beta^*$. We know that it is positive, but there could be a jump to a higher level of investment depending on the precise format of the investment and utility functions.

8 Conclusion

This paper captures the government decision problem between public investment and public consumption in a simple model of political instability. The chance of another government being in power and taking undesirable decisions in the future produces a negative spill-over onto today's government. This is the basis for the result of myopic government behavior in the literature.

In this paper, it is actually optimal for the current government to totally refrain from spending on public investment, if enough myopia is produced by political instability. As we increase political stability, we reach a threshold above which it is optimal to increase investment. At first, marginal investment is strong, because additional political stability effectively increases the discount factor for the future. Then, however, the additional investment increments become smaller, because marginal investment profitability goes down.

The paper offers an (alternative) explanation for appalling levels of public investment in some countries and/or governments' unwillingness to invest in the fight against corruption. For several reasons, the model is particularly relevant for certain developing or transition countries. First, political instability in some of these countries is inherent to the political structure of the country rather than caused by electoral uncertainty as in Western democracies. Second, the disregard for private sector decisions on labor, consumption and investment would certainly not be suitable simplifications for industrialized countries, but may be seen as a first approximation in some developing or transition countries, where there is either no economic growth or it depends on external factors (like foreign direct investment).

However, relaxing these assumptions offers scope for future research. A possible extension would be to model the effect of public investment on growth, when the private sector optimizes its investment and consumption decisions. A further extension might be to capture the interaction between growth and political instability. It is, however, not obvious how to do this, because the typical median voter approach (as, for instance, in Tabellini and Alesina's political instability model) may not be suitable for less democratic countries. It may also be worth while exploring if there are any trade-off effects when other sources of government revenue are included.

Finally, this model could be tested empirically. Countries could be placed in different groups according to their level of investment. It could then be studied, if their investment behavior changes as their level as political instability changes over time. The model predicts that moderate changes of political instability would not affect the investment behavior of low investment countries.

Appendix A: Optimal Public Goods Spending

The following exposition draws on Cukierman, Edwards, and Tabellini (1992). The same approach is also used in Svensson (1998). For convenience, polarisation assumption (2) which is embedded in the government utility function H for public goods spending is restated for the type i government:

$$H^i(G^i, F^i) = \frac{1}{\alpha(1-\alpha)} \min\{\alpha G^i, (1-\alpha)F^i\} \tag{A.1}$$

Since (A.1) contains a minimum function, optimality can only be achieved for

$$(1-\alpha)F^i = \alpha G^i \tag{A.2}$$

As the utility function H for the type k government is symmetrical according to its definition in section 2, so is the optimal distribution between F^k and G^k: $(1-\alpha)G^k = \alpha F^k$.

Government i's optimal total public goods spending Xi can be written as

$$X^i := F^i + G^i = \frac{G^i}{1-\alpha} = \frac{F^i}{\alpha} \tag{A.3}$$

By reinserting into utility function (A.1) the optimal values for F and G in terms of X ($G^i=(1-\alpha)X^i$, $F^i=\alpha X^i$) a simple result for total public goods utility H is obtained:

$$H^i(G^i, F^i) = \frac{1}{\alpha(1-\alpha)} \min\{\alpha(1-\alpha)X^i, (1-\alpha)\alpha X^i\} \tag{A.4}$$
$$= X^i = F^i + G^i$$

We can now see that the denominator in equation (A-1) was chosen as a normalisation such that the marginal public goods utility is unity. Furthermore, given that utility function (A.1) is symmetrical for both types of government, the optimal values for F and G are crosswise identical ($F^i=G^k$ and $G^i=F^k$) and

$$H^i(G^i, F^i) = X^i = X = X^k = H^k(G^k, F^k) \tag{A.5}$$

Appendix B: Second Order Condition

For (9) to be a well-specified maximisation problem, the second derivative with respect to I must be smaller or equal to 0:

$$\rho * V''((1-\tau)Y(I)) * ((1-\tau) * Y'(I))^2 \tag{B.1}$$

$$+ \rho * V'((1-\tau)Y(I)) * ((1-\tau) * Y''(I)) \tag{B.2}$$
$$+ \rho * \beta(\alpha, \pi) * \tau * Y''(I) \leq 0$$

<=>

$$\underbrace{\left(\rho * V''((1-\tau)Y(I))\right)}_{-} * \underbrace{\left(((1-\tau) * Y'(I))^2\right)}_{+} \tag{B.3}$$
$$+ \underbrace{\left(\rho * Y''(I)\right)}_{-} * \underbrace{\left(\tau * \beta(\alpha,\pi) - (1-\tau) * V'((1-\tau)Y(I))\right)}_{?} \leq 0$$

A sufficient condition for this to hold is:

$$\tau * \beta(\alpha,\pi) \geq (1-\tau) * V'((1-\tau)Y(I)). \tag{B.4}$$

Given that the marginal utility of H is normalised at unity, the condition could be rewritten as:

$$\tau * \beta(\alpha,\pi) * H'(G_2,F_2) \geq (1-\tau) * V'((1-\tau)Y(I)). \tag{B.5}$$

If we ignore the tax rate for a moment (set $\tau = .5$), condition (B.4) requires the effective marginal public goods utility in period 2, β*H'_2, to be greater or equal to second period marginal private sector utility V'_2. Given some political instability ($\beta < 1$) this means that, at the margin, the policy maker must attribute less importance to private consumption than to total public goods provision.

Equation (B.2) does, however, hold for weaker conditions as well. The marginal private sector utility V'_2 could also be greater than the effective marginal public goods utility β*H'_2, as long as β*H'_2 is sufficiently close to V'_2. For V'_2 above (but close to) unity, β must be relatively close to 1, where 1 signifies perfect political stability (no polarisation and/or no chance of government change). For V'_2 below unity, the following holds: the farther V'_2 from unity (i.e. the less important private consumption is relative to public consumption), the more political instability is permitted.

In fact, equality in (B.2) defines β^*, a threshold level for β. For $\beta > \beta^*$ the government choice problem (9) is a well-defined maximisation problem producing an interior solution for the optimal level of public investment I.

Appendix C: Perturbation Results

Proposition 1 (i) – given $\beta > \beta^*$:

$$\frac{dI}{d\beta} = -\frac{\frac{\partial W_I}{\partial \beta}}{\frac{\partial W_I}{\partial I}} = -\frac{\overbrace{\rho * \tau * Y'(I)}^{+}}{\underbrace{\frac{\partial W_I}{\partial I}}_{-}} > 0 \tag{C.1}$$

Proposition 1 (ii) – given $\beta > \beta^*$:

$$\frac{d\dfrac{dI}{d\beta}}{d\beta}=\frac{\overbrace{-\rho*\tau*Y''(I)*\dfrac{\partial W_I}{\partial I}}^{-}--\overbrace{*\tau*Y'(I)*\rho*\tau*Y''(I)}^{-}}{\underbrace{\dfrac{\partial W_I^2}{\partial I}}_{+}}<0 \tag{C.2}$$

References

Aghion, P. and P. Bolton (1990), "Government Domestic Debt and the Risk of Default: a Political-Economic Model of the Strategic Role of Debt", in Rudi Dornbusch and Mario Draghi (eds.), Public Debt Management: Theory and History, Cambridge: Cambridge University Press.

Beck, P.J. and M.W. Maher (1986), "A comparison of bribery and bidding in thin markets", Economics Letters, 20, 1-5.

Bohn, F. (2000), "The Rationale for Seigniorage in Russia – A Model-Theoretic Approach", in Paul Welfens and Evgeny Gavrilenkov (eds.), Restructuring, Stabilizing and Modernizing the New Russia – Economic and Institutional Issues, Heidelberg: Springer.

Cukierman, A., S. Edwards, and G. Tabellini (1992), "Seigniorage and Political Instability", American Economic Review, 82, 537-555.

Devereux, M. B. and J.-F. Wen (1998), "Political Instability, Capital Taxation, and Growth", European Economic Review, 42, 1635-1651.

Huntington, S.P. (1968): Political order in changing societies, New Haven: Yale University

Press. Lien, D.H.D. (1986): "A note on competitive bribery games", Economics Letters, 22, 337-341.

Lui, F.T. (1985): "An Equilibrium Queuing Model of Bribery", Journal of Political Economy, 93, 760-781.

Mauro, P (1995): "Corruption and Growth", Quarterly Journal of Economics, 110, 681-712.

Méon, P-G. and K. Sekkat(2003), "Corruption, growth and governance: Testing the 'grease the wheels' hypothesis", paper presented at the Annual Meeting of the European Public Choice Society in Aarhus, Denmark, 26-28 April.

Svensson, J. (1998), "Investment, Property Rights and Political Instability: Theory and Evidence", European Economic Review, 42, 1317-1341.

Tabellini, G. and A. Alesina (1990), "Voting on the Budget Deficit", American Economic Review, 80, 37-49.

Institutional Issues of Transport Policy Implementation in Russia

Nina Oding

1 Introduction

Russia is enjoying the most encouraging external economic environment of the last 15 years. The world economy has recovered from stagnation, and all major world economies are looking forward to further growth. Russia is demonstrating dynamic development with new types of demands on the transport industry services. Higher needs in business trips and cargo shipments are part and parcel of growing business operations. The Russian economy is witnessing an upsurge accompanied with growing exports and relative production-cost reduction. With annual growth rates exceeding 7%, the country has escaped from its debt quagmire. Another important feature of the present situation is that the material-intensive economies of China, India, and other Asian states show growing demand for raw materials, with raw material prices continuing to ride high. With respect to this, the issue of Russia's integration into the international transport services market acquires special significance. The main goals are to secure Russia's present position in the traditional sales markets and enter new markets while ensuring independence and reliability of the transportation links. The plans include export flows' diversification and switching over to the east and northwest directions with a focus on exports through Russian ports, coal export through Russian ports, and marine shipments of natural gas.

At the same time, with the impressive growth rates largely fueled by a favorable external situation, the Russian economy continues to face a number of serious challenges. Despite an inspiring upturn in the internal market, processing industries, and the services sector, the economy's dependence on resource exports remains high. Today, the fuel-and-energy complex accounts for around 30% of Russia's total manufacturing output, 32% of the consolidated budget revenues, 45% of federal budget revenues, 54% of the exports and about 45% of all hard-currency earnings. These trends are expected to remain unchanged in the short-term as well. (Osnovnyje Pokazateli Socialno-Ekonomicheskogo RazvitiJa Rossii, 2003).

The globalization trends that gained momentum at the end of the last century significantly aggravated the problems of Russia's competitiveness. The solution to these problems will largely depend on whether the country can diversify its economic structure, increase the share of products with high-added cost, and stimulate high-tech export growth. This can only be done if the country opens its national economy, joins the WTO and competes successfully with the developed economies. The economy and external trade diversification will require significant expansion of the transportation services exports and an adequate updating of the existing transport infrastructure.

The Transport Strategy of Russia approved by the RF State Council in late 2003 is to become a long-term basis for state policies in this domain. In order to see if that strategy can help meet the acute infrastructure development challenges in the country, one has to analyze the current state and development trends of the transport complex, identify the key components of the country's transport policies, and review the existing institutional problems of their implementation.

The analysis should address the transport system's strengths and weaknesses, and the factors blocking massive investments and large-scale structural changes in the transport industry.

2 External Economic Activities

In 2002 and 2003, the external economic sector continued to be one of the most dynamic industries in the country. Its development unfolded against a background of surging business activities, expanding internal demand, and a favorable global general economic and commodity situation. Crude oil production swelled in 2003, as oil companies were eager to take advantage of high world market prices. According to preliminary information from the Ministry of Energy, crude production throughout 2003 averaged 8.46 million barrels per day (bpd), up 11 % from 2002.

In the last three years, the share of exports in the Russian GDP amounted to about 40% (as specified by the official Ruble-USD exchange rate). In the past four years, Russian crude oil exports have risen 66% and oil products 38%. Natural gas exports were up 2% last year. Strong export volume growth was also seen in coal production, some metals, and certain chemical and forest products. The development of export prices in 2003 largely depends on the currency in which they are measured (BOFIT Weekly, 11, 2003). Russian export earnings increased by a quarter and export prices rose over 10% in dollar terms. Crude oil brought in 30% of Russia's export earnings, followed by natural gas (15%) and oil products (10%).

In 2002, the Russian foreign trade turnover grew 44.6% (from \$115.1 billion to \$166.4 billion) in comparison to that in 1999 with the foreign trade surplus amounting to \$45.8 billion in 2002 (Figure 1). The substantial surplus of exports over imports provided a precondition for ensuring a black-ink balance of payment of the country, a stable situation in the domestic currency market, and a record-high hard-currency reserve. This enabled Russia to cover its debt liabilities in a timely fashion without resorting to debt-service loans from international financial institutions.

As a result of favorable raw material prices (primarily prices on energy resources), the RF external trade proceeds substantially increased to about one-third of the total federal budget revenues. Today, fuel and energy account for around 30% of Russia's total manufacturing output, 32% of consolidated budget revenues, 45% of federal budget revenues, 54% of exports and about 45% of all hard-currency earnings. These trends are to remain stable in the short-term perspective as well.

By some estimates[1], Russia's foreign-trade turnover in 2003 jumped 23.7% to \$172.9 billion, with the trade balance surplus amounting to \$53.7 billion and exports exceeding imports by a factor of 1.9. In the last three years, the commodity

[1] Estimates by the RF Ministry for Economic Development and Trade (MERT) based on the State Statistic Committee's data.

structure of exports to non-CIS countries has not shown any noticeable change. Mineral products continue to make up over 50% of exports, with machines and equipment accounting for no more than 8% of total exported goods.

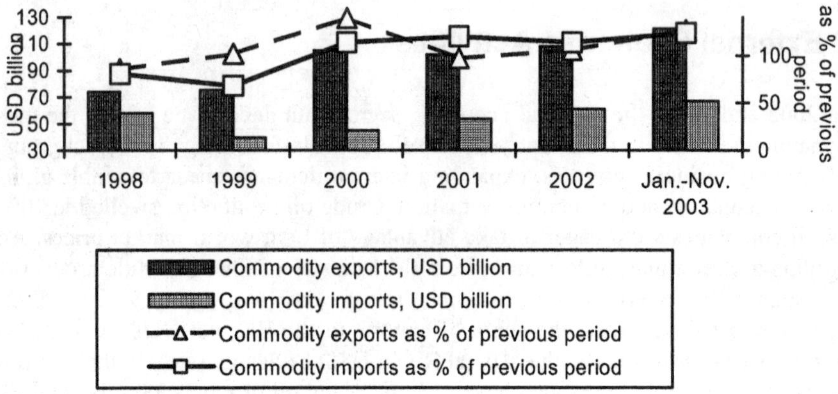

Fig. 1. RF External Trade Turnover

Source: RF State Statistics Committee.

Data by the RF State Customs Committee show that between January and November 2003, the share of fuel and energy resource exports grew to 60.2% of the total or 3.5 percentage points up from January to November 2002. The exported items composition did not change and continues to include energy resources, basic metals, round timber, saw timber, and chemical industry products (Appendix 1).

The recent signs of buoyancy in the world economy and an increasing demand from China pushed up world prices for ferrous and non-ferrous metals as well as gas. Correspondingly, the share of ferrous and non-ferrous metals in Russian exports amounted to 14.2%, the share of pulp-and-paper products 4.6%, and chemical industry products 7%, while the share of high added-value products (machines, vehicles, light-industry goods and other manufactured commodities) declined. Specifically, the share of machines, equipment and vehicles in total exports fell from 10.5 in 2002 to 9.5%.

Russia's imports from non-CIS countries in 2003 have been estimated at $59.6 billion or 22.1% higher than seen in 2002. The main factors behind the high import rates in 2003 were internal demand growth, real strengthening of the ruble, and improvements in the organization of trade. The imports of expensive consumer goods grew substantially following solvent consumer demand growth as well as broader and cheaper consumer loan arrangements.

In the last three years, the commodity structure of imports from non-CIS countries to Russia continued to be dominated by machines and equipment (30-40%), foodstuffs and agricultural materials for food production (over 20%) as well as chemical industry products (over 18%). The share of foodstuffs and raw materials for food production amounted to 21.3%. The imports of machines, equipment and vehicles reached $15.6 or 26% up from January to November 2002.

Growth was propelled by the 50 % volume increase in passenger car imports in the machinery and equipment category as well as a boom in cellular phone imports. However, approximately one-quarter of goods imports are not recorded by Russian customs.

The increased economic activities pushed up the demand for transport services. At the same time, a substantial growth of foreign trade volumes exposed a deficit of specialized facilities at marine ports and access rail capacities in the country.

Russia's reorientation from imports to exports and expansion into new international markets will require a systemic diversification of the infrastructure of all types of transport involved in foreign trade. A delay in resolving this problem can hamper the use of the existing foreign trade potential of Russia. This means that the transport sector is to be updated regardless of what the actual foreign trade structure will be. In the first place, this should be strategic modernization and development of the existing system of trunk pipelines and the transport infrastructure supporting oil, petroleum, coal, and natural gas exports.

3 Transport Sector

Russia's large size underscores its need to develop means of transportation for both goods and passengers. However, the huge territory with different climate conditions could be an obstacle to interregional exchange. Railways provide the main part of freight and passenger turnover. Due to excessive natural resources (oil and gas), pipeline transport is very significant for the economy. Automobile and air transportation serve as the main means for passenger transport.

The degree of development of Russia's transport system varies a lot by region. The most developed transport network can be found in the European part of Russia: the Central, North-West, North-Caucasus, and Volgo-Vjatka regions. There is also a difference in terms of the structure of turnover. Pipelines and railways are developed in the regions of raw materials (West Siberia), inner water transport is developed in the forest resources regions, and railways dominate in regions with manufacturing industries.

In 2003, the transport complex of the RF Ministry for Transport had to cope with, and develop against a background of, increasingly growing major macroeconomic indices. In 2003, the cargo flows through the ministry's sectors grew 3%, with the transit cargo shipment earnings amounting to about $900 million.

Notably, the transport has so far been operating in a growth-market situation with increasing returns, falling numbers of loss-generating enterprises, and mounting investments and tax proceeds (Appendix 2).

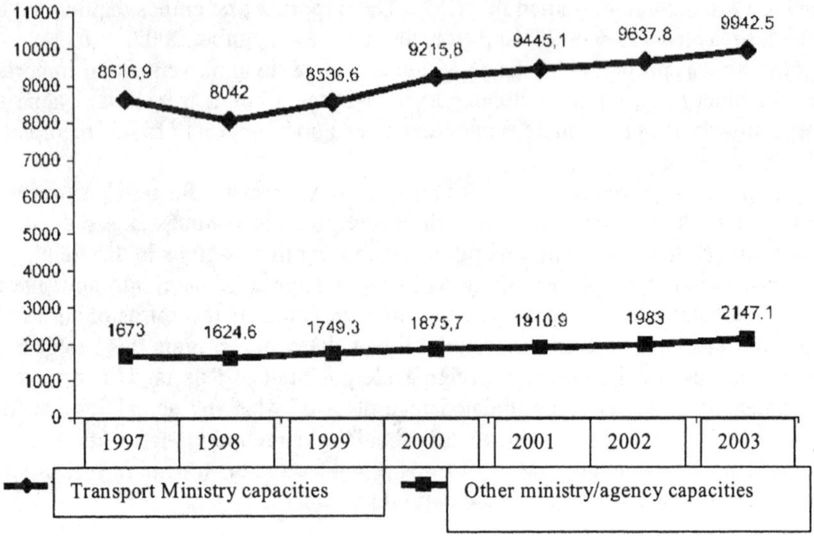

Fig. 2. Cargo shipments, million tons.

Source: RF Ministry of Transport.

According to the forecast of the Ministry of Transportation, the volume of cargo shipment (without pipelines) will increase from 3.1 billion tons in 2004 to 3.2-3.3 billion tons in 2006. The railways and aviation have contributed significantly to this growth, 18-21% and 15-19 % over 2002 levels, respectively.

Unfortunately, the existing technological/ organizational level of Russia's transport systems does not facilitate bringing transportation costs below 30% (compared to 13% in the EU countries). In Russia, the commercial speed of producer-consumer cargo flows is two to three times slower than in Europe and the USA.

The exports of transportation services amount to 9-10 % of the total transportation services provided. In recent years, this index has shown an upward trend, increasing from $3.006 million in 1999 to $5.492 million in 2002 (based on data taken from balance-of-payment statements). This fairly dynamic growth trend continued into 2003 as well. In the first quarter of 2003, exports increased by 11% from the corresponding period in 2002. At the same time, imports of transportation services showed significantly smaller rates. In 2002, such imports increased by $2.862 million from 1999, representing less than a 30% growth, not even reaching thereby pre-crisis 1997 figures (Transportnaja Strategija, 2003).

Russia's transport system which supports the national foreign trade turnover has certain features which bring about specific problems. Rail is the main type of transport in Russia accounting for over one-half of all traffic, while the world transportation system is dominated by marine transport.

Russia's main non-CIS trading partners are East and West European countries, the rail access to which is possible only through Belarus and/or Ukraine. The lay-out of the Russian European rail system is characterized by a radial pattern, whereby all railways go to Moscow, the central transport hub, which is thus con-nected to all economic regions of Russia and to other countries of the world.

The Kaliningrad railways provide direct access only to the West. Russia is also cut off from the railway marine crossing, Illichevsk-Varna, belonging to Ukraine.

Estimates and forecasts show that the current aggregate cargo turnover rates in the country correspond to those worldwide, and that demand for transportation services is to grow 4-5% annually. Apart from providing direct transportation ser-vices to commodity producers, Russia's transportation system has considerable transit potential stemming from the country's lucrative geographic location be-tween the main world-trade growth centers found in the EU, Asia, and the USA. This potential can be realized by using a system of international transport corri-dors (ITC) being laid across Russia (North-South, Transsib, and Northern Mari-time Corridor). Apart from additional transit cargo flows and corresponding reve-nues for the country's coffers, this will result in developing the entire transport infrastructure along the ITCs, thereby strengthening Russia's international and in-terregional ties (Nasonov, 2000). In particular, the Northern Maritime Corridor will provide a shortcut between Northwest Europe, Southeast Asia, and North America as well as a transport route for oil pumped at the Yamal and Prirazlom-noye oil fields.

The North-South ITC goes from the northwest borders of Russia to the Caspian ports and crossings following via the Caspian countries to the Gulf, the Arabian Sea, and India and thus almost halving cargo shipment time. The extreme North-South ITC points in Russia are the St. Petersburg Port in the Northwest and the Olya Port on the Caspian Sea. Russian transport development strategies for the pe-riod up to 2025 plan to attract 5-7% of the current Eurasian transit cargo flows to Russian transport corridors with an annual profit of over $3.0 billion. This will re-quire measures to provide for the development of the country's port infrastructure and maritime transport as well as for the expansion of interaction with the EU and its new members (Ruksha, 2003).

4 Maritime Shipments

Over one-half of Russian imports arrive by sea, with only less than one-quarter of this figure coming through Russian ports. The FSU Baltic states and Ukraine now own a significant proportion of former USSR modern cargo ships and tankers, in-cluding the large ports of Tallinn, Klaipeda, Riga, Ventspils, Odessa, and others. Kaliningrad is Russia's most western port (and the only port which remains unfro-zen year-round). The main Baltic Naval Base is located in Baltijsk, and the St. Pe-tersburg and Vyborg ports stand on the Russian shore of the Gulf of Finland. The main petroleum port of Russia is Novorossijsk on the Black Sea. The only Russian port on the Sea of Azov is Taganrog. Other relatively large ports include Murmansk, Nakhodka, Archagelsk, Vladivostok, and Vanino. The rest (around 30) are small-size ports. With the loss of its Danube Fleet, Russia's trade, transport, passenger and tourist ties with the Danube countries have been severed. In the northwest and in the south, Russia has only a few sites convenient for new port development. At present, three new ports are being built on the Gulf of Finland, and one port on the Sea of Azov.

The backbone of Russia's maritime transport today consists of 14 large state-owned and private shipping companies, 44 maritime ports, 13 dockyards, four R&D institutes, three marine academies, a maritime law institute, and six maritime colleges, with 260 independent ship-owners operating 1,100 vessels with an aggregate deadweight of 13 million tons. The fleet provides export services for an annual amount of around $2.0 billion in a stiff competitive environment of the global freight market. The existing economic conditions force Russian ship-owners to keep most of their vessels under foreign ship registers.

Data from the official national ship register place Russia in the 25th position worldwide in 2002 based on its aggregate merchant fleet tonnage. However, taking into account the actual number of vessels controlled by Russian ship-owners (including those operating under "convenient" flags), foreign experts believe Russia to occupy the 13th place on this index, immediately after Great Britain and Denmark, but ahead of such countries as Italy, Turkey, and Sweden.

When estimating cargo shipments and the marine cargo turnover, one should take into account the recent trend of time-charting Russian vessels to foreign freighters, which means that Russian statistics do not take cargo handled by these ships under consideration. For example, the fleet of Russian marine shipping companies spent 34.5% of their operating time in 2003 on time-charter shipping for foreign freighters.

In 2002, Russian marine ports handled 260.9 million ton of cargo, 30% higher than was seen in 2001 (Ministry of Transport, 2003). This record growth was achieved after the launching of new and revamped transshipping facilities and an increase in production output and exports flows (mostly of bulked cargo). Another factor behind export growth was government protectionism aimed at luring cargo flows to domestic ports by cutting rail cargo tariffs. When handling foreign-trade cargoes carried through Russia, other CIS countries and the Baltic States, Russian railways cooperate with 22 marine and five river ports (Filina, 2004, p. 121).

As noted in (Semenikhin, 2003), one of the factors expected to boost Russia's marine fleet development is the use of an alternative international ship register which would reduce dependence on foreign ship-owners' import service and offer Russian ship-owners better economic conditions than those currently provided in offshore zones. Vessels registered in an alternative ship register would be exempt from all taxes and custom duties and would only have to pay registration and annual fees which are not tied to the ships' financial results. This would put them on equal competitive footing with other maritime shippers in the international market and increase their own funds available for fixed-asset renovation by a factor of 1.5-1.8 compared to Russian shipping companies operating under "standard registration conditions."

At the same time, developing the marine fleet means more than just increasing the tonnage and the number of ship-owners. With its tremendous cargo base, growing export volumes, and an army of highly qualified seamen, Russia can efficiently develop a wide range of services, including professional and management personnel training, the improvement of ship and port operations, ship-management and freight services as well as the provision of ice-breakers owned by various public agencies.

A reorientation of the Russian economy from import to export activities and Russia's entry into new international markets will require systemic diversification of the infrastructure for all types of transport engaged in foreign-trade operations. So far, as noted in IZVESTIA[2], Russian cargo carriers have thus far been guided by the principle, "First grab as much as you can and think afterwards." For example, one of the worst problems today is demurrage. In early 2003 alone, Russian railways lost R300 million following the demurrage of 163 trains with 1.5 million tons of cargo[3].

This situation was seen once again in 2004, when ports and port access roads were badly congested after shippers had attempted to grab the opportunity offered by a delay in the introduction of higher rail tariffs. As the result, in the first half of January cargo inflows into ports jumped by 20%, catching port facilities totally unaware. Stormy weather aggravated the situation even more, as ports could not handle neither incoming nor outgoing vessels. Railways were forced to stop accepting cargo bound for such destinations as Kaliningrad, Novorossijsk, Tuapse and Murmansk (Pletnev, 2004).

This problem could pose a serious hurdle to the further development of Russia's foreign-trade potential. Many of these obstacles could be eliminated by establishing contract relations between ports and railways (especially after the foundation of the JSC Russian Railways, RZhD), with the defaulting party obliged to cover the losses it has caused.

This impressive growth exposes not only the lack of port capacities but also the problem of competition based on tariffs and service quality. Following tariff adjustments, exporters switched cargo flows over to Russian ports while importers continue to favor Baltic (Finnish) ports. Consumer and investment goods from Russia's main partner, the EU, arrive in Russia within containers, while raw materials, oil and gas are exported through pipelines, ports, and by rail. Correspondingly, import deliveries are fairly flexible, whereas exports are tied to a rigid transport infrastructure. Developing new routes for export flows will therefore require significant investments. M. Khodorkovsky (Khodorkovsky, 2003) believes that oil production in Russia is hindered by the insufficiently developed transport infrastructure. Existing oil pipelines have limited capacity and are connected to a limited number of countries, while shipments through Black Sea channels are restricted by safety regulations. Any further expansion of the Baltic coast capacities is potentially limited by environmental regulations established for the Danish

[2] IZVESTIA (2004), Russian ports do not stand competition, 28 January.

[3] IZVESTIA (2003), Steam Engines Ask for Ships, 16 January.

straits. Thus the main export restraints exist for oil/petroleum products, Russia's most important export items.

5 Tariffs

The RF government regulates tariffs for airport services, cargo/passenger rail tariffs (with cross-subsidies), and tariffs in marine/river ports (foreign-trade cargo transshipment and vessel duties in marine ports charged by marine port administrations). Structural natural monopoly reform allows for a gradual change from rigid tariff regulation to tariff deregulation.

In 2003, cargo tariff indices in the RF Transport Ministry sectors did not exceed the manufacturers' price indices and, consequently, did not contribute to inflation rates in the economy. Marine transport tariffs declined 2% compared to a 23% rise across the industry. Within cargo flows with strong price elasticity like river coal shipments, tariff rates have not changed for years. The same stability is characteristic of (the more socially-sensitive) passenger transit. In those cases when service prices are regulated by the state (e.g., port charges or cargo handling tariffs), the transport industry pursues market-oriented policies. For example, the state stopped foreign vessel discrimination in Russian ports, a problem that had hindered negotiations on Russia's joining the WTO.

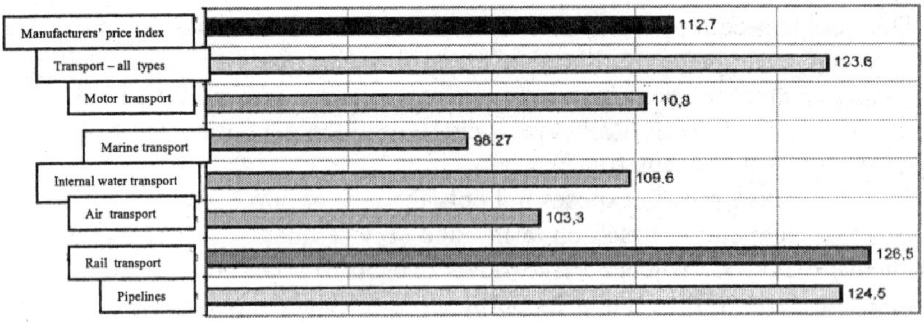

Fig. 3. Cargo tariff indices in 2003

Source: RF Ministry of Transport.

Rail tariff policies are to take into account the interests of cargo owners/carriers in their competition with foreign ports. The plans include unification of rail tariffs that should accommodate the problems of VAT repayment, differences in customs procedures for cargo leaving Russian ports, and also establish approximately equal conditions for all Russian ports within the same basin in order to avoid spasmodic cargo flow changes and the potential blocking of surface border crossings.

Notably, the government has enhanced a protectionist trend in its transport policies by using special tariff regulation for Russian cargo carriers. For example, promotional rail tariffs were instrumental in bringing the share of ports in foreign-trade cargo handling up from 69% to 73% by 2001. As a result, international marine export flows grew significantly against the background of a general contraction of cargo carried and decreased traffic through Ukrainian ports and land crossings.

Today, Russian businesses and the country in general are very much interested in modern tariff policies that would provide incentives to both large-sized or small-sized businesses and individual entrepreneurs. There is no doubt that the national transport strategies must include tariff-policy development principles. Meanwhile, according to forwarders' and cargo-owners' associations, the new freight and railway service tariff list (№ 10-01) has significantly contributed to a hike in both tariffs and non-tariff charges.

6 Transport Strategy

The economic growth in Russia stimulates the demand for transport service, however it makes the problems of transport sector crucial.

The mobility of the Russian population is 2-3 times lower than in the developed countries. The constituent of transportation in the cost of the goods exceeds 15-20%. The insufficiently developed transport infrastructure is the main obstacle to increasing the export of main goods. The transit potential of the transport corridors is not used. There are also troubles with regards to the security and environmental impact of transport in some regions of the country. Besides weaknesses of domestic constituencies for continued institutional reform, transport development in Russia is also aggravating.

All of these problems are connected with inefficiency in the operation of state-run monopolies, especially as regards overmanning and requirements to maintain unprofitable but politically sensitive services.

The Transport Strategy of the Russian Federation for a period of up to 2025 is the main document determining the long-term development of transport in the country. Apart from the state policies (its main component), the strategy defines two other basic components: a transport reform program and a plan for transport infrastructure development. In the first place, the state transport policies are aimed at ensuring marketwise reforms and competition development. On the other hand, the state is to participate in the strategic planning and funding of transport system development. At the same time, the government's primary responsibilities in the transport sector remain those of safety and environment protection provision along with providing for economic efficiency of the industry. The transport strategy was formulated at a period, when Russia's large businesses had gained enough power to share its responsibilities for public welfare with the state. The corporate social responsibility doctrine is transforming itself into a concept of corporate citizenship. Notably, the transport sector is one of the first industries in the country demonstrating successful examples of private-government partnership in new infrastructure facility development. The second constituent of the transport strategy is a package of programs for structural changes in different transport sectors (the federal railways, the air traffic organization and inland waterways management).

Pipelines	▪ State property, not permitted to build private pipelines ▪ State regulations: prices and access
Railways	▪ Government-owned railway systems ▪ Start of the Reform: Ownership is separated from regulation
Aviation	▪ Uncompleted of privatization of airports and airlines
Sea transport	▪ Uncertainty in relations of the state and business guards of seaports ▪ Registration of ships
River transport	▪ Part of activity are fulfilled by state organizations subsidized by budgets
Automobile transport	▪ Liberalized ▪ Needs simple and efficient regulation ▪ Private road-building

Fig. 4. Main problems of transport sector

The third constituent of the Transport Strategy of Russia is a long-term plan for national transport infrastructure development. This plan is tied with the country's productive force development scenarios, and it will be achieved based on the Eurasian transport-corridor development concept.

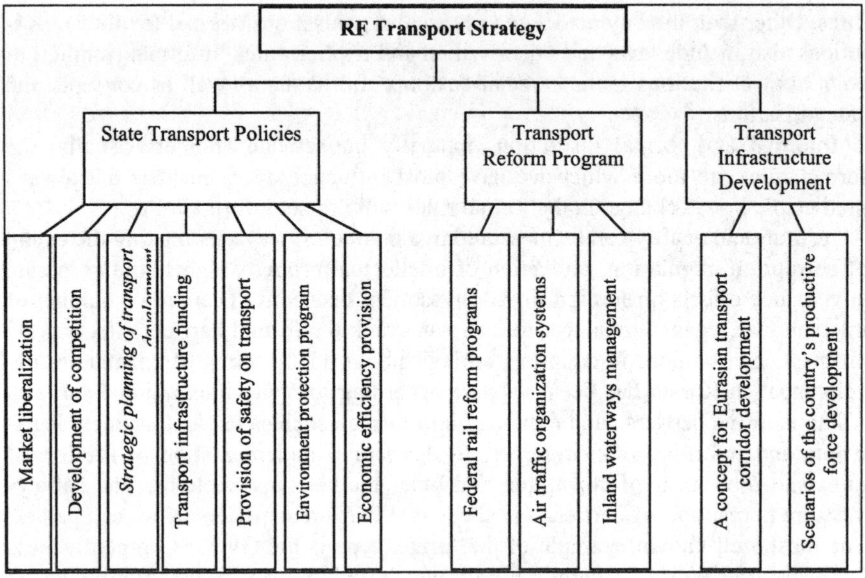

Fig. 5. RF Transport Strategy

The main priorities of the transport strategy include developing a reliable transport system to ensure the economic unity of the country and providing for increased population mobility and national security. Reliable external communications must guarantee Russia's external trade independence and provide for transit flows growth. A comprehensive solution of motorization and road development problems is to become an important factor of economic growth, life quality improvement, and conservation of the environment. These goals are to be achieved through joint efforts by federal and local governments, businesses, transport science and education institutions, professional associations, trade unions, the media, and millions of rank-and-file transport workers. The transport strategy implementation will require bringing together complex and the sometimes diametrically-opposed interests of all transport-process participants: cargo owners and consignees, freighters and cargo carriers, cargo operators and insurers.

7 Organisations, Actors and Institutions

A general definition of institutions is characterised as formal and informal social rule structures with associated standing patterns of behaviour and procedures. An important characteristic of institutions is that they define actor relations and organise their interaction. Generally speaking, institutions can be said to arise or to be developed in order to reduce uncertainty and provide stability for socio-economic interaction, through regular and repetitive ways of conduct. The term institution covers both formal institutions and organisations and informal social rule structures. Other than the key actors and physical organisations, formal (explicit) institutions also include laws and other written and explicit rules. Informal (implicit or cognitive) institutions include social customs and habits as well as concepts and categorisations.

Informal and formal institutions mutually impact one another. Usually, the formal rules are those which we have most influence over, but it is not always predictable how a change in the formal rules will impact informal rules.

Institutional quality can be measured in a number of ways, estimating the extent of corruption, regulation, protection of intellectual property rights, and corporate governance effects on foreign firms' investment decisions. There are a number of international organizations that measure and rank the formal barriers affecting the business environment in countries around the world. In terms of corruption, development in Russia has been negative according to many international surveys. Administrative barriers can be divided into formal, such as tax and business legislation, and informal, often referring to the actual implementation of the formal rules and the extent of corruption and other market imperfections. The surveys measure perception of barriers and the actual barriers experienced by companies. The most well-known example of the former type is the Global Competitiveness Report by the World Economic Forum which includes a very comprehensive set of indicators on perceptions of the business and investment climate.

A whole range of organizations, or actors, are involved in the development and implementation of transport policy in Russia. The key actors include governments and politicians, other governmental organisations, transport service and infrastructure producers, transport users, interest groups, and the public. A list of actors at the international, national, regional and local level can be seen in the table below.

International level	⇨ International public authorities (EU, UN, OECD) ⇨ Multinational companies ⇨ Populations and individuals
National level	⇨ Governments and ministries ⇨ Trade unions, producers of different economic sectors and industrial lobbies, associations ⇨ Mass media ⇨ Citizens
Regional and local level	⇨ Regional or federal authorities ⇨ Municipal authorities ⇨ Large private companies ⇨ Citizens

Fig. 6. Actors in the European transport context

EU strategy toward Russia in the transport sector firstly includes the use of the mechanisms incorporated in the Partnership and Cooperation Agreement to help Russia optimally utilize its transport infrastructure by applying modern management techniques and expertise in a competitive market environment. This will enable Russia to choose its own strategy in the transport sector, evaluate the infrastructure development proposals and identify its own priorities. This was the fist time that the European Commission put the users' needs in the focus of its strategy and proposed measures to address that goal (De Palacio, 2003). The first measure was designed to change the balance between the types of transport by boosting rail traffic, promoting marine and inland waterway shipments, and integrating different types of transport. Simultaneously with this new transport policy, the EC proposed an Action Plan for substantial improvement of transport quality and efficiency in Europe. The strategy is designed to reduce the impact on the environment and prevent road jams while preserving economic competitiveness. Within the Trans-European Transport Network (TEN), the EU is forming new transit thoroughfares based on the integration of different types of transport in a multimodal transport system to be expanded eastward (first into Russia itself) and to be connected with the transport networks of third countries. In particular, Russia participates in developing the following transport corridors: Corridor 1 (Helsinki-Kaliningrad-Gdansk), Corridor 2 (Berlin-Minsk-Moscow-Nizhni Novgorod), and Corridor 9 (Helsinki-St. Petersburg-Moscow-Pskov-Kiev-Aleksandropol).

The EU and Russian transport strategies are being brought together along the lines of transport safety and integrated investments in Russia's international transport projects. The latter include: coasting trade development, ice-breaker services in the Gulf of Finland, and the development of a multi-purpose cargo/passenger/motor/rail ferry line between Ust-Luga, Baltijsk, and German Baltic ports. At present, the first priority problems in Russia's interaction with the EU with respect to the transport sector deal with:

- Environmental hazards posed by shipments through Danish and Black Sea straits, and
- More active protectionist tariff policies aimed at luring cargo flows within Russian ports.

There is also cooperation with international organizations including the European Conference of Ministers of Transport within the Committee for Transport of European Economic Commission to the UN. In the framework of the European Economic Commission, Russian authorities are in the process of considering and adopting 14 agreements and conventions related to transportation in Europe.

Negotiations about joining the WTO and access to the Russian transport market are currently being considered. There are some institutional and organisational barriers on the national level defined as inefficient co-ordination and co-operation among different branches and levels of government and inefficient consultation and communication between government and private sectors.

One of the most important issues is to establish a balance between the state and private sectors in view of the forthcoming structural reforms in the rail transport and electric power production as well as in light of administrative and inter-budget relation reforms.

Firstly, the lack of co-operation among different Ministries with an interest in or responsibility for transport (e.g., Transport, Antimonopoly, Land use, Finance, State Property).

Secondly, transport planning involving urban areas is undertaken at local, regional and national levels (depending on the type of project or investment), while urban land-use planning remains to a large extent a local issue, although there is growing recognition that strategic spatial planning must occur at a national level.

Thirdly, the issues yet to be addressed are certain problems of state regulation, when public bodies use tariffs as an instrument of unfair competition between state-owned and private enterprises to the detriment of natural economic efficiency stimuli.

The recently launched state governance reform is another additional factor in the formation of an institutional environment for transport industry participants.

During the days of the Soviet Union, each form of traffic had a ministry of its own. Since 1991, all forms of transport such as river transport, mercantile shipping, aviation, and road making are under the jurisdiction of the Ministry of Transport of Russian Federation (MINTRANS). Only the Ministry of Railways remained separate.

The Ministry of Transport is comprised of the Service of Automobile Transportation, managing the governmental supervision of road transport, and the Russian Transportation Inspection authorities (RTI), which is authorized to supervise traffic along the roads.

The RF Ministry of Transport is in charge of formulating and implementing concepts and programs for the social and economic development of the transport sector as well as developing and implementing inter-state and inter-industry programs. The ministry implements measures to develop and improve transport and freight operations, deploy a ramified network of transport terminals, and acts furthermore as a state customer for targeted inter-state and federal transport development programs organizing expert reviews of such programs and projects.

In the 1990s, the legal base for transport services was substantially updated. Now practically every transport sector has a new basic law of its own. The RF Air Code was adopted in 1997, the Merchant Marine Code in 1999. A number of draft laws are currently at different stages of legislative preparation, including the inland Water Transport Code, a set of basic motor transport laws, as well as industrial transport, road system, passenger city transport, transport insurance, and other laws. The concepts for marine shipping policies and air traffic and aviation development have been prepared for approval, while a number of federal laws are already in place. These include the Federal Laws "On Technical Regulation", "On Transport and Freight Activities", "On the Russian International Ship Register", and the Motor Transport Code. The Draft Federal Law "On Maritime Ports in the Russian Federation" has been passed in its first reading. The Ministry of Transport is the only Russian ministry to have proposed cutting two-thirds of its licensed activity types.

Until recently, one of the central challenges to actual transport policies was the organization of joint transport infrastructure development efforts by the Railway and Transport Ministries, especially as regards integration and coordination of maritime port operations (Transport Rossii, 2001).

In March 2004 as part of Russia's on-going administrative reforms, a new three-tier system of federal organizations has been announced. Central authority will be represented by ministries, federal services (*sluzhba*) and federal agencies (*agentstvo*). Federal ministries, the number of which has been reduced from 23 to 14, are responsible for setting policy and adopting regulations. While most federal services are supervisory bodies, several of them are special services reporting directly to the president. Federal agencies produce state services and administer state property. The reform seeks to distinguish regulatory, supervisory and service functions of administrative bodies. Following the changes, ministers' political responsibility will be enhanced. In addition to being accountable for their particular ministry, they will be accountable for operations of services and agencies under their ministries. A commission made up of representatives of ministries, the presidential administration and government staff has two weeks to submit proposals putting the government reform into practice. The number of bodies within the central administrative bureaucracy (including ministries) has risen from 58 to 76. The Ministry of Industry has experienced the biggest changes. It took over the energy ministry, atomic energy ministry, and space agency. It will also be responsible for production-sharing agreements. The industry and energy ministry together with transportation and telecommunication ministry will deal with reforms of monopolies in their sectors.

Under the ongoing administrative reform, the RF President's Decree №314 of 9 March 2004 revamped the country's transport management bodies by pooling the Railway, Transport and Telecommunications Ministries into a super-ministry in charge of railways, roads, transport and telecommunications. The ministry defines state policies and state/legal regulations. The federal services under the ministry carry out control and supervision functions, while federal agencies are in charge of public services and public property management. The provisions for the ministry, its federal services and agencies are to be adopted by May 2004. Meanwhile the ministry is fine-tuning its structure to avoid controversies between the ministry, service and agency functions.

Further plans include preparation and adoption of provisions for the executive bodies after their functions are specified and finalized. These provisions are to be used as a basis for developing administrative regulations for agencies and their departments, which will include procedures for relevant planning, organization, execution and recording activities. The regulations are to determine not only the document turnover formats and directions, but also methods for managerial decision preparation and execution.

In accordance with a new decree of the president on 20 May 2004, the Ministry of Transport and Telecommunications will be reorganized into Ministry of Transport and Ministry of IT and Telecommunications, including both the Federal Transport Supervision Service and Federal Telecommunications Agency as well.

The Federal Geodesic and Cartography Agency will be added to the structure of new Ministry of Transport. At moment, the final structure looks like this:

FR Ministry of Transport

- Federal Transport Supervision Service

- Federal Air Transport Agency
- Federal Road Agency
- Federal Railroad Agency
- Federal Marine and River Transport Agency
- Federal Geodesic and Cartography Agency

Fig. 7. FR Ministry of Transports

The regional administration is organized very much like the federal government, although some committees are also subordinate to the central government of the Federation.

The Russian Constitution provides for a wide range of joint powers of authority shared by the Russian Federation and its administrative regions. These powers include:

- The ownership, use and disposal of land, minerals, water and other natural resources,
- The establishment of common principles for organising the system of public authorities and local government, and
- Co-ordination of the international and foreign trade links between the Russian Federation and it regions.

The Ministry of Transport is a very much centralized organization with regional representative offices all over Russia. There are also departments comprising several subjects of Federation in the framework of seven rather newly established *okrugs*.

There is the general notion that transport, especially maritime transport, is by and large market driven. In Russia, there is considerable state influence, real or potential. Competition between ports, therefore, is not entirely a game between private actors obeying the rules of the market. To some extent, this competitive game also involves local authorities, regional authorities and federal authorities.

There are a lot of regional divisions of the federal bodies (Ministry of Transport and MPS) on the regional level. On the regional level, the committee for transport is also included in the structure of the administration. The local transport authorities participate in the discussion of the investment projects providing their resolutions and permissions. Public actors at various administrative levels plan mostly the infrastructure. In St. Petersburg, for instance, there are more than 10 transport administration bodies at the federal and local level, and coordination between them is poor.

However, the port authority intends to operate a "port conglomerate" where national actors co-operate with local/regional actors in providing the central functions including investments and financing of infrastructure both ashore and at sea. This is often financed via the national budget, while the port's terminal services etc. are privatised.

Investors deals with regional authorities in the sphere of socio-economic development, urban development and environmental development.

8 Investments

Despite the oil earning prop-up, government budgets have proven to be unreliable sources of funds for sufficient investments at maintaining and improving transport services and infrastructure. The RF transport industry accounts for 12% of the country's fixed assets and for about 20% of all investments (Table 1).

Table 1. Structure of investments by industry, as percent of the total

	Investments in fixed assets					Foreign investments				
	1998	1999	2000	2001	2002	1998	1999	2000	2001	2002
Investments total	100	100	100	100	100	100	100	100	100	100
Manufacturing	33.3	37.2	38.5	38.7	42.7	39.9	51.0	43.1	39.7	37.1
Transport	14.1	18.5	21.1	20.7	19.1	2.7	5.5	9.3	5.3	0.9
Trade and catering*	2.5	2.4	2.8	3.0	2.4	10.2	17.0	17.8	37.1	44.5
Housing & utilities	24.7	20.7	18.0	16.5	15.4	0.2	0.2	0.4	0.2	
Other industries	25.4	21.2	19.6	21.1	20.4	47	26.3	29.4	17.7	17.5

* "Investments in fixed assets" capture only wholesale trade in industrial goods

Source: The RF State Statistics Committee.

Compared to other Russian industries, investments in the transport sector are growing at extremely high rates. The main factors determining the industry's attractiveness are huge fixed assets, the irreversible character of the country's integration in the system of global economic relations, and the predictability of the results of new capacities launched. Capital investments in the industry (without consideration of the motorway system) increased by 17% from 2001 to 2002. In absolute figures, aggregate capital investments in transport system development (without railways and pipelines) from all sources amounted to R158 billion in 2002, with R48.3 billion or 30% coming from the federal budget, R72.4 billion or 46% from regional and local budgets, and R37.7 billion or 24% from extra-budgetary sources.

Maritime transport organizations continue to lead in luring investments from extra-budget sources. According to (EAST, 2003), they attracted R20.2 billion. Investments in 2002 somewhat exceeded those in 2001, while foreign loans attracted by Russian companies for marine transport development increased substantially. Overall, marine transport attracted R21 billion from all sources, or 13% of total investment in the country.

The total capacity of port terminals built in 2002 amounted to around 4.0 million tons. Turnover of Russian ports grew by almost one-third in one year. Moreover, the ports' role as the country's "trade windows" into the global economy is projected to grow. The 19% growth of investments in the transport sector was largely accounted for by investments from the regional and local budgets. New port developments play a special role in the drive to expand an export outlet to Europe. After launching a number of new projects implemented in the last 2 to 3 years, Russia has taken a large step in providing for its transport independence. In that sense, the country now holds a sort of a "controlling stake," with 75% of all Russian marine foreign-trade cargoes handled in Russian ports. At the same time, growth in exports of (especially) oil, petroleum products, grain and coal is significantly hindered by the lack, or poorly organized use of, port and other related transport infrastructure capacities. This is true not only for capacities alone, but for different trade sectors as well. For example, the additional 120 million tons of oil exports declared to be provided by 2010 would require revising the throughput capacities of pipelines and ports projected in the 1990s. The discussion of projects to lay a trunk oil pipeline to the nonfreezing Barents Sea, where a port may be built to handle tankers with deadweight of 250,000-300,000 tons, reveals the necessity of ensuring transport balance for integrating the development of transport, power production, and foreign trade. Similar projects for the Pacific coast are also in the works.

The main factors of restraining investment activity include:

- High dependence of national economy, public finance and payment balance on prices for oil, gas and raw materials;
- Excessive administrative barriers for the business, weak protection of property rights;
- Luck of law enforcement;
- Weak incentives for investors in terms of high bank loan rates;
- Underdeveloped banking system.

The state continues to play a significant role in the investment process. The RF Government approved a targeted federal program "Russian Transport System Modernization in 2002-2010" prepared by the Transport and Railways ministries. The program includes a number of subprograms: rail transport, motorways, civil aviation, a unified air traffic system, maritime transport, inland waterway transport, inland waterways, public passenger traffic reform, motor traffic security, informatization, and international transport corridors. The ten-year program was allocated R4646.3 billion, including R822.5 billion from the federal budget and R1385.8 billion from regional budgets. R337.3 billion in capital investment have already been spent in 2003.

In 2003, the ***Maritime Transport Subprogram*** spent R24.058 billion, including R 1.41 billion from the federal budget. The facilities launched included transshipment capacities for 4.89 million tons and 526 rm of berths (in Makhachkala, Olya, Murmansk, Vostochny, Ust-Luga and Kaliningrad Ports). In 2003, 15 transport vessels with an aggregate deadweight of 1,271,600 tons and nine support vessels were built. Construction on the atomic ice-breaker "50 Years of Victory" is underway.

In 2003, the ***Inland Waterway Transport Subprogram*** launched 16 new vessels, including 12 vessels with a 57,200 ton capacity for international cargo shipments, and four vessels for the Far North. Nineteen vessels with an aggregate capacity of 54,800 tons were modernized and re-equipped as oil tankers. Three passenger vessels were refurbished and equipped with more comfortable passenger cabins.

The projected overall economic growth with the corresponding increase in cargo turnover requires renewal of the transport fleet to a scale which cannot be funded by the transport enterprises themselves. Therefore, an important goal (apart from improving the efficiency of the existing capacities) is to lure private investment in the development of transport infrastructure. Investments of that scale will require new investor-related laws on concessions and on such arrangements like the currently popular "build-operate-and transfer" system. Under this system, the investor agrees to develop a turnkey infrastructure project (a port, container terminal, airport, bridge, toll-road, etc.) and operate it for 20 to 30 years. After that term, the state will have the right to buy out the controlling stake in the facility from the investor at a mutually-beneficial price established at the moment the agreement is signed. The Transport Strategy envisions different types of public-private partnerships like concession arrangements for such projects as toll roads or city transport development, port and airport modernization, and the establishment of free economic zones and industrial parks in large transport hubs. Under this strategy, the government is to specify the division of federal and regional authority.

Some of the arrangements to be used to attract investments include the following:

- Investments by cargo owners in the infrastructure used for promoting their products in various markets (LUKOil, Surgitneftgaz, Rosugol, and Yukos Companies);
- Loans from international lending organizations against federal guarantees (an EBRD loan for the project "A Regional System of Navigation Safety in the Eastern Part of the Gulf of Finland";
- State-private partnership arrangements funded by loans provided against Russian bank guarantees;
- Issues of bond liabilities planned in the draft federal budget for 2004.

At the same time, one should admit that by joining government and market forces (under the pretext that the infrastructure they jointly develop has a special status since it will serve other types of economic activities as well), one hardly solves the existing development problems in the longer perspective. As noted in (Kuznetsov Yu., 2003, p.60), such arrangements will make it impossible to determine the market prices for road, bridge, and rail services, or to calculate the charges for areas under the traffic infrastructure. Given the scale and the long-term character of government investments in the transport sector, any designers' mistake may lead to colossal losses, incomparable to potential losses by private companies investing in a single road or port.

The transportation services market is currently in the making (like the majority of Russian markets in general). Cargo turnover rates grow largely due to favorable conditions in the raw material markets and protectionist tariff policies by the government. As for shipment costs, they remain excessive by world standards and show no signs of reduction.

Developing new transport routes is impossible until the idea of economic efficiency is firmly adopted in the sector. The still-applied principle of special (geopolitical, ideological, etc.) status for transport infrastructure does not allow for the estimation of the actual cost of the use of land under transport facilities, which leads to inefficient utilization of resources due to designer mistakes and/or bureaucratic ambitions. Therefore, one can step up present investment rates only on the condition of a significantly increased private capital participation in the sector. One should not forget that over R2.0 billion of the R4.5 billion projected for the federal program, "Modernization of the Russian Transport System," is expected to come from extra-budgetary sources. To make that happen, the state must not only provide propitious conditions, but it must primarily limit its own participation in the transport development process.

9 Anti-Monopoly Policy and Privatization

It is important to note here that among the issues currently pushed to the forefront of Russia's transitional-economy challenges are those related to the still-debated problem of the state's role in the economy and the formation of a system of state intervention in the economy. The special acuteness of the issue of state supervision over natural monopoly activities arises not only from the fact that the former system of management has been annihilated, but also from a certain delay in a much needed reform of the natural monopoly sector. The general concept of a natural monopoly reform calls for curtailing state regulation to be replaced by competition between economic agents. In 2002, the reform of the Russian railway system began. The basic principals of the reform include:

- Single state-owned infrastructure,
- Centralized traffic control,
- Sustainability and security.

The actions of reforming the Russian railway system are based on Program of Structural Reform of Railways, approved by the Decision of the RF government on 18 May 2001 № 384 and Action Plan of the program for 2003 to 2005, approved upon decision of the RF government on 6 May 2003, № 283.

The Medium-Term Program for the Social and Economic Development of the Russian Federation from 2003 to 2005 plans the following steps during the first phase of the reform:

- Division of state governance and economic management functions in rail transport with simultaneous unbundling of competitive services from the monopoly structure;
- Phased elimination of the cross-subsidizing of passenger services at the expense of cargo operations, as well as the cross-subsidizing of internal operations at the expense of export and import shipments; and
- Provision of guaranteed non-discriminatory access to the federal rail infrastructure for independent cargo and passenger operators and rolling-stock users;
- Removal of social, individual-services and other (non-specialized) facilities from the federal rail balance in order to cut non-productive costs as well as provision for financial transparency of all economic activities in the transport industry, including the introduction of separate financial accounting.

The three-stage reform plan most closely resembles the "vertical access" model. The infrastructure has been opened to independent train operating companies, which pay a published, transparent access fee for their use of the infrastructure. Shippers may direct their rail carrier to use the shippers' own rolling stock, and the carrier receives a discount on the infrastructure access fee for using privately-owned rolling stock rather than RZhD-owned rolling stock. RZhD will nevertheless still operate the railway infrastructure and remain in the train operating business. RZhD owns at least fifty percent of the rolling stock in the system.

However, as pointed out by Russell Pittman* (Pittman, 2004), there is one very important sense in which the reform plan, at least so far and apparently through the second stage of reform as well, differs from the usual "vertical access" model. In Russia, legislators and regulators do not rely on competition among train operators or from motor or water carriers to protect shippers from monopolistic railway rates. Rather, the rates paid by shippers using RZhD trains remain strictly regulated with very specific commodity, location, and distance parameters set out in Tariff Price List 10-01.

Despite the adoption of the Transport Strategy aimed at developing competition in the transport sector, a trend toward increased government intervention is still in place. For example, the draft law "On Marine Ports in the RF" currently tabled at the Federation Council includes provisions determining state participation in port administration rather than defining ports as legal entities in the general system of civil and legal relations in the domain of marine port services. The draft defines

* Director of Economic Research and Director of International Technical Assistance, Economic Analysis Group, Antitrust Division, U.S. Department of Justice, and Visiting Professor, New Economic School, Moscow.

every port as a "complex of structures," the property of which (waterworks and berths) remains under federal ownership. Without a clear definition of ports as legal entities in the general system of civil and legal relations, one is not be able to distinguish between port administrations, operators, consignors, cargo carriers, etc. The draft (sent back for revision) also proposed to retain state regulation of port activities based on natural monopoly laws. In practice, this provision would only stifle competition between maritime ports, push up prices and degrade the quality of services.

When infrastructure monopolies operate in environments combining monopoly and potentially competitive types of activities, the distribution of a large share of economic resources is affected through non-market mechanisms. This calls for immediate implementation of the main infrastructure monopoly reforms planned in power industry, railways and telecommunications. The only path monopolies choose in the absence of competitors or market-demand constraints is that of pushing up their costs and prices; their growing needs in long-term investment funding are also covered by higher consumer tariffs, which leaves the financial system resources of a country practically unused.

Antimonopoly regulation in Russia has to define and prevent an abuse of dominant positions as well as agreements between firms and financial organizations. The current rules for the control of economic concentration, however, are rather complicated and non-transparent in terms of procedures.

In order to facilitate the development of the market, the Ministry of Economic Development and Trade has prepared an amendment to the law "On competition and restriction monopolistic activity on the markets," thereby introducing new criteria for the control of economic concentration on the market power. The main approach to the new order is to diminish the number of transactions under control of antimonopoly regulation, to simplify the application to the antimonopoly body, and to create an information system of antimonopoly legislation and practice.

Privatization is one of the main areas of institutional development and private investment mobilization strategy. Its goal is the marketwise transformation of state-owned enterprises which do not perform state functions while enhancing the efficiency of state property management and transport activities regulation. Despite 10 years of privatization of the state property, the significant part of the Russian GDP is produced in the non-market sector. Besides there are a lot of minor shares of the commercial enterprises belonging to the state without any real state participation in the company's governance.

Today, the federal government holds stakes in 187 JSCs, only 30 of those being with controlling staked and 70 with blocking stakes. However, even minority or golden-share participation of the state represents a constraint for private investors.

The majority of transport enterprises in the country have been privatized, and over 90% of cargo shipments (without consideration of the Ministry of Railway Operations) are accounted for by the non-government sector. Before the Transport Strategy was adopted, privatization in the industry had moved at a snail's pace.

Of 35 enterprises earmarked under the program for divestiture in 2002, only one was actually privatized. The sale of state stakes in JSCs was also slow, with only three stakes (out of the 137 offered) sold in 2002. The privatization plan for 2003 included 44 federal state unitary enterprises (FGUP) and stakes in 175 JSCs (with only 30 FGUPs finally transformed into JSCs). The privatization program for 2004 includes 69 FGUPs (47 in the commercial aviation, 20 in motor transport, nine in maritime services, three in river transport, and six in road maintenance services), and stakes in 59 JSCs (15 in air transport, nine in motor transport, 16 in the river transport, and 19 in maritime services).

The RF Transport Minister, S. Frank, noted in (Frank, 2003) that "with [privatization] rates like that, the government will be doomed to participate in JSCs for another 50 years. By putting the brake on privatization, we conserve a huge passive non-market layer in the transport industry. There can be but one conclusion: we need private investments."

In practice, however, the transport authorities are not happy about the initiatives of the Russian Government (Ministry state property management) to sell shares of the seaports. Just after special auctions, where 34.5% of Taganrog seaport and 22% of Murmansk and Tuapse seaports were sold, the Ministry of Transport had lost the majority stock. The Ministry has therefore initiated consideration of a draft on a new law with the main idea being to allow the state to maintain its grasp on seaports. The second direction of the Ministry activity is the creation of the federal state unitary enterprise "Rosmormort" in order to control state property in the seaports.

All transport industry sectors must create competition-friendly conditions by unbundling potentially competitive activities from natural-monopoly sectors. The government should focus on regulating the (land, water, and air) space of transport corridors, while management of these corridors must be turned over to private hands. These may be transport infrastructure management companies (in charge of rail, road, and pipeline operations), dispatcher/controller companies (including those in air transport), or companies operating various types of terminals (berths, runways, etc). As for state-owned companies, they should be managed under the existing legal (but not administrative) arrangements, i.e. through stakeholder meetings, Boards of Directors and appointed company presidents. The cost of state company services operating infrastructure facilities must be determined at organized markets. Of equal importance, all newly-created assets must be legally declared free of any state-participation or "social" encumbrances (Zavadnikov, 2003).

Administrative reform should specify the division of authority between the RF and federation entities, as many regions even today continue financing the maintenance and development of waterways, airfields and the like in violation of laws adopted back in 1993. Another method to lure investment would be the creation of a favorable climate for registering transportation services and vessels in Russia (e.g., in a Russian international maritime register).

10 Conclusion

Transport is to become one of the main instruments for Russian integration into the global economy, strengthening its position in traditional markets and ensuring entry into new ones. Russia's updated transport policies must take into account long-term global trends as well. The main approaches with respect to the future development of the transport system must include: de-monopolization and competition, replacement of licensing with more efficient arrangements to ensure civil liability, disclosure of information on government activities, separation of the state from economic activities, and simplification of tax treatment. These measures will help Russia take advantage of its propitious conditions for developing transit services.

At present, administrative structures and economic mechanisms created under the planned economy still survive to a large extent in the transport industry. Under the previous economic system, the transport sector had a commodity-distribution function without taking into account the actual market requirements. Even now, there is still an excessive presence of the state in the transport businesses and excessive state regulation of certain transport activities. In the railway sector, market reforms are only in their early phases of inception. Certain types of transport services show low economic efficiency and give no appeal to private investors and entrepreneurs. The main approach to developing a transport system of the future must be based on clear-cut principles and uniform treatment of structural changes aimed at enhancing the sector's competitiveness and customer satisfaction capabilities. In the short-term, however, the government is pursuing a politically-motivated strategy aimed at complete autonomy of foreign trade and transport activities by applying methods of state regulation, subsidies, and new capacity development.

Appendix 1

Table 2. Russian Foreign Trade Turnover*

	UAD million						As % of previous period					
	1998	**1999**	**2000**	**2001**	**2002**	**Jan.-Nov. 2003 ****	**1998**	**1999**	**2000**	**2001**	**2002**	**Jan.-Nov. 2003 ****
Russian foreign trade turnover total												
Commodity exports	74.4	75.6	105.0	101.9	107.9	121.5	85.7	101.5	139.0	97.0	105.6	126.2
Commodity imports	58.0	39.5	44.9	53.8	61.0	67.1	80.6	68.1	113.5	119.8	113.4	123.1
Russian foreign trade turnover with non-CIS countries												
Commodity exports	58.7	63.6	90.8	86.6	91.2		86.5	108.4	142.8	95.4	105.3	
Commodity imports	43.7	29.2	31.4	40.7	48.8		81.9	66.7	107.8	129.6	119.9	
Russian foreign trade turnover with CIS countries												
Commodity exports	15.8	12.0	14.3	15.3	16.4		82.8	76.0	118.8	107.2	107.2	
Commodity imports	14.3	10.4	13.4	13.0	12.2		76.9	72.6	129.4	97.1	93.2	

Sources: *Voprosy statistiki (Statistics Issues), №1, 2004, pp. 79-81;

** http://www.gks.ru/scripts/free/1c.exe?XXXX05R.1.1

Table 3. Commodity Structure of Russian Exports (in actual prices)

	1995		1997		1998		1999		2000		2001		2002	
	USD million	as % of the total	USD million	as % of the total	USD million	as % of the total	USD million	as % of the total	USD million	as % of the total	USD million	as % of the total	USD million	as % of the total
Exports total, including	*78217*	*100*	*85096*	*100*	*71314*	*100*	*72885*	*100*	*103093*	*100*	*99970*	*100*	*106154*	*100*
Foodstuffs and raw materials (except textiles)	1378.2	3.3	1600.2	1.9	1461.7	2.1	976.0	1.3	1623.2	1.6	1886.7	1.9	2732.6	2.6
Mineral products	33278.0	42.0	41100.9	48.4	30508.3	42.8	32689.0	44.9	55487.7	53.8	54653.3	54.7	58626.3	55.2
Chemical industry products, Indian rubber	7842.5	9.9	7100.8	8.3	6149.9	8.7	6177.0	8.5	7392.3	7.2	7480.5	7.5	7381.0	7.0
Hide, fur and hide/fur articles	313.2	0.4	399.8	0.5	389.3	0.6	207.0	0.3	269.7	0.3	228.7	0.2	268.5	0.3
Timber and pulp & paper goods	4362.7	5.6	3600.5	4.2	3532.7	4.9	3716.0	5.1	4460.1	4.3	4426.8	4.4	4908.3	4.6
Textiles and footwear	1153.5	1.5	931.5	1.1	842.8	1.1	811.0	1.1	816.5	0.8	798.2	0.8	883.3	0.8
Metals, precious stones and articles	20900.8	26.1	20400.9	24.0	19650.1	27.6	19017.0	26.1	22369.7	21.7	18797.9	18.8	19742.9	18.6
Machines, equipment and vehicles	7962.3	9.9	9160.4	10.7	8151.4	11.4	7958.3	10.9	9070.9	8.8	10471.0	10.5	10063.1	9.5
Other commodities	1025.8	1.3	800.7	0.9	627.6	0.8	1334.0	1.8	1602.8	1.5	1226.5	1.2	1548.3	1.4

Source: Russian Statistical Yearbook. 2003: Statistical Bulletin, Moscow: RF State Statistics Committee, 2003, p. 637.

Table 4. Commodity Structure of Russian Imports (in actual prices)

	1995		1997		1998		1999		2000		2001		2002	
	USD million	**as % of the total**	**USD million**	**as % of the total**	**USD million**	**as % of the total**	**USD million**	**as % of the total**	**USD million**	**as % of the total**	**USD million**	**as % of the total**	**USD million**	**as % of the total**
Imports total, including	*46709*	*100*	*53123*	*100*	*43580*	*100*	*30278*	*100*	*33879*	*100*	*41881*	*100*	*46153*	*100*
Foodstuffs and raw materials (except textiles)	13152.2	28.2	13278.4	25.1	10820.1	24.8	8073.0	26.7	7384.1	21.8	9204.9	22.0	10363.1	22.5
Mineral products	3001.2	6.4	3106.2	5.8	2324.3	5.4	1207.0	4.0	2136.7	6.3	1699.7	4.1	1713.8	3.7
Chemical industry products, Indian rubber	5088.3	10.9	7625.6	14.4	6578.5	15.1	4869.0	16.0	6080.4	18.0	7631.7	18.2	7711.6	16.7
Hide, fur and hide/fur articles	166.5	0.4	180.6	0.3	125.1	0.3	87.0	0.3	126.3	0.4	220.5	0.5	206.0	0.5
Timber and pulp & paper goods	1103.6	2.4	1863.3	3.6	1675.3	3.8	1077.0	3.6	1293.3	3.8	1687.2	4.0	1999.6	4.3
Textiles and footwear	2643.8	5.5	2435.1	4.5	1789.7	4.1	1583.0	5.2	1990.7	5.9	2296.5	5.5	2438.6	5.3
Metals, precious stones and articles	3956.3	8.4	3830.9	7.1	3165.2	7.2	2223.0	7.3	2824.4	8.3	3113.9	7.4	2961.1	6.4
Machines, equipment and vehicles	15704.1	33.7	18709.2	35.3	15500.2	35.6	10071.4	33.3	10648.2	31.4	14230.5	34.0	16720.9	36.2
Other commodities	1893.0	4.1	2094.1	3.9	1601.1	3.7	1086.4	3.6	1394.3	4.1	1796.4	4.3	2038.3	4.4

Source: Russian Statistical Yearbook. 2003: Statistical Bulletin, Moscow: RF State Statistics Committee, 2003, p. 639.

Appendix 2

Table 5. Cargo Shipments by Types of Public Transport, million ton

	1998	1999	2000	2001	2002
All types of transport total,	*2349*	*2428*	*2560*	*2610*	*2613*
including:					
railways	835	947	1047	1058	1084
motor transport	593	556	550	561	503
pipelines	790	802	829	853	899
maritime transport	36	31	27	24	26
inland water transport	94	91	106	113	100
air transport[3)]	0.6	0.7	0.8	0.9	0.9

Source: Russian Statistical Yearbook. 2003: Statistical Bulletin, Moscow: RF State Statistics Committee, 2003, p. 451.

Table 6. International Cargo Turnover by Some Types of Public Transport [1)] (billion ton/km)

	1995	1996	1997	1998	1999	2000	2001	2002
Motor transport[2)]	2.4	2.2	2.3	1.7	1.5	1.7	1.6	1.6
Maritime transport total,	286.7	218.7	201.8	144.6	114.7	93.6	87.5	87.3
including:								
Exports	...	43.1	37.6	27.3	24.8	30.0	31.2	31.7
Imports	...	6.7	6.3	5.0	3.1	3.7	4.0	3.0
Shipments between foreign ports	...	169.0	158.0	112.3	86.8	59.9	52.3	52.5
Inland water transport total,	40.3	38.4	38.9	32.6	27.2	31.3	42.2	45.9
including:								
Exports	21.6	17.7	17.8	13.4	14.3	18.7	29.3	36.2
Imports	2.1	1.8	2.2	1.6	0.8	1.5	2.2	2.1
Shipments between foreign destinations	16.5	18.8	18.4	17.2	10.0	9.1	9.6	7.3
Transit	0.1	0.1	0.5	0.5	2.1	2.0	1.1	0.4
Air transport	0.9	1.4	1.8	1.4	1.6	1.7	1.7[3)]	1.8

[1)] As of 1996 – including communication with CIS countries (for motor transport, as of 1997).

[2)] As of 1995 – by organizations of the Motor Transport Subsector.

[3)] In comparative conditions, the cargo turnover amounted to 94.1% of the 2000 level.

Source: Russian Statistical Yearbook. 2003: Statistical Bulletin, Moscow: RF State Statistics Committee, 2003, p. 454.

References

BOFIT Weekly, 11, 2003.

De Palacio Loyola, European Commission, http://www.eur.ru/ru/p_304.htm#top.

EAST (Vestnik Evroaziatskogo transportnogo sojuza), May-June 2003, №3 (10).

Filina, V. (2004), Transport Logistics: Modern Challenges and Development Areas, Problemy prognozirovanija, No1, 110-130.

Frank, S. (2001), Kaliningrad's pulse is under permanent control, Transport Rossii, No.5.

Frank, S. (2003), Transport Strategy, Ekonomika Rossii: XXI Century, No. 12.

Khodorkovsky, M. (2003), Verbatim report of the NK YUKOS President Mikhail Khodorkovsky at the Second Annual Meeting of the International Public Committee "Russia in the United Europe". Helsinki, 17 – 18 May 2003, Russian Expert Review, http://www.rusrev.org/BlazeServer/page.jsp?pk=node_1056100739877.

Kuznetsov, Yu. (2003), Infrastructure as business, Expert, No. 45, 60.

Nasonov, A. (2000), Transit is a Priority Area, Transport Rossii, No.32.

On the Transport Strategy of the Russian Federation. A Report by a task group of the RF State Council Presidium. 2003.

Osnovnyje pokazateli socialno-ekonomicheskogo razvitija Rossii (2003), BIKI, №100.

Pittman, R. (2004), Structural Reform of Railways: The Devil in the Details Remarks prepared for the conference "Reform and Privatization of Russian Railways"17-18 February 2004, Moscow.

Pletnev, S. (2003), V rossijskikh portakh probivajut "probki", http://www.strana.ru/print/205144.html.

RF Ministry of Economic Development and Trade. On the Social and Economic Development Results in the Russian Federation for 2000-2002, http://www.economy.gov.ru/merit/73.

RF Ministry of Transport. Development of the transport industry is a national target, (2001), Transport Rossii, No.12.

RF Ministry of Transport. The Transport Complex Results in 2003, and Priority Targets for 2004, http://www.mintrans.ru/pressa/Itogy_TK_2003.pdf.

RF State Statistics Committee. Information on the social and economic situation in Russia, January-December. Moscow: RF State Statistics Committee. 2003.

Ruksha, V. (2003), The Russian Fairway,Rossijskaja biznes-gazeta, No46.

Semenikhin, A. (2003), The key role belongs to ports, Far East Federal District, No.9.

Zavadnikov, V. (2003), De-monopolization is the future for the Russian transport industry. An interview for Rosbalt Agency (interviewed by Shatrov I.), Moscow, 07.04.2003.

Human Capital and Growth: A Panel Analysis for the EU-15, Selected Accession Countries and Russia

Dora Borbély and Christopher Schumann

1 Introduction

Since 1989, the year in which the political and economic transition in Central and Eastern Europe began, a lot has changed. While the geographically Western transition countries are facing EU-membership (Poland, Czech Republic, Slovakia, Hungary, Slovenia and the Baltic States), some are in a queue (Bulgaria, Romania) and some are not taking part in the enlargement process of the EU (e.g. Russia, Ukraine, Belarus). The decision for or against EU accession is generally one of a political nature, but without economic growth and development, none of the transition countries would even have the opportunity to join the club.

All transition countries experienced a phase of recession after the breakdown of their systems (see e.g. Kornai 1996). Only in the course of the 1990s were they able to return to positive growth rates with high variation between the countries. Some countries reached dynamic growth in the early 1990s while others had much longer recessions or set-backs in economic development. Table 3 in the annex shows the growth rates in real GDP per capita of selected transition countries and the Euro Area in the 1990s.

This discussion paper is an empirical analysis of the factors that have contributed to the growth of transition and EU countries in the course of the 1990s. We use the same methodology as Bassanini, Scarpetta and Hemmings (2001) who analyzed growth in OECD countries in the course of the 1970s and 1980s with respect to human capital, and several other variables that represent the influence of politics and institutions. In the framework of a panel model, we analyze growth in the EU-15 and four transition countries – Poland, Hungary, the Czech Republic and Russia – in the period of transition up to 2002.

The paper is organized as follows: In chapter 2 the theoretical background of the determinants of economic growth is described. In chapter 3 the model is presented, and chapter 4 then gives an overview on the underlying data. The empirical results are presented in chapter 5 and finally, chapter 6 concludes this discussion.

2 Determinants of Economic Growth

2.1 Accumulation of Capital and Labour

There are many determinants of economic growth. In his famous "Inquiry to the Causes of the Wealth of Nations," Adam Smith found several factors that foster economic growth (Smith, 1993 [1776]). A framework for empirical analyses of economic growth was later developed by Robert Solow. In his neoclassical growth model, accumulation of physical capital and labor are the main determinants of economic growth (Solow, 1956). While savings and investments foster growth, population growth was identified as having a negative impact on national income per capita. But Solow himself already recognized that the simple neoclassical model was insufficient to explain long and short term economic growth. Searching for other determinants, the theory of human capital was born.

2.2 Human Capital and Economic Growth

The term human capital is based mostly upon the work of Gary Becker, Jacob Mincer and Theodore W. Schultz. According to Becker, all "activities that influence psychic and monetary income by increasing the resources in people [...] are called human capital" (Becker, 1964, p.1). But because of methodological problems and a lack of data, the influence of human capital on economic growth could still not be analyzed empirically. Only in the mid-1980s were consistent growth models developed that overcame these difficulties. Paul Romer (1986) and Robert Lucas (1988) are known to be the founding fathers of the "new growth theory". In their models, external effects in the process of formation and diffusion of knowledge as well as investments in the educational sector enhance economic growth. In the following years, much empirical work confirmed these relations. One of the most well-known is the contribution of Mankiv/Romer/Weil (1992), in which the neoclassical model has been extended by human capital as a separate factor. But a special problem exists in the measurement of human capital (e.g. Schumann 2002). Although the understanding of the term human capital in the sense of Becker's definition is quite wide, the empirical measurement is often limited to the extent of formal schooling. In macroeconomic empirical analyses, enrolment rates as well as the average number of years that the population has spent in schools, is widely used. Meaningful indicators that reflect the quality of education and the usability of this acquired knowledge are still not available. The OECD plays an important role in gathering the necessary data in this field, for example via the "PISA study".

In the course of the 1990s, the influence of many other variables on economic growth were analyzed and proven correct. Some of these will be elaborated on in the following paragraphs.

2.3 Macroeconomic Stability

A stable macroeconomic framework is often considered a precondition for sustainable economic growth. The extent to which a country concentrates on macroeconomic stability can be grasped by looking at the inflation rate. In the literature, the following arguments can be found to enlighten the relationship between inflation and economic growth:

- Inflation acts as an additional tax on investment. The return of an investment must exceed not only the costs but also the devaluation of the currency in order to be profitable. A high degree of inflation lowers the probability of positive returns on investments in the medium and long run. And when investments become unprofitable, the growth process loses its central force.

- Inflation causes uncertainty. As a result, price signals are weak and long term calculations are difficult to pursue. This mechanism is obvious for a high inflation country, but not so obvious for a country with low or moderate inflation. It is argued that a stable moderate inflation process is better than a permanently changing level of inflation, even if this level is rather low.

Low inflation is of course not the only result of an economic policy that aims to create stability. But among others, Fischer (1991) justifies the focus on inflation in this context, because it can be used as an indicator for the ability of a government to steer its country's economy.

2.4 Size of Government

The activity of governments is an important determinant for the economic framework in which growth should take place. But in this context, the direction of the effect is not clear. On the one hand, a minimum degree of governmental activity is necessary to build and keep a reliable framework that enhances a minimum level of welfare and social peace. Another example is the legal system that does not function without state interference.

But beyond these basic functions, state activity does not necessarily have a positive impact. State interference must be considered to be positive if it helps to overcome negative external effects or economically unfavorable market situations or if it reinforces the effect of positive externalities. On the other hand, exaggerated state activity is counterproductive, if private economic actors are crowded out or a vast bureaucracy is established.

Not even the direction of the causality is clear cut. Growing state expenditures do not necessarily yield a higher national product, but on the contrary, a higher national product is often connected to a higher level of welfare which can be followed by higher state activity and bureaucracy.

In the framework of this paper, the size of government is measured by government consumption in relation to GDP. Generally, we expect a negative correlation between the size of government and growth. For the transition countries in our panel, this effect should be even stronger. They started off with an oversized public sector and mostly experienced a rather speedy contraction of government activity mainly through privatization, which at the same time had a positive impact on growth.

2.5 International Trade

In the context of the discussions on globalization, it is often said that there is a positive relationship between openness and economic growth. In particular, the transition countries that were in the process of major changes were consulted by international organizations to open up their markets. In the scientific sphere, the following advantages of openness appear:

- the expropriation of comparative advantages,
- the adoption of conditions of international competition,
- the acquisition of knowledge through the import of technology intensive products,
- the inflow of foreign capital,
- the access to foreign capital markets.

But there are counterarguments as well. Especially in the short run, the opening up of markets can result in a crowding out of domestic production and a decline of employment. In our analyses, we use, as Bassanini/Scarpetti/Hemmings (2001), a general indicator of trade openness that is constructed on the basis of imports and exports in relation to the GDP.

3 The Model

The starting point for estimating economic growth is the basic assumptions of a standard neoclassical growth model. It contains physical capital K labor and L as the main factors influencing production. Assuming constant returns to scale, as described by a Cobb-Douglas type of production technology, the simple production function Y is as follows:

$$Y_t = K_t^{\alpha} L_t^{1-\alpha} \tag{1}$$

In addition, our standard equation accounts for economic catching up. This is done by including the level of GDP of the previous period. A plausible explanation for different economic growth rates among countries is provided by the absolute convergence hypothesis. It states that in the long-run, all economies reach the same growth equilibrium. Thus, growth differences are explained by the catching-up process of less developed countries in order to reach the level of more developed economies. Equation (2) shows a standard form of a cross-country estimation that is often used in the empirical literature.

$$\ln(y_t) = a + \alpha \ln(y_{t-1}) + \beta \ln(s_t{}^K) + \gamma(n_t) + \varepsilon_t \tag{2}$$

Here, s^K stands for accumulation of physical capital, n for population growth and ε is the error term. Subtracting the level of GDP of the previous period leads to an estimable transformation in growth rates.

$$\Delta \ln(y_t) = a + \phi \ln(y_{t-1}) + \beta \ln(s_t{}^K) + \gamma(n_t) + \varepsilon_t \tag{3}$$

where $\phi = -(1-\alpha)$.

The speed of convergence is given by parameter ϕ. The results of such a cross-country analysis, however, ignore country-specific differences such as the access to different levels of technology, since the intercept and the estimated coefficients are assumed to be identical across countries; thus the differences are summed up in the error term. To be able to account for county-specific characteristics, we will now turn to a panel analysis.

Due to the two-dimensionality of a panel – time and cross-country dimension –, the number of observations is increased, as compared to a pure cross-country estimation. Depending on the estimation method used, the quality of estimation can also improve. The underlying sample allows us to use data for different time periods *t* (years), and for different countries *i*. The annual variation of GDP growth rates also contains, however, short-run, so called business cycle influences. This is not explained by the use of level variables, as shown in equation (3). Therefore we include the first differences of the exogenous variables into the regression to account for the short-run variability. A standard specification of panel estimation is shown in equation (4).

$$\Delta \ln(y_{i,t}) = a_{0,i} + \phi_i \ln(y_{i,t-1}) + a_{1,i}t + a_{2,i} \ln(s^K_{i,t}) + a_{3,i}n_{i,t} + b_{2,i}\Delta \ln(s^K_{i,t}) + b_{3,i}\Delta n_{i,t} + \varepsilon_{i,t} \quad (4)$$

The equation contains an intercept $a_{0,i}$ and a coefficient $a_{1,i}$, which measures the influence of time *t*. The coefficients $a_{2,i}$ and $a_{3,i}$ measure the long-run influence of physical capital and population growth on per capita GDP growth rates, whereas the coefficients $b_{2,i}$ und $b_{3,i}$ measure these variables' short-run influence.

Generally speaking, equation (4) can be estimated in two different ways. Using one extreme and assuming all coefficients to be completely independent among the countries under study, one can estimate the influence for each country separately by running *i* separate regressions. In this case, the average of the estimates is of special interest, which is usually called the Mean Group (MG) estimator. It ignores, however, the cross-country interdependence of the influencing variables. In addition, *t* must be large enough such that we can estimate the model for each country separately. Using the other extreme is applying the traditional pooled estimators, such as the fixed and the random effect estimators. These set all short and long-term parameters identical across the countries, except for the intercepts. The assumptions of this method also use very strong *a priori* restrictions on the coefficients, which in many cases are unlikely to be reflected by the data.

Imitating Bassanini, Scarpetta and Hemmings (2001), we will now apply a method situated between the two extremes. We use a Pooled Mean Group (PMG) estimator. The name highlights both the pooling and the averaging of the estimator. Accordingly, the PMG estimator constrains long-run coefficients for all countries to be the same, but allows the intercepts, short-run coefficients and error variances to differ freely across countries. It is assumed, that in the long-run, the influence of the variables on GDP growth is the same in every country, but not in the short-run. The explanation aims at the convergence hypothesis: economies, which are situated at a similar stage of development – just like the OECD countries or the European countries – have similar access to common technologies and to foreign capital. Furthermore, they have a similar intensity of intra-industry trade, which indicates how intense the economies are integrated.[1] It is noteworthy

[1] For a more detailed analysis of intra-industry trade in accession countries, see Borbély 2004.

that the speed of absolute convergence differs across countries, since the economies' positions differ with respect to the common long-run steady state. Also, there is difference in the speed of population growth.

In order to get a consistent estimation, the PMG estimator adopts a likelihood approach. The likelihood of the panel data model is then written as the product of the likelihoods for each country. The PMG calculations are made by using the Newton-Raphson algorithm, which uses both the first and the second derivatives of the log-likelihood function.[2]

The PMG specification of equation (4) is shown in equation (5) as follows:

$$\Delta \ln(y_{i,t}) = \phi_i \left[\ln(y_{i,t-1}) + \theta_1 t + \theta_2 \ln(s^K_{i,t}) + \theta_3 n_{i,t} + \theta_{0,i} \right] + b_{2,i} \Delta \ln(s^K_{i,t}) + b_{3,i} \Delta n_{i,t} + \varepsilon_{i,t} \qquad (5)$$

where $\theta_{0,i} = \frac{a_{0,i}}{\phi_i}$, $\theta_1 = \frac{a_{1,i}}{\phi_i}$, $\theta_2 = \frac{a_{2,i}}{\phi_i}$, $\theta_3 = \frac{a_{3,i}}{\phi_i}$.

The hypothesis of the long-run homogeneity of the variables is merely assumed ex-ante, however, we test for the correctness of the hypothesis in each specification. This happens by using a Likelihood Ratio and a Hausman test.

First we estimate equation (5) as our standard specification, and then we augment the specification with human capital as written in equation (6).

$$\begin{aligned} \Delta \ln(y_{i,t}) = {} & \phi_i \left[\ln(y_{i,t-1}) + \theta_2 \ln(s^K_{i,t}) + \theta_3 n_{i,t} + \theta_4 \ln(h_{i,t}) + \theta_{0,i} \right] \\ & + b_{2,i} \Delta \ln(s^K_{i,t}) + b_{3,i} \Delta n_{i,t} + b_{4,i} \Delta \ln(h_{i,t}) + \varepsilon_{i,t} \end{aligned} \qquad (6)$$

The time trend is excluded from this estimation. Including human capital causes the time trend in most empirical works to become insignificant, since in many countries, the average number of schooling has steadily increased in the sample period.[3]

We then augment equation (6) with the additional exogenous variables, which have already been explained in chapter two. Unfortunately, due to limited degrees of freedom, it is not possible to estimate the coefficients of these three variables simultaneously: inflation p, government consumption g, and trade intensity x. In equation (7) these variables are included in $Z \in \{p, g, x\}$.

$$\begin{aligned} \Delta \ln(y_{i,t}) = {} & \phi_i \left[\ln(y_{i,t-1}) + \theta_2 \ln(s^K_{i,t}) + \theta_3 n_{i,t} + \theta_4 \ln(h_{i,t}) + \theta_Z \ln(Z_{i,t}) + \theta_{0,i} \right] \\ & + b_{2,i} \Delta \ln(s^K_{i,t}) + b_{3,i} \Delta n_{i,t} + b_{4,i} \Delta \ln(h_{i,t}) + b_{Z,i} \Delta \ln(Z_{i,t}) + \varepsilon_{i,t} \end{aligned} \qquad (7)$$

Obviously, all exogenous variables appear both in the short-run and in the long-run. Hereby the lag order is being chosen for each country by the Schwarz Bayesian Criterion (SBC), which in our case is subject to a maximum lag of one.

---

[2] For a detailed description of the PMG Estimator see Pesaran et al. 1998a.

[3] This finding corresponds to Bassanini and Scarpetta (2001).

4 The Data

Having explained the model, we now turn to the description of the data. The endogenous variable – $\Delta\ln(y_{i,t})$ – represents in every specification the logarithm of the real GDP per capita growth rates. Physical capital accumulation – $\ln(s_{i,t}^{K})$ – is measured by the logarithm of the ratio of real gross capital formation in real GDP. Labor as an input of the production function is proxied by the rate of population growth, $n_{i,t}$. For Human Capital – $\ln(h_{i,t})$ – the logarithm of the average number of years of schooling of the population between 15-64 years of age is used. For the EU-15, annual data has been kindly provided by Bassanini, which is based on the Barro/Lee (2001) data set and adjusted according to De La Fuente and Domenech (2000). For the other countries we also interpolated and adjusted data from Barro/Lee (2001), which is originally given for every 5 years. Inflation – $p_{i,t}$ – is measured as the annual percentage change of the consumer price index. The size of the government – $\ln(g_{i,t})$ – is proxied by the logarithm of the ratio of nominal government consumption in nominal GDP. Finally, trade intensity – $\ln(x_{i,t})$ – is calculated according to the following formula, where we use the logarithm of all variables:

$$\text{"Trade Intensity"} = \frac{\text{Exports}}{\text{GDP}} + (1 - \frac{\text{Exports}}{\text{GDP}}) * \frac{\text{Imports}}{\text{GDP} - \text{Exports} + \text{Imports}}$$

To avoid a bias due to the differences in country size, the trade measure was adjusted for the country size.

We estimate equations (5), (6) and (7) for a pool of 19 countries for a maximum time period of 16 years, 1987-2002. In addition to the 15 current EU members, we include three accession countries – Poland, Hungary and the Czech Republic – and Russia in the analysis. Our panel is not balanced, because for the accession countries and Russia data availability is a problem, especially for the beginning of our sample. For these countries, reliable data is only available some years after the beginning of transition.

Table 4 in the annex gives an overview on the sources of the database used in this analysis.

5 Regression Results

The following chapter presents the results of the estimations. First, the focus is on the PMG estimates to draw conclusions on the country pool, and then we turn to the country-specific OLS regressions in order to compare the implications on an inter-country basis.

5.1 Pooled Mean Group Estimator

Table 1 contains the estimated coefficients for the standard equation and the human capital augmented equation for the pool of 19 countries. For the model specification, see equations (5) and (6). The table contains only the long-run impact of the variables, which have been restricted to be the same for all countries, but besides the equations all contain country-specific intercepts and short-run coefficients. The latter is expressed by the first difference of the variables. In addition, the standard equation contains a time trend, which can be interpreted as common technological progress in the context of a growth model. The time trend is, however, not significant. Thus it is dropped in the augmented model specifications.

Table 1. Pooled Mean Group Estimator: The Role of Convergence, Capital Accumulation, Population Growth and Human Capital for Economic Growth

Estimated Coefficients	Standard Equation	Human-Capital augmented
$\log(y_{t-1})$	-0.271*** (0.092)	-0.567*** (0.100)
$\log(s^K)$	1.624*** (0.114)	0.457*** (0.014)
n	-0.143*** (0.021)	-0.027*** (0.005)
$\log(h)$	-	1.272*** (0.028)
Joint Hausman-test	1.71	3.21
Number of observations	257	255

Standard errors in brackets.

In both estimations, all the long-term variables have a significant impact with the expected sign. Thus, the lagged per capita GDP has a negative impact on growth. The closer the economy is to its steady-state level, the slower the convergence process becomes. The existence of a convergence process is seen as a necessary requirement for a long-run relationship of the variables. Including human capital as an explanatory variable accelerates the convergence process.[4] In accordance with our expectation, accumulation of physical capital plays an important enhancing role for growth in both estimations. The coefficient in the human capital augmented equation for physical capital is broadly consistent with the empirical literature: one percent increase in the investment share brings an increase in steady state GDP per capita of about 0.5 percent. On the other hand, high population growth impedes a rise in GDP per capita significantly. Human capital has –

[4] This finding corresponds to the existing empirical literature. See e.g. German Council of Economic Experts (2002).

with an error probability of 1% – a significant positive impact on growth. The coefficient implies a very high return on investment in human capital: One extra year of average schooling, which corresponds to a rise in human capital by approximately 10 percent, raises steady-state output per capita by about 12%. In the pool of OECD countries, this value accounts for approximately 10% (Bassanini et al. 2001).

Two alternative tests are applied in all estimations to prove whether homogeneity of long-run coefficients is permitted: the Likelihood Ratio test and the Hausman test. The latter is applied both for each exogenous variable separately and for the combination of all exogenous variables as a joint Hausman test. In the case of these kind of panel studies, the Likelihood Ratio test usually rejects equality of long-run coefficients. This is also the case for all of our estimations.[5] On the contrary, the Hausman type of test statistic, which is applied to the difference between the MG estimator – here calculated as the unweighted average of the individual country coefficients – and the PMG estimator is not significant and thus does not reject the H_0-Hypothesis of the equality between the MG and the PMG, allowing the constraint of long-run coefficients' homogeneity.[6]

Table 2 shows the results for the macroeconomic and policy variables augmented specifications. The average schooling variable remains in all equations, in order to control for the constancy of human capital's influence on economic growth. Except for inflation, all variables are highly significant and appear with the expected sign all three estimations. The speed of convergence remains rather stable throughout the estimations, such as the highly significant positive influence of investment on economic growth. The coefficient for population growth persists at a very low level. The effect of the human capital variable is subject to variability. Depending on which macroeconomic variable is included in the equation, the impact of an extra year of average schooling varies significantly. Surprisingly, we do not find any significant influence of the level of inflation on economic growth. This contrasts to some studies carried out for the OECD countries, which find a strong negative effect on economic growth.[7] The impeding effect of a large government sector is, however, much more distinctive. For the underlying sample it proves that high government consumption expenditure tends to crowd out private economic activity. Unsurprisingly, the positive correlation between trade intensity and GDP per capita growth is strongly positive.

[5] This is also the case in both case studies done by Pesaran et al. (1998a). Implications and interpretation of these features can be found in Pesaran et al. (1998b).

[6] In table 1, the figure for the joint test for all long-run coefficients can be found. We have also tested for each long-run coefficient separately. There is no evidence that constraining any of the used exogenous long-run coefficients may cause problems.

[7] See e.g. Andres, J. and I. Hernando (1997).

Table 2. Pooled Mean Group Estimator: The Role of Macroeconomic Variables and Human Capital for Economic Growth

Estimated Coefficients	Human Capital and Inflation augmented	Human Capital and Government Expenditure augmented	Human Capital and Trade Intensity Augmented
$\log(y_{t-1})$	-0.314*** (0.098)	-0.412*** (0.099)	-0.523*** (0.092)
$\log(s^K)$	0.844*** (0.122)	0.474*** (0.030)	0.509*** (0.030)
N	-0.043*** (0.012)	-0.069*** (0.011)	-0.005*** (0.002)
$\log(h)$	2.983*** (0.157)	1.203*** (0.035)	0.798*** (0.050)
p	0.000 (0.000)	-	-
$\log(g)$	-	-0.128** (0.059)	-
$\log(x)$	-	-	0.357*** (0.028)
Joint Hausman-test	na	na	5.37
No. of observations:	252	255	255

Standard errors in brackets.

In the inflation and the government expenditure augmented equations, the joint Hausman test faces severe problems with the long-run homogeneity assumption. However, the PMG does pass the respective Hausman test for each exogenous variable separately. The trade augmented specification even passes the joint Hausman test.

5.2 Country-Specific Results

To allow comparisons of the country-specific long-run coefficients and the PGM estimations, we now turn to the results of the OLS regressions run for each country separately, which were used for calculating the MG estimator. The same error-correction specification has been applied to the country-specific estimations than to the PGM estimation. Also, the choice of the optimal lag structure – with a maximal lag order of 1 – is done by means of the Schwarz criterion mentioned above.

Following Pesaran et al. (1998), extreme outliers are identified by contrasting the country-specific coefficients to the MG estimator. If the fit is very poor and the country-specific coefficient distorts the MG estimates, the respective country is left out of the estimation. It turns out that the PMG estimator is very robust to outliers. Dropping extreme outliers from the sample changes the MG estimator substantially; however, it hardly changes the PMG estimator.

Some caution is required when interpreting the country-specific results, because sometimes problems occurred with convergence. However, as in the case of the PMGE estimations, convergence is a prerequisite for interpreting long-run coefficients.

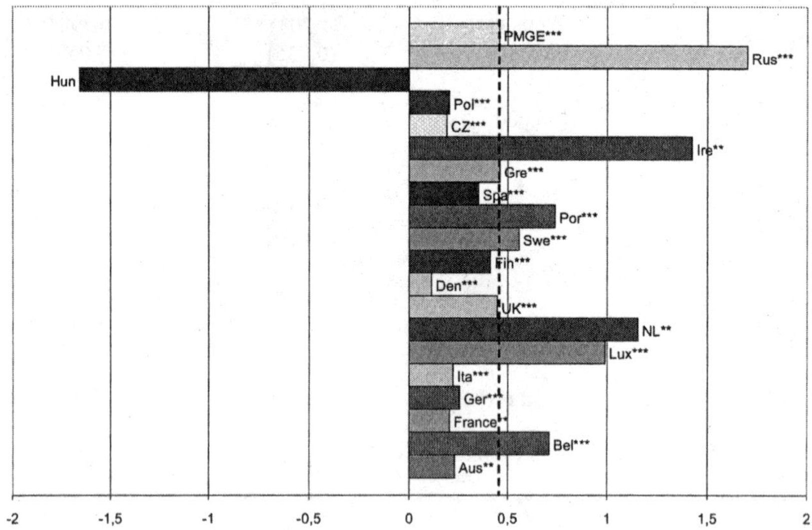

Fig. 1. Investment – Country-Specific and PGM long-run coefficients

In Figures 1-6 the country-specific long-run coefficients are contrasted to the PMG estimators. For investment, population growth and human capital, the human capital augmented basic specification results are used; For inflation, government expenditure and trade, the respective augmented models. Country groups are ordered in the same way in all figures. The top bar corresponds to the PMG estimator, below this is Russia, followed by the three EU accession countries: Hungary, Poland and the Czech Republic. Further down there are the four EU cohesion countries: Ireland, Greece, Spain and Portugal; followed by the Scandinavian EU countries: Sweden, Finland and Denmark. The rest of the European Union is ordered alphabetically at the lower end of the figure.

The influence of investment in most countries is, just as in the pool, significant, positive and rather strong (figure 1). Merely one outlier distorts the picture: Hungary, although the coefficient is not significant. The positive effect of investment is much higher in some cohesion countries – Ireland and Portugal – and in all the Benelux countries, than in the pooled mean. However, the strongest significant influence of investment on economic growth is generated in Russia. A one percent increase in investment share in Russia leads to a rise of steady-state GDP per capita by more than 1.5%. This is three times as much as the PMG estimator predicts. On the contrary, the effect of investment in accession countries is generally much lower than the PMG estimator.

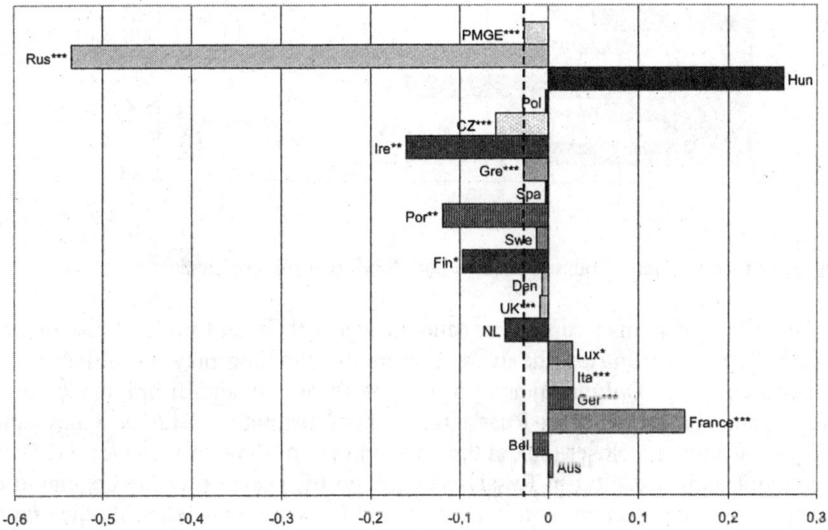

Fig. 2. Population Growth – Country-Specific and PGM long-run coefficients

Also concerning the impact of population growth, the Russian coefficients exceed those of the other countries (figure 2). This strong negative figure is due to a deep and continuous decline in the Russian population, which is accompanied by a simultaneously strong rise in GDP per capita values in the respective time period. This tendency is also valid for the Czech Republic. Negative coefficients, which are stronger than the pool average, result in some other countries as well, just as in Ireland, Portugal, Finland and the Netherlands, however, the explanation is very different. In these countries positive population growth is accompanied by a decline in GDP per capita growth rates. On the contrary, there are five countries with a significantly positive coefficient. Here, both GDP per capita growth rates and population growth rates are positive, whereby the former apparently exceeds the latter. Again, the Hungarian coefficient is not significant.

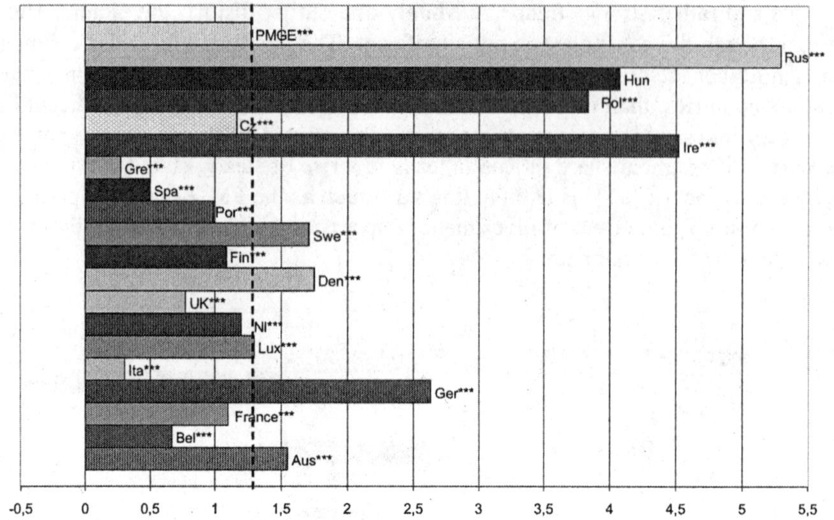

Fig. 3. Human Capital – Country-Specific and PGM long-run coefficients

The effect of human capital on economic growth is uniform and pronounced (figure 3). In all countries, the average years of schooling play a positive role in enhancing growth. Only in Hungary is the coefficient not significant, though positive. Again, the influence in Russia is the most distinctive. This becomes especially clear taking a closer look at the development of the two variables, GDP per capita and human capital in Russia. The period of recession at the beginning of transition is accompanied by a decline in average schooling years. At the end of the 1990s, the indicator for human capital reaches its initial level of 1990. This development falls into a period of strong economic growth. But also in Poland, Ireland, Sweden, Denmark, Germany and Austria, the growth enhancing power of human capital is higher than in the pool average. The influence of human capital on growth is relatively low in most cohesion countries – Greece, Spain and Portugal – as well as in some other European countries, just like Italy or Belgium. Generally speaking, our estimates confirm the findings of many growth regressions, stating that a high education level is essential for economic prosperity. This is especially true for transformation countries. For the remaining three macroeconomic and policy variables, inflation, government expenditure and trade exposure, country-specific effects are more ambiguous.

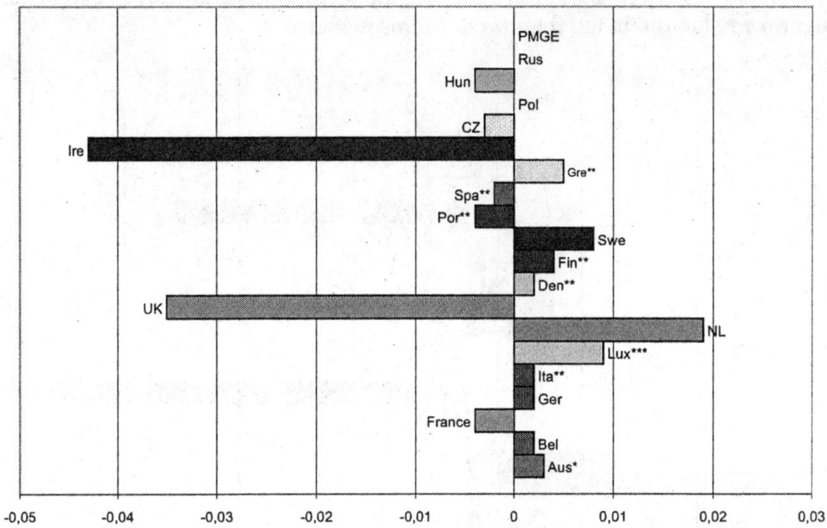

Fig. 4. Inflation – Country-Specific and PGM long-run coefficients

Concerning inflation (figure 4), we can not interpret any deviation from the pool, since the PMG estimator is not significant. Nevertheless, the cross-country regressions reveal only very low and often insignificant estimates. According to most of the existing literature, the level of inflation should be negatively correlated with the steady state GDP per capita. It is quite significant that economic policy aiming for macroeconomic stabilization, such as a low level of inflation, boosts economic growth. A significant and negative coefficient can be found only in Spain and Portugal in our sample. In Ireland and the UK, the distinctive negative correlation is not significant. On the other hand there is a range of countries – Greece, Finland, Denmark, Luxemburg, Italy and Austria – with a significant positive coefficient. Unfortunately, a significant coefficient is not found for either any of the accession countries, or for Russia.

As already described in chapter 2, the effect of government expenditure on economic growth is less clear cut (figure 5). However, the hypothesis that the size of government has an impact on growth receives some empirical support. The PMG estimator yields a significant and negative impact of government consumption on economic growth, indicating that government consumption causes some crowding-out effects of private activity. Basically, this corresponds to the findings of Bassanini et al. (2001). It is, however, noteworthy that - controlling for the financing of total government expenditure - they find a positive significant impact of government consumption on output per capita for the pooled average. We get this result for some of the countries, such as the Czech Republic, the UK and the Netherlands. In the Scandinavian countries, which are known as economies with a relatively large governmental sector, a negative influence of government consumption on growth cannot be asserted, with the exception of Finland. The anticipation, that in eastern European countries the effect is significantly negative, does not prove to be true in the framework of this model.

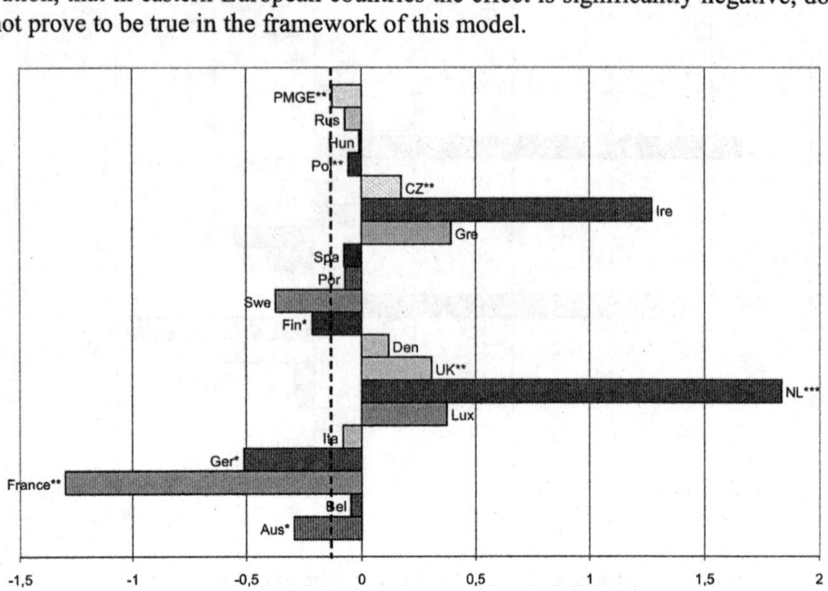

Fig. 5. Inflation – Country-Specific and PGM long-run coefficients

Last but not least, figure 6 shows the coefficients for the trade intensity. In accordance with the PMG estimator, most country-specific coefficients implicate a positive and significant impact of trade intensity on economic growth (figure 6). By far the highest impact is in Belgium, where a one percent increase in trade intensity leads to a rise in steady state GDP per capita of more than 3 percent. Also in Hungary, Poland, Portugal, Sweden, Germany and France, the positive impact is higher than in the average of the pool. Surprisingly, there are four countries, Czech Republic, Ireland, Greece and Luxemburg, where an increase in trade intensity significantly hinders economic growth. For Russia, the coefficient is not significant.

It would be interesting to simultaneously analyze the impact of macroeconomic and policy variables. According to the analysis of Bassanini et al. (2001) for the OECD countries, it turns out that there is considerable interaction between these variables, and the coefficients alter significantly depending on the change of model specification. Unfortunately, due to short time series and difficulties in data availability in transition countries, this is not possible. Technically, there are too little degrees of freedom in our country sample.

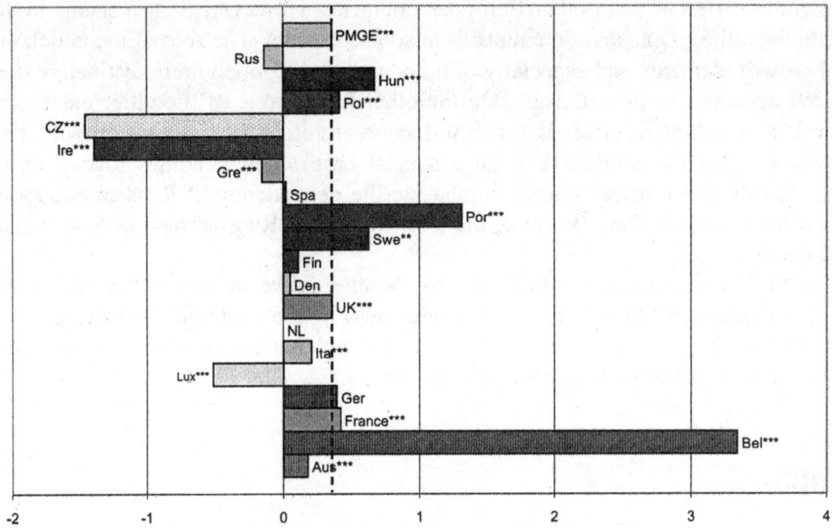

Fig. 6. Government Consumption – Country-Specific and PGM long-run coefficients

6 Conclusion

This paper analyses the links between accumulation of physical and human capital as well as some other macroeconomic and policy variables and economic growth. Using a Pooled Mean Group Estimator and taking into account a pool of all EU-15 countries plus three accession countries – Hungary, Poland and the Czech Republic – plus Russia, we find strong empirical support for the neoclassical elements of growth theory, such as physical capital and population growth. Furthermore, the analysis confirms the hypothesis that the accumulation of human capital is extremely important for enhancing economic growth. In the framework of our model, we find strong evidence for convergence in economic growth. For the pool, the level of inflation does not have a significant influence on growth. This finding is contradictory to most of the empirical literature, which finds a clear negative impact of inflation. The data supports the hypothesis that government consumption may hinder growth by crowding-out private economic activity. On the contrary, foreign trade intensity is beneficial for enhancing growth.

As far as country-specific impacts are concerned, the picture is quite clear for physical and human capital as well as for population growth. The impact of the remaining three analyzed variables – inflation, government consumption and trade intensity - is not as clear. Focusing on transition countries, we find that the basic interaction between the variables is not too different from the current EU countries. Thus, the mechanisms of economic growth in transition countries are not generally different from other European countries. However, Russia seems to deviate from the EU accession countries in some respects. The role of the neoclassical growth elements and especially of human capital is much more distinctive than in Western and Eastern Europe. On the other hand, none of the other macroeconomic and policy variables is found to have a significant impact on growth. This might either indicate Russia to be a special case when it comes to explaining growth. Many empirical studies emphasize the dependency of Russian economic growth on the oil price. But also, the poor quality of Russian data may influence the results.

In further research, we would like to use alternative indicators for the exogenous variables in order to prove the robustness of the findings. Furthermore, we would like to extend the set of countries and explanatory variables to shed more light on the determinants of economic growth.

Annex

Table 3. Percentage change of real GDP per capita for selected countries, (y-o-y)

	Russia	Poland	Czech Rep.	Hungary	Euro Area
1988					3.8
1989					3.5
1990					3.2
1991	-5.3	-3.3	-5.1		2.1
1992	-14.6	0.9	-0.3	-1.3	0.9
1993	-8.6	1.5	0.0	-0.1	-1.3
1994	-12.5	2.1	0.9	1.4	2.0
1995	-4.0	2.9	2.5	0.4	2.0
1996	-3.1	2.5	1.9	0.7	1.1
1997	1.2	2.8	-0.3	2.0	2.1
1998	-4.6	2.0	-0.4	2.2	2.6
1999	5.8	1.7	0.2	1.9	2.5
2000	8.9	1.7	1.4	2.3	3.2
2001	5.0	0.4	1.5	1.7	1.2
2002	4.3	1.1	0.9	1.6	0.5

Source: OECD, World Bank.

Table 4. Overview of data used in the sample

Variable	Description	Country	Source	Time horizon
Real GDP	Real GDP expressed in millions of national currency, 1995 prices, (Russia: in US-Dollar)	EU-15	OECD	1987-2002
		Russia	World Bank, EBRD	1990-2002
		Hungary	OECD	1991-2002
		Poland	OECD	1990-2002
		Czech Rep.	OECD	1990-2002
Population	Total population in thousand persons	EU-15	OECD	1987-2002
		Russia	Goskomstat, EBRD	1990-2002
		Hungary	OECD	1987-2002
		Poland	OECD	1987-2002
		Czech Rep.	OECD	1987-2002
Investment	Ratio of real gross capital formation in real GDP	EU-15	OECD	1987-2002
		Russia	World Bank	1990-2002
		Hungary	OECD	1991-2002
		Poland	OECD	1990-2002
		Czech Rep.	OECD	1990-2002
Human Capital	Average number of years of schooling of the population from 15-64 years of age	EU-15	Bassanini	1987-2002
		Russia	Barro/Lee	1990,1995,2000
		Hungary	Barro/Lee	1990,1995,2000
		Poland	Barro/Lee	1990,1995,2000
		Czech Rep.	Barro/Lee	1990,1995,2000
Government Consumption	Ratio of nominal government consumption in nominal GDP , (Russia: government expenditure)	EU-15	OECD	1987-2002
		Russia	World Bank	1990-2002
		Hungary	OECD	1991-2002
		Poland	OECD	1990-2002
		Czech Rep.	OECD	1990-2002
Inflation	Percentage of change of consumer prices (y-o-y)	EU-15	OECD	1987-2002
		Russia	EBRD	1991-2002
		Hungary	EBRD	1991-2002
		Poland	EBRD	1991-2002
		Czech Rep.	EBRD	1991-2002
Trade Intensity	Weighted average of export intensity and import penetration, See formula on page 9. Data needed: exports and imports	EU-15	OECD	1987-2002
		Russia	World Bank	1991-2002
		Hungary	OECD	1992-2002
		Poland	OECD	1991-2002
		Czech Rep.	OECD	1991-2002

References

Andres, J. and I. Hernando (1997). Does Inflation Harm Economic Growth? Evidence for the OECD. NBER Working Paper No. 6062.

Becker, G. (1964): Human Capital – A Theoretical and Empirical Analysis with Special Reference to Education, New York: National Bureau of Economic Research.

Borbély, D. (2004). EU Export Specialization Patterns in Selected Accession Countries. EIIW Working Paper No. 116, Wuppertal (forthcoming).

Barro, R.J. and X. Sala-i-Martin (1995). Economic Growth, McGraw-Hill.

Barro, R.J. and J.W. Lee (1996). International Measures of Schooling Years and Schooling Quality. American Economic Review, Papers and Proceedings, 32(3), 363-394.

Barro, R. J. and J.W. Lee (2001). International Data on Educational Attainment: Updates and Implications. Oxford Economic Papers, July, 53(3), 541-63.

Bassanini, A. and S. Scarpetta (2001). Does Human Capital Matter for Growth in OECD Countries? Evidence from PMG Estimates. *OECD* Economics Department Working Papers, No. 282, Paris.

Bassanini, A., S. Scarpetta and P. Hemmings (2001). Economic Growth: The Role of Policies and Institutions. Panel Data Evidence from OECD Countries. OECD Economics Department Working Papers, No. 283, Paris.

EBRD (1999). Transition Report – Ten Years of Transition, European Bank for Reconstruction and Development, London.

EBRD (2002). Transition Report – Agriculture and Rural Transition, European Bank for Reconstruction and Development, London.

Fischer, S. (1991). Growth, Macroeconomics and Development". NBER Macroeconomics Annual. 329-364.

Fuente, A. De La, and Domenech, R. (2000). Human Capital in Growth Regressions, How Much Difference Does Data Quality Make ? CSIS, Campus de la Universidad Autonome de Barcelona, mimeo.

German Council of Economic Experts (2002). Einflussfaktoren des Wirtschaftlichen Wachstums in Industrieländern: Eine Panelanalyse. In: Annual Report 2002/2003. Zwanzig Punkte für Beschäfigung und Wachstum. 316-355. http://www.sachverstaendigenrat-wirtschaft.de/gutacht/themen/z594_613j02.pdf.

Goskomstat (2002). Rossiisky Statistichesky Eshegodnik, 2002

Kornai, J. (1996). Unterwegs – Essays zur wirtschaftlichen Umgestaltung in Ungarn; Marburg: Metropolis.

Lucas, R. (1988): On the mechanics of economic development; in: Journal of Monetary Economics, 22, 3-42.

Mankiv, N.G.; Romer, D.; Weil, D.N. (1992): A Contribution to the Empirics of Economic Growth; in: Quaterly Journal of Economics 107 (2): 408-437.

OECD (2004). Statistics, Paris http://www.oecd.org/statsportal/0,2639,en_2825_293564_1_1_1_1_1,00.html.

Pesaran, M.H., Y. Shin and R.P. Smith (1998a). Pooled Mean Group Estimation of Dynamic Heterogenous Panels. http://www.econ.cam.ac.uk/faculty/pesaran.jasaold.pdf.

Pesaran, M.H., R.P. Smith and T. Akiyama (1998b). Energy Demand in Asian Economies, Oxford University Press.

Romer, P. (1986): Increasing Returns and Long-Run Growth; in: Journal of Political Economy, 94, 5, 1002-1037.

Schumann, C. (2002): Measuring human capital – old and new approaches and their suitability for growth analysis in transition countries, in: Raudjärv, Matti (eds.). The Effect of Accession to the European Union on the economic policy of Estonia. Berlin/Tallinn, 200-208.

Smith, A. (1993). An Inquiry into the Nature and Causes of the Wealth of Nations; [1776], Oxford: Oxford University Press.

Solow, R. (1956). A Contribution to the Theory of Economic Growth. In: Quarterly Journal of Economics, 70, 1, 65-94.

World Bank (2002). World Development Indicators, CD-Rom.

Telecommunications, Trade and Growth: Gravity Modeling and Empirical Analysis for Eastern Europe and Russia

Albrecht Kauffmann

1 Introduction

During the re-orientation of the economic systems of post-socialist countries which were highly integrated in the former Council of Mutual Economic Aid, foreign trade relations have had to be settled in a new way after the breakdown of communist order in Eastern Europe. The states at the western margin of the former Eastern Bloc searched – and have quickly found – the political, military and economic connection to western alliances that already existed, and to the economic area of the West. Successors of former Soviet Republics (FSU) did not have this ability in the majority of cases. Moreover, not only had the foreign trade channels to the former CMEA partners outside the Soviet Union been cut, the political decay of the USSR was simultaneously the end of the former highly integrated economic area of the Soviet Union. The centrally coordinated, excessive domestic trade between former Socialist Republics came to a standstill, the new foreign trade, created by disintegration of the former single market, and was hindered by many barriers resulting from non-cooperation of the monetary authorities (Gross/Steinherr 1995, ch. 13). Simultaneously, the development of foreign trade based on economic principles of the use of comparative advantages caused by national experience and factor properties was a chance to participate in the grid of international economic connections as a prerequisite to taking part in international labor division that promotes economic growth.

Particularly, Russia meets some requirements for taking up and enhancing foreign trade as a base of economic growth. Besides large natural resources, a level of education in all layers of the population exists as well as a readiness to put its labor force into economic activity. A part from trade barriers caused by institutional affairs of law and security, non-utilization of the existing potential of foreign trade may be caused by antiquated, expensive, and/or a non-existing infrastructure for the transfer of goods and information.

The ability to meet quantitative statements regarding the possibility of connection between international trade volumes on the one hand and progress in extension of infrastructure of information and telecommunication (ICT) on the other, have improved at the start of the 21st Century, particularly as a result of improved data availability. The concept of measurement of influence of ICT networking on foreign trade volume is based on the assumption that the improvement in transmission of information is helpful to overcome the "economic distance," which includes the geographical distance as one of many parts, between economically acting subjects. The inclusion of data that indicates the state of networking of information by ICT into well-known foreign trade models regressing international trade volumes to economic weight of trading partners and the (economic) distance between them could prove to be reasonable.

The gravity approach was named after the physical phenomenon of gravity and found its way from economic geography into spatial economic modeling in the first quarter of the 20th century. Linnemann (1966) was the first to apply the approach to international trade. The popularity of the gravity model may be caused by its simplicity and robustness. On the other hand, the advocates of gravity have had to deal with the reproach of a lack of reference to economic theory. Gravity modeling experienced some theoretical foundations during the last twenty years, e.g. by the works of Bergstrand (1985 and 1989), Deardorff (1998), Evenett/ Keller (1998) and Feenstra et al. (1998).

Welfens/ Jungmittag (2001) made a first analysis of bilateral trade volumes between 12 OECD countries, integrating annually cumulated duration of bilateral telephone connections into a gravity model as distance overcoming quantity. Separate estimations for 1995, 1996 and 1997, provide evidence of telecom utilization at a 5 percent level; in addition, the inclusion of these variables improves the coefficient of determination. In Welfens et al. (2003), the relation between national ICT infrastructure indicators and foreign trade volumes is analyzed by the inclusion of network densities of cable and mobile phones and the Internet into the gravity equation. The influence of ICT indicators cannot be rejected in a panel regression for 27 OECD countries for the period of 1995–2001, after consideration of strong multicollinearity between ICT-variables. In Von Westernhagen (2002), the inclusion of Internet host density into OLS gravity regression for some OECD and Eastern European countries shows significant positive influence on bilateral foreign trade volume. Further investigation of foreign trade between Eastern European transition and other countries under consideration for ICT networking aspects has so far not been done; there is a certain necessity to do this in face of the meaning of foreign trade for economic growth on the one hand and the current dynamic development and spreading of modern information and communications technologies on the other.

My investigation is restricted by data availability: First, for Russia and some other countries of the FSU, bilateral trade data were available only for 1998 and 1999; therefore, I will estimate gravity equations for these two periods separately. Second, my analysis is confined to existing foreign trade, as non-existing trade is not identified in the dataset. For this reason, the important question of whether the commencement of trade could be influenced by improved information and communications networking cannot be answered here. This should be done in the framework of a Tobit model (see e.g. Rohweder 1988). I will apply OLS methods for the estimation of bilateral trade volumes between all members of a group of countries, consisting of 24 transition countries and 33 of its main trading partners, and some subgroups of these two, by two connections; the aim of the investigation is to find an answer to the question if it is possible to ease existing bilateral trade by the improvement of national ICT infrastructure.

The following section deals with the ability to influence telecommunication networking on foreign trade theoretically. Section 3 gives an overview of the development of bilateral trade between the Eastern European transition countries and its main trading partners, and between subgroups of these. Section 4 describes some developments of national ICT indicators of these countries, while section 5 looks at a possible connection between bilateral trade and national ICT indicators in pairs and analyzes this in the framework of the gravity model. Finally, section 6 draws conclusions pertaining to this analysis.

2 Telecommunications, Foreign Trade, and Globalization

The technological advancements of the past three decades, with the introduction of the first microprocessors, the digitalization of media transmissions and the world-wide linking of information channels bringing about a continuous opening-up of new possibilities, has palpable consequences for all areas of life, in which information as input, output or as a helping factor plays an important role. Many authors claim that the information sector has established itself as a fourth sector of economic activity alongside the traditional sectors of agriculture and mining, manufacturing and services, and that its importance will only increase (see, for instance, Nefiodow 1994). The importance of quicker, more secure and more reliable information for trade in goods has grown steadily since the invention of pen and paper and has ensured that progress in the development of technologies for the transfer of information has been achieved. The expenses linked to the transfer of information should be considered transaction costs; through bundling, transactions costs for single trades are reduced. This can be considered a rationale for the establishment of organized markets.

As a result of the economies of scale connected with large networks, a result of the high level of investment and sunk costs involved in constructing and maintaining such networks, information network industries as with transport or energy networks are seen as natural monopolies. More in-depth analysis has revealed, however, that this is only valid in certain core sectors of these networks, whereas other services within this sector, such as information and transfer services, are subject to competition resulting in more efficient provision of service. The liberalization of telecommunications markets, based on such well founded theoretical considerations, for instance in the USA and other countries of the European Union has led to dramatic drops in prices in many sectors of the telecommunications markets, as well as to an increase in the variety and quality of services and products offered.

Parallel to this, developments occurred in two new communications networks, the separation of which in the not too distant future will be purely perfunctory: mobile telephony and the Internet. Both media have changed the shape and structure of the lives of the individuals who have access to the new technology. They have influenced developments in the nature of work and due to the reproducibility of digital content have opened up unthought-of possibilities in the transfer, storing and replication of information. This has had both desirable and undesirable consequences. Whereas demand for fixed-line connections in developed industrial countries stagnates because of market saturation, in markets for mobile and Internet services, including the necessary hardware and software, demand remains dynamic and growing.

The effect of the relatively uninhibited flow of information on foreign trade (also on other key areas of foreign trade such as international capital flows) has been dubbed "globalization" in colloquial speech. This term represents most vividly perhaps the most importance consequence of this intertwining: the coming together of the continents, in the sense that the individual's scope for decision-making and acting, previously separated and unaware of the others existence through barriers of distance, oceans, physical blockades, customs etc., are suddenly almost pervading each other. In other words, that once again a part of the economic distance, which limits the economic power of the individual and therefore protects his sovereignty and individuality, has been overcome.

If foreign trade hindered by all types of barriers is captured by the concept of economic distance, then the approach presented by the gravitation model, extended to include indicators for information and communication, attempts to quantitatively account for the overcoming of this particular aspect of economic distance.

An attempt to evaluate the phenomenon of globalization is difficult because it represents a collection of dynamic processes, the effects of which are felt in the most varied areas of society and the economy and are often unpredictable. To what extent the benefits realized from this opportunity are able to achieve the gains that globalization is perceived to offer, is just as difficult to predict as weighing up its potential benefits versus potential risks. It can, however, be stated with certainty that the expansion and modernization of existing information and telecommunications networks as with the construction of new networks, represents a necessary, although not sufficient, requirement for participation in the opportunities offered by globalization. The failure or delay in developing the ICT sector on the other hand offers no protection against the risks associated with globalization. State control over the "economy of networks", which exhibit the characteristic of a natural monopoly, in terms of an efficient regulation of private network monopolists would however be desirable and make economic sense.

3 Foreign Trade of Transition Countries

3.1 Choice of Countries to be Included in the Investigation

The choice of countries to be included in the quantitative analysis was determined by different requirements. It should contain all European and Central Asian countries that were integrated in the former CMEA and those countries that were most frequently "main trading partners" of them in 1998 and 1999. The main trading partners of a certain transition country are those countries with a sum of bilateral trade volume with this transition country between 90 to 95 % of its whole foreign trade volume during the periods 1998 and 1999. Another restriction of country choice was the availability of bilateral trade data.

Data foundation of this analysis was the voluminous dataset that Prof. Andrew K. Rose kindly placed at disposal on his homepage.

The dataset does not contain original data on the Direction of Trade (DoT) database by IMF, but it contains already well-prepared data of bilateral trade and other features needed for gravity modeling for 178 countries. The trade data of DoT – two each on FOB export and CIF import values for every couple of trading partners – are averaged and then deflated by the American CPI for all urban consumers (1982-1984=100; taken from www.freelunch.com); for every pair of countries $i,j = j,i$ **one** logarithm of bilateral trade volume in US Dollar is available. The reader can find the comprehensive description of this dataset in Rose 2003.

The investigation of trade volumes between each single transition country of the group

Armenia	Uzbekistan
Belarus	Czech Republic
Azerbaijan	Slovak Republic
Georgia	Estonia
Kazakhstan	Latvia
Kyrgyz Republic	Hungary
Bulgaria	Lithuania
Moldova	Mongolia
Russian Federation	Slovenia
Tajikistan	Poland
Turkmenistan Ukraine	Romania

with all other 177 potential trading partners led to a choice of 57 countries that became the object of our further analysis (see Tab. 1). Some dichotomous variables stand for membership in a main subgroup of our country choice: *transec* means, that the country belongs to the group of post-socialist transition countries, *fsu* stands for FSU-countries, *eucand* for EU member-candidates, and *eu* for EU members.

By combining these grouping variables with each other, bilateral subgroups of trading partners can be identified: e.g., pairs of trading partners stemming one from *transec*-group, the other from *nontransec*-group, we can put in a *transec.nontransec* group, with its own dummy variable; pairs of trading partners stemming from one group itself we name with the suffix *p*, e.g. *fsup* (see fig. 1 and fig. 2). This allows us to determine the influence of a trading partner pair's membership in one or more bilateral subgroups, and to estimate the gravity equation with data restricted by membership in one of these subgroups.

Table 1. Choice of countries included

		transec	fsu	eucand	Eu
USA	USA	0	0	0	0
United Kingdom	GBR	0	0	0	1
Austria	AUT	0	0	0	1
Belgium	BEL	0	0	0	1
Denmark	DNK	0	0	0	1
France	FRAU	0	0	0	1
Germany	DEU	0	0	0	1
Italy	ITA	0	0	0	1
The Netherlands	NLD	0	0	0	1

		transec	fsu	eucand	Eu
Norway	NOR	0	0	0	0
Sweden	SWE	0	0	0	1
Switzerland	CHE	0	0	0	0
Canada	CAN	0	0	0	0
Japan	JPN	0	0	0	0
Finland	FIN	0	0	0	1
Greece	GRC	0	0	0	1
Ireland	IRL	0	0	0	1
Spain	ESP	0	0	0	1
Turkey	TUR	0	0	0	0
Brasilia	BRA	0	0	0	0
Mexico	MEX	0	0	0	0
Cyprus	CYP	0	0	1	0
Iran	IRN	0	0	0	0
Israel	ISR	0	0	0	0
Egypt	EGY	0	0	0	0
Hongkong	HKG	0	0	0	0
India	IND	0	0	0	0
Indonesia	IDN	0	0	0	0
South Korea	KOR	0	0	0	0
Pakistan	PAK	0	0	0	0
Singapore	SGP	0	0	0	0
Thailand	THA	0	0	0	0
Armenia	ARM	1	1	0	0
Azerbaijan	AZE	1	1	0	0
Belorus	BLR	1	1	0	0
Georgia	GEO	1	1	0	0
Kazakhstan	KAZ	1	1	0	0
Kyrgyz Republic	KGZ	1	1	0	0
Bulgaria	BGR	1	0	0	0
Moldova	MDA	1	1	0	0
Russian Federation	RUS	1	1	0	0
Tajikistan	TJK	1	1	0	0
China	CHN	0	0	0	0
Turkmenistan	TKM	1	1	0	0
Ukraine	UKR	1	1	0	0
Uzbekistan	UZB	1	1	0	0
Czech Republic	CZE	1	0	1	0
Slovak Republic	SVK	1	0	1	0
Estonia	EST	1	1	1	0
Latvia	LVA	1	1	1	0
Hungary	HUN	1	0	1	0
Lithuania	LTU	1	1	1	0
Mongolia	MNG	1	0	0	0
Croatia	HRV	1	0	0	0
Slovenia	SVN	1	0	1	0
Poland	POL	1	0	1	0
Romania	ROM	1	0	0	0

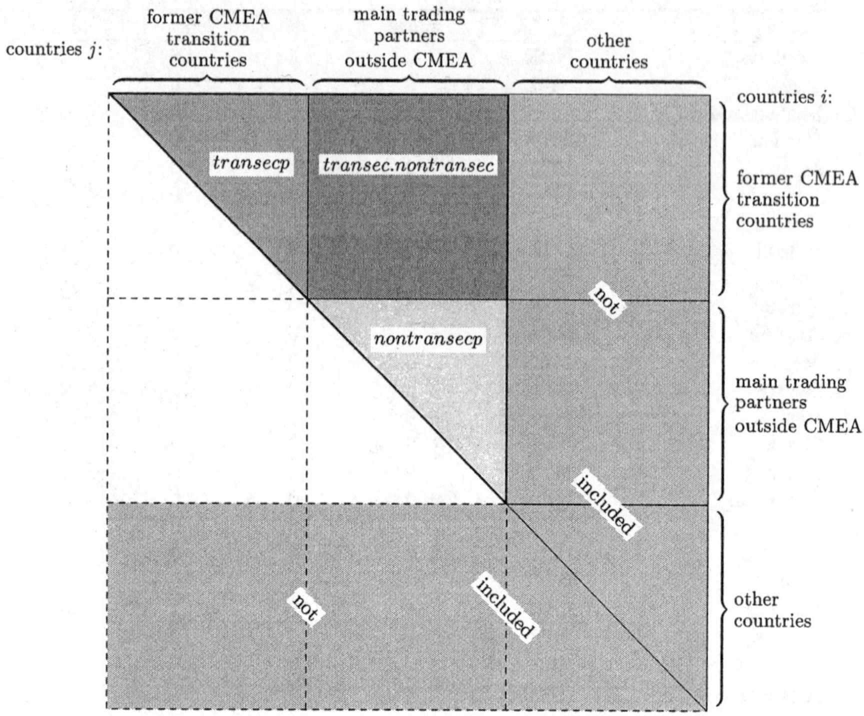

Fig. 1. Main subgroups of pairs of 178 countries

3.2 Development of Foreign Trade of Selected Country Groups

Even though we will specify the gravity equation with cross section data for 1998 and 1999, we have to take a glance at development of foreign trade over as long a period as possible. For this purpose, the graphics in fig. 3-8 show the aggregated trade volume as a percent of GDP of each member country of one group with all member countries of another group or with all other member countries of the same group, respectively. In this way, we gain an impression of the different trade development patterns, particularly of countries of the FSU and those transition countries that did not belong to the former USSR. Note that the trade volumes are taken from averaged values of the ROSE dataset, re-inflated by the US-CPI (see above) and divided by nominal GDP data from WDI 2002. In spite of possible strong differences in data of other sources, the relations, tendencies, and turning points should be the same.

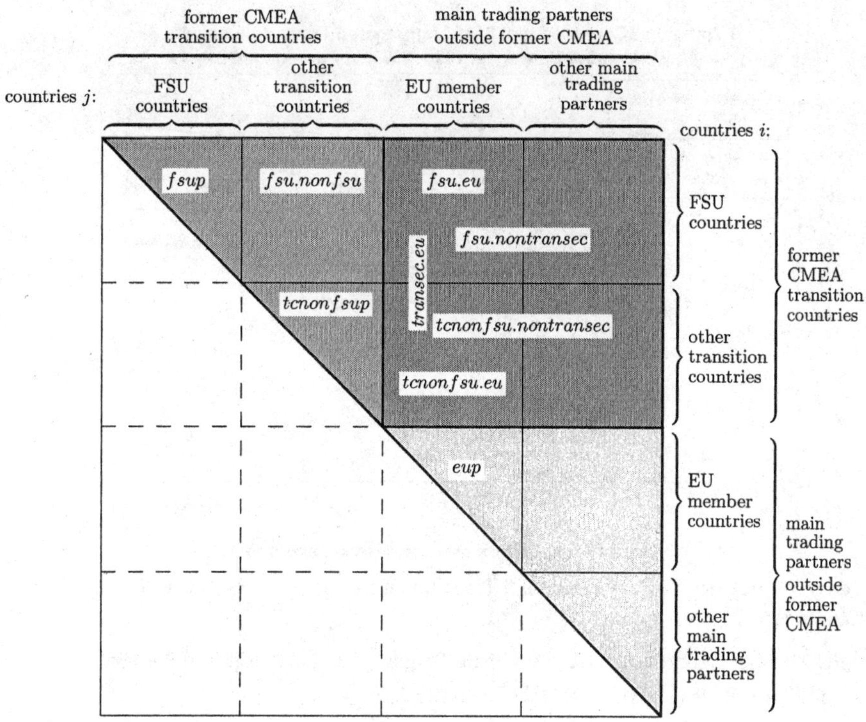

Fig. 2. Subgroups of selected 57 countries

One first finding is the higher share of trade of GDP of EU-member candidates with EU members than trade of FSU countries with the EU member group. Simultaneously we can see a lag of about five years in the trade development of FSU countries with EU members. Next, we should state that all plots of trade of FSU members show a turning point after the financial crisis in 1997; this bend is weaker in the charts of the former Baltic Soviet Republics. Third, foreign trade within the FSU group has a smaller mean value, but its relative standard deviation is high and growing. In comparison with this, the foreign trade within the group of other transition countries has a bigger share of its GDP, with decreasing dispersion. Finally, trade between FSU and Non-FSU transition countries shows a heterogeneous pattern. While amongst FSU country members only the Baltic Republics show stable development with a slightly increasing tendency, the other FSU country members show more staggering courses, with some cases possibly being caused by the Russian financial crisis. The share of trade of GDP of Non-FSU countries with FSU countries is small and decreasing; the synchronous development together with increasing foreign trade with EU member (and other OECD) countries may be an indication of trade diversion caused by integration of the EU-member candidates.

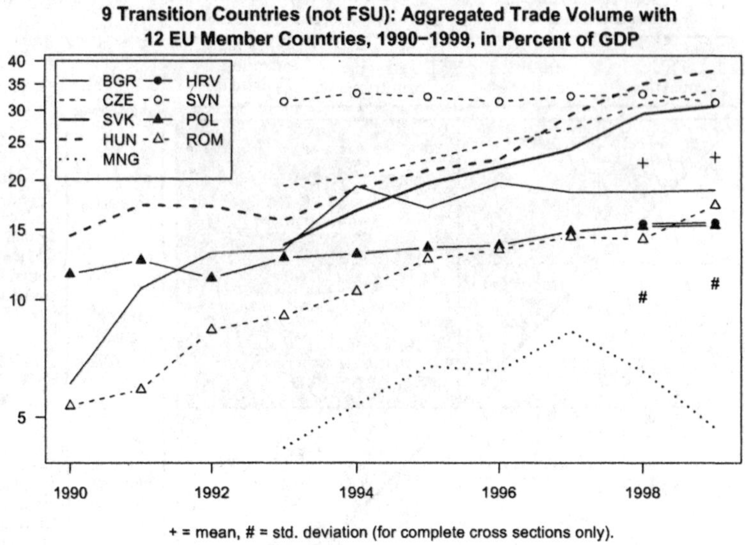

Fig. 3. Aggregated Trade Volume of 9 Transition Countries (not FSU) with 12 EU Member Countries*

* EU Member Countries are EU-15 without Belgium, Luxembourgh and Portugal.

Data Source: Rose (2003), WDI 2002, own calculations.

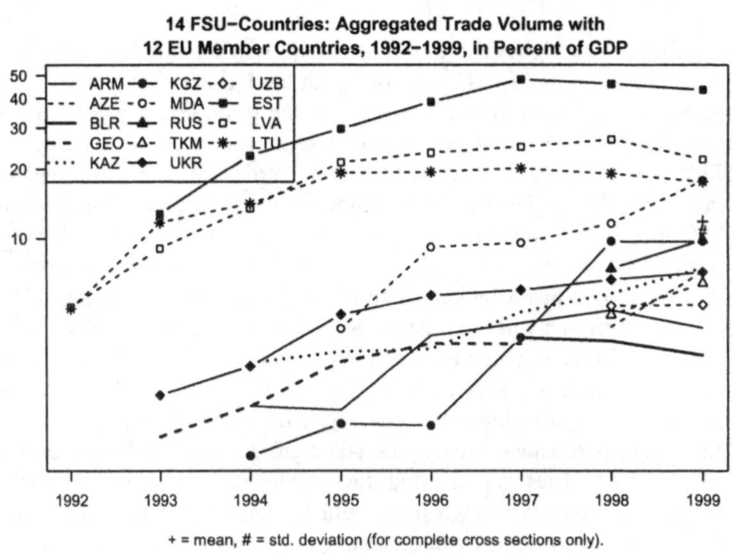

Fig. 4. Aggregated Trade Volume of 14 FSU Countries with 12 EU Member Countries*

*see note to Fig. 3.

Data Source: Rose (2003), WDI 2002, own calculations.

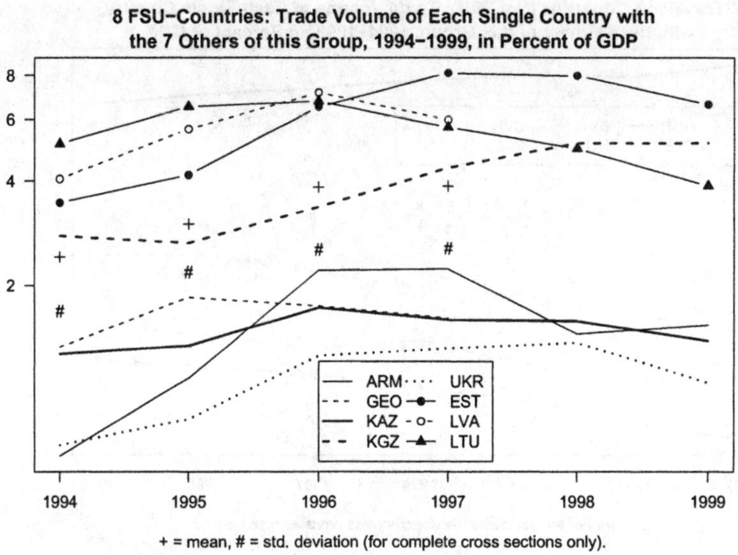

Fig. 5. Aggregated Trade Volume of 8 FSU Countries with Each 7 Other Members of this Group

Data Source: Rose (2003), WDI 2002, own calculations.

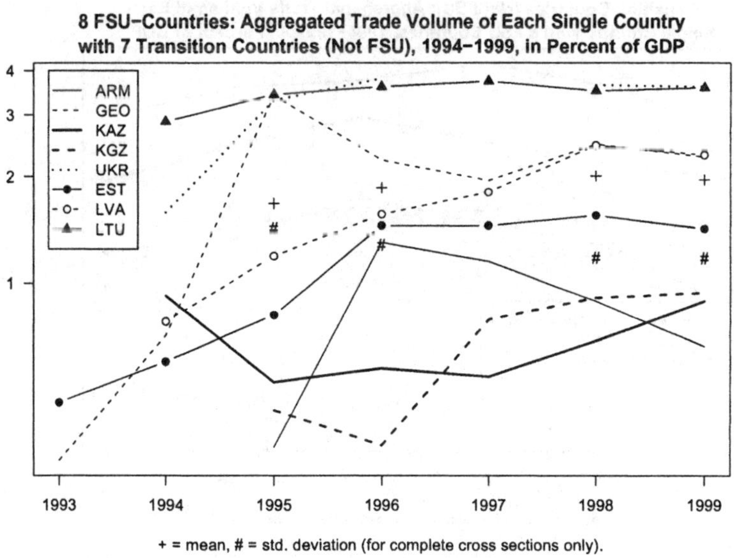

Fig. 6. Aggregated Trade Volume of 8 FSU Countries with 7 Transition Countries*

* Transition countries are BGR, CZE, SVK, HUN, SVN, POL, ROM.

Data Source: Rose (2003), WDI 2002, own calculations.

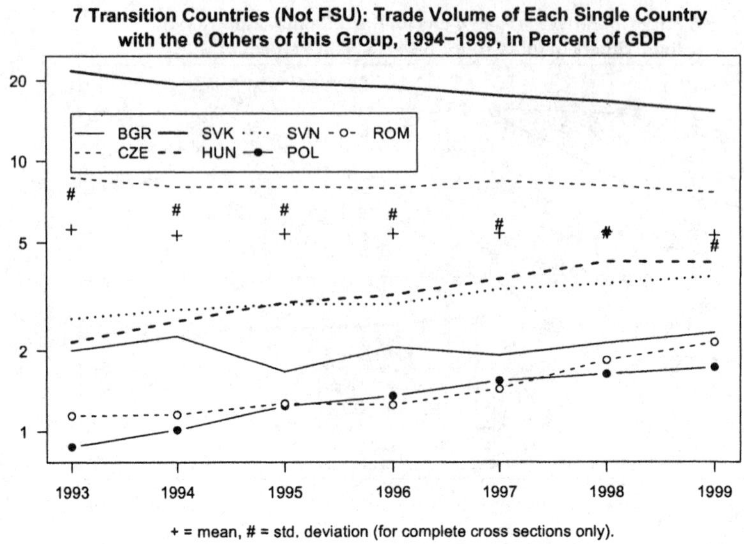

Fig. 7. Aggregated Trade Volume of 7 Transition Countries (not FSU) with Each 6 Other Members of this Group

Data Source: Rose (2003), WDI 2002, own calculations.

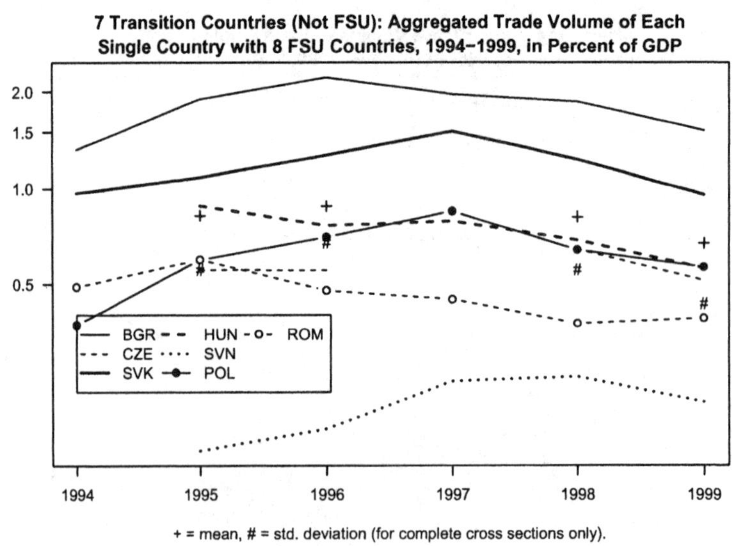

Fig. 8. Aggregated Trade Volume of 7 Transition Countries with 8 Countries of FSU*

* FSU Countries are: ARM, GEO, KAZ, KGZ, UKR, EST, LVA, LTU

Data Source: Rose (2003), WDI 2002, own calculations.

4 Developments of ICT Infrastructure in Selected Groups of Countries Included Into Investigation

We will confine ourselves to a short comparison of four well-documented ICT indicators by subgroups of countries for the period 1990-1999: telecom subscribers per 100 inhabitants (or telecom subscribers density), mobile telecom subscribers density, Internet host density and Internet users density. The development of ICT that has occurred throughout the last decade of the last century in all countries of our selection was aimed in the same direction, but took place with different speed and – particularly in the countries of FSU – with a time lag of up to 10 years. Only the Baltic republics are an exception in this country subgroup. A glance at the subgroup of EU members of our selection (fig. 9) indicates the leading position of Scandinavian countries in all four ICT density indicators.

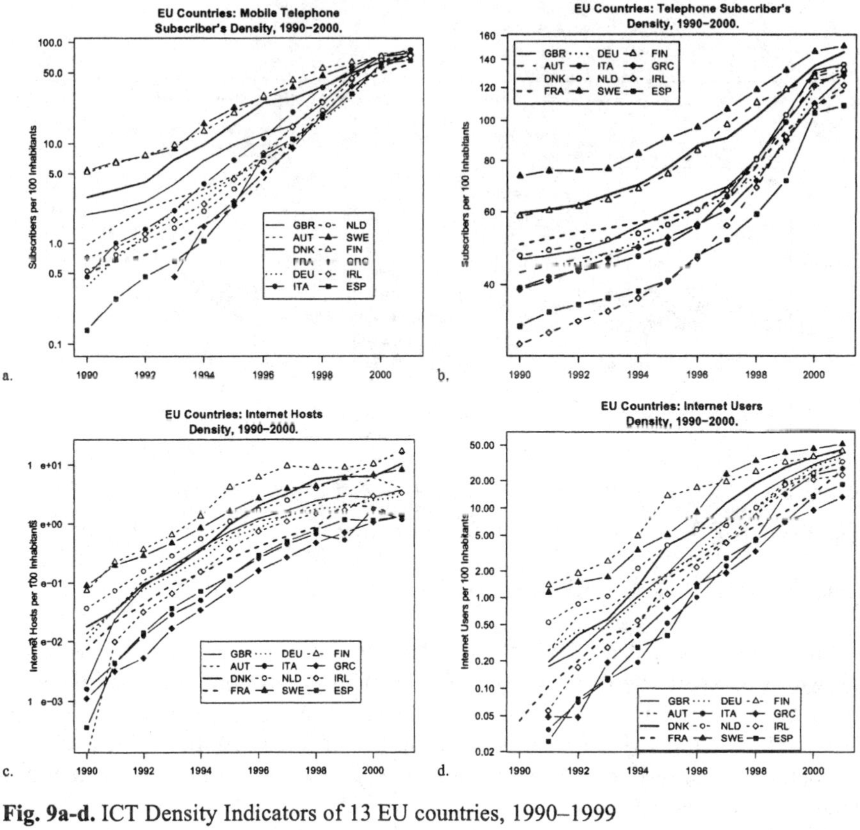

Fig. 9a-d. ICT Density Indicators of 13 EU countries, 1990–1999

Data Source: ITU Telecommunications Database 2002.

The diminished increase of charts for telephone and mobile telephone subscribers density may be interpreted as an indication of the first stages of the saturation of markets for these services in this country subgroup. The Internet host density as a proxy of supply of Internet services and the share of population using the Internet had grown during the whole period with almost undiminished speed.

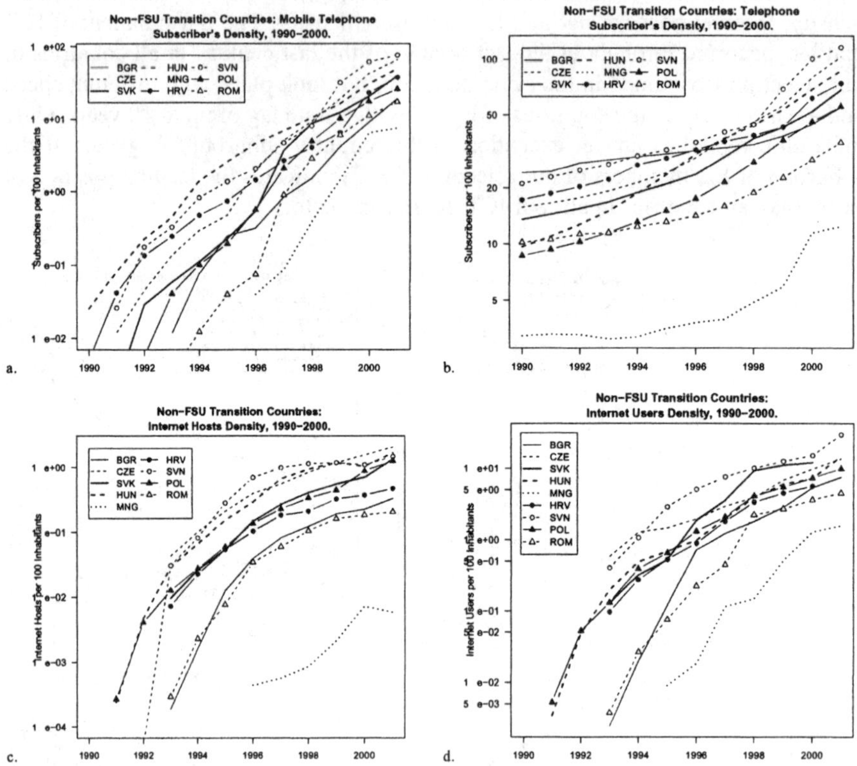

Fig. 10a-d. ICT Density Indicators of 9 Transition countries (not FSU), 1990–1999

Data Source: ITU Telecommunications Database 2002.

In transition, countries that do not belong to the group of FSU countries, the growth process of telephone and mobile telephone grids continues undiminished (see fig. 10). We can thus observe a slight decline in the development of ICT infrastructure by the level and course of the charts of these countries. The evolution of Internet use and supply clearly lags behind the performance of the EU member countries, but has progressed compared with FSU countries (fig. 11). In graphs reflecting the development of ICT density indicators of FSU countries, the striking difference in the dynamics of telephone and mobile telephone densities attracts attention, together with their high dispersion caused particularly by the high performance of the ICT sector in the Baltic republics. While the mobile phone grid is growing at high rates at a density of about 5 percent, the development of cable grids shows negligible progress during the decade under observation. This can become a serious disadvantage of location in attracting foreign direct investment, and should be deemed an important obstacle for economic growth.

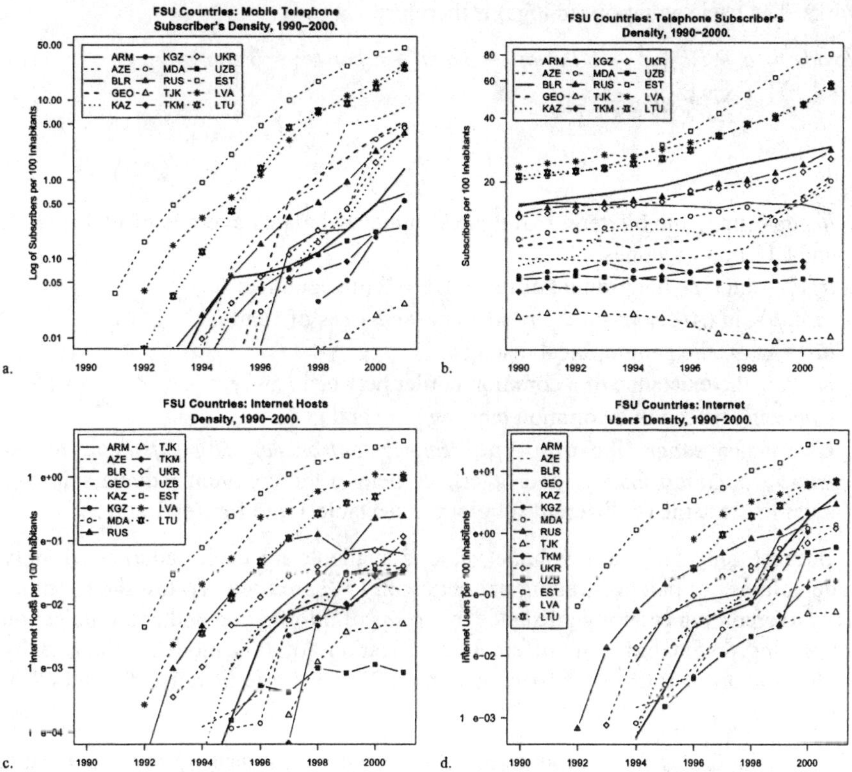

Fig. 11a-d. ICT Density Indicators of FSU successors, 1990–1999

Data Source: ITU Telecommunications Database 2002.

5 ICT Infrastructure and Foreign Trade: Extended Gravity Model

5.1 Overview

To combine foreign trade and ICT development and to show the possibility of influence on each other, we will start with a traditional gravity model for the selected 57 countries that regresses the bilateral volume of trade T_{ij} on the product of i's and j's real GDP, the product of their land areas, their geographical distance, the existence of a common border and/or language, as well as the membership to subgroups of countries characterized by membership of both trading partners to one economic integrated area (e.g. *fsup*) or to different economic integrated areas (like *fsu.eu*). The application of products of real GDPs, areas, etc. should be justified because it approximates economies of scale of trade and/or information networks. The basic equation (in logs) is therefore

$$ltrade_{ij} = \beta_0 + \beta_1 lrgdp_{ij} + \beta_2 lareap_{ij} + \beta_3 dist_{ij} + \beta_4 border_{ij} + \beta_5 comlang_{ij} + \sum_k \beta_k \, subgr_{k,ij} + u_{ij} \tag{1}$$

with

- *ltrade* = ln T_{ij} the bilateral real trade volume as deflated average of FOB export and CIF import values,
- *lrgdp* = $\ln(Y_i Y_j)$ the product of real GDP of both countries *(i,j)*
- *lareap* = ln $(Area_i Area_j)$ the product of land areas of *i* and *j*,
- *dist*= ln D_{ij} the geographical distance,
- $border_{ij}$ the existence of a common border between *i* and *j*,
- $comlang_{ij}$ speech in a common language in *i* and *j*,
- *k* variables *subgr* like $transecp_{ij}$, $transec.nontransec_{ij}$, $fsup_{ij}$, $fsu.eu_{ij}$, $tcnon\text{-}fsu.eu_{ij}$, $fsu.nontransec_{ij}$, (and other, see below) the common membership of *i* and *j* to the same or different subgroups (see table 1 and figures 1 and 2).

Because only one trade volume value is available for each pair *(i,j=j,i)*, only trade volumes of pairs of trading partners with $i < j$ are used. To test the hypothesis of overcoming economic distance by means of information and communication networking, estimations of different specifications of this model, enhanced by products *ictdp* of four quantitative national ICT density indicators of *i* and all in logs follows as shown below:

- *ltsdp* =$\ln(TSD_i\, TSD_j)$ –product of cable telephone subscribers per 100 inhabitants of *i* and *j*,
- *lmtsdp* = $\ln(MTSD_i\, MTSD_j)$ – product of mobile telephone subscribers per 100 inhabitants of *i* and *j*,
- *lihdp* = $\ln(IHD_i\, \mathrm{IHDj})$ – product of Internet hosts per 100 inhabitants of *i* and *j*, and
- *liud* = $\ln(IUD_{i\,,} IUD_j)$ – product of Internet users per 100 inhabitants of both countries.

With this, the enhanced model can be formed to the equation

$$ltrade_{ij} = \beta_0 + \beta_1 lrgdp_{ij} + \beta_2 lareap_{ij} + \beta_3 dist_{ij} + \beta_4 border_{ij} + \beta_5 comlang_{ij} + \sum_k \beta_k \, subgr_{k,ij} + \sum_l \beta_l ictdp_{l,ij} + u_{ij} \tag{2}$$

All trade, real GDP product, land area product, distance, common border and common language data are taken from Rose (2003). ICT density indicators are computed by use of ICT and population data from ITU (2002).

Due to the data restrictions mentioned above, eq. (1) and (2) are estimated separately for 1998 and 1999, at first with data of the whole group of selected countries. We will see shortly that due to strong multicollinearity between single ICT-density-variables, it is impossible to provide evidence of a certain impact of ICT variables putting all of them together in the model. One possible way to deal with multicollinearity is to create a common variable for cable and mobile telephone density:

smttsd = *m*obile *t*elephone *s*ubscr. *d*ens. + (cable) *t*elephone *s*ubscr. *d*ens.,
in logs, for pairs (i,j): $lsmttdp_{ij} = \ln(smttsd_i * smttsd_j)$,

Implicitly, this re-parameterization is based on the substitution of cable telephone transmission by mobile telephone (see Sung/ Lee, 2002). We therefore estimate the enhanced model with 5 ICT density variables for 1999 (for 1998 the variable *liudp* is not available for the whole country set) in separate equations including each ICT indicator variable successively.

Another problem of multicollinearity deserves our attention: GDP, land area, and ICT variables are correlated, so that the sign of parameters of the ICT-variable changes in cases of dropping out the *lareap* variable. In the basic model, the influence of the latter variable on trade volume may be due to ambiguous reasons. It can work as an additional distance variable because of the proportionality of distance and square root of areas of two adjacent countries, and it can work as a substitute for economic weight, if all countries have similar population densities. We will see this, if we drop out the data of city-countries Hong Kong (HKG) and Singapore (SGP).

While estimating eq (1) and (2) for the whole country set, we include those dummy variables for membership in subgroups of trading partners with significant influence on bilateral trade volume. This leads over to the next part of our empirical analysis, the estimation of the basic and the enhanced gravity model with data from subgroups (and subgroups of subgroups) of trading partners.

5.2 Model Specifications for the Whole Country Set

Table 2 and 3 show the results for both the basic model and its enlargements for the 1998 period, and for 1999 respectively. The results for both years are very similar, with slightly different parameter values for the ICT variables. While in 1998, the elasticity of *lmtsdp* and *ltsdp* variables are roughly equal, the influence of the mobile phone density in 1999 clearly seemed to dominate one of the cable phone variables. This could be a cautious hint for substitution phenomena between both kinds of telephony.

Influence of gravity and distance variables matters according to expectations. The negative sign of the *lareap* variable depends strongly on the inclusion of data of the small but economically very strong countries of Hong Kong and Singapore in the sample. If we exclude the data of these countries, the significant negative influence of *lareap* gets lost in the basic model but changes to significant positive influence if we introduce some ICT variables (tables 4 and 5). The intensity of influence of ICT variables changes slightly, but its relations to other ICT variables remains the same.

Table 2. Estimation results of the basic and the enhanced model for all selected countries, 1998[1)]

ICT-Variable	*none*	*all*	*lmtsdp*	*ltsdp*	*lmttsdp*	*lihdp*
Constant	-28.36 -29.94***	-27.01 -26.06***	-27.25 -28.55***	-28.04 -29.61***	-28.02 -29.61***	-27.16 -27.29***
lrgdp	0.97 50.54***	0.94 42.3***	0.92 42.36***	0.94 40.94***	0.94 40.95***	0.94 42.33***
lareap	-0.073 -5.46***	-0.04 -2.57***	-0.03 -1.89*	-0.05 -2.81***	-0.04 -2.65***	-0.05 -2.92***
ldist	-0.82 -20.04***	-0.81 -19.84***	-0.79 -19.61***	-0.79 -19.22***	-0.79 -19.32***	-0.80 -19.55***
border	0.87 6.22***	0.86 6.31***	0.89 6.55***	0.90 6.51***	0.90 6.52***	0.90 6.54***
comlang	0.52 4.63***	0.58 5.13***	0.58 5.14***	0.55 4.84***	0.55 4.87***	0.53 4.64***
transecp	0.88 5.88***	1.05 6.57***	0.93 6.23***	0.84 5.63***	0.85 5.71***	0.81 5.47***
trasec.nontransec	-0.28 -3.00***	-0.25 -2.65***	-0.27 -2.93***	-0.29 -3.11***	-0.28 -3.05***	-0.31 -3.32***
fsup	1.42 8.85***	1.65 9.96***	1.55 9.78***	1.42 8.90***	1.42 8.94***	1.44 9.06***
fsu.eu	0.53 4.45***	0.52 4.48***	0.49 4.25***	0.50 4.24***	0.50 4.22***	0.50 4.25***
tcnonfsu.eu	0.27 2.49**	0.24 2.24**	0.23 2.12**	0.24 2.26**	0.24 2.23**	0.24 2.20**
Fsu.nontransec	-0.60 -5.26***	-0.43 -3.68***	-0.50 -4.45***	-0.60 -5.30***	-0.60 -5.28***	-0.59 -5.16***
lmtsdp		0.13 4.27***	0.076 4.72***			
ltsdp		-0.13 -2.13**		0.075 2.65***		
lsmttsdp					0.076 2.86***	
lihdp		-0.00 -0.03				0.034 3.15***
liudp		-				
F-Value:	816.9 on 11 and 1525 DF	657.3 on 14 and 1522 DF	763.6 on 12 and 1524 DF	752.3 on 12 and 1524 DF	753 on 12 and 1524 DF	754.2 on 12 and 1524 DF
$R^{2\ korr}$	0.8539	0.89	0.8563	0.8544	0.8545	0.8547

1) All t values of these and of the following estimations are adjusted for heteroskedasticity (WHITE heteroscedasticity consistent estimator, see Green (2000) and David/MacKinnon (1993)). t values and abbreviations for the level of significance are printed below parameter values; the meaning of the abbreviations is:

*** 0.1 %, ** 1 %, * 5 %, and "." 10 %.

This finding also holds if we remove the *lareap* variable from our equations (1) and (2), see table 6 and 7. For now, there is no cause to drop any variable, but in subgroups particularly *lareap* seems to be highly correlated with ICT variables. Furthermore, in many estimations with data restriction for members of subgroups only, the influence of *lareap* is significantly positive. For the whole set, it seems to be an important finding that firstly influences all ICT variables and is significantly positive if we introduce each and every one of them, and this holds independently from dropping or the introduction of the *lareap* variable. Secondly, in regressions with data of countries without HKG and SGP, it is striking that the influence of *lareap* changes from zero to positive values since ICT variables are introduced, while the influence of *ldist* declines slightly, and the parameter values of *border* and *comlang* increases. This could be a serious indication for a reduction of economic distance by means of ICT.

On the other hand with the introduction of any ICT variable, the influence of *lrgdp* decreases. GDP is correlated with all ICT variables – this has to be in part by nature of GDP growth that is highly induced by development of ICT. In the present framework, it seems to be impossible to distinguish direct effects of ICT on trade volume from effects of ICT on GDP or of GDP on ICT, or from effects of both on trade. What we can do is to search contradictions in this line of reasoning and attempt to solve them. It appears to support our alternative hypothesis that the adjusted coefficient of determination increases after introducing ICT density variables.

Plotting the cumulated trade volume relative to GDP of each single country of the whole country selection exchanged with every other of the 56 countries of this set (so far the data are available) against ICT density indicators of these countries, we can clearly identify two subgroups (see fig. 12), one with relatively low ICT density and high trade-GDP-ratio, and another with relatively high ICT density and a lower trade-GDP ratio. The first subgroup looks very similar to our group of *transec* countries, while in the second group we can only find countries with developed market economies – the core of our *nontransec* subgroup. There are missing values for 25 countries, nevertheless we get an impression of contrary forces affecting the specification of our model oppositely.

Table 3. Estimation results of the basic and the enhanced model for all selected countries, 1999

ICT-Variable	*None*	*All*	*lmtsdp*	*ltsdp*	*lmttsdp*	*lihdp*	*liudp*
constant	-29.25 -30.02***	-28.29 -26.51***	-28.26 -29.12***	-28.96 -29.64***	-28.93 -29.68***	-28.47 -27.6***	-28.32 -28.26***
lrgdp	1.0 51.02***	0.98 42.3***	0.94 43.31***	0.97 41.06***	0.96 41.04***	0.97 43.33***	0.96 42.73***
lareap	-0.07 -5.43***	-0.05 -3.05***	-0.03 -1.72*	-0.05 -2.88***	-0.05 -2.62***	-0.06 -3.46***	-0.05 -2.75***
ldist	-0.865 -20.7***	-0.87 -20.67***	-0.83 -20.17***	-0.84 -20.07***	-0.84 -20.09***	-0.85 -20.51***	-0.85 -20.47***
border	0.81 5.69***	0.785 5.622***	0.83 6.04***	0.83 5.94***	0.83 5.96***	0.83 5.88***	0.83 5.96***
comlang	0.56 5.02***	0.60 5.34***	0.63 5.58***	0.59 5.24***	0.60 5.29***	0.57 5.07***	0.57 5.08***
transecp	0.81 5.33***	1.06 6.53***	0.86 5.69***	0.77 5.10***	0.78 5.15***	0.77 5.07***	0.77 5.16***
transec. non-transec	-0.29 -3.12***	-0.27 -2.96***	-0.29 -3.19***	-0.3 -3.24***	-0.30 -3.20***	-0.30 -3.29***	-0.32 -3.47***
fsup	1.45 9.2***	1.83 10.77***	1.63 10.36***	1.46 9.34***	1.47 9.43***	1.47 9.37***	1.54 9.78***
fsu.eu	0.32 2.51**	0.32 2.61***	0.27 2.19**	0.29 2.31**	0.28 2.26**	0.29 2.36**	0.30 2.34**
tcnonfsu.eu	0.24 2.37**	0.23 2.17**	0.19 1.88*	0.22 2.14**	0.21 2.07**	0.22 2.15**	0.22 2.14**
fsu. nontransec	-0.49 -4.35***	-0.20 -1.72*	-0.36 -3.21***	-0.48 -4.31***	-0.48 -4.26***	-0.48 -4.26***	-0.43 -3.85***
lmtsdp		0.17 5.24***	0.085 5.18***				
ltsdp		-0.22 -3.05***		0.068 2.34**			
lsmttsdp					0.073 2.71***		
lihdp		-0.03 -1.22				0.024 2.18**	
liudp		0.05 1.13					0.053 3.25***
F-Value:	845.4 on 11 and 1525 DF	643.5 on 15 and 1521 DF	793.8 on 12 and 1524 DF	777.7 on 12 and 1524 DF	778.9 on 12 and 1524 DF	777.3 on 12 and 1524 DF	643.5 on 15 and 1521 DF
$R^{2\,korr}$	0.8581	0.8625	0.861	0.8585	0.8587	0.8585	0.8625

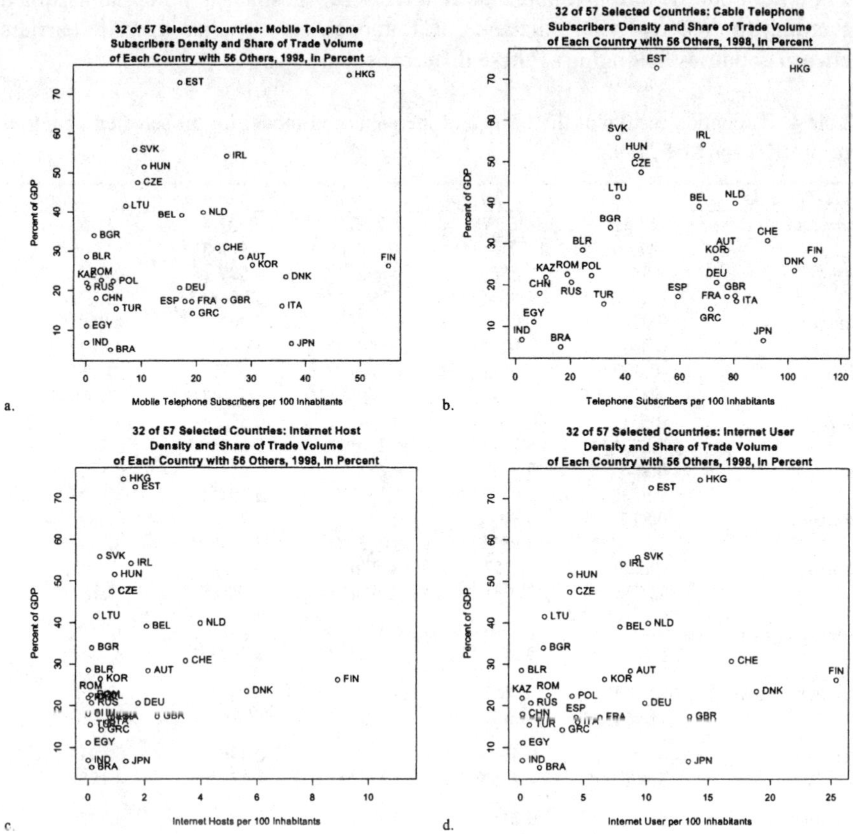

Fig. 12a-d. 32 Selected Countries: ICT Density Indicators and Trade Volume–GDP ratio of Each with 56 Other Selected Countries, 1998

Data Source: ITU Telecommunications Database 2002, ROSE (2003), own calculations.

By means of country pair dummy variables, we can control and quantify these influences. Thus the next matter that deserves an explanation is the introduction of country subgroup variables. Because several of them are perfect complements, not all of them can be introduced simultaneously into the model. I decided in favor of *transecp* and *transec.nontransec* that include implicitly the *nontransecp*–couples of trading partners as well. Each of these dummy variables has significant influence in all estimation regressions: *transecp* with positive and *transec.nontransec* with negative values. The positive influence of the former variable means that the trade volume exchanged between trading partners both stemming from the transition country group should be relatively high, even if their real GDP is relatively low. This may be an aftermath of former CMEA integration. On the other hand, the negative value of *transec.nontransec* variables – which means that the trade volume between two trading partners stemming one from transition and the other from other countries group should be relatively low despite its potential assumed according to their real GDP, distance, ICT impact, etc. – points to trade barriers between countries belonging to these different subgroups.

Table 4. Estimation results of the basic and the enhanced model for all selected countries except HKG and SGP, 1998

ICT-Variable	*none*	*lmtsdp*	*ltsdp*	*lmttsdp*	*lihdp*
constant	-27.616	-26.178	-27.102	-27.074	-25.65
	-29.405***	-27.842***	-28.991***	-29.003***	-26.064***
lrgdp	0.943	0.876	0.892	0.889	0.881
	48.354***	39.666***	37.912***	37.966***	39.2***
lareap	0.016	0.079	0.061	0.064	0.069
	0.951	3.923***	2.959***	3.098***	3.493***
ldist	-0.997	-0.983	-0.969	-0.971	-0.983
	-21.585***	-21.876***	-21.156***	-21.284***	-21.684***
border	0.651	0.66	0.684	0.682	0.686
	4.873***	5.141***	5.278***	5.269***	5.267***
comlang	0.206	0.271	0.237	0.241	0.195
	1.933*	2.637***	2.259**	2.305**	1.85*
transecp	0.812	0.873	0.742	0.758	0.688
	5.474***	5.933***	5.063***	5.187***	4.757***
transec.nontransec	-0.259	-0.252	-0.276	-0.267	-0.308
	-2.735***	-2.681***	-2.914***	-2.823***	-3.267***
fsup	1.34	1.494	1.335	1.341	1.37
	8.653***	9.822***	8.705***	8.761***	8.978***
fsu.nontransec	-0.583	-0.467	-0.59	-0.587	-0.566
	-4.962***	-4.057***	-5.083***	-5.054***	-4.888***
fsu.eu	0.532	0.496	0.492	0.49	0.491
	4.408***	4.269***	4.133***	4.122***	4.172***
tcnonfsu.eu	0.261	0.215	0.226	0.221	0.215
	2.423**	1.988**	2.093**	2.051**	2.007**
lmtsdp		0.094			
		5.871***			
ltsdp			0.117		
			4.126***		
lsmttsdp				0.115	
				4.328***	
lihdp					0.054
					5.043***
F-Value:	810.6 on 11 and 1418 DF	768.1 on 12 and 1417 DF	752.9 on 12 and 1417 DF	753.9 on 12 and 1417 DF	758.1 on 12 and 1417 DF
$R^{2\ korr}$	0.8617	0.8656	0.8633	0.8634	0.8641

Table 5. Estimation results of the basic and the enhanced model for all selected countries except HKG and SGP, 1999

ICT-Variable	*none*	*lmtsdp*	*ltsdp*	*lmttsdp*	*lihdp*	*liudp*
constant	-28.624 -29.386***	-27.364 -28.372***	-28.13 -28.903***	-28.095 -28.97***	-27.186 -26.466***	-27.344 -27.441***
lrgdp	0.969 48.766***	0.901 40.592***	0.919 38.058***	0.914 38.011***	0.923 40.524***	0.918 40.548***
lareap	0.014 0.822	0.079 3.887***	0.057 2.695***	0.063 2.952***	0.054 2.765***	0.058 2.977***
ldist	-1.043 -21.937***	-1.024 -22.092***	-1.017 -21.632***	-1.018 -21.725***	-1.039 -22.139***	-1.033 -22.047***
border	0.59 4.319***	0.599 4.592***	0.617 4.665***	0.614 4.657***	0.609 4.545***	0.611 4.588***
comlang	0.25 2.336**	0.32 3.097***	0.286 2.718***	0.294 2.803***	0.25 2.365**	0.248 2.38**
transecp	0.754 4.986***	0.808 5.421***	0.69 4.591***	0.702 4.691***	0.673 4.496***	0.706 4.74***
tran-sec.nontransec	-0.279 -2.996***	-0.287 -3.109***	-0.298 -3.191***	-0.292 -3.126***	-0.309 -3.318***	-0.323 -3.48***
fsup	1.379 9.043***	1.583 10.507***	1.393 9.261***	1.407 9.387***	1.408 9.342***	1.485 9.839***
fsu.nontransec	-0.441 -3.84***	-0.285 -2.544**	-0.433 -3.814***	-0.423 -3.737***	-0.423 -3.717***	-0.362 -3.199***
fsu.eu	0.303 2.404**	0.257 2.133**	0.265 2.129**	0.259 2.085**	0.272 2.196**	0.284 2.294**
tcnonfsu.eu	0.253 2.45**	0.197 1.89*	0.219 2.106**	0.21 2.015**	0.216 2.098**	0.223 2.164**
lmtsdp		0.103 6.356***				
ltsdp			0.11 3.837***			
lsmttsdp				0.114 4.256***		
lihdp					0.043 3.949***	
liudp						0.07 4.445***
F-Value:	848 on 11 and 1418 DF	808.1 on 12 and 1417 DF	786.2 on 12 and 1417 DF	788.5 on 12 and 1417 DF	786.5 on 12 and 1417 DF	789.8 on 12 and 1417 DF
$R^{2\ korr}$	0.867	0.8714	0.8683	0.8686	0.8684	0.8688

Table 6. Estimation results of the basic and the enhanced model without *lareap* for all selected countries, 1998

ICT-Variable	*none*	*lmtsdp*	*ltsdp*	*lmttsdp*	*lihdp*
constant	-27.096 -30.209***	-26.612 -30.291***	-27.292 -30.782***	-27.312 -30.768***	-25.896 -29.163***
lrgdp	0.927 55.354***	0.898 53.601***	0.9 52.829***	0.9 52.956***	0.896 52.478***
ldist	-0.887 -23.263***	-0.805 -20.507***	-0.802 -19.515***	-0.803 -19.69***	-0.815 -20.408***
border	0.738 5.408***	0.863 6.439***	0.866 6.42***	0.868 6.436***	0.871 6.401***
comlang	0.591 4.661***	0.62 5.254***	0.603 4.99***	0.603 5.023***	0.568 4.642***
transecp	0.646 4.489***	0.881 5.93***	0.709 4.959***	0.736 5.119***	0.662 4.671***
transec.nontransec	-0.351 -3.673***	-0.292 -3.109***	-0.327 -3.475***	-0.315 -3.343***	-0.357 -3.815***
fsup	1.315 8.627***	1.553 9.866***	1.378 8.926***	1.388 8.982***	1.414 9.113***
fsu.nontransec	-0.706 -6.264***	-0.506 -4.517***	-0.645 -5.791***	-0.638 -5.724***	-0.62 -5.55***
fsu.eu	0.579 4.899***	0.494 4.321***	0.495 4.222***	0.492 4.203***	0.494 4.279***
tcnonfsu.eu	0.257 2.353**	0.215 1.987**	0.22 2.029**	0.216 1.998**	0.213 1.975**
lmtsdp		0.094 7.191***			
ltsdp			0.133 5.887***		
lsmttsdp				0.128 6.07***	
lihdp					0.054 5.894***
F-Value:	872.6 on 10 and 1526 DF	830.5 on 11 and 1525 DF	814.8 on 11 and 1525 DF	816.2 on 11 and 1525 DF	816.5 on 11 and 1525 DF
$R^{2\ korr}$	0.8502	0.8559	0.8535	0.8538	0.8538

Table 7. Estimation results of the basic and the enhanced model without *lareap* for all selected countries, 1999

ICT-Variable	*none*	*lmtsdp*	*ltsdp*	*lmttsdp*	*lihdp*	*liudp*
constant	-27.964 -30.216***	-27.708 -30.703***	-28.165 -30.771***	-28.218 -30.796***	-27.011 -29.244***	-27.275 -30.012***
lrgdp	0.95 55.793***	0.921 54.74***	0.922 53.355***	0.922 53.545***	0.925 52.963***	0.922 53.446***
ldist	-0.935 -23.956***	-0.847 -21.078***	-0.853 -20.312***	-0.852 -20.425***	-0.881 -21.736***	-0.87 -21.599***
border	0.676 4.867***	0.804 5.935***	0.798 5.833***	0.8 5.854***	0.781 5.659***	0.794 5.798***
comlang	0.631 5.01***	0.666 5.667***	0.648 5.413***	0.652 5.469***	0.617 5.089***	0.603 5.09***
transecp	0.571 3.922***	0.804 5.41***	0.638 4.408***	0.666 4.58***	0.602 4.162***	0.66 4.539***
transec.nontransec	-0.361 -3.788***	-0.315 -3.39***	-0.341 -3.631***	-0.329 -3.511***	-0.358 -3.827***	-0.368 -3.968***
fsup	1.347 8.955***	1.637 10.466***	1.432 9.403***	1.451 9.512***	1.44 9.416***	1.54 9.912***
fsu.nontransec	-0.597 -5.38***	-0.356 -3.226***	-0.52 -4.724***	-0.505 -4.588***	-0.517 -4.68***	-0.437 -3.949***
fsu.eu	0.366 2.932***	0.269 2.23**	0.282 2.272**	0.275 2.219**	0.294 2.385**	0.305 2.482**
tcnonfsu.eu	0.234 2.212**	0.183 1.746*	0.197 1.879*	0.19 1.811*	0.193 1.86*	0.204 1.956*
lmtsdp		0.102 7.706***				
ltsdp			0.129 5.743***			
lsmttsdp				0.126 6.057***		
lihdp					0.048 5.133***	
liudp						0.082 6.066***
F-Value:	903.1 on 10 and 1526 DF	863.7 on 11 and 1525 DF	841.7 on 11 and 1525 DF	844.1 on 11 and 1525 DF	838.7 on 11 and 1525 DF	846.1 on 11 and 1525 DF
$R^{2\,korr}$	0.8545	0.8617	0.8576	0.8579	0.8571	0.8582

The influence of *fsup* and *fsu.nontransec* variables points to the same phenomenon now indicated in the smaller subgroups. *Tcnonfsup* is the complement of *fsup*; while *tcnonfsu.nontransec* is together with *fsu.nontransec* complementary to *transec.nontransec*. Replacement of *fsu.nontransec* by *tcnonfsu.nontransec* shows similar results with the same always-significant values. The dummy variable for trading partners coming both from EU member countries, *eup*, did not show any significant influence in both regression periods. Country pair variables for membership of one trading partner country in the EU, while the other is resident in a FSU or another transition country are *fsu.eu* and *tcnonfsu.eu*. Both variables show significantly positive influence in all regressions, which should be interpreted in connection with the relatively high trade volume between former CMEA countries and EU member countries compared with the trade volume between countries in transition and their trading partners outside the EU.

The different direction of influence shown by dummy variables for subgroups, raises the question as to how our model would behave if we estimate parameters for data of country pairs of single subgroups. Looking at the different parameter values, we can expect some differences of behavior between equations tested by data of different subgroups.

5.3 Model Specifications for Subgroups of Trading Partners

There are a large number of possibilities for combining subgroups of countries to subgroups of trading partners. Therefore, I must confine the set of results reported here to the most striking ones regarding the aim of investigation – to reject or to accept the claim that the spread of ICT does not matter to the dynamics of international trade. In fact, regression results for some subgroups show none or even negative influence of ICT density variables on bilateral trade volume under certain conditions.

Many of the findings of model estimations can already be supposed upon closer inspection of the results for the whole country selection. The most stable impact of ICT variables are found in those subgroups where the sign of the parameter of subgroup dummy variable is significantly negative. This refers specifically to the *transec.nontransec* and *fsu.nontransec* variables and the couples of trading partners within them. Table 7 shows the main results of estimated equation parameters for data of the *transec.nontransec* group. Estimation results for the *fsu.nontransec* subgroup are quite similar.

The causes for the clear and stable impact of ICT variables on trade volume in this subgroup can be underlined by some figures that show the high correlation between the telephone density and trade volume of each transition country with all countries outside this country subgroup ("nontransition" countries). See fig. 13.

Table 8. Regression results for trading partners of *transec.nontransec* group[1)]

a) equation contains *lareap:*

	ict-var	*lrgdp*	*lareap*	*ldist*	*border*	*fsu.nte*[2]	*tr.eu*[3]	*fsu.eu*	*euc.eu*[4]	$R^{2\ korr}$
lmtsdp	0.14	0.89	0.044*	-1.1	1.32	-0.46	-0.3**	0.6	0.21*	0.79
ltsdp	0.19	0.89	(0)	-1.05	1.34	-0.66	-0.37**	0.65	0.44	0.78
lsmttsdp	0.18	0.89	(0)	-1.06	1.34	-0.65	-0.37**	0.645	0.42	0.78
lihdp	0.08	0.89	(0)	-1.08	1.41	-0.62	-0.34**	0.63	0.32	0.785
without	-	0.97	(0)	-1.09	1.3	-0.67	-0.31**	0.67	0.48	0.78
	ict-var	*lrgdp*	*lareap*	*ldist*	*border*	*fsu.nte*	*tr.eu*	*fsu.eu*	*euc.eu*	$R^{2\ korr}$
lmtsdp	0.15	0.91	0.05**	-1.14	1.23	-0.29**	-0.38	0.44	0.27**	0.79
ltsdp	0.18	0.92	(0)	-1.1	1.25	-0.53	-0.42	0.475	0.49	0.78
lsmttsdp	0.18	0.915	(0)	-1.1	1.24	-0.51	-0.42	0.47	0.47	0.78
lihdp	0.06	0.94	(0)	-1.14	1.27	-0.515	-0.395	0.48	0.43	0.78
liudp	0.1	0.93	(0)	-1.14	1.27	-0.43	-0.38	0.48	0.42	0.78
without	-	0.99	(0)	-1.14	1.21	-0.56	-0.36	0.5	0.55	0.78

b) *lareap* excluded:

1998

	ict-var	*lrgdp*	*ldist*	*border*	*fsu.nte*[2]	*tr.eu*[3]	*fsu.eu*	*euc.eu*[4]	$R^{2\ korr}$
lmtsdp	0.11	0.93	-1.08	1.38	-0.45	-0.29**	0.58	0.21*	0.787
ltsdp	0.15	0.92	-1.045	1.375	-0.63	-0.35**	0.63	0.42	0.782
lsmttsdp	0.14	0.92	-1.05	1.37	-0.63	-0,34**	0.63	0.4	0.782
lihdp	0.066	0.92	-1.07	1.41	-0.59	-0.33**	0.62	0.32	0.783
without	-	0.95	-1.11	1.23	-0.705	-0.32**	0.7	0.515	0.777

1999

	ict-var	*lrgdp*	*ldist*	*border*	*fsu.nte*	*tr.eu*	*fsu.eu*	*euc.eu*	$R^{2\ korr}$
lmtsdp	0.13	0.95	-1.12	1.3	-0.28**	-0.36	0.41	0.27**	0.789
ltsdp	0.14	0.95	-1.09	1.28	-0.51	-0.4	0.46	0.48	0.7815
lsmttsdp	0.135	0.95	-1.1	1.28	-0.49	-0.4	0.46	0.455	0.782
lihdp	0.051	0.955	-1.135	1.29	-0.5	-0.39	0.47	0.43	0.781
liudp	0.083	0.95	-1.13	1.295	-0.42	-0.37	o.47	0.41	0.782
without	-	0.97	-1.15	1.16	-0.59	-0.375	0.53	0.585	0.777

[1)] In these tables all results without additional "*" or "." are significant at 0.1 % level. ** means 1%, * stands for 5 %, and "." for 10 % level of error probability. (0) stands for not significant at 10 % level.

[2)] fsu.nontransec

[3)] transec.eu

[4)] eucand.eu

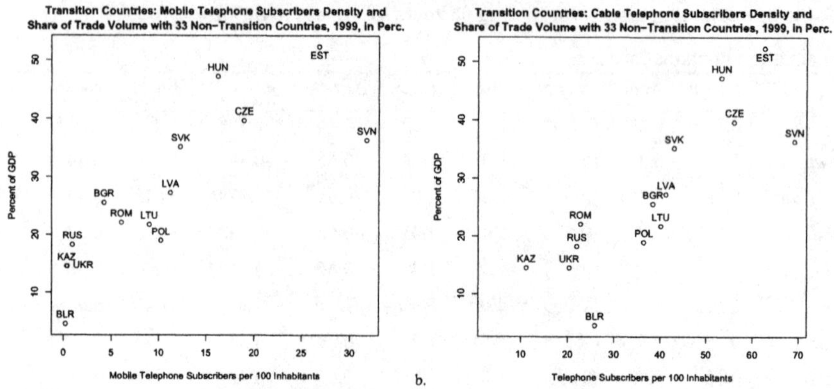

Fig. 13a-b. Transition Countries: Cable and Mobile Telephone Subscribers Density, and share of Trade Volume with 33 Non-Transition Countries at GDP, 1999.

Data Source: ITU Telecommunications Database 2002, ROSE (2003), own calculations.

Fig. 14 shows the same graphics for the *transecp* subgroup of trading partners, both of which stem from transition countries. Here we cannot recognize any tight linear correlation between cumulated trade volume of trade with the other members of the group and telephone subscribers density. Table 8 shows estimation results for two different estimations with data of this subgroup. At first, including *lareap* variable, one could assume a relatively reliable impact of some ICT density variables. Excluding *lareap* leads to a change of direction of impact of ICT variables. Yet nothing can be said to the elasticities of trade volume referring to ICT density variables, because a multicollinearity problem is perhaps covering the background.

Even more distinctly, the results for *fsu.tcnonfsu* trading partner group show that results of equations containing *lareap* have to be analyzed very cautiously (see table 9 and fig.15). From the graphs, we can conclude that the Baltic Republics are too different a group compared with the other former Soviet Republics. However, even regressing the same independent variables on trade volume of FSU countries without the Baltic Republics, we get quite similar results. In principle, two processes that matter simultaneously but not synchronously could cause this behavior. At first, there is the process of either disintegration or trade diversion in light of the EU Eastern enlargement that was perhaps already noticeable during the late 1990s. Secondly, the process of modernization of ICT infrastructure runs with different lags and speeds in different countries and has started from different levels. So we are faced with the situation that some countries with completely backward telephone grids are supporting active trade connections, while other potential trading partners cannot utilize their trade possibilities, perhaps favored by good ICT networks but hindered by other trade barriers.

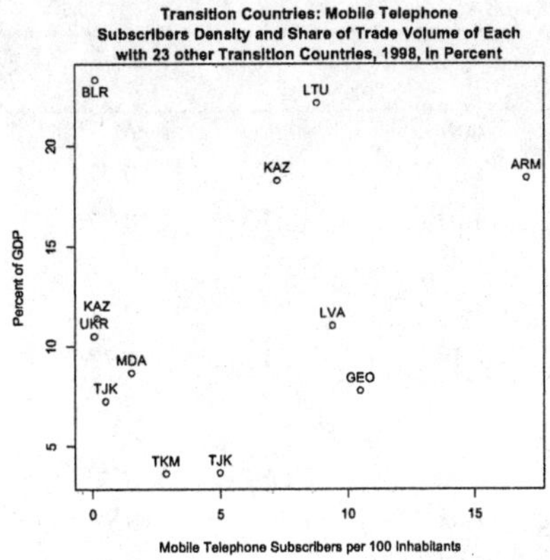

a.

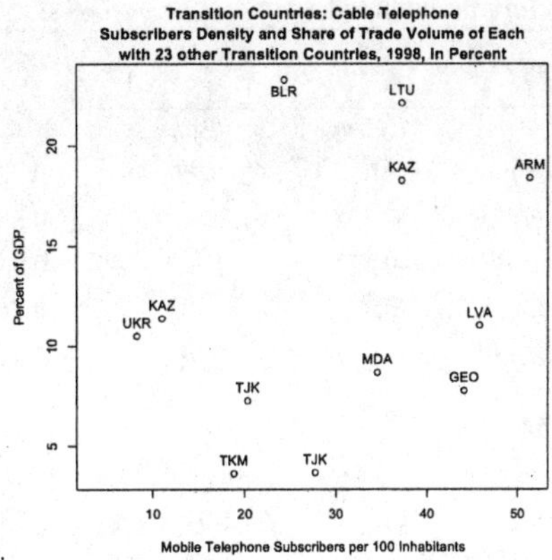

b.

Fig. 14a-b. Transition Countries: Cable and Mobile Telephone Subscribers Density, and share of Trade Volume of Each with 23 other Transition Countries at GDP, 1998

Data Source: ITU Telecommunications Database 2002, ROSE (2003), own calculations.

Table 9. Regression results for trading partners of *transecp* group

a) equation contains *lareap*

1998

	ict-var	*lrgdp*	*lareap*	*Ldist*	*border*	*Fsup*	$R^{2\ korr}$
lmtsdp	0.055*	0.79	0.31	-1.09	0.66	1.07	0.80
ltsdp	0.195*	0.75	0.34	-1.09	0.68	1.0	0.80
lsmttsdp	0.19*	0.75	0.34	-1.09	0.675	1.01	0.80
lihdp	0.075**	0.74	0.35	-1.11	0.65	1.03	0.80
without	-	0.83	0.27	-1.1	0.67	0.98	0.80

1999:

	ict-var	*lrgdp*	*lareap*	*Ldist*	*border*	*fsup*	$R^{2\ korr}$.
lmtsdp	0.07**	0.81	0.31	-1.14	0.59	1.16	0.81
ltsdp	0.22*	0.76	0.34	-1.14	0.61	1.08	0.81
lsmttsdp	0.22**	0.75	0.35	-1.14	0.6	1.1	0.81
lihdp	0.07**	0.79	0.325	-1.15	0.585	1.1	0.81
liudp	(0)	0.83	0.29	-1.15	0.59	1.09	0.81
without	-	0.85	0.26	-1.15	0.6	1.03	0.81

b) *lareap* excluded

1998

	ict-var	*lrgdp*	*ldist*	*border*	*Fsup*	$R^{2\ korr}$
lmtsdp	(0)	0.99	-0.73	1.14	1.25	0.77
ltsdp	-0.195**		-0.8	1.04	1.23	0.775
lsmttsdp	-0.17*	1.02	-0.8	1.06	1.23	0.775
lihdp	(0)	1.01	-0.76	1.1	1.24	0.775
without	-	0.98	-0.69	1.18	1.33	0.77

1999

	ict-var	*lrgdp*	*ldist*	*border*	*Fsup*	$R^{2\ korr}$
lmtsdp	(0)	1.01	-0.77	1.08	1.34	0.78
ltsdp	-0.15	1.04	-0.85	0.985	1.26	0.785
lsmttsdp	(0)	1.03	-0.83	1.0	1.27	0.785
lihdp	(0)	1.02	-0.81	1.03	1.285	0.785
liudp	(0)	1.02	-0.82	1.03	1.22	0.785
without	-	1.01	-0.76	1.09	1.36	0.78

Table 10. Regression results for trading partners of *fsu.tcnonfsu* group

a) equation contains *lareap*

1998

	ict-var	*lrgdp*	*Lareap*	*ldist*	*R-Q.*
Lmtsdp	(0)	0.87	0.31	-1.24	0.769
Ltsdp	(0)	0.84	0.33	-1.24	0.768
Lsmttsdp	(0)	0.85	0.32	-1.22	0.768
Lihdp	(0)	0.84	0.33	-1.21	0.768
Without	-	0.85	0.33	-1.22	0.77

1999

	ict-var	*lrgdp*	*Lareap*	*ldist*	*R-Q.*
Lmtsdp	(0)	0.86	0.32	-1.19	0.778
Ltsdp	(0)	0.85	0.33	-1.18	0.778
Lsmttsdp	(0)	0.85	0.33	-1.19	0.778
Lihdp	(0)	0.86	0.33	-1.2	0.778
Without	-	0.87	0.31	-1.2	0.78

b) *lareap* excluded

1998

	ict-var	*lrgdp*	*ldist*	*R-Q.*
Lmtsdp	-0.14	1.07	-0.96	0.729
Ltsdp	-0.46	1.12	-1.08	0.733
Lsmttsdp	-0.44	1.12	-1.09	0.735
Lihdp	-0.143	1.12	-1.0	0.733
Without		1.04	-0.78	0.715

1999

	ict-var	*lrgdp*	*ldist*	*R-Q.*
Lmtsdp	(0)	1.07	-0.89	0.731
Ltsdp	-0.38	1.13	-1.04	0.743
Lsmttsdp	-0.34	1.12	-1.03	0.743
Lihdp	-0.122	1.1	-0.96	0.742
Without	-	1.06	-0.79	0.729

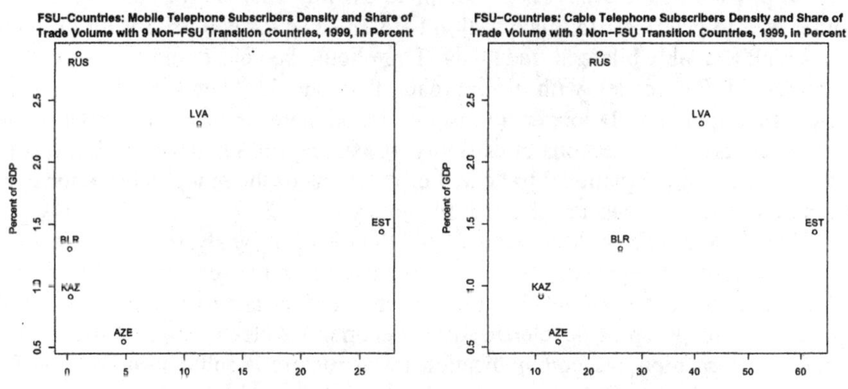

Fig. 15a-b. Countries of FSU: Cable and Mobile Telephone Subscribers Density, and share of Trade Volume of Each with 9 other Transition Countries at GDP, 1999

Data Source: ITU Telecommunications Database 2002, Rose (2003), own calculations.

6 Conclusion

This first attempt to show possible links between the expansion of national ICT infrastructures and the intensity of bilateral trade between the post-socialist transition countries themselves and with their main trading partners outside the former CMEA, and to reject the zero hypothesis of absence of such links can only partially provide evidence of its claims. For the whole set of (already existing) bilateral trade connections, the traditional gravity equation successively enhanced one-by-one of several ICT density indicators rejects the zero hypotheses at a high level of significance. This also holds for such subgroups of pairs of trading countries where one of them belongs to the subgroup of transition countries or one of its subgroups, while the other is part of the complementary subgroup of countries outside the former CMEA. Testing the enhanced gravity equation with data of bilateral trade between countries that both belong to the subgroup of countries in transition, results do not confirm any connection between foreign trade and ICT development. Nevertheless, one important result of investigation is that the role of the land area variable in the enhanced gravity model is ambiguous not only in its meaning swaying between mass and distance, but also because its strong influence on the indicated direction of ICT impact on bilateral trade and its significance. This influence is also found in the estimation results for data from trading partners both belonging to the subgroups of non-transition or EU member countries (not documented here). Its causes should be the topic of further investigations of this kind of modeling.

Another question remaining open is the possible impact of ICT development on bilateral trade connections that have until now had the value zero. To deal with it requires data that distinguish between "not any trade" and "not reported trade". It would probably be a large task to complete existing datasets for zero values. Another way to get closer to this question is to enhance the country set for all countries with available bilateral trade data. This should be considered for further estimations of the model with recent data that should likewise allow a panel regression approach. If longer time series for bilateral trade were available, one could set about the questions of causality of existing links between ICT spreading and intensity of international trade and of reactions of the model's behavior in response to discrete measures of economic policy.

What conclusions could be drawn from the results of analysis for practical policy? The findings especially for the investigated link between ICT infrastructure and foreign trade intensity between transition countries and its trading partners belonging to the group of developed market economies clearly suggest that a modernized information and communication infrastructure is suitable to promote foreign trade activities. Besides the progressing developments of disintegration and new orientation of foreign trade of the former CMEA countries on the one hand and the processes of privatization, liberalization and modernization of its ICT sectors that are obviously dominant over the rather weak links between ICT infrastructure and foreign trade within these groups on the other, it should be clear that the modernization of national networks of information and telecommunication would also promote foreign trade within the former CMEA area.

Confirmation of assumed distance overcoming and trade creating effects of ICT underlines the necessity for politics of natural monopoly regulation to consider carefully between the sometimes-contradicting goals of cheaply using ICT infrastructure and its modernization. The experiences of many countries that have already privatized and liberalized their former national telecommunication companies should be carefully analyzed regarding the quality of supply of the new ICT businesses and their incentives to invest. Policy measures affecting the modernization of ICT infrastructure should be seen as measures directed to the promotion of economic growth; therefore government policies that only pursue a goal of skimming off monopoly rents is very shortsighted and irresponsible, particularly if the state is unable to finance ICT modernization.

References

Bergstrand, J. H. (1985): The gravity equation in international trade: some microeconomic foundations and empirical evidence. – Review of Economics and Statistics 67, 474–481.

Bergstrand, J. H. (1989): The generalized gravity equation, monopolistic competition, and the factor-proportions theory in international trade. – Review of Economics and Statistics 71, 143–153.

Davidson, R., MacKinnon, J. G. (1993): Estimation and Inference in Econometrics. New York: Oxford University Press.

Deardorff, A. V. (1998): Determinants of bilateral trade: does gravity work in a neoclassical world?. – Frankel, J. A. (eds.): The Regionalization of the World Economy. Chicago and London: The University of Chicago Press, 7–31.

Evenett, S. J., Keller, W. (2002): On theories explaining the success of the gravity equation. – The Journal of Political Economy 110, 281–316.

Feenstra, R. C., Markesan, J. A., Rose, A. K. (1998): Understanding the Home Market E_ect and the Gravity Equation: the Role of Differentiating Goods. NBER Working Paper 6804: National Bureau of Economic Research.

Greene, W. H. (2000): Econometric Analysis. Vierte Auflage. New York: Prentice Hall.

Linnemann, H. (1966): An Econometric Study of International Trade Flows. Amsterdam: North Holland Publishing.

Nefiodow, L. A. (1994): Informationsgesellschaft – Arbeitsplatzvernichtung oder Arbeitsplatzgewinne?. – Ifo Schnelldienst 47/12, 11–19.

Rohweder, H. C. (1988): Ökonometrische Methoden zur Schätzung von Gravitationsmodellen des internationalen Handels -- Darstellung, Kritik und Alternativen. Allgemeines Statistisches Archiv 72, 150–170.

Rose, A. K. (2003): Which International Institutions Promote International Trade? CEPR discussion paper 3764: Centre for Economic Policy Research. http://faculty.haas.berkeley.edu/arose/ RecRes.htm#GATTWTO.

Sung, N., Lee, Y.-H. (2002): Substitution between mobile and fixed telephones in Korea. – Review of Industrial Organization 20, 367–374.

Welfens, P. J. J., Jungmittag, A. (2001): Liberalization of EU Telecommunications and Trade: Theory, Gravity Equation Analysis and Policy Implications. EIIW Discussion Paper 87: European Institute for International Economic Relations at Potsdam University.

Welfens, P. J. J., Jungmittag, A., Beckert, B., Joisten, M., Zoche, P. (2003): Internetwirtschaft 2010 – Perspektiven und Auswirkungen. Vorläufige Fassung: mimeo.

Westernhagen, N. von (2002): Systemic Transformation, Trade and Economic Growth: Developments, Theoretical Analysis and Empirical Results. Heidelberg: Physica

Russia's Integration Into the World Economy: An Interjurisdictional Competition View

Alexander Libman

1 Introduction

Russia's integration into the world economy has been one of the most important topics for political and scientific discussion in Russia and abroad during this decade. The system transformation of the Russian economy and politics determines important changes in Russia's position in the global economic and political system. Of course, the Soviet Union was not a real autarky, closed economy, and even the socialist block remained part of the global economy. In fact, Wallerstein (2001) considered the USSR to be one of the core countries of the economic world system after World War II. However, the creation of market institutions means a new quality with respect to Russian integration into the world economy. First, more companies participate directly or indirectly in global competition. Second, the decisions of Russian actors in the world economy are met decentralized and by every enterprise. That's why there is a broader spectrum of interests of different groups and individuals affecting Russia's position in the world economy, not only that of the bureaucracy and politicians like in the Soviet Union.

The objective of this paper is to analyze Russia's integration into the world economy from the point of view of the theory of interjurisdictional competition. In Section 2, we provide a brief overview of the theory of interjurisdictional competition. Section 3 deals with the main effects of the interjurisdictional competition for the Russian economy, and in Section 4 we develop a set of possible explanations for the economic problems of Russia from the point of view of the interjurisdictional competition. Section 5 offers conclusions to our analysis.

2 Theory of the Interjurisdictional Competition: A Brief Overview

From an economic point of view, the relation between governmental structures and private actors can be described as a market. The government offers certain goods (including public goods, formal institutions enforced by the public authority, and even private goods like assets in the privatization process) to private actors, charging a fee in the form of taxes for its consumption. In a closed economy, the government is a natural monopoly.

There are many governments in an open economy with free capital and labor movement between countries offering different packages of goods of different quality and price. That means that individuals and companies can chose the optimal variant, investing in that country (or settling in a country) which is most attractive for them. The companies chose an "exit" from the countries with lower quality or higher price of public and institutional goods. The tax base is reallocated to the countries with better institutions or lower taxes. Other countries suffer under negative economic processes.

This means there are reasons for the government to try to attract mobile factors under different theoretical assumptions. A "benevolent dictator" is concerned with negative trends in the national economy. An egoistic "Leviathan" government loses the main income source for bureaucrats and politicians (in form of taxes and even in the form of bribes – there is no reason to bribe the government if a company does not plan on investing in the country). In the democratic regime, politicians can lose the elections. One more factor which can be important for the government is the declining influence in the international relations system. The governments also **compete for mobile factors of production (capital and labor).** As the mobility of capital in the modern world is higher than that of labor, governments compete for capital rather than for both production factors.

This process is called **interjurisdictional competition**. The main instruments used by the state to attract mobile factors and to prevent "exit" are fiscal policy, especially taxation (*fiscal competition; tax competition)* and institutional policy (quality, ecological and social standards, competition law etc.) (*institutional competition*).

The model of interjurisdictional competition is usually used to describe relations between subnational jurisdictions in a federative state like the US or Switzerland. The globalization process means a higher level of mobility of production factors through national borders. For this reason, the theory of the interjurisdictional competition can be used to describe relations between states in a world economy. Some studies provide empirical evidence for the existence of competition between OECD and EU states. Another point involves competition between mature market economies and developing countries (the problem of "ecological dumping" and "social dumping"). One more case for international interjurisdictional competition is the existence of offshore financial centers and tax heavens (the so-called "harmful tax competition").

The theory of interjurisdictional competition is another way to deal with competitiveness than that which was criticized by Krugmann (1994). This theory deals not with the competitiveness of the national economy, but the competitiveness of government (or, in broader sense, of immobile production factors). Interjurisdictional competition is not a zero-sum game. Even a weak competition position of a national government can induce changes in governmental policy enforced by competition forces that improve the quality of life of all citizens.

Depending on theoretical assumptions, however, there are many different positions on economic and social effects of institutional competition. The basic neoclassical tax competition model describes the behavior of benevolent states using only tax competition to attract capital. The result is the so-called "**race to the bottom,**" taxation of mobile factors (capital) declines to the zero level. The result is either the underprovision of public goods or the tax shift to immobile factors like labor (Zodrow, Miesckovski 1986). Until now, there has been little empirical evidence for "race to the bottom" (see Krogstrup 2003 and Feld 2001) (An example of this process is the MERCOSUR (Baer, Cavalcanti, Silva 2003). Assuming, that governments use both taxation and production of public goods and institutions to attract capital and that companies are interested not only in the law "price" of public services but in their high "quality" as well, some scholars make the conclusion that interjurisdictional competition leads to a more efficient provision of public goods (the **Tiebout hypothesis**)[1].

Strong support for positive effects of interjurisdictional competition is based on the evolutionary economics and the public choice theory (Streit 1996). Competition between states (as well as competition between companies) has a control function and a discovery function. First, the states are not benevolent; the politicians and bureaucrats try to improve their wealth rather than support public needs. The failure of democratic procedures (like the paradox of voting and the influence of interest groups) and even the absence of democracy in an autocratic political regime prevents citizens from influencing governmental policy. "Exit" is an additional instrument of control. Second, competition can be described as a discovery process. Governmental policies are hypotheses about the possible needs of individuals. The competition process tests this hypothesis, selecting out the less efficient ones.

But some arguments criticize the efficiency of the control and discovery function. There are market failures in interjurisdictional competition as well as in competition between private actors. For example, governments can create a type of "cartel," harmonizing price and the quality of goods. The information asymmetry between private and public actors prevents them from meeting optimal decisions. The "competition order" (or the main institutions impacting the behavior of supply-side and demand-side agents) influences the effects of the interjurisdictional competition (Leipold 1997a).

3 "Exit" in the Russian Economy

Russia's integration into the world economy means an active participation in the interjurisdictional competition. The investment (divestment) decision patterns of Russian and foreign companies include the consideration of the "price" and the "quality" of the institutions and public gods. And even individuals (especially wealthy ones) can "exit" or "enter" Russia.

To measure the effect of "exit" and "entrance" in the Russian economy, we use three indicators:

1. Capital flight. Despite strict capital controls, capital outflow continued during the 1990s (see Figure 1). Official statistics do not represent the illegal and "half-legal" channels of capital flight. Under expert opinion, capital flight can be even larger than is represented in Figure 2. Both graphs (Figure 1 and 2) show a decline in capital outflow after 1998. In Q2 2003, net capital inflow amounting to $3.6 bln was registered. Because of the *Yukos* deal, this inflow was replaced by capital outflow (Q3 – $8.7 bln).

[1] For an overview of interjurisdictional competition theories see: Kenyon 1997; Wilson 1999; Feld 2001; Krogstrup 2002; Schenk 2002; Janeba, Schjelderup 2003.

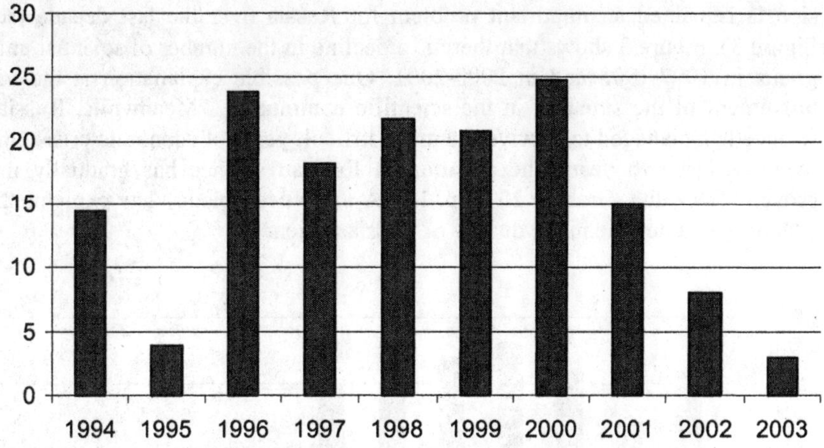

Fig. 1. Net Capital Export by Private Sector ($Billion)

Source: Central Bank of the Russian Federation 2004.

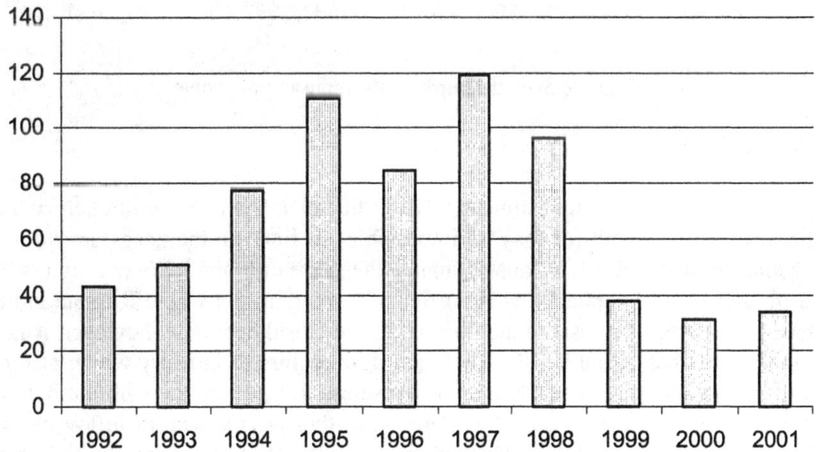

Fig. 2. Capital flight from Russia ($Billions, average expert assessment without extremely high and low assessments).

Source: Lopashenko 2002, pp. 22-23.

2. The "brain drain". The emigration of scientists and other high-qualified professionals remained an important problem for Russia over the last decade (see Figure 3). Figure 3 shows that there is a decline in the number of scientist emigrants in 1997-1998 and in 2000-2001. One possible explanation is the improvement of the situation in the scientific community. "Meanwhile, Russian science has managed to survive the most difficult years of economic crisis, and over the last two years, the situation in Russian science has gradually improved" (Dezhina, Graham 2002, p. 14). A more pessimistic view explains the situation by a decline in the quality of Russian science.

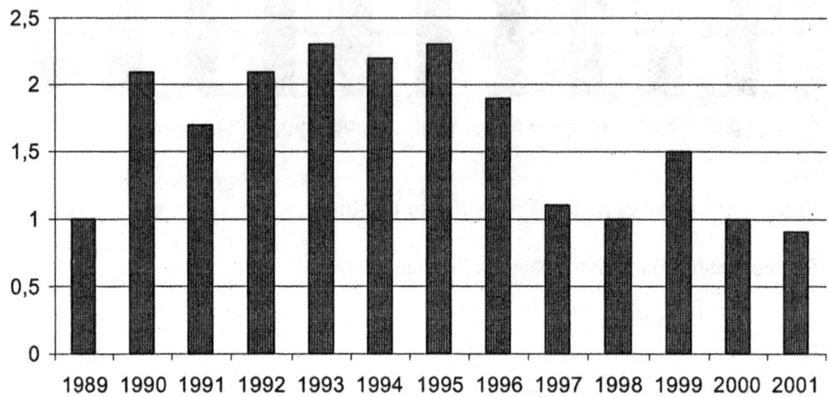

Fig. 3. Number of Russian Scientists Emigrants, thousand of people

Source: CRSS 2003.

3. The deficit of foreign investments. This indicator is the most contradictory one, because it is difficult (or may be impossible) to find out the necessary volume of foreign investments, because human wishes are unlimited. Some scholars believe that inward capital flow is sufficient to reequip the whole Russian industry. The degree of Russian integration into the world economy, however, is now higher than that of the USSR. There are new sectors of industry which also require investments. For this reason, it is useless to build up the whole industrial complex of the former Soviet Union. Nevertheless, the capital inflow within Russia was most certainly limited (see Figure 4). If we identify the "peer group" of competitors for the Russian government in global interjurisdictional competition, it is important to notice that there is no direct competition between Russia and OECD countries from the point of view of foreign investors (both transnational corporations with FDI and portfolio investors). Russia competes only with other emerging markets (Loukashov, Arinin, Kocheshkova, Isahanian 2003, p. 4). Compared with other transformation countries, Russia's inflow of FDI was relatively low (Figure 5).

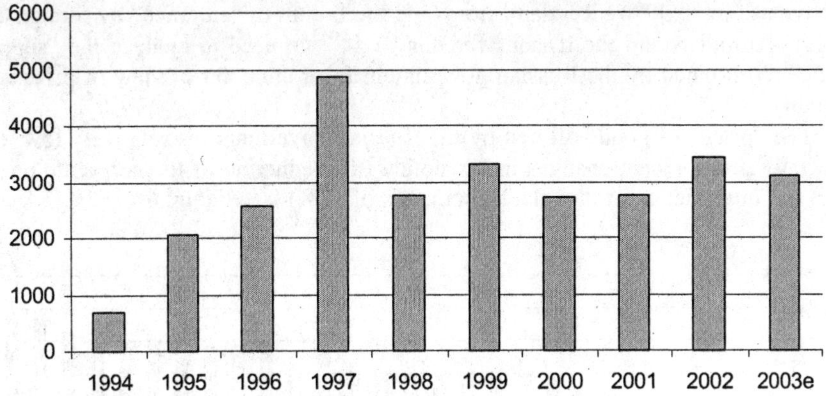

Fig. 4. FDI Inflow, $Million[2]

Source: Central Bank of the Russian Federation, 2004.

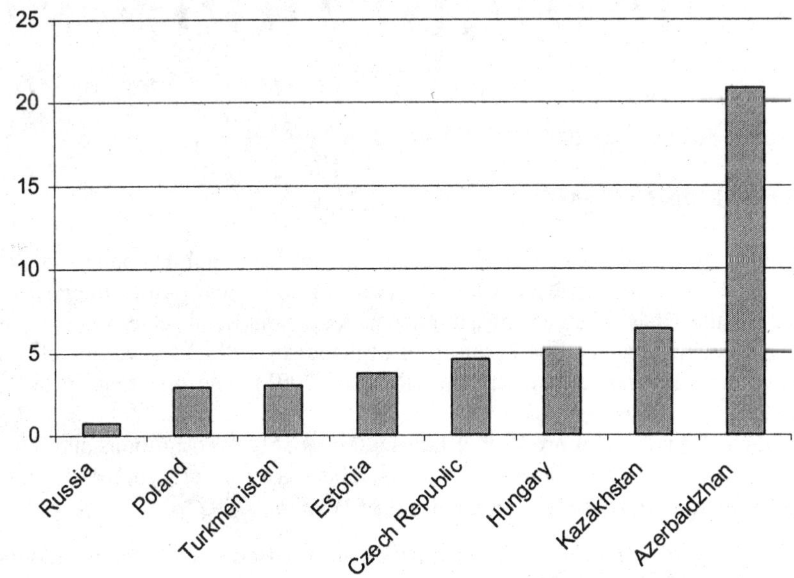

Fig. 5. FDI in % of GDP, 1996-1999

Source: Dabrowski, Gortat 2002, p. 564.

[2] For 2003 only a 9-month-result was available. The annual result is calculated as a 9-month result * 4/3.

Capital flight, brain drain and the deficit of foreign investments demonstrate an active use of "exit" by Russian actors (and the failure of "entrance" by foreign actors). To understand the reasons for this "exit," we need to analyze the "supply side" represented by the Russian government from the point of view of price and quality.

The "price" of goods offered by the Russian government is relatively low, especially under recent changes in tax policy (the reduction of the corporate profit tax and introduction of the "flat" income tax of 13%) (see Figure 6).

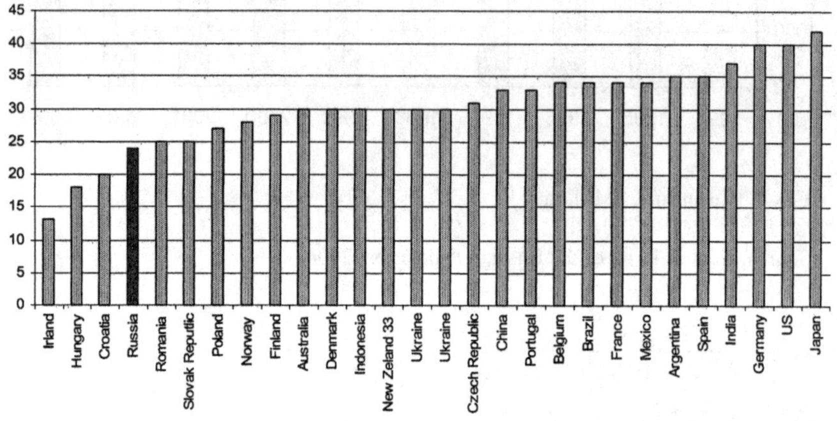

Fig. 6. Corporate Tax Rate 2003, %

Source: KPMG 2003, pp. 3-4.

But there is an additional problem regarding the price of public goods and institutions in Russia, the existence a huge number of additional (partly illegal) payments. On the basis of some measurements, for example, an entrepreneur pays about 10% of the deal's value in the form of bribes to different government (federal, regional and municipal) officials (INDEM 2001). The resulting "price" is higher than the official one.

But the most important problem remains a law quality of institutions and public goods. It is difficult to measure these factors. There are 5 criteria for assessing the quality of institutions described in the paper of Welfens (2003, p. 3):

- *Consistency of institutions.* First, the problem of Russian law is the parallel existence of different partly contradictory norms. For example, there are important differences between the Civil Code as the basic act of civil law and special acts on insurance, acts on leasing etc. Moreover, there are even greater differences between acts of the Parliament and those of Ministries and other public agencies. Second, may be a more important case of inconsistency of Russian institutions is the difference between legal and unofficial institutions. A good example can be seen in the high degree of corruption. Russia ranks 86 under the

Transparency International Corruption Perception Index 2003 (Transparency International 2003, p.4) and 92 under the World Democracy Audit Corruption Ranking (World Democracy Audit 2003). Third, an inconsistency exists between the law (and even the informal institutions) and its application by powerful (private and public) agents. Sometimes public authority applies existing legal norms differently for different actors. The case of *Yukos* is one of the recent examples of this feature of the Russian institutional system[3].

- *Legitimacy of institutions.* First, the differences between official and unofficial institutions reduce the legitimacy of both. Second, the deficit of democratic procedures reduces the legitimacy of the law. And third, the fragmentation of Russian society leads to a kind of "institutional interregnum" (see Brockmeier 1997). Even the informal institutions are used only by small groups of people.
- *Reduction of the set of rules to the minimally efficient one.* Russian law is a sophisticated system of different acts and regulations. However, the situation is not quite different from that in developed countries. The complexity of Russian law is an additional feature making its inconsistency a more important problem.
- *General rules rather than individual rules.* The Soviet economy with its huge monopolies determined the importance of certain enterprises for the Russian economy. These companies are often regulated by other sets of rules than are their smaller competitors. For example, there are different terms for accounts submission set for *Sberbank* and other Russian banks.
- *Completeness.* A paradoxical feature of the Russian set of institutions is its combination between the complexity of existing rules and the deficit of necessary rules and institutions. For example, there is still a deficit of rules regarding the protection of shareholders' rights (corporate governance).

An often-used indicator for the quality of economic institutions is the index of economic freedom. The Heritage Foundation ranks Russia 114 ("mostly unfree") based on characteristics like "law level of property rights protection," the "high level of restrictions in banking & finance" and the "high level of regulations" (Heritage Foundation 2004, pp. 339-341). Under the Fraser Institute report "Economic Freedom of the World," Russia ranks 112 of 132 countries (Fraser Institute 2003, p. 12).

We believe there to be an excellent criterion for the quality of private goods (i.e., the market and the competition as the discovery process). We can accordingly assert that the quality of institutions and public goods is indicated by market reactions in the form of exits.

[3] The resulting deficit of confidence between economic agents is an important problem for the Russian economy as well as for some other transition economies (Leipold 1997, p. 61). For empirical evidence of the deficit of confidence, see Oleinik 2001, p. 137

4 Effects of the Interjurisdictional Competition for the Russian Economy

To analyze the reasons for the inefficiency of interjurisdictional competition in Russia, we use the model of the "market for public goods and institutions" described in the Section 2. The economic performance of interjurisdictional competition in Russia depends on the behavior of main actors on both the supply and demand side of the market.

4.1 Demand Side of the Market for Institutions and Public Goods

A surprising result of some recent studies of the transformation is that private actors do not necessary require better institutions and public goods. On the contrary, they are interested in the persistence of the inefficient equilibrium. There are different explanations for this fact in economics and political science.

1. Hellmann (1998) reveals that the first stage of the transformation with inefficient and incomplete market order and weak government creates transformation rents for some economic actors. The winners of this transformation are interested in a long-term institutional interregnum as a source for their rent income.
2. Path dependence is also an important factor influencing the behavior of Russian companies and households. Many scholars refer to "long-term traditions of the centralized economy and corrupt governments" (e.g. Panther 1998) which created a kind of QWERTY effect, Russian managers are able to act only in a system of institutional interregnum. Their knowledge of this generally inefficient system is a competition advantage for them which they want to use[4].
3. An important feature of the Russian economy is the domination of a small number of huge business groups. In 2002, 85% of the largest private Russian companies were under control of 6 groups of shareholders (Boone, Rodionov 2002). Large companies have different opportunities to protect their property. They can invest in a private protection system (e.g., hire a security firm) or use their "exit" option to influence the government's behavior and to ensure a better public protection system. Under a deficit of public protection, rich agents can gain from redistribution due to improper protection of property rights, because they have a significant advantage over the weaker agents. Thus, they become "natural opponents in improvement in public protection" (Sonin 2002)[5].

---

[4] However, there is a general problem associated with all path dependencies and cultural effects. As culture and history are specific for each country, it is very difficult to make generalized statements about their economic effects. The existing phenomena are declared to be the only possible. Another problem is the complexity of the historical processes and difficulties with the separation of different factors.

[5] Rajan, Zingales (2003) provide an example of this effect, comparing economic development in the US with a majority of small farmers in Latin America with big landowners.

Due to these three factors, we can assume that a better supply of institutions afford both advantages and disadvantages for Russian companies. In fact, the gains may even be smaller than the losses. Thus, companies do not generally use the "exit" option to improve institutional quality of the Russian economy. Mummert, Mummert (2000) describe a possible situation in a developing or transformation economy, in which the same interest groups transfer capital from the country because of the inefficiency of its economy but at the same time are interested in the persistence of the inefficient economy. We believe a similar situation exists in Russia.

An interesting question from the normative point of view is to prove the existence of a "dumping strategy" option for the Russian government. Is it possible to lower taxation under the current low quality of institutions and still attract foreign investments? There is no clear theoretical and empirical support for this option, especially for large countries. However, even if this strategy is successful, bad institutions prevent capital from long-term investments in the Russian economy because of high uncertainty. For this reason, the positive effects can only be short-term.

Paradoxically, the "exit" of efficient companies can even strengthen inefficient companies. After most efficient companies leave the country, the remaining inefficient ones become the main source of income for politicians and bureaucrats (legally and illegally). As such, they have a considerable impact on political decisions.

It is more difficult to explain the behavior of foreign companies which make investment (or divestment) decisions. In section 3, we provided an overview of investment deficit of the present-day Russian economy. However, there are companies investing even under these circumstances. Many scientists hope that these companies can create a kind of "countervailing power" which is able to encourage the government to provide better institutions. Unfortunately the experience of some CIS countries does not justify these hopes. For example, Kazakhstan managed to attract the highest per-capita value of FDI in the CIS. The FDI share in tangible asset formation in Kazakhstan is 3 to 4 times as high as in Russia (see Figure 7).

However, the quality of institutions in Kazakhstan remains as low as in Russia (or even lower). The grade of corruption is also very high (Transparency International 2004; Heritage Foundation 2004). Hellmann, Jones and Kaufmann (2000, p. 5) show that foreign companies are often engaged in corruption networks in host countries. Even the privatization of assets started with different corruption scandals involving the participation of foreign investors (see Brill Olcott 2003).

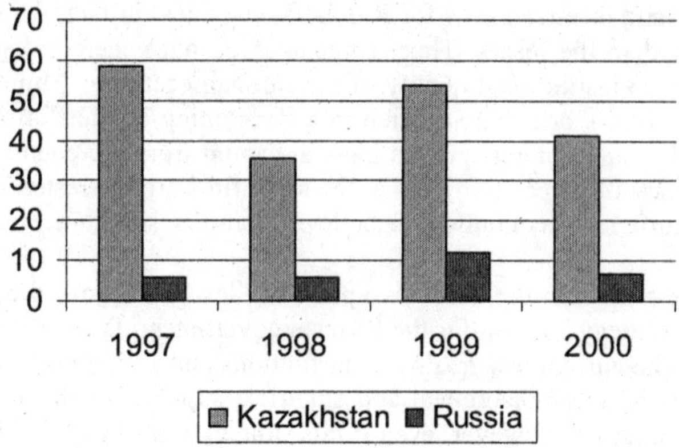

Fig. 7. FDI share in the formation of tangible assets.

Source: UNCTAD 2002.

There are at least two explanations of this. First, inefficient and corrupt economies (as is the case is Russia and Kazakhstan) often attract inefficient investors, companies which are ready to work within corruption and criminal networks (Akhmetova 2002, p. 62). This fact creates a kind of adverse selection. The governments receive foreign investments, even providing bad institutions and public goods. Second, huge natural resources can partly substitute for the inefficiency of institutions, especially if foreign investors are certain of their property protection and profit repatriation rights.

4.2 Supply Side of the Market for Institutions and Public Goods

It is easier to explain the reasons the government has for providing law quality institutions and public goods. Actually, there are two main logics explaining the government behavior: the power logic and the income logic. The government tries to ensure its power position and to receive pecuniary gains from its position. The power logic is at the center of the political analysis of the relations between state and business; the income logic is a popular explanation of the government's behavior in economics.

From the point of view of the **power logic,** the government requires certain instruments of influence which can be used to control private actors and to prevent them from investing in the political opposition. A possible means to achieve this is through the bad specification of property rights. In case of a conflict, the government can easily enforce its will, using formally legal instruments (Furman 2003). The case of *Yukos* may perhaps be one of the best examples for this power instrument.

The **income logic** explains the behavior of public actors with the same instruments as those of private actors. Bureaucrats and politicians maximize their income, not the wealth of the nation. There are many options for rent seeking and rent creating in an economy with bad institutions: a huge number of governmental interventions and administrative barriers (like licenses, standards and a sophisticated registration system) and a lack of control over the government are one of the main reasons for the dominating corruption.

Under realistic assumptions, however, all governments are interested in profit maximizing and income maximizing. That is the reason for interjurisdictional competition to create an additional control instrument over the government. That means that the power logic and the income logic do not explain the reasons for the failure of interjurisdictional competition. They only describe the behavior of the government. There are, however, two other factors influencing the supply side of the market for institutions in Russia. The first one is the political system which is characterized by a lack of democratic control over the political decisions.

In a recent study, Popow (2003) demonstrates that countries with "bad democracies" (democratic regimes which fail to ensure the economic rights of their citizens) are even less efficient than autocratic regimes. In a democratic regime (even in the case of a bad democracy like Russia), economic policy is determined by both power and income logics. In an autocratic regime, the government does not need to ensure its power by changing economic institutions, because the main source of power is pure violence. As such, there are fewer reasons for the government to create bad institutions in an autocratic regime than in a bad democracy, and there are more possibilities for the government to create bad institutions in a bad democracy than in a good democracy.

The second factor involves oil and gas export. First, under high prices on the international markets, it can soften the negative processes in the Russian economy. Second, it creates additional influence potential for the government in international relations. For this reason, the government does not necessarily need economic development to maximize its power in international relations.

Both the government and private actors have certain reasons for encouraging bad institutions and for supporting bad institutions. This means an existence of an institutional trap (a stabile inefficient equilibrium) which prevents interjurisdictional competition from influencing the Russian economy and politics.

5 Conclusion

Russian integration into the world economy requires its participation in global interjurisdictional competition. However, the competition position of Russia is rather bad than good because of the low "quality" of institutions and public goods and a relatively high (partly informal) "price" for them. This inefficiency leads to a deficit in foreign investments and a "brain drain" and capital flight as well. However, interjurisdictional competition does not execute its control function due to specific behavior of private and public actors. Both the supply side and the demand side support the existing inefficient equilibrium.

The first conclusion is that the ongoing integration of Russia in the world economy is not sufficient to move its economic system to a better equilibrium. The "exit" option is useless if economic agents do not use it to enforce better institutions for the national economy, and the government does not depend upon the decisions of private actors due to specific features of political system. Integration can only be efficient if efficient political institutions are created and current sources of power in the private sector are weakened.

The second point we wish to make is that the main problem with the Russian economy is not the high price of goods and services offered by the government but the law quality of institutions, goods and services. The potential of pure tax reforms for attracting investors and preventing illegal practices as well as "exit" is limited. Additional institutional reforms for improving the quality of institutions and public goods are required.

References

Akhmetova, G. (2002) Corruption in Oil-Extracting Countries. Almaty: Kuldzakhan (in Russian).

Baer W., Cavalcanti T. and P. Silva. (2003). Economic Integration without Policy Coordination: The Case of MERCOSUR, in: Schüller A., Thieme J. (Eds.) Ordnungsprobleme der Weltwirtschaft. Stuttgart: Lucius & Lucius.

Boone, P. and D. Rodionov (2002). Rent seeking in Russia and in CIS. Moscow.

Brill Olcott, M. (2003). Kazakhstan: The Unfulfilled Way. Moscow, Gendalf (in Russian).

Brockmeier, TH. (1997). Wettbewerb und Unternehmertum in der Systemtransformation – Das Problem des institutionellen Interregnums im Prozess des Wandels von Wirtschaftssystemen. Stuttgart.

Central Bank of the Russian Federation (2004). Statistics. www.cbr.ru

CSRS (Center for Statistics and Research of Science) (2003). The Science of Russia, Moscow (in Russian).

Dabrowski, M. and R. Gortat (2002). Political Determinants of Economic Reforms in Former Communist Countries. Economicheskiy Vestnik, Vol.2, No.4 (in Russian).

Dezhina, I. and L. Graham (2002). Russian Basic Science after Ten Years of Transition and Foreign Support. Carnegie Endowment for International Peace Working Paper No.24.

Feld, L. Eine empirische Analyse der Auswirkungen des internationalen Steuerwettbewerbs. Gutachten zuhanden der UBS AG.

Fraser Institute (2003). Economic Freedom of the World: Annual Report.

Furman, D. (2003). Political System of the Modern Russia and its Live Cycle. Svobodnaya Mysl, No. 11 (in Russian).

Hellman, J. (1998). Winners Take All: The Politics of Partial Reform in Postcommunist Transitions. World Politics, Vol. 50.

Hellmann, J., Jones, G. and D. Kaufmann (2000). Are Foreign Investors and Multinationals Engaged in Corrupt Practices in Transition Economies? // Transition, May-Juny-July.

Heritage Foundation (2004). Index of Economic Freedom 2004.

Indem Foundation (2001). Diagnostics of Russian Corruption: A Sociological Analysis. Moscow.

Janeba, E. and G. Schjelderup (2003). Tax Competition: A Review of the Theory. Report No. 3 in the Globalisation Project, commissioned by the Norwegian Ministry of Foreign Affairs.

Kenyon, D. (1997). Theories of Interjurisdictional Competition. // New England Economic Review, March/April.

KPMG (2003). Corporate Tax Rate Survey.

Krogstrup, S. (2002). What Do Theories of Tax Competition Predict for Capital Taxes in EU Countries: A Review of Tax Competition Literature. HEI Working Paper, No. 05/2002.

Krogstrup, S. (2003). Are Capital Taxes Racing to the Bottom in the European Union. HEI Working Paper, No.1/2003.

Krugman, P. (1994). Competitiveness: A Dangerous Obsession. Foreign Affairs, Vol.73, No.2.

Leipold, H. (1997): Der Zusammenhang zwischen gewachsener und gesetzten Ordnung: Einige Lehren aus den postsozialistischen Reformerfahrungen, in: Cassel, D. (Ed.): Institutionelle Probleme der Systemtransformation, Berlin, Duncker&Humblott.

Leipold, H. (1997a) Der Zusammenhang swischen dem Entstehen und dem Wettbewerb von Ordnungen, in Von Delhaes, K. and U.Fehl (Eds.) Dimensionen des Wettbewerbs. Stuttgart: Lucius&Lucius Verlag.

Lopashenko, N. (2002). Problems of Capital Flight from Russia and Options for Its Recurrence. Saratov (in Russian).

Loukashov, D., Arinin, S., Kocheshkova, N. and M. Isahanian (2003). From Private Property to the Market: Equity Market Strategy, Moscow: FINAM Research (in Russian).

Mummert, A. and U. Mummert (2000). Institutioneller Wettbewerb in Entwicklungsländern im institutionellen Wettbewerb. Max-Planck Institut zur Erforschung von Wirtschaftssystemen Diskussionsbeitrag 03-00.

Oleinik, A. Costs and Perspectives of Russian Reforms – An Institutional Approach. Istocki, Vol.3 (in Russian).

Panther, S. (1998). Historisches Erbe der Transformation: „Lateinische" Gewinner – ortodoxe Verlierer?, in: Wegner G., Wieland J. (Eds.) Formelle und informelle Institutionen – Genese, Interaktion und Wandel, Marburg, Metropolis.

Popow, W. (2002). State, Democracy and Economic Growth. Moscow, Instiute for Complex Strategic Studies (in Russian).

Rajan, R. and L. Zingales (2003). Saving Capitalism from the Capitalists: Unleashing the Power of Financial Markets to Create Wealth and Spread Opportunity. New York : Crown Business.

Schenk, M. (2002). Effiziente Steuersysteme und internationaler Steuerwettbewerb. Frankfurt/Main, Berlin: Peter Lang.

Sonin, K. (2002). Why the Reach May Favor Poor Protection of Propery Rights. William Davidson Working Paper No. 544.

Streit, M. (1996). Systemwettbewerb und Harmonisierung im europäischen Integrationsprozess, in: Cassel D. (Ed.) Entstehung und Wettbewerb von Systemen. Berlin: Duncker&Humblott.

Transparency International (2003). Transparency International Corruption Perception Index. Press Release, October 7.

UNCTAD (2002). Kazakhstan Country Fact Sheet.

Wallerstein, I. (2001). Analysis of World Systems and Situation in the Modern World. St.-Petersburg: Letniy Sad (Russian Edition).

Welfens, P.J.J. (2003). Regionale Integration in der Ordnungs-, Außenwirtschafts- und Wachstumtheorie. Paper presented at the Radain Seminar on Institutional Economics.
Wilson, J. (1999). Theories of Tax Competition. National Tax Journal, Vol.52.
World Democracy Audit (2003). Corruption Ranking. http://www.worldaudit.org/corruption.htm.
Zodrow, G. and P. Mieszkovski (1986). Pigou, Tiebout, Property Taxation and the Underprovision of Local Public Goods. Journal of Urban Economics, Vol.19, No. 3.

Panel Discussion: Perspective on Russia

Telecommunications, Trade and Growth: Gravity Modeling and Empirical Analysis for Eastern Europe and Russia

Tiiu Paas

Interesting research topic having relationships to the economic growth and convergency problems and the increasing role of information and telecommuniation in these processes. The main (possible) research hypothesis of the paper[1]: 1) Development of the ITC has a statistically significant positive impact on foreign trade. This impact varies between the countries and country groups (transitional countries, FSU, EU-15, AC10, EU-25), depending on the level of economic development, investments and innovations. 2) The influence of ITC (information and telecommunication) networking on foreign trade volume takes place through a transmission of information, and this transmission is helpful in overcoming "economic distance" (geographical distance) between economically acting countries. (Geographical distance *versus* virtual distance).

If the aim of the paper is to check the validity of the conclusions presented in the papers of Jungmittag and Welfens[2] and to develop these research results, then choosing the gravity equation analysis as the main methodological approach of the study seems to be appropriate. However, it is recommendable to place more attention on analyzing theoretical foundations of the gravity models in order to apply

---

1 Unfortunately, the aim of the study and the main research hypothesis are not clearly presented in the introductory part of the paper, therefore, it is possible that the reviewer of the paper cannot fully understand the intensions and the main research questions of the author.

2 P. Welfens, A. Jungmittag. Europäische Telekomliberalisierung und Aussenhandel: Theory, Gravitationansatz und Implicationen, EIIW Discussion Paper 85, Juni 2001. – A. Jungmittag, P. Welfens. Liberalization of EU Telecommunications and Trade: Theory: Gravity Equation Analysis and Policy Implication. EIIW Discussion Paper 87, October 2001.

this approach for testing the research hypotheses.[3] For instance, how the including of the ITC indicators in the augmented gravity equation fits to the theoretical foundations of this model, etc.

By the way, Tinbergen, not Linnemann, was the first who applied the gravity model based approach to exploring international trade flows. Following the work of Tinbergen (1962) and Pöyhönen (1963), Linnemann (1966) added more variables in the gravity equation and went farther toward a theoretical justification in terms of Walrasian general equilibrium system. Therefore, Linnemann's model is sometimes called the augmented gravity model. Linnemann pointed out that, when considering the theoretical aspects of a gravity model for trade, there are three main factors to be taken into account: 1) the total potential supply, or exports, of a country to the world market; 2) the total potential demand, or imports, of a country to the world market; 3) those factors that create resistance to trade and thus, affect the degree of trade intensity. These ordinarily include tariff barriers and transportation costs.

It is a natural question whether the ITC variables are endogenous variables within the specified gravity equations (Jungmittag and Welfens, 2001). If they are not, then OLS estimators of a gravity equation may no longer be consistent. Therefore, it recommendable to include the lagged variables into the equations and to use endogeneity tests (e.g. Hausman specifications tests, using instrumental variables, etc).

It should be taken into account that when analyzing telecommunication problems based on the data of the years 1998 and 1999, and trying to take some policy advice for 2004, the conclusions may be misleading. The situation in the quickly developing ITC sector was not the same in 1998 and 1999 as in 2004. It is not convincing that the investigations are restricted to the analysis of the situation during the years of 1998 and 1999, only by data availability. It is certainly possible to use trade data later than 1998 and 1999 for Russia and other FSU countries (See IMF trade statistics, databases 2002 and 2003). Of course, if the main aim of the author is only to consider some theoretical and methodological questions of gravity modeling and empirical analysis for Eastern European and Russian telecommunications as well as trade and growth problems and not to make any remarkable policy implications, then the author's approach regarding the time horizon seems to be appropriate. In this case, it is recommendable to restructure the paper to place figures and tables in the appendix, and to give more explanation of the research hypothesis, theory, specification and estimation problems in the body of the paper.

It is reasonable to make some corrections in the classification of the countries' groups. After May 2004, some countries are no longer candidate countries, and therefore, in the paper, which is to be published in 2004 or 2005, it is recommendable to make respective corrections, for instance, using dummies for EU15 and AC10 or CC12, etc.

---

[3] The theoretical foundations of the gravity models are based on 1) microeconomics; 2) regional science and new economic geography; 3) trade theories. All these theories and discussions related to them explain the existence of trade from different viewpoints.

U.S.-Russian and U.S.-Ukrainian Trade Relations and Foreign Direct Investment Effect

Tatiana Sedash

The following article provides a general analysis of modern trade relations and foreign direct investment between Russia, the Ukraine and the USA. The beginning of the article discusses foundations of new trade theory and its application in Russian and Ukrainian trade relations with the USA. The author then examines specifics of U.S.-Russian and U.S.-Ukrainian trade performance and structure and proceeds to discuss foreign direct investment and its connections with foreign trade. The article provides an economic model that reflects linkages between foreign direct investment, trade balance and a number of other key economic factors. In summary the article draws conclusions and gives recommendations on economic policy objectives that are essential for encouraging greater levels of foreign direct investment and stimulation of foreign trade in Russia and Ukraine.

Prof. Nosova points to the inadequacy of a classical approach to trade relations between the developing and developed countries. There is a discussion of the findings of modern academics that discovered new trade patterns in countries where an assumption of perfect competition is inapplicable, such as the effects of clustering and internet penetration as causes of export growth. Based on these findings, the article outlines a need to develop a new trade model for countries with transitional economies. Such a model would account for the restricted mobility of factors, asymmetrical information flows, technological gaps and other factors that are typical for a developing economy.

A detailed analysis is given of U.S.-Russian, U.S.-Ukraine trade relations. From the year 1994 onwards Russia enjoyed a growing trade surplus with the United States. The author pays substantial attention to U.S. trade performance and suggests that some of this surplus may be due to a possible loss of competitiveness of US industry. In addition growth in the trade surplus is due to the growing export-orientation of the Russian economy.

The article states that import substitution as a means of early development was pursued by countries in the 1950s and 1960s. Export oriented policies are more widely pursued by countries in transition today. The growth in exports of industrial goods by the countries in transition increases competition with developed countries and provides for growth in efficiency, while the reduction of trade barriers encourages the growth of trade.

The author then proceeds to discuss foreign direct investment from the U.S. to Russia and Ukraine. Admittedly, the U.S. is a major exporter of capital to both Russia and Ukraine. Prof. Nosova gives a general overview of the foundation of foreign direct investment, such as ample investment opportunities in the natural-resources industry, an abundance of qualified and inexpensive labor and bilateral treaties that provide stability to a legal framework for foreign investments.

The author proposes an autoregression distributed lagged model (ARDL) that defines FDI as a function of several economic variables, such as GDP, real exchange rate, trade balance and country risk. The model attempts to explain certain lags in the economic performance of the Ukraine. Since the short-term multiplication is equal to minus 0.67 (zero point sixty seven), increased FDI inflow into the Ukraine is not accompanied by growth in investment capitalization at the present time. However, more methodological and mathematical justification is needed to assess the accuracy of ARDL.

In conclusion the author draws several policy implications, in particular the continuation of diversification of the export structure in Russia and the Ukraine, the formulation of specific goals and objectives for Russian and Ukrainian policy makers coupled with an appropriate monitoring system, greater transparency, a favorable legal environment to attract FDI and encourage trade with developed countries. While most of these suggestions are undoubtedly very accurate for the Russian economy, it would be interesting to see deeper discussion of the specifics of export diversification. Does export diversification imply diversification from primary exports to industrial exports? And to what extent is diversification in industrial exports as opposed to concentration on a hand-full of industrial exports compatible with and beneficial to economies of scale?

The article draws upon the most recent data on both FDI and trade relations between the countries in question and provides a very interesting overview of this data. However, a link between FDI and trade between the countries in question requires more discussion. The author mentions a well-known connection between tariffs and FDI in capital intensive industries. Prof. Nosova further mentions the study by Wada, Graham (2000) which found that «US exports and US direct investment abroad are net complements» However, no data is given to illustrate this connection in either the U.S.-Russian or U.S.-Ukrainian relationship. The article leaves a reader with several questions - would it be worthwhile to sacrifice some trade by the imposition of tariffs for the purpose of attracting capital-intensive FDI? Or would it perhaps be more wise to encourage industrial growth by greater orientation toward trade openness and stability?

The article by Prof. Nosova is very thought-provoking and raises important issues for discussion about the economic future of the relationship between the U.S. and CIS countries.

Sustainability of Growth and Development of Financial System in Russia

Ralf Wiegert

Since 1999, Russia has been experiencing a period of rapid economic growth, fuelled by high oil prices, an initial push through a sharp real devaluation and low real wages. While oil prices have been volatile recently, but at a fairly high level, real wages as well as the real value of the Ruble has gained ground again and almost reached or surpassed pre-crisis levels. Russia's export revenues, consisting to some 55% of transactions related to the mineral ressources sector, surged in the last five years, and the current account recorded extraordinarily high surpluses.

Providing a comprehensive view on the origins of GDP growth in Russia since the 1998 financial crisis and in the recent past, Evgeny Gavrilenkov refers to the correlation between the price level for Urals crude oil and Russia's GDP growth rate. He points out to the dependence of the Russian economy on natural resources exports and hence on the international oil price, and acknowledges that, for the sake of sustained high economic growth, the origins of growth have to shift from the dependency on the oil price toward a more balanced and diversified structure of the economy. However, such a restructuring can only be achieved by high investment, which currently is impeded by ongoing capital flight, adverse investment climate and, being Gavrilenkov's main concern, the low monetization of the economy. As a consequence, he argues, banks are quite reluctant to lend money to private borrowers and play therefore an almost neglectable role for investing in the restructuring of Russia's economy.

Without doubt, the dismal state of Russia's banking sector impairs restructuring and modernization considerably. A recent study by the World Bank (2004) revealed that economic growth in Russia after 1998 is more a function of intra-sectoral restructuring and modernization rather than intersectoral. Moreover, the most part of intersectoral restructuring – the rise of market services at the expense the industry's share among the value added total and employment – took already place before growth actually took off in 1998. Since then, intersectoral restructuring slowed down, and growth became a mere result of intra-sectoral restructuring and modernization. This means that large industrial plants have eventually made investment in order to keep their production going, not to mention the oil and gas sector, which considerably upgraded its capital stock as regards production as well as transport, but a surge of the market services sector at the expense of the industry's share of the economy largely failed during the recent economic boom.

In contrast, many central European transition countries shut down the old industrial behemoths during transition, expanded the services sector instead, and the most advanced ones have already built up an industrial cluster of their own, but Russia still more or less sticks to its industrial structure inherited from Soviet times, laying even higher weight on natural ressources extraction.

The structure of investment financing, that Gavrilenkov provides in his paper makes the nature of the problem and the link between lagging restructuring and the banking sector obvious. Own-retained earnings were by far the largest source for investment financing (45.6% of total funds), while bank loans equalled a mere 5.3% of total funds in 2003. The public budget comes second, with roughly 20% of total funds, when encompassing off-budget funds as well. Thus, investment financing in terms of bank loans or equity shares, of predominant importance in developed market economies, are nearly negligible from a macroeconomic point of view.

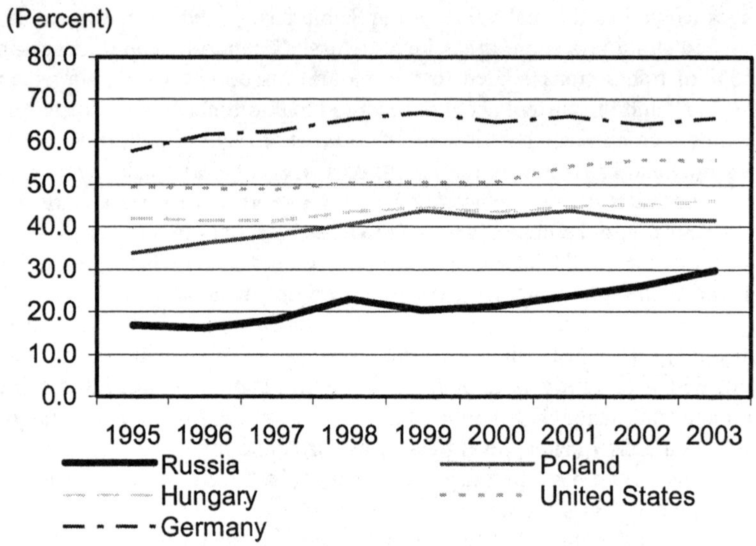

Fig. 1. M2 to GDP in Selected Countries

Source: Global Insight.

Gavrilenkov identifies the overall weakness of the banking sector, i.e. the inability to perform its role as a financial intermediary due to low competition, lack of risk assessment instruments, legal shortcomings, shortage of skilled personnel etc., as an origin of this dismal situation. However, he stresses that almost as important as the weakness of the banking sector from his point of view, the low degree of monetization of Russia's economy is responsible for the shortage of investment funding from banks. From an international perspective, Russia's degree of monetization is still comparably low (see chart above). However, one has to acknowledge that liquidity is concentrated in the key financial centres, mostly in Moscow, and the overwhelming share of regions are actually still quite short of liquidity. During the recent economic boom, asset prices have been soaring in Moscow, largely due to increased liquidity as a result of strong export revenues.

Given the highly unequal regional distribution of liquidity, increasing monetization alone will not help to cure the investment funding problem, so is it right to link monetization to economic growth? In the case of Russia, there is no doubt about it up to a certain point. Russia's rate of monetization was painfully low, and it was set to rise after the last financial crisis. However, with a growing loans volume recently, and interest rates on the decline – becoming even negative in real terms –, one has to ask whether the recent credit boom, triggered by surging monetization of the economy, is still healthy indeed.

To answer this question, it seems appropriate to ask for the origins of growing monetization. At times, the windfall oil revenues would have forced the Ruble to appreciate considerably against the Dollar, but, due to the efforts of the Russian Central Bank, buying dollars on a grand scale during the last couple of years, this failed to happen. Only since March/April 2003, the ruble was allowed to appreciate against the dollar, leading to an nominal appreciation of some 10% in March 2004 compared to the same period a year ago. However, as proper instruments to sterilize foreign exchange market transactions were not available for some time, the dollar purchase of the Russian central bank led to a robust expansion of Ruble money supply.

The key problem is that liquidity flows into a financial sector which seems quite ill-prepared to stomach additional funds at such a scale. Due to a lack of investment opportunities, cash among banks is piling, or, alternatively, liquidity is used to invest in assets already available, such as shares, housing and government bonds. As a consequence, share prices are soaring. At the beginning of 2004, however, it seems premature to talk of a full-fledged asset-price bubble in Russia or in Moscow alone, but further liquidity injection will drive asset prices further upwards. Without promoting development of banks in Russia's regions, a paradoxical situation will be locked in: while Moscow's asset prices, including the stock market, are rising to unprecedented levels, the regions are quite short of liquidity. Hence, it does not look reasonable to further increase the degree of monetization at the same pace as during 1999-2003. For the sake of macroeconomic stability, Russia's central bank and government policymakers should link rising levels of monetization with eliminating banking sector's weaknesses.

References

World Bank (2004), From Transition to Development. A Country Economic Memorandum for the Russian Federation, Moscow, draft.

List of Contributors

NOER AZAM ACHSANI
University of Potsdam, Germany, e-mail: achsani@rz.uni-potsdam.de

FRANK BOHN
University College Dublin, Ireland, e-mail: frank.bohn@ucd.ie

DORA BORBÉLY
European Institute for International Economic Relations (EIIW) at the University of Wuppertal, Germany. e-mail: dora.borbely@wiwi.uni-wuppertal.de

HARRY G. BROADMAN
The World Bank, USA, e-mail: HBroadman@Worldbank.org

IRINA ELISEEVA
St. Petersburg State University of Economics and Finance, Russia, e-mail: eliseeva@finec.ru

EVGENY GAVRILENKOV
Troika Dialog, BEA Bureau of Economic Analysis Vysshaja Shkola Ekonomiki, Russia, e-mail: gavrilen@beap.dol.ru

ROLAND GÖTZ
German Institute for International and Security Affairs, Germany, e-mail: roland.goetz@swp-berlin.org

RUSLAN GRINBERG,
Institute for International Economic and Political Studies, Russian Academy of Sciences, Russia, e-mail: grinberg@transecon.ru

THORVALDUR GYLFASON
University of Iceland, Iceland, e-mail: gylfason@hi.is.

ALBRECHT KAUFFMANN
European Institute for International Economic Relations (EIIW) at University of Wuppertal and EIIW Research Center at Potsdam University, Germany, e-mail: alkauffm@rz.uni-potsdam.de

ALEXANDER LIBMAN
Center for CIS and Baltic States of the Institute for International Economic and Political Studies, Russia, e-mail: Libman@rambler.ru

OLGA NOSOVA
National University of Internal Affairs, Ukraine, e-mail: nosovaov@yahoo.com

NINA ODING
International Centre for Social and Economic Research "Leontief Centre", Russia, e-mail: oding@leontief.spb.su

TIIU PAAS
University of Tartu, Estonia, e-mail: tiiu.paas@mtk.ut.ee

CHRISTOPHER SCHUMANN
European Institute for International Economic Relations (EIIW) at the University of Wuppertal, Germany, e-mail: chr.schumann@uni-wuppertal.de

TATIANA SEDASH
St. Petersburg University of Economics and Finance, Russia, e-Mail: tse-dash@yahoo.com

HANS GERHARD STROHE
University of Potsdam, Germany, e-Mail: strohe@rz.uni-potsdam.de

PAUL J.J. WELFENS
European Institute for International Economic Relations (EIIW) at the University of Wuppertal, Germany, e-mail: welfens@uni-wuppertal.de

RALF WIEGERT
Global Insight, Germany, e-mail: ralf.wiegert@globalinsight.com

Further Publications by *Paul J. J. Welfens*

P. J. J. Welfens
Market-oriented Systemic Transformations in Eastern Europe
Problems, Theoretical Issues, and Policy Options
1992. XII, 261 pages. 20 Figs., 29 Tab., Hardcover, ISBN 3-540-55793-8

M. W. Klein, P. J. J. Welfens (Eds.)
Multinationals in the New Europe and Global Trade
1992. XV, 281 pages. 24 Figs., 75 Tab., Hardcover, ISBN 3-540-54634-0

P. J. J. Welfens (Ed.)
Economic Aspects of German Unification
Expectations, Transition Dynamics and International Perspectives
1996. XV, 527 pages. 34 Figs., 110 Tab., Hardcover, ISBN 3-540-60261-5

R. Tilly, P. J. J. Welfens (Eds.)
European Economic Integration as a Challenge to Industry and Government
Contemporary and Historical Perspectives on International Economic Dynamics
1996. X, 558 pages. 43 Figs., Hardcover, ISBN 3-540-60431-6

P. J. J. Welfens (Ed.)
Economic Aspects of German Unification
Expectations, Transition Dynamics and International Perspectives
2nd revised and enlarged edition
1996. XV, 527 pages. 34 Figs., 110 Tab., Hardcover, ISBN 3-540-60261-5

P. J. J. Welfens
European Monetary Integration
EMS Developments and International Post-Maastricht Perspectives
3rd revised and enlarged edition
1996. XVIII, 384 pages. 14 Figs., 26 Tab., Hardcover, ISBN 3-540-60260-7

P. J. J. Welfens (Ed.)
European Monetary Union
Transition, International Impact and Policy Options
1997. X, 467 pages. 50 Figs., 31 Tab., Hardcover, ISBN 3-540-63305-7

P. J. J. Welfens, G. Yarrow (Eds.)
Telecommunications and Energy in Systemic Transformation
International Dynamics, Deregulation and Adjustment in Network Industries
1997. XII, 501 pages. 39 Figs., Hardcover, ISBN 3-540-61586-5

P. J. J. Welfens, H. C. Wolf (Eds.)
Banking, International Capital Flows and Growth in Europe
Financial Markets, Savings and Monetary Integration in a World with Uncertain Convergence
1997. XIV, 458 pages. 22 Figs., 63 Tab., Hardcover, ISBN 3-540-63192-5

P. J. J. Welfens, D. Audretsch, J. T. Addison, H. Grupp
Technological Competition, Employment and Innovation Policies in OECD Countries
1998. VI, 231 pages. 16 Figs., 20 Tab., Hardcover, ISBN 3-540-63439-8

P. J. J. Welfens, G. Yarrow, R. Grinberg, C. Graack (Eds.)
Towards Competition in Network Industries
Telecommunications, Energy and Transportation in Europe and Russia
1999. XXII, 570 pages. 63 Figs., 63 Tab., Hardcover, ISBN 3-540-65859-9

P. J. J. Welfens
EU Eastern Enlargement and the Russian Transformation Crisis
1999. X, 151 pages. 12 Figs., 25 Tab., Hardcover, ISBN 3-540-65862-9

P. J. J. Welfens
Globalization of the Economy, Unemployment and Innovation
1999. VI, 255 pages. 11 Figs., 31 Tab., Hardcover, ISBN 3-540-65250-7

P. J. J. Welfens, J. T. Addison, D. B. Audretsch, T. Gries, H. Grupp
Globalization, Economic Growth and Innovation Dynamics
1999. X, 160 pages. 15 Figs., 15 Tab., Hardcover, ISBN 3-540-65858-0

R. Tilly, P.J.J. Welfens (Eds.)
Economic Globalization, International Organizations and Crisis Management
Contemporary and Historical Perspectives on Growth, Impact and Evolution of Major Organizations in an Interdependent World
2000. XII, 408 pages. 11 Figs., 20 Tab., Hardcover, ISBN 3-540-65863-7

P.J.J. Welfens, E. Gavrilenkov (Eds.)
Restructuring, Stabilizing and Modernizing the New Russia
Economic and Institutional Issues
2000. XIV, 516 pages. 82 Figs., 70 Tab., Hardcover, ISBN 3-540-67429-2

P.J.J. Welfens
European Monetary Union and Exchange Rate Dynamics
New Approaches and Applications to the Euro
2001. X, 159 pages. 26 Figs., 12 Tab., Hardcover, ISBN 3-540-67914-6

P.J.J. Welfens
Stabilizing and Integrating the Balkans
Economic Analysis of the Stability Pact, EU Reforms and International Organizations
2001. XII, 171 pages. 6 Figs., 18 Tab., Hardcover, ISBN 3-540-41775-3

P.J.J. Welfens, B. Meyer, W. Pfaffenberger, P. Jasinski, A. Jungmittag
Energy Policies in the European Union Germany's Ecological Tax Reform
2001. VII, 143 pages. 21 Figs., 41 Tab., Hardcover, ISBN 3-540-41652-8

P.J.J. Welfens (Ed.)
Internationalization of the Economy and Environmental Policy Options
2001. XIV, 442 pages. 57 Figs., 61 Tab., Hardcover, ISBN 3-540-42174-2

P.J.J. Welfens
Interneteconomics.net
Macroeconomics, Deregulation, and Innovation
2002. VIII, 215 pages. 34 Figs., 30 Tab., Hardcover, ISBN 3-540-43337-6

D.B. Audretsch, P.J.J. Welfens (Eds.)
The New Economy and Economic Growth in Europe and the USA
2002, XII, 350 pages. 28 Figs., 59 Tab., Hardcover, ISBN 3-540-43179-9

C.E. Barfield, G. Heiduk, P.J.J. Welfens (Eds.)
Internet, Economic Growth and Globalization
Perspectives on the Digital Economy in Europe, Japan and the U.S.
2003. XII, 388 pages. 34 Figs., 67 Tab., Hardcover, ISBN 3-540-00286-3

J.T. Addison, P.J.J. Welfens (Eds.)
Labor Markets and Social Security
Issues and Policy Options in the U.S. and Europe, 2nd edn.
2003. X, 402 pages. 56 Figs., 52 Tab., Hardcover, ISBN 3-540-44004-6

T. Lane, N. Oding, P.J.J. Welfens (Eds.)
Real and Financial Economic Dynamics in Russia and Eastern Europe
2003. XII, 293 pages. 50 Figs., 63 Tab., Hardcover, ISBN 3-540-00910-8

J.E. Gavrilenkov, P.J.J. Welfens, R. Wiegert (Eds.)
Economic Opening Up and Growth in Russia
2004. IX, 298 pages. 61 Figs., 70 Tab., Hardcover, ISBN 3-540-20459-8

P.J.J. Welfens, A. Wziatek-Kubiak (Eds.)
Structural Change and Exchange Rate Dynamics
The Economics of the EU Eastern Enlargement
2005. VI, 288 pages. 26 Figs., 58 Tab. Hardcover, ISBN 3-540-27687-4

E.M. Graham, N. Oding, P.J.J. Welfens (Eds.)
Internationalization and Economic Policy Reforms in Transition Countries
2005. XI, 340 pages. 77 Figs., 28 Tab. Hardcover, ISBN 3-540-24040-3

P.J.J. Welfens, F. Knipping, S. Chirathivat, C. Ryan (Eds.)
Integration in Asia and Europe
Historical Dynamics, Political Issues and Economic Perspectives
2006. VI, 284 pages. 32 Figs., 30 Tab. Hardcover, ISBN 3-540-28729-9